DUTY, HONOR, EMPIRE

DUTY, HONOR, EMPIRE

The Life and Times

OF

Colonel Richard Meinertzhagen

John Lord

RANDOM HOUSE · New York

Library of Congress Catalog Card Number: 77–85600

Acknowledgment is gratefully extended to the following for permission to reprint from their works:

Dodd, Mead & Company: "Peace" from *The Collected Poems of Rupert Brooke*. Copyright 1915 by Dodd, Mead & Company, Inc. Copyright 1943 by Edward Marsh.

Doubleday & Company, Methuen & Co. and Mrs. George Bambridge: From Rudyard Kipling's "Recessional" and "White Man's Burden" in *The Five Nations*.

Master and Fellows of Magdalene College, Cambridge: From "Pomp and Circumstance" by A. C. Benson.

Oxford University Press: From "The Windhover" in *Poems*, by Gerard Manley Hopkins.

All photographs courtesy of the Meinertzhagen Estate except as noted.

Manufactured in the United States of America
by Haddon Craftsmen, Inc., Scranton, Pennsylvania

9 8 7 6 5 4 3 2

FIRST EDITION

ACKNOWLEDGMENT

First thanks are due to Colonel Richard Meinertzhagen, who not long before his death permitted me to use his diaries. Dr. Theresa Clay, as his Trustee, thereafter helped me in every way without once placing restriction or imposing opinions upon my work: for her trust and kindness I am deeply grateful.

Miss Margaret Gale of the British Information Services Library and Miss Mildred Joy of the National Broadcasting Company's Library have been of more assistance than they know. Throughout, Mr. Robert D. Loomis of Random House has displayed that most precious talent of the editor—patience—and for that I am greatly in his debt.

To My Mother & Father

CONTENTS

PREFACE

Richard Meinertzhagen never came to terms with the modern world. For nine decades he watched the changes in public and private conduct that placed expediency before principle in matters of high policy as well as in domestic life. He never accepted those changes, and in that lies his relevance to our times. His vision was pure, constant and without cynicism, his judgment uncompromising; above all, he was never afraid of being honest, and that may be a saving virtue in any time and any place.

J. L.

DUTY, HONOR, EMPIRE

PROLOGUE

All night long the noise of crowds tramping through the city sounded like the far insistence of the sea. They were massing for a glimpse of a somber little lady in her seventy-ninth year whose soft wrinkled hand uplifted could call down tempests. More power pulsed in that dumpy figure than any tsar or kaiser could hope to command. She was a symbol of preeminence and the repository of her people's pride. So they were walking in the darkness toward a moment of glory when they could see her open carriage pass close by, watch the frail arm wave, and know themselves for an instant to be a part of majesty. They had been singing for weeks a song the music halls had taught them:

> *In every heart she has fashioned her throne,*
> *As Queen of the Earth she reigneth alone.*

Strict historical accuracy apart, the sentiment was true. The year of Queen Victoria's Diamond Jubilee, the sixtieth of her reign, had more claim than most to be the climax of the century. To her people the Queen was living evidence that the belief they all held in the progress of mankind was being realized. They had forgotten the years when the royal coaches flashed by at a gallop for fear of jeering hooligans and the cannon held ready in Buckingham Palace loaded with grapeshot for the Chartist mob. Now her likeness hung venerated over the humblest mantelpiece. It was ironic that neither the Queen nor her common subjects had any idea of what was meant by "democracy," but it was not important. What bound them was pride and a measure of unreasoning affection. So the crowds were filling the streets to celebrate the achievement of their nation, but also to seek from the presence of that indomitable old grandmother some affirmation of their own convictions, which these days pomp and circumstance alone were not always enough to sustain.

Since it fell on a Sunday, the real anniversary of the Queen's accession could not be celebrated in anything but pious fashion. At eleven o'clock that morning in 1897 every church in the land began its service of thanksgiving, during which without false humility praise was rendered with Bishop How's Jubilee Hymn "Thou hast been mindful of Thine own." The service in St. George's Chapel at Windsor also included the Prince Consort's *Te Deum,* a reminder of the Golden Jubilee of ten years before. That had been a royal occasion, certainly. But the dreams of 1887 were now accomplished fact. This occasion was imperial and the Queen herself had approved its name with an initialed Victoria Regina Imperatrix. When she arrived in London the next day it was as though every race on earth had sent a representative to do her homage. Clouds of goodwill swirled everywhere as dense as a London particular. Even far-off America had caught some of the enthusiasm. President McKinley, fresh from dedicating Grant's Tomb on the Hudson River, dispatched by the hand of his special ambassador Mr. Whitelaw Reid a letter of state which began, "Great and good Friend," and which continued in slightly hortative mood, "May liberty flourish throughout your empire under just and equal laws, and your government continue strong in the affections of all who live under it." There was every likelihood that this last hope would be realized, one way or another, for in the heydey of British rule those who did not like it were quickly forced to lump it. In the last three decades of the nineteenth century the British fought and won one hundred and ten wars of assorted sizes, not counting mere confrontations and local rebellions.

The morning of Tuesday, June 22, 1897, the day of secular celebration, was as dull as lead. The air was hot and still and the sky a sullen gray. By eight o'clock the crowds were beginning to settle into solid lines along the miles of the procession's route. By eight-thirty troops had begun to line the streets, horse and foot, regulars and volunteers. The Hampshire Yeomanry had bivouacked the night before in Hyde Park, but now they were mounted in a line of dark blue and gold at the bottom of St. James's Street. Staring up toward Piccadilly, Second Lieutenant Richard Meinertzhagen was delighted with the excellence of his view. From under the steel V of his dragoon's helmet, its white horsehair plume hissing softly against the metal when he moved his head, he would be able to watch unobstructed the gradual descent of Her Majesty's carriage down St. James's. His hunter Melksham had been promoted to charger for the occasion and seemed for the moment to be impressed by that dignity. Richard had breakfasted well before it was light in the Yeomanry Mess in the Park, he was conscious that his short jacket with its crusted braid at the throat suited his broad shoulders, and even his new moustache felt a little less wispy this auspicious morning. For once all was well with Richard Meinertzhagen's nineteen-year-old world, particularly his present location, for he intended to take a picture of Her Majesty, in outright defiance of Her Majesty's Regulations for the Army, with his new camera. He hoped he would not be noticed. With each man close enough to touch the next, twelve miles of troops settled in the saddle or stood loosely at ease in the heavy air.

At a quarter to ten, an hour and a half early to be on the safe side, His Royal Highness Field Marshal Prince George William Frederick Charles, Duke of Cambridge and Knight of the Garter, known more familiarly throughout the army as "dear old Garge," arrived at the royal mews to pick up his chestnut charger Rifleman. Slightly oversized in every detail, from his snowy mutton-chop whiskers to the sparkling decorations riveted to his extensive chest, the duke was the apotheosis of a soldier. He had served the Queen, his cousin, as commander in chief of her army for thirty-nine conservative years and today, though no longer in office, he would serve her again by riding on the left of her carriage. After all, though seventy-eight, he was only a couple of months older than she was.

He sat Rifleman like a rock, watching the parade form in the distance. It was four miles long.

This was a family affair, so the colonial contingents were given pride of place at the head of the procession. They were so novel and so magnificent as to make what followed seem in danger of anticlimax. There were roughriders from the shadow of the Zulu hills, slouch-hatted and tanned; casual, smiling men from the tin-hutted towns of New South Wales and Victoria; dominion troops from a Canada that now stretched solid from ocean to ocean; gunners, cavalry and infantry from the booming settlements that England had fed with emigrants and treasure and now guarded with her ships. The smallest colonies and protectorates were represented. Malays, West Indians, Cypriots, Nigerians and Chinese marched, rank on rank of horsemen, police and riflemen in uniforms as multitudinous as fancy could envision. And then, resplendent and climactic, the cavalry of India clattered by in their long coats of dark green or blue or blazing scarlet, turbans striped and gleaming with gold, white-breeched and black-booted, sabers and scimitars smacking the leopard skins or gold emblazonry of their saddle cloths, their gauntlets a flash of white against their cummerbunds of silk, their shoulder chains bunched and glinting as they swung in their saddles. They were native officers, most of them, senior Risaldar-Majors of long and valiant service in such regiments as the 2nd Bengal Lancers (Gardner's Horse), and their beards were curled with the fastidiousness of dancing masters.

Behind them marched the regulars, the steady enduring instrument of England's will. They were quiet and sober, well drilled, and if they did not swagger like Prussians they were still purposeful men. Every regiment was there, dark highlanders slow-paced to their barbaric music, infantry of the line from Devon, London and the hills of Wales; some detachments were fusiliers, some light infantry, all had some singular mark of distinction or behavior. And every regiment represented had fought at some time in some place in the Queen's service. Precedence in this part of the procession belonged to the cavalry and among these the Household Regiments were first; no man there that could not swipe a sheep in half with a single backswing at sword practice. They were followed by lancers and hussars as dapper as money could make them, men who firmly believed that their prime purpose in war was to give tone to what might otherwise degenerate into a vulgar brawl. It stretched, this fantasy of a demonstration, as far as any eye could see and as it moved into position it waited, a great cataract of men and horses, for a low open carriage to emerge at the smartest pace consistent with dignity from the gates of Buckingham Palace.

The Queen had dressed that morning in her customary black. She wore full skirts and a bodice buttoned down the front and cut high and square at the neck, the whole lightened by fine white lace. Her stockings, which presumably only the eyes of God and her maid had ever seen *in situ,* were of the finest black silk with white soles. Bracelets of gold chain, hung about with lockets containing the hair of various children and grandchildren, jingled at her wrists, and round her neck she wore as usual her double-sided miniatures of Alice, Grand Duchess of Hesse, and the Duke of Albany. She settled her black bonnet, trimmed for the occasion with white feathers, firmly on her head and went out to face her ordeal. On her way to the landau with its eight white Hanoverian ponies docile in the traces, she caused to be dispatched a message to be telegraphed across the world. It read: "From my heart I thank my beloved people. May God bless them." She climbed stiffly into the carriage and took the gray silk parasol presented by her Members of Parliament. It was precisely fifteen minutes past eleven o'clock and until that moment no one among the tens of thousands waiting in the city had seen the sun. The first fulmination of the guns of the royal salute clouted the sky, the postillions and the footmen leaned forward, the carriage began to glide, and at that instant the sun came out in glory. It was "Queen's weather" again, and it could only be a prophecy.

Prince George cantered heavily but neatly to the side of the carriage and was the recipient of a gracious nod. On the other side rode the Earl of Dundonald of the 2nd Life Guards, commander of the Sovereign's Escort. In front of the carriage tittuped gallant Lord Wolseley, Prince George's successor at the head of the army, and a stirring sight with his plumes and his keen expression for any occasion. Behind came a flock of princes and personages feathered and multicolored and adazzle with honors. The crowd, which had spilt its ecstasy once already on the colonial troops far ahead, had had time to catch its breath by the time the Queen drove by. The cheering was a wave, changing as she approached into a roar of "God Save the Queen!" and the sonorous rhythm of the national anthem. So pressing was their enthusiasm that one senior courtier was unable to control his horse. It suddenly bolted clean past the royal carriage, found itself blocked by a wall of yelling faces, stopped dead and precipitated its eminent rider head first onto the roadway, where his cuirass, helmet and sword created a din, as Lord Dundonald put it, "such as a gigantic lobster might have made when dropped on a stone slab." Alarmed at such a clatter, the Queen stopped her carriage to ask how the victim was. Lord Dundonald assured her that no vital part had been injured. At this intelligence, Dundonald recorded, "Her Majesty with her usual kindness at once made Lord Howe a Grand Cross of the Victorian Order."*

By the time Her Majesty left Buckingham Palace, Richard Meinertzhagen had already drunk the glory of the colonial and empire troops. His years of scanning the atlas had finally come to life with a flash of lanceheads and a rumble of gun carriages. Behind him the darkened bricks of St. James's Palace echoed the

---

* Dundonald himself received a lesser decoration in the same Order, which proved of some value to him later for, as he said, "a short time afterwards the station-master at Nice received it, and was thereby inclined to give his brother in chivalry a seat in the express." A whimsical and imaginative fellow, Dundonald was the inventor of a waterproof canvas bag large enough to hold three men. Once occupied, the bag was tied at the top and could be hauled across a river on an endless rope, air being supplied through an india-rubber tube suported by a cork. His lordship demonstrated its utility for conveying the wounded by having himself pulled across the Thames, but his idea was never taken up. He earned distinction in the Boer War as one of the most vigorous and efficient of commanders in the field. At the outbreak of the First World War he unearthed his grandfather Admiral Cochrane's Secret Plans evolved in 1811 "to Secure at one Blow the Maritime Supremacy of England," presented them to Winston Churchill at the Admiralty, and became one of the pioneers of the tactical use of smoke screens.

cantering hoofs and the crunch of boots. In front of him file after file wheeled round from Piccadilly and down the hill toward his line of troopers. There was a slight brake in the flood, and there she was, coming straight at him, so small and so awe inspiring. Gingerly Richard raised his camera. The royal party turned past him into Pall Mall and the rhythm of the marching men resumed. The beat and the color clamored in Richard's head, waking thoughts not far removed from those of the journalist who wrote, reflecting on the imperial message, "You begin to understand, as never before, what the Empire amounts to. We send out a boy here and a boy there, and the boy takes hold of the savages and teaches them to march and shoot and believe in him, and die for him and the Queen." Even to a foreign eye the total effect was much the same. "All the nations seemed to be filing by," Mark Twain wrote. "It was a sort of suggestion of the Last Day." To Richard Meinertzhagen it was a kind of new day; the resolve he had begun to form to serve the Queen became a little more firm that morning. His resolution was soon put to the test: before the Yeomanry were dismissed from further duty, his squadron leader hauled him savagely and at length over the coals for so far having forgotten the duty and bearing of an officer as to take a photograph while on duty. It left Richard feeling tender and the experience was not at all mitigated when the photograph was developed and turned out to be an excellent close-up of his horse's ears.

Chastened but not wholly subdued, Richard joined the rest of the family at their town house in Rutland Gate. The excited chatter of aunts, uncles and a few cousins, as well as of the large band of sisters and brothers, soon put Richard in the best of spirits. He knew that he looked superb in his uniform and for once he allowed himself the luxury of feeling proud. It was as if he had been swimming all his life against an icy tide of criticism from his mother and disapproval from others, his every desperate lunge bringing him only closer to the numbing heart of loneliness, and now he had suddenly broken into a warm and silken lagoon. He basked like a porpoise. It was then that he suffered the most disastrous clash he had ever had with his mother. Outside the drawing room there was a veranda decorated for the occasion like almost every house in London with a number of big Union Jacks. The evening air was benign and the party had spilled out onto the veranda, conversing quietly, the men smoking cigars and cigarettes, except for Richard, who did not smoke. Someone threw a match over the balcony. It was still lit and set one of the flags ablaze. Richard seized the flag and began to crumple it in his bare hands to extinguish the flames. At that instant, with all her strength, his mother hit him across the face. His father shouted, "Georgie! Georgie!" Richard said not a word. Silent, shocked and agonized, he went up to his room and took off his uniform. Then he walked out of the house.

CHAPTER 1

What Nerve! What Muscle! What Energy!

The year of Richard Mein-ertzhagen's birth was a great one for daffodils. It was the Sunday before Lent, March 3, 1878; spring was already established across England and a mist of green buds danced along her southern hedgerows. Though pale, the sun was strong, the air clean and fresh as country churchbells climbed and tumbled, calling the English to stern duty and the visible practice of humility before an Almighty who in His wisdom had seen fit to favor this people above all others, and to Whom all nature gave obedience, in spite of Charles Darwin. To Victorians, the multitudes of daffodils afforded a double pleasure. The annual reappearance of their deep, serene yellow gave proof that all was for the best in the best of all possible worlds; it also provided opportunity for reflection on mortality, since by popular belief a flower that hung its head portended death. Fortunately, on this particular morning, the daffodils trumpeted certainty toward the sky and birth was in the air.

So a thousand rural clerics meditating among tombstones and the last of the snowdrops, much strengthened by the eloquence of spring, gathered about them their vestments of white lawn and, as the bells' clamor sank to a single striding note, rustled in to their crepuscular chancels. There they delivered their messages of divine love, of human duty, of just reward and of a smiling future that could be marred only by insensitivity or ingratitude or, worst of all, by radicalism. Soft-voiced and slow, their rural congregations sought blessings on the Queen and, separately, on the Prince of Wales who, if he lived long enough, would succeed her. They sang Mrs. Alexander's graceful hymn, popular at this season, which began:

> *All things bright and beautiful,*
> *All creatures great and small,*
> *All things wise and wonderful,*
> *The Lord God made them all,*

and which continued:

> *The rich man in his castle,*
> *The poor man at his gate,*
> *God made them high or lowly*
> *And ordered their estate.*

The farm laborers accepted Mrs. Alexander's detached view of things because it seemed to express the facts of life. They were realists, their ancestry too was bound to the rituals of the soil; in any case it would be best to go along with the service in the hope of a good seed-time and a better harvest than last year's. No one, certainly, was greatly disturbed, even if he knew of it, that other voices among the druid-haunted mineshafts of South Wales and in the grimy valleys of the North were singing with greater fervor quite different songs of praise. The England of the last quarter of the nineteenth century had numerous voices, and most were the voices of change.

The voice of Richard Meinertzhagen, which was to be heard for nine decades, made its first intimation of life that gentle morning at 10, Rutland Gate in Kensington, London, a royal borough which was then, if not the hub of the universe, at least within easy reach of it. He had been born, as it happened, on the brink of the greatest change of all, a tide that was carrying England to an Empire, and his voice would record its rise and fall; for, having arrived at the upsurge of that huge wave, he would ride its crest as it gathered, foamed and thundered reluctantly toward oblivion. The past, for this Sunday's child, meant privilege and wealth which, with some distinction on the part of various ancestors, had bred authority. To Victorians there was nothing squalid about money, though to care too much about it was vulgar. The wealth of Richard's father, Daniel, was solidly and respectably based on the great merchant banking firm of Frederick Huth and Company, then the leading acceptance house in the City of London and concerned mainly with the financing of foreign trade, an activity in which the City had become preeminent in the world. This connection, with others no less admirable, placed the Meinertzhagens firmly in the upper middle class which, though they could never have been crude enough to suggest it, was in practice the new aristocracy. The blood that mattered in this climax of the Victorian age was no longer blue; what coursed through the veins of the new imperialists and the loudest of the new moralists was the same color as the tinge that was spreading slowly across the map of the world—a full and uncompromising red.

In this carminization, Richard Meinertzhagen was to play a sturdy part, directed partly by environment and the virile currents of the times, and partly by an adventurousness inherited from both sides of his parentage and peppered on his mother's with a strain of eccentricity and a liberal measure of independence of mind. His mother's great-grandfather, a Yorkshire farmer turned draper, refused to light his windows to celebrate a British victory in the American War of Independence and lost them to the stones and cudgels of the mob. However, he prospered, as indeed he had to, being obliged to support four sons and four daughters. Two of the sons grew into pillars of that most monumental of cities, Manchester. When they first established their textile business there, Lancashire was already the altar of King Cotton; by 1836, the year before the teen-age Victoria came to the throne, the Potters were rich and confident enough to build a mammoth warehouse six stories high, each floor devoted to a different stock—fine wool, hosiery, silks, haberdashery, worsteds and cottons. They shipped anywhere from the

Yangtze ports to the Levant, but they always shipped exactly what was needed. Both were radicals in politics. One of them, Sir Richard Potter, sat in Parliament for Wigan, and the other, Sir Thomas, sat in the brand-new mayoral chair of Manchester; it would be hard to assess who, in those years, was the prouder.

Sir Richard Potter married a tall, dark woman, Mary Seddon, who revealed a wildness in her veins and a certain quixotic flair that came from either gypsy or Jewish breeding. A Hebrew scholar, she once bought a white donkey and, heeding the dictates of the Good Book as she construed them, assembled a small group of Jews behind her and rode off to reestablish them after two thousand years in the Holy Land. Her inspiration was not sufficient, however, to kindle much national pride in her bedraggled following, and by the time she reached Calais she was alone with her donkey, whence both were rescued by the more practical Sir Richard. Lapsing into sadder eccentricities, she died four years before the birth of her great-grandson Richard, in whom her plan and her initiative were oddly reincarnated.

The Potters' eldest son was, naturally enough, another Richard, who eventually shook off both the harsher climate of the North and the arduous liberalism of his father. Settling in Gloucestershire, a soft county of sighing woods and rich pastures, he married Lawrencina Heywood, daughter of yet another radical merchant and Member of Parliament, and a woman of great intellectual force. Richard became chairman of the Great Western Railway, the father of nine daughters, and a timber magnate. This last activity flourished by the fruition of a scheme to supply wooden huts to the army, then rotting and starving on the wintry beaches of the Crimea. He later conceived the idea of gouging out a canal from the Mediterranean through Syria to compete with the Suez Canal and wrung a concession to do so from the sultan, only to be frustrated by the leading British contractor of the day (in whom envy vied with cupidity) on the grounds that the canal would take forty years to fill and would submerge the Holy Places. But Richard Potter's greatest achievement was his daughters, once described by a distracted husband of one of them as a monstrous regiment. The fourth daughter, Georgina, was to become Richard Meinertzhagen's mother and her gift to him would bring both agony and love.

Richard was the second son born to Daniel and Georgina, but he was none the less welcome for that. His older brother, named after the father, could be expected to assume the responsibilities of the first-born. Victorian parents longed for sons because they meant security. A son could carry on the family name and protect the family fortunes if anything should happen to the father, which was not unlikely. The Victorians were not oppressed by any fears of annihilation but the minatory presence of fevers and disease nagged at them constantly. The typhoid that had carried off the Prince Consort and almost accounted for his son the Prince of Wales cut down one out of every three adults; though it was called by different names, its effect was universally recognized as deadly. Prince Albert had very likely contracted it at Windsor Castle itself, parts of which were rendered uninhabitable by the odors of ancient cesspits. Prince Edward, who had emerged from his delirium on the tenth anniversary of his father's death (a fact not unnoticed by the funerary Queen), had caught the fever during a visit to a house in Yorkshire which, though undeniably noble, had lethally bad drains.*

Sewage disposal was one of the last problems to be tackled in this era of immense technological advance, but what was still missing was any real knowledge of the true nature of illness and its cause. It was still customary in 1878 to locate a hospital by its stench. So likely was the probability of infection that surgeons hesitated to operate; their patients' death rate was as high as forty per cent even for minor operations, when even small incisions rapidly

---

* In 1858 London had suffered an epic visitation called the Great Stink, so pungent a miasma that the House of Commons itself was forced to rise early when even curtains doused in chlorinated water could not keep the fumes out of the Chamber. As late as the 1890s the main sewer of Cambridge still emptied into the slow-moving Cam. Her Majesty, visiting the bucolic university town, happened while crossing a bridge to glance down at the water and was prompted by what she saw floating there to ask her guide, the ingenious Master of Trinity College, a question. "Those, Ma'am," the Master answered, "are notices forbidding bathing."

turned green and black from what some described vaguely as a miasma in the air and some more specifically as a malignant effect of oxygen. In the month Richard Meinertzhagen was born, there appeared a better hope, though few recognized it at once. Joseph Lister, newly installed in a chair of surgery at King's College Hospital, published in *The Lancet* his report on the use of carbolic acid as an antiseptic. But Lister was a lonely pioneer. Considering the dangers still floating unseen in the Victorian air—diphtheria (the Queen's second daughter died of it that year after nursing her family in her palace in Hesse) and tuberculosis were common, as well as scarlet and other fevers, killers all—the remarkable thing was that so many had survived rather than that the mortality rate had fallen.

The Meinertzhagens eventually provided their own insurance in the form of four sons and six daughters. Richard was preceded by Daniel and Barbara, and followed by Margaret, Frederick, Lawrencina, Beatrice, Louis, Mary and Betty. They made a fine family—buoyant, vigorous and fortunate. They were lucky in their parentage and they were lucky to be born at a time when there was a high romance shining over the child's world. As well as the wonder of country things close at hand, theirs was the golden age of knightly chivalry. Between them, Lord Tennyson and William Morris had transformed the sordid facts of the Middle Ages into a land of perennial youth and perpetual innocence. Even false knights could behave sportingly on occasion, and castles were hygienic and their inhabitants well-groomed at all times, especially spiritually. Not long after the Meinertzhagens had set up house at Rutland Gate the Aesthetic Movement, which Morris' designs had largely inspired, became the rage and every fashionable wall bore some of his elaborate designs. Though Morris yearned after an age that had never really existed, and though his visual interpretation of it could be complicated, his verse ran with a fine simplicity:

> *Swerve to the left, son Roger, he said,*
> *When you catch his eyes through the helmet-slit,*
> *Swerve to the left, then out at his head,*
> *And the Lord God give you the joy of it!*

It was heady stuff for children. It sounded a bit like bayonet practice. The English were very fond of the expression "the Lord God" at this point; the addition of a peerage gave the Deity a majesty He probably did not enjoy in other countries. It made Him theirs.

When Victorian children tired of jousting there were other games. An educational system predominantly classical in tone furnished numerous tales of sunlit odysseys and Greeks and Trojans, and indeed the predilections formed in these early years often carried over into maturity, so that the administrators of the future might judge a man according to whether he seemed to belong temperamentally on the embattled walls of Troy or beneath them with sulky Achilles. Then there were the home-grown legends of Sir Walter Scott, which left many a child gasping his last among the rhododendrons with the dying words of Marmion on his lips: "Charge, Chester, charge! On, Stanley, on!" The situation was not dissimilar from those such children would have to face as adults while confronting hordes of Afghans or dervishes or Africans or, as it seemed at the time, Russians. Many Englishmen were still to die far off—Gordon under the broad spears in Khartoum, Scott in the ice of the South Pole, an entire army of Old Contemptibles within the first few weeks of the Great War in the poppy fields of Flanders—and they owed some of the dignity of their passing to manners assimilated in childhood.

The Victorians invented, after all, the Stiff Upper Lip, an endowment that has no description in anatomy. It was a means of withstanding the buffetings of a physical world which, with all their wealth and technology and steam power, they realized they could not completely control. So, with wisdom and a certain bravery, they committed the future to God and faced the storm. As their ancestors had bitten on bullets in the hills beside Corunna or on the littered fields of Waterloo to stop their wounded flesh from screaming, so Richard Meinertzhagen's contemporaries would remain mute under hardship, concerned first with enduring and second with betraying no evidence of weakness. Control was everything to the Victorians, and self-mastery under the awful eye of God was the first lesson they pressed upon their children. They flaunted nothing, neither riches nor pain nor intellect nor passion, and that made them seem men of ice. To adult Victorians the same Arthurian legend that gave their children simple pleasure held a stern and central moral. When Tennyson's Guinevere surrendered to the glamorous Sir Lancelot, she placed self-indulgence before self-sacrifice and by this loss of self-control and reversal of rectitude she broke faith with King Arthur. She thus destroyed the whole fabric of honor, truth and trust which the men of Daniel Meinertzhagen's time were at such pains to build and protect. Manliness could be measured by the progress the individual made toward this moral ideal, the visible evidence of which was a high seriousness in thought and act. Men lived and died by this difficult standard and its romanticism was intensely masculine. It was the force that drove men as different as Lawrence of Arabia and his friend Richard Meinertzhagen.

The Victorians were heavyweights in many ways, not only in their ethics. Their humor was lumpish, finding hilarity in brussels sprouts and rolling pins and the quaint remarks of precocious urchins and green curates, and above all in anything that seemed avant-garde. They giggled for hours over appalling conundrums like the one the Queen's private secretary put to his wife in a bad year for the cattle plague: Q. "Why is the rinderpest like a mouse?" A. "Because the cat'll get it." There were sharper wits than that, of course. The sanitary innovator Edwin Chadwick, upon being created a Knight Commander of the Order of the Bath, observed that it was to distinguish him from the great unwashed.

As for diet, great reliance was placed on boiled puddings, both savory and sweet, and the heavier the better. Breakfast in a home like the Meinertzhagens' was spread out on the sideboard in a variety of heated silver platters which, when uncovered, revealed deviled kidneys, kedgeree (a concretion of fish and eggs derived from India), lamb chops, steaks and occasionally a curry as well as staples like ham, eggs and sausages. Daniel Meinertzhagen would commonly take three or four courses, with a couple of boiled eggs and some marmalade as an afterthought. One great delicacy provided by Fortnum and Mason was hung beef, grated into a fluffy pile, then eaten by overturning pieces of buttered toast onto it. This was a great treat in the nursery, where small children took all their meals. Dinner, even in a home of moderate means, could extend over eleven courses, beginning with soup and moving inexorably through fish, fowl, meat and game to pudding, cheese, fruit and nuts, with bottle after bottle of claret.

This solidity of the Victorians accompanied them wherever they went. Even on its annual trips to the seaside, a reasonably affluent family would fill half a baggage car with necessaries, including a hip bath. However far afield they ventured, they were disinclined to travel light or to live in any way like the natives. Ladies retained their layers of petticoats and their tight-laced corsets even on the equator, and soldiers slogging up the Nile were issued with thick, sausage-shaped pads of kapok to keep the sun from striking the spine through their scarlet broadcloth tunics. Solid old-fashioned plum puddings, as devastating in the heat as cannonballs, followed Richard Meinertzhagen into the sweltering African bush and generations of Englishmen in forlorn outposts sat down thankfully to local versions of suet pudding and trifle sickly with sherry. Victorians abroad—and abroad began on the far side of the English Channel—settled firmly inside invisible stockades where they could practice their stolid habits without bothering, or being bothered by, the inhabitants. For many, the last word on foreigners and their light customs had been spoken by Mr. Podsnap: "They do—I am sorry to be obliged to say it—as they do. For this island was blessed, Sir, to the direct exclusion of such other countries as there may happen to be." For others, including Charles Dickens, it was not enough to cultivate, as Podsnap did, a flourish of the right arm, which would clear the world of its most difficult problems by sweeping them behind them. Though the English stayed inside their compounds, they were not all unaware of what was going on outside, and if many vacationed abroad in bizarre outfits, carrying umbrellas to beat the porters with, there were others who caricatured them as oafs. What was universal, however, was the sense of mission. Victoria's people did not expect foreigners to copy them faithfully, but they certainly believed in setting an example for those who wished to have the right guideline through life. That example was based on habit, on decorum and on the desirability, above all, of avoiding any fuss.

When a fuss happened they acted. They were incisive and swift in execution and their methods were as ruthless as need be to restore the status quo. Almost all their policies until late in the century were aimed at protecting the tranquility of Europe and, incidentally, of India. Politicians, historians, philosophers and essayists spent much energy examining alternatives to any imaginable set of disruptive circumstances; when the unforeseen appeared they stopped talking and loaded the troopships. In 1878 the Indian Mutiny was still an alarming memory. Its heroes were now senior officers, many with the dull crimson ribbon of the Victoria Cross on their chests, among them Major General Sir Sam Browne, who had lost an arm charging the rebel guns at Sirpura and who passed into eternity as the inventor of a military belt. The Mutiny was alarming because it demonstrated to the British that their presence was unwelcome, that the frenzied outburst of their sepoys was more than a Muslim reluctance to bite cartridges smeared with pork fat or a Hindu antipathy to beef dripping. More dangerous still, it showed up their rule as incompetent. They took steps to change things. Having put down the rebellion, they exterminated its leaders by hanging them or, more dramatically, by strapping their arms to the wheels of cannon to bring their chests snug up against the muzzles, then blasting them into red mist. Thereafter they disbanded the Honorable East India Company and substituted a new government designed to canalize national feelings, and administered by an elite civil service which comprised no more than a thousand men. But each was an autocrat, even the most junior being expected to rule single-handedly a territory bigger than most English counties. They did so because they were capable, dedicated men.* They were

---

* They were men of a type that could quell a revolt with a swagger cane and a cold stare. In 1924 one like them, Hubert Jervoise Huddlestone, then chief of staff and adjutant general of the Egyptian army, ended a mutiny among Sudanese infantry in Khartoum by walking toward them alone and unarmed across a bridge. They surrendered and walked back to barracks,

supported, as was only wise, by a reinforced white garrison of considerable strength and by an infrastructure of public works of irrigation and famine relief. By 1878 Simla, Delhi and the Punjab were names as well known in English homes as Manchester or Dover, and Richard Meinertzhagen would not be very surprised later to find himself visiting all of them.

On the day Richard Meinertzhagen was born, March 3, 1878, a peace was signed between Russia and Turkey at San Stefano, somewhat to the relief of the latter and the annoyance of the former. The Russians had swept victoriously through the Balkans, leaving a great deal of blood on the snow, and had pressed on for the Golden Horn, only to espy, riding at anchor in Besika Bay with the minarets of Constantinople in the distance, the admonitory, squat black shapes of British ironclads. That disposition had been the inspiration of Her Britannic Majesty's Prime Minister, Mr. Benjamin Disraeli.

San Stefano was less a conclusion than a prelude. For the balance was too obviously in Russia's favor and the Powers of Europe moved to adjust the scale with Disraeli's fingers on the weights, capable of manipulations as byzantine as any managed from St. Petersburg. In June 1878 a Congress assembled in Berlin, where that most honest of brokers Prince Bismarck supervised a revision of the Treaty of San Stefano, the amputation of a large part of Russia's gains and the partial dismemberment of the Ottoman Empire. Disraeli bore away with Cyprus, a joint protectorate of Egypt to safeguard the Suez Canal, and a commitment in the greater part of Arabia—circumstances that fore-ordained the careers of many young men like Richard Meinertzhagen.

Disraeli and his Foreign Secretary, Lord Salisbury, returned to a delirious London. Potted palms, banks of geraniums and roses twined round a forest of cast-iron pillars, had turned Charing Cross station into an immense red hothouse to welcome the Prime Minister. The statesmen drove to Downing Street, swathed from end to

---

treading delicately. In 1946 Huddlestone was governor general of the Sudan and when asked how he could have done such a thing explained, "It never occurred to me that they would do otherwise."

end in scarlet cloth, in a carriage kindly loaned by Lady Aber-
gavenny, and Dizzie appeared on the balcony to announce, "We
have brought you back, I think, Peace with Honor!" The rosy glow
of these events warmed the Queen. "High and low the whole
country is delighted," she wrote, "except Mr. Gladstone, who is
frantic." Disraeli heard all summer the roar of popular opinion
behind him. The people had picked up from The Great Macdermott,
their music-hall idol, a song that was even quoted amid suitable
hilarity in the House of Commons. "The rugged Russian Bear," it
proclaimed, was "full bent on blood and robbery." There was only
one answer to *that*:

> *We don't want to fight, but by Jingo if we do,*
> *We've got the ships, we've got the men,*
> *We've got the money too.*
> *We've fought the Russian Bear before,*
> *And while we're Britons true*
> *The Russians shall not have Constantinople.*

It was the first rumble of the imperial theme.

That jingo summer was also the fourth in a row in which the
wheat had rotted in the harvest fields, beaten down and blighted by
continuous rains. What little had been gathered steamed dankly in
the ricks. For the second year merchantmen were unloading American wheat into British ports, fat-grained and beautiful to mill,
straight from the new prairie lands that had no need of fertilizer.
Ironically, it had been carried out of the Middle West on tracks
made of British rail forged and finished years before in Dowlais
and Middlesborough. English farmers had begun to turn over their
land to grass and sheep, but now a plague of liver-rot had hit the
flocks and they were dying by the hundred. The depression in agriculture was accompanied by a short recession in industry and trade
which brought wage cuts to Wales and the North. At the beginning
of the year there were deserted ironworks at Merthyr and Aberdare,
production of coal in Cardiff alone had fallen off a hundred thousand tons a month and, out of five hundred pits in two counties,
only twenty were working full time. People were feeding on

potato peelings, raw cabbage leaves and brewers' grains. By the
year's end only one in four of the blast furnaces that had scorched
the skies of the Midlands was still alight. Just before Christmas
sixty thousand textile workers in Manchester huddled in their
shawls on the relief lines provided by charity. The structure of the
modern economic state was shaping itself around their unconscious
heads: Marx had not yet been published in English, and Henry
George, who was to be a prophet to Richard Meinertzhagen's Aunt
Beatrice Webb and those socialist friends of hers young Richard
would later abhor, was far off in New York, busily preparing
Progress and Poverty for his publisher.

The emphasis in England, particularly, but not exclusively, for
the lower orders, was on self-help, individually and collectively, but
there were thousands upon thousands, caught up in the satanic
mills and the robot life of the machines, who could not now hope to
emulate the mid-Victorian paragons of Samuel Smiles.* For these
the hope was education and beneath their longing for that and their
struggle to gain it shone always the central mid-Victorian conviction
that good must come of effort, an ethic which was preached at
them twice on every Sunday.

Nonconformity was now a broad movement and Charles
Haddon Spurgeon, the greatest of its leaders, had been publishing
a sermon a week for twenty years. At the century's end there
were still two thousand five hundred of them on sale. Spurgeon
drew six thousand people to every service in his Metropolitan
Tabernacle, binding them with his rich voice and awesome bulk,
and even more by the fervor of his appeals to their consciences. He
would take his Calvinistic texts from the harsh verses of Ecclesiastes,

---

* Smiles's *Self Help,* published in 1859, gave inspiration and fifty million
readers to Horatio Alger. It was followed by *Character, Thrift* and *Duty.*
Smiles's noble theme was that the mass was composed of individuals and that
the failure or success of each individual affected society as a whole. His later
works were popular biographies of workingmen who had made good. Smiles
achieved one beautiful definition: "The capitalist is merely a man who does
not spend all that is earned by work. He is a man prepared to forego present
satisfaction in the hope of future reward."

enjoining, "Whatsoever thy hand findeth to do, do it with all thy might," with the awareness of the grave always behind his sonorous rhetoric, but always, too, with the hope of salvation through Christ. In a sense, Victorian religion was class-conscious. In the raw chapels of the industrial towns they thought of the Savior; in the proper churches of the middle classes, of the Lord; and before the private altars of the aristocracy the spirit was addressed to God Almighty. Spurgeon's austere teaching infused generations beyond his own, yet like many of his persuasion, he was neither ascetic nor humorless. He once presided over a banquet arranged by the Butchers of London, where all present chose to sing the hymn "There is a fountain filled with blood."

The Victorians' preference, naturally, was for the heaven-directed. In architecture they turned to the aspiring pinnacles and arrowheads of stone of the Gothic style, rejecting the more earthbound massiveness of the neoclassic affected by their grandfathers. The comfortable, even lavish, Meinertzhagen home lay on the edge of that huge complex of museums and institutions, including the Albert Hall, with which the Queen planned to calcify the memory of her departed Consort. From the end of Rutland Gate the young Meinertzhagens could see, two blocks away, the great symbol of the age, completed six years before Richard's birth. The Albert Memorial was regarded by its architect, Sir Gilbert Scott, as his masterpiece. In his lengthy career he had restored no fewer than eleven cathedrals; now he restored a memory and laid bare a nation's dreams. His exuberant stalagmite, polychromatic with tile and marble, mosaic, granite, bronze and building stone, was an encyclopedia of Victorian attitudes and Victorian hopes. Mythologies were ransacked for deities to guard the central brooding figure, history and the arts and sciences emptied of their heroes to fill the carved relief below him, while beasts and divinities from every continent proclaimed the far-flung sway of the Prince's mourning wife.

In 1878, however, the sway was not as extensive as it would shortly be. Though the soldiers of the Queen were marching hilltop by hilltop through the tribesmen of Afghanistan, and though her representative in South Africa had won the Ninth Kaffir War and was arranging the destruction of the Zulu King, many officials in Her Majesty's Colonial Office were contemplating a complete withdrawal from West Africa. That year the Anglo-American adventurer Henry Morton Stanley, whom Richard Meinertzhagen would one day befriend, published *Through the Dark Continent*, which, though accepted as a tale of heroic endeavor, illuminated the future hardly at all. For the British, nothing much had changed in West Africa since their squadrons had lain in wait there for slave ships. It had been said then:

> *Beware and take care of the Bight of Benin:*
> *There's one comes out for forty goes in.*

And it was still true. There was enough trouble on the other side of the continent, where a joint commission of British and French was trying to find a way of keeping the Sultan of Turkey's vassal, the Khedive of Egypt, and his miserable country out of debt. Before Richard Meinertzhagen reached his fifth birthday the British would enter Egypt with the bayonet, and before he reached his teens new territories fifty times the size of the British Isles would have been added to the Empire.

Such things were not accomplished by milksops. The Victorians —even the late ones—were hard men with a brutal heritage. Young men just entering on their careers could remember public executions and the white-capped bodies of murderers hanging outside Newgate Prison at the top of Ludgate Hill. Flogging was still lawful in the army on active service and a man who deserted, if he escaped the rope, would still be left with a black D branded on his chest. Not only the lower orders suffered. The public schools could be purgatories of discipline imposed in the name of character-building. The eminent Victorians were no Pickwickians. Their portraits show them as lean men, firm-lipped, searching and certain of eye, bony and imperative, capable of any exertion of thought or action. When Disraeli frothed, "What nerve! What muscle! What energy!" after an audience with the Queen in 1879, he implied far more than an individual picture.

Victoria and her people, largely unknowing, were at the doorway to another world. It was a world substantially at peace, but arms maintained it. It was an age of expansion that brought imbalance, of profit that brought new inequality. It was the beginning of a time when certainties were questioned and doubts began to have their reasons. The earlier Victorians had been the most religious people of modern times, believing wholeheartedly in their God and in salvation through work. Their deepest longings and their most precious ideal had been expressed by Winwood Reade in his strange book *The Martyrdom of Man*: "Not only will man subdue the forces of evil that are without; he will subdue those that are within. He will repress the base instincts and propensities which he has inherited from the animals below him; he will obey the laws written in his heart; he will worship the divinity that is within him." Reade foretold the conquest of disease, the division of space, planet by planet, and the ultimate mastery of the forces of nature. His vision—based as it was within the human mind and heart with their powers of self-control and self-expression, passionate and pure—lay at the core of the Victorian ideal. When Reade's book was published in 1872, the dream was already slipping away. Though thousands upon thousands would live and die by what they saw of that ineffable vision, it was already being eroded, not by the forces of nature or of economics, but by the ancient weaknesses of the human spirit. Richard Meinertzhagen would be one of those who swam against the current, for, in a sense, he was born already an anachronism.

CHAPTER 2

I Never Saw Such
a Perfect Little Animal

I f Daniel Meinertzhagen had a grand passion, other than for rectitude, it was for fishing. Soon after his marriage to Georgina Potter, who never liked London but who grew equally restless in the country, he rented a house some sixty miles away from the city, deep in the bare wolds and dark woods of Hampshire, and near the River Test, a chalk stream famous for its trout. He did not care that his sons, with the dispositions and appetites of poachers, could take more fish with wire or spear than he could with an Olive Dun or March Brown flicked sweetly below the willows. Daniel Meinertzhagen had to satisfy only himself in matters of judgment, and no one else. His temperament, calm, patient, and well supplied with relevant knowledge, was perfectly suited to his pastime, which provided him more with the remote satisfaction of the artist than with the sensuous thrill of the hunter.

The equilibrium of Daniel Meinertzhagen's life was not universal in his family, nor had it always been. The liveliest eccentric young Richard remembered was his father's uncle Louis Huth, who at the time of Richard's birth was Sheriff of the neighboring county of Sussex. Born and raised to wealth,* C'lou, as he was called,

* His father, Frederick Huth, C'lou once hopefully hinted to Richard, was perhaps the clandestine son of a Spanish grandee of superior rank. What

greatly preferred using money to making it and, released from previous restrictions by his father's death, concentrated on the former art, though not, of course, to excess. He satisfied an exquisite taste by collecting *objets,* particularly Chinese porcelains, which he protected from the multitudinous children of the family, after one costly accident, by banning them entirely from his house. Much loved by all who knew him, C'lou was extremely generous to others and by no means unkind to himself, feeling no scruple about indulging his own simple whims as they came upon him. After dinner he would take out his false teeth for comfort and hygiene and clank them about in his fingerbowl, somewhat to the embarrassment of his guests but not to himself, since he had grown rather deaf. It was his habit, when finding himself in boring company, to call out, "All right, I'm coming!" and swiftly disappear, a technique which could not have offended acquaintances and certainly saved C'lou much wear and tear. He was a tall man, thin and rigid, who carried his head at a slightly quizzical angle. His face was aquiline, with a firm mouth bracketed by deep lines curving inward to a great fierce nose; and it usually wore an expression at once imperious and inquisitive. His eyes, hooded and pouched, were those of a hanging judge, but all this forbidding exterior hid the nature of an elf. C'lou was unpredictable, save for one outward expression of mood, which he indicated by means of wigs. Left bald by sickness at an early age, C'lou's normal wig was dark brown; he had a blond one for frivolous occasions, a black one for times of mourning, a white one for other catastrophes, all superbly made and attractively natural, and a matted wig of blazing red which he wore only in his short-lived moments of rage. Even this device was not enough to reveal with absolute certainty C'lou's moods at all times, for he would occasionally discover in the middle of dinner that the ambience had altered his feelings and he would have to retire to his dressing

---

was indisputable was Huth's intimacy with the royal family of Spain. He rescued the queen's jewels from Napoleon's columns and was given the profitable responsibility of paying the salaries of Spanish embassies and consulates all over the world. Old Mr. Huth died in 1864 worth over a million pounds and still, like a good Victorian, innocent of any kind of ostentation.

room for a change. Toward the end of his long life, his capricious-
ness was further clouded by absence of mind. Driving one afternoon
with his great-nephew Richard, C'lou noticed a familiar figure on
the road and was worried that the name escaped him. The carriage
was stopped, the dignified old man raised his hat, peered into the
pedestrian's face, and said agreeably, "I know your face very well,
sir, but cannot for the life of me recollect your name." It was his
butler.

C'lou's sister Amelia, named after the queen of Spain, was
wooed and won by Richard Meinertzhagen's grandfather Daniel,
an immigrant from Germany. In 1833 Daniel and Amelia Meinertzhagen settled into the unpretentious mode of the Huth family and
began to build the English branch of the Meinertzhagens. By the
time their fifth offspring and first son, Daniel, arrived on October
28, 1842, Daniel and Amelia had moved to a larger house at 25
Devonshire Place in Marylebone, behind the stucco and serendipity
of the Nash terraces arcing round Regent's Park, and very close to
the house in which Elizabeth Barrett was defying sickness and her
tyrannical father. Daniel was not yet a year old when his father
began wondering what to make of him, observing with paternal
prejudice that the infant was "decidedly too clever for a merchant."
Daniel's delicate feelings were near the surface as a child; even the
unexpected repainting of the door at Devonshire Place was shock
enough to move him to tears. His schooldays were not remarkable
and no record was left of them by that uncommunicative man. Like
most of his class, he was sent away to boarding schools, but not, as
might have been expected, to one of the great public schools then
beginning to come into their own as forcing-houses for the new
leaders. Whatever the nature of his early education, it accomplished
enough to get him into Oxford in his eighteenth year.

Oxford and Cambridge were then the only universities, though
there were reported to be seats of learning elsewhere in the country.
Cambridge, isolated in its East Anglian swamps, was somewhat
quicker to embrace the new science, while disputatious Oxford
tended to concern itself more with the controversy then beginning,
after Darwin's *Origin of Species* appeared in 1859, about the no-

man's-land between scientific and theological interpretations of the universe. Oxford was superbly fitted for such a contest. Each side of the argument could recruit from platoons of eminent scholars capable of chopping any logic, with a knot of eccentrics on the sidelines swift enough to run down the most sophistical hare. What Oxford eventually offered was a middle way between the materialists and agnostics, which, because of its heritage, it had been well suited to build. It allied Hellenism with Christianity and produced John Ruskin to write the marriage lines.

Oxford in Daniel Meinertzhagen's time was, as ever, the home of professionals masquerading as amateurs. It was easy for Daniel to float on the charmed stream of privileged life that flowed, unhurried and delectable, past its medieval walls, curling and eddying round the memories and testaments of vanished bishops and regretted patrons. A fourteenth-century foundation, Daniel Meinertzhagen's college still owned in the 1860s the silver-gilt cup given it by Edward II; it was still accused of having stolen that famous relic, the skin of Saint Bartholomew, and it still spoke proudly of its great alumnus Sir Walter Raleigh, deceased in 1618 after an encounter with the headsman's ax. More recently, its common room had sheltered the leaders of the Oxford, or Tractarian, Movement* and still retained a faint tang of the schismatic smoke of the fires they had started there. Ecclesiastical argument was never to Daniel Meinertzhagen's taste, but there was much else to occupy him.

On the river, oars flashed and dipped past college barges clotted with heraldry, and punts slid through shadowed backwaters on afternoons that had no end. On May Morning the choristers sang to the dawn from Magdalen's tower as they had for four hundred years, and the Morris Dancers clacked prancing down the High Street as they had for even longer. Men swam naked at Parson's

---

* The chief of these was John Henry Newman, who changed his cloth from that of the Church of England to that of Rome in a cloud of obloquy and glory. Newman was the author not only of the hymn "Lead, Kindly Light," with its intensely poignant burden ("The night is dark, and I am far from home"), but also of thoughts of inspired grace: "It is almost a definition of a gentleman to say that he is one who never inflicts pain."

Pleasure, or they hunted or professed poetry or took up manly exercises or entertained in their oak-lined rooms, or practiced with friends the difficult art of argument. Study could be avoided and many undergraduates never took degrees. Of those who did, the elite followed the classics or "Greats," as Oxford called it. This was Daniel's subject for three years, by which time he was enough of a scholar to read Sophocles, Plato and Aristotle with ease. He also contracted a love for French and English literature and history, and had picked up as well one cap for sculling and another for billiards. In later life he never spoke about his Oxford years to his children, but some observations his son Richard made point to what they gave him. They confirmed in him a belief in the privilege of birth backed by tradition, they trained his mind in analysis, they taught him to distrust the pseudo-intellectual, they impressed on him the necessity for work, and, with typical irony, they injected into him a faint strain of fatalism. His Oxford was not only the Oxford of ancient dons muttering at long-dead enemies, it was the Oxford of Jowett, the maker of proconsuls.

Benjamin Jowett came from nothing and died the Vulcan of the Victorian mind. No academic exercised over his times the ascendancy of the pink-cheeked, blue-eyed autocrat with the cherub's face who lived in Balliol as a snail lives in its shell. When Daniel Meinertzhagen was at Oriel, Jowett was at the peak of his years as a classical tutor at Balliol and his influence spread through the university. In all, Jowett spent fifty-seven of his seventy-six years in the college. He had never played a game or danced; he had once smoked a cigarette "abroad"; and he died a virgin. His genius and his passion were for teaching and his religion was work. "Cease to drift!" he exhorted. He had no time for show or transient popularity. Numbers of his students encountered his disapproval of any tremor of the will; one of them, confessing one morning that he had lost his faith, was told, "I hope you will be able to find it again before twelve o'clock tomorrow, or you will have to go down from this college." Jowett was traduced for his "rationalism" by inferior clerics and denied his reward for a time, but it was his integrity and energy that gave to a series of Victorian bishops, cabinet ministers, governors and senior civil servants the sense of purpose that helped renew the Church and re-create the machinery of government. Though Daniel Meinertzhagen was never Jowett's pupil, he took away with him from Oxford that teacher's principles, which later made him known for his probity throughout the City of London.

He also took with him another Oxford characteristic, a faint air of aestheticism spiced with an exotic aroma from the East. During Daniel Meinertzhagen's university years, Edward FitzGerald's strange and slender work *The Rubaiyat of Omar Khayyam* became the rage, and Oxford's undergraduates, with palates avid as usual for new sensations, tasted, gulped, and grew intoxicated on its subtle essences. Though he had never seen Asia, FitzGerald had caught the shifting vagueness of Omar's habitudes and milieu and with it the clear tinkling echoes of the good life in a Persian courtyard. He passed on Omar's easy reflections, each quatrain self-sufficient, but all adding up to an epicurean view of life and a fatalistic attitude toward the hereafter, both accompanied by the faintest air of melancholy. Certainly this epicurism would have appealed to Daniel Meinertzhagen, who, though he would never believe that life's highest good was happiness, enjoyed luxury as much as C'lou. There was, too, a dreaming quality about him, in the eyes, as if his senses were at play with something seductive and far-off.

In 1864 Daniel joined his father at Huth's. By then they were living in their new mansion, Belmont, in Wimbledon, heavy with mahogany and sparkling with chandeliers. Careful of expense, his father went in to the office by train. Daniel had grander ideas. Refusing to ride in such a filthy thing, he traveled to London daily in a mail phaeton. The extravagance, not unnaturally, irked his father, but an ultimatum was reached only after two years of argument. Daniel answered it by resigning from the firm and starting to hunt for a house in the center of London. His father bought him an apartment in Albany, a discreet courtyard off Piccadilly given over to bachelors and reticence, and allowed him two thousand pounds a year, of which less than forty disappeared in income tax. He kept three fine horses and a groom, hunted, shot, ambled through the glittering London season, and traveled, whenever the fancy took him, to Paris, Vienna or Budapest. They were years of unimaginable ease and pleasure, unclouded and unregretted, and few other times, before or since, could have afforded them to Daniel Meinertzhagen. In 1869 his father died and the idyll ended. Daniel had to consider where his best interests and his duty lay. He went back to Huth's, who sent him off at once on a tour of South America, part of it by pack mule, to learn the business. His other notable tour for the firm was to Russia, where he shot bears and enjoyed a banquet in the Kremlin. He never talked much about these journeys, or about his life as a conspicuously eligible bachelor, which he continued until the fall of 1872, when he was invited to Richard Potter's home in Gloucestershire, Standish House. Potter had a business connection with Frederick Huth and Company, and Frederick's son Henry was friendly with the philosopher Herbert Spencer, who was so close to the Potters as to rate almost as a member of the family. Whatever its genesis, the first confrontation of this fashionable man with the redoubtable Potter sisters was no contest. He was thirty years old, exquisitely dressed, polished in manner, adorned with a full beard and blatant whiskers. He wore a sleepy expression and used a monocle. The nine sisters stared, sniffed and marked him firmly in their critical minds as a fop. Out hunting, Daniel took a bad fall and broke some of his elegant bones; while he was convalescing at Standish House, Georgina Potter began to recognize his real worth. Early in the next year the Potter girls were brought to London, and Georgina and Daniel rode together in Rotten Row. One morning in a downpour that had discouraged other riders, finding the Potters' groom out of earshot, Daniel proposed.

Their first child, Daniel VII, was born at the start of the third year of their marriage; the next year came Barbara and then Richard, or Oliver as he was first called. His birth had been registered in that name, but almost at once the choice was questioned. Just before the christening his mother suggested Henry and wrote, "I like Harry very much; he is such a splendid person, sleeping and growing like a creature without a brain to worry it. I never saw such a perfect little animal." At the church door Daniel Meinertz-hagen, who could not dissociate the little animal's name from Oliver Cromwell's, whom he regarded as a tyrant and a revolutionary, insisted on a change but would not accept Henry. A rapid compromise produced Richard, after Georgina's father, a credit to Meinertzhagen diplomacy. The infant's godparents were Richard Potter, his mother's sister Margaret and his father's brother Ernest.

Uncle Ernest's most spectacular gift to his godson was an elephant. His life was of generous proportions in more ways than one. He early displayed the Meinertzhagen love of food by inexplicably bursting into tears one day, after suddenly remembering that he had not eaten asparagus for a whole year. Though delicate as a child, in manhood he was immensely strong; bearded at the age of seventeen, he never shaved, though he lived to be seventy-nine. He had worked briefly at Huth's, the universal providers, but quit to satisfy a great lust for travel. His first burst took him through Chile and the Isthmus, the islands of the South Pacific and the Antipodes, where he met his future wife, Richard's Aunt Gwavas. There was an interlude spent practicing law, then the couple married and at once began a series of wanderings in Alaska, Japan, Southeast Asia and the jungle frontiers of China. All their lives they were kind friends to Richard, as munificent in warmth of spirit as they were lavish with presents, wise advice and religious precept. Richard was also fortunate in his other godparents. Aunt Margaret, the most vivacious of the Potter sisters, though she had seven children of her own, gave him the affection he craved. Richard Potter taught him to pray, simply by kneeling down beside the child as he gabbled away and explaining what the words meant, and showed him how to ask for special guidance, a practice he never forgot. A little wooden chair, a china mug and a framed photograph he gave his grandson were still treasured by that grandson nine decades later.

The infant Richard was suckled by a wet nurse, a fairly common custom then, especially in more well-to-do families, since it relieved the sociable mother of the more exacting of her maternal duties soon after her confinement. In Georgina's case, the substitution was made for medical reasons. When Richard was visited by his former foster mother at around the age of four, he ran out of the room, alarmed either by some atavistic memory or by her obtrusive appearance. In fact, alternatives were not much more agreeable. Cow's milk, even if not considered too strong for infants, was by no means guaranteed pure, or even fresh, in the cities. Richard's sister Beatrice was fed on donkey's milk from the Donkey Dairy at Marble Arch. Asses' milk cost nearly twenty times as much as cows' milk but it was in heavy demand from valetudinarians and babies, who drank it, from beauties who bathed in it, and from one Member of Parliament who used it for shining his boots because his valet insisted there was nothing like it for getting up a high gloss.

Fortunately, by the time Richard was even dimly aware of his surroundings, the wet nurse had been supplanted by a goddess of a type often worshiped in Victorian families. At least a generation of England's leaders owed as much to these women as they did to their putative mothers. Sarah Peacock ruled in the nursery with the same air of benevolent despotism that Her Majesty the Queen spread over the rest of the realm. If Georgina made a sally into her fiefdom and there was a disagreement, Sarah would clap on an old bonnet and leave, only to return within minutes and declare, "No, I shall not leave my children to the mercy of Mrs. Meinertzhagen." In thirty years Sarah never took an afternoon off for sickness or for relaxation, disdained any help, and seldom ventured as far as the lower floors of the house. She served the Meintertzhagens for over fifty years and Richard owed her more than he could ever repay.

Richard's world for his first few years was a large room dominated by Sarah's enormous bed, usually sprinkled with small children. Twice a day their father flitted in, always smiling, if otherwise undemonstrative, and occasionally threatening, "I'll bring Bony to you!", a deterrent he remembered from his own youth but which was quite lost on his offspring, who had never heard of the dreadful Napoleon Bonaparte.

Beyond the railings at the front of the house was the hard

mud of Rutland Gate, which led up to Knightsbridge and James, the crossing-sweeper. James kept a path clear for the thin shoes of the gentry and was awarded a few pence for it; he was noteworthy not only for his age but also because he swung about, wielding his broom with the help of crutches, having lost a leg at Balaklava. He charged with the Light Brigade, but his horse was shot from under him, threw him and broke his leg, which was amputated without anaesthetic. "Oh, Master Dick," he would recall, leaning on his broom, "it gives me the shivers whenever I think of it; the pain was summat awful!" and the quivering little boy would ask again and again for the terrible tale. When Frederick was born, James's domain was strewn for sixty yards with a carpet of straw to deaden the noise of carriages passing by, not an infrequent custom during a confinement expected to be difficult. Frederick's arrival turned the scale and the family moved to a larger house in the same street. By the time Richard was old enough to ride in the park, which the Meinertzhagen children enjoyed daily in the company of a groom who led them solemnly along Rotten Row, the old stone setts of major carriageways like Knightsbridge and Piccadilly had been replaced by wooden paving. The children saw nothing incongruous in the men with dust pans and brooms stationed every two hundred yards, whose duty was the instant removal of horse droppings. On Sundays the great treat was a ride in a hansom cab to the zoo in Regent's Park, home of the eponymous pachyderm Jumbo. In his seventeen years at the zoo Jumbo, an African bull elephant, had carried tens of thousands of wriggling children on his amiable back, and when he was sold to P. T. Barnum's American Circus in 1882 there was a national outcry.*

Two or three times a week old Amelia Meinertzhagen would come swinging into Rutland Gate in her landau with the spotted dog running under it, to see her grandchildren and bring them presents. Some days there would be a German brass band, noisy but

---

* Three years later, in a moment of elephantine forgetfulness, Jumbo tried conclusions with a train in Ontario, Canada, derailed the locomotive, and died of wounds.

unpopular. The Italian barrel organs with monkeys in green jackets to take the pennies were greatly preferred, at least by the children. Georgina Meinertzhagen would send out a footman with sixpence as a bribe to move off, but it was usually matched by a similar donation from her children entreating the organ grinder to stay. The last of the performing bears sometimes shambled into London, clinking money boxes round their necks, and one autumn evening in Knightsbridge there was a man who made a hare dance on a tambourine. Some of the old street vendors with their distinctive cries still made their rounds with bunches of lavender, fresh herrings, or shallow baskets of muffins to be eaten dripping with butter in front of comfortable nursery fires. There was the rumble of the fire engine, brass bell clanging and firemen shouting to their galloping grays. And every evening came the newsboys shrilling as they ran down Rutland Gate.

On February 11, 1879, they sent a shiver down that stately preserve with tidings of disaster at a forlorn place called Isandhlwana in the green rolling hills of Zululand, quite unknown to the mass of taxpayers. There the black regiments of Cetshwayo, the Zulu King, an unfamiliar monarch, had wiped out a force of nine hundred red-coated infantry sent to depose him. For a while the volley fire of the British had held off Cetshwayo's warriors, but when it slackened, the Zulu regiments had stood one by one, drummed on their oxhide shields, stamped the hard earth in unison, for the first time uttered their deep and sibilant war cry, and surged onward in an arc almost a mile across. They carried the heavy, broad-bladed assegai they called *iKlwa* (after the noise it made when plucked out of a wound), and after the killing split open each corpse at the belly, after their fashion, to release the spirit. The British shipped out ten thousand regulars as fast as they could get them to the troopships, and by midsummer their cavalry had ridden down the running warriors of Cetshwayo's last shattered regiment as if they were ground game. Even so, the army's showing against a power that, however gallant, remained barbaric, had not been such as to encourage much confidence. The Queen, once more the nation's voice, wrote to her prime minister: "If we are to maintain our position as a first-rate Power . . . we must, with our Indian Empire and our large Colonies, be prepared for attack and wars somewhere or other continually. And the true economy will be to be always ready. . . . It will prevent war."

It was the first whisper of the deterrent theory, but the problem was to know how, when and where to apply it. There was even an irritating difference of opinion as to whether it should be applied at all. In November 1879 William Ewart Gladstone began in his new constituency of Midlothian the first courtship of the mass of the British electorate and the most devastating political attack of modern times. The Queen noted sourly in her journal, "Mr. Gladstone is going about Scotland like an American stumping orator, making most violent speeches." It was something of an understatement. Mr. Gladstone was going about Scotland like the wrath of God, with approximately the same effect. Arches hung with flags and garlands welcomed him everywhere; his arrival was watched from the rooftops, his departure was accompanied by files of torch bearers and signaled by bonfires. In dour Dalkeith he rumbled: "Remember the rights of the savage, as we call him. Remember that the happiness of his humble home, remember that the sanctity of life in the hill villages of Afghanistan,* among the winter snows, is as inviolable in the eye of Almighty God as can be your own." He described Disraeli's expansionism as "false phantoms of glory" and savagely dismissed the Queen's assumption of the Crown of India as "theatrical bombast and folly." He derided Disraeli's efforts to profit from the seeming decay of the Ottoman Empire, pounding again and again at the recklessness of Tory policy. The fierce moral ardor of his liberalism illuminated with glaring light the issues of justice, humanity and freedom and won him the election. It was a high irony that his own administration would soon draw the country into Egypt as well as a complex of international reactions which

---

* Gladstone was referring to the bloody progress of British columns through the hateful mountains of Afghanistan with the object, as Disraeli saw it, of pacifying Kabul, avenging the slaughter of the British Resident there, maintaining a puppet amir on the throne, and, above all, excluding the Russians.

would embroil for years not only Richard Meinertzhagen but millions of others.

In 1879 the Khedive Ismael of Egypt had abdicated in favor of his son Tewfik, taking with him forty-one of the forty-two dinner services of solid gold and a fortune of sixteen million pounds. The new khedive, Tewfik, wandered through his palace snuffing out candles in empty rooms, but his economies could not ameliorate the country's ills. His embittered army threw up a nationalist champion, Colonel Ahmed Arabi, known as El Walid, "the unique," who was born a peasant and nursed a peasant's anger. Superficially, Arabi's coup early in 1882 expressed dissatisfaction with the army's lack of pay and the privileges of Turkish and Circassian officers; in fact, it was a national movement with neither strong roots nor real hope. Just as a precaution the British and French Mediterranean fleets were ordered to Alexandria. After a spasm of rioting in that city, Arabi began to arm the Alexandrian forts. The French sailed away on July 10, 1882, an action they were later to regret, and next morning the British squadron of fifteen vessels, nine of them ironclads, reduced the forts and Arabi's future. By an historic irony, this show of imperial force had been ordered by the great liberal whose mandate from the people had rested on his revulsion at Disraeli's aggressiveness in the poor but sovereign state of Afghanistan. None could see to what immense distances the gun flashes pointed: whether they liked it or not, Gladstone and the British had been sucked into the vacuum of Egypt and of Africa.

One small result was that Richard Meinertzhagen cried himself to sleep in his nursery three years later. It was February 11, 1885, and his mother, hearing the newsboys shouting catastrophe yet again in Rutland Gate, had brought the evening newspaper up to her children. The headline, huge and irrevocable, was "Death of General Gordon." It was more than an insult to English pride; it was as if the nation's soul had been ravaged, for to Englishmen, not excluding Richard Meinertzhagen, aged six, Gordon seemed to embody everything that was noble and heroic in the race. In 1881 there had appeared in the Sudan, nominally a protectorate of Egypt and the sultans but actually a million square miles of anarchy, a

prophet by the name of Mohammed Ahmed, a Sufi Muslim claiming descent from the Prophet himself. Announcing that he was the
Mahdi, Mohammed's successor, he exhorted all true believers to
abandon themselves to God, abjure worldly pleasures, and join in
his holy war. He encouraged cooperation with hippopotamus-hide
whips, loyalty by chopping off a hand or a foot from the lukewarm,
and purity of thought by executing the profane. To quench this fire,
eight thousand reluctant Egyptians commanded by Colonel William Hicks were sent plodding into Kordofan at the end of 1883.
Fifty thousand of the Mahdi's dervishes caught them in a forest of
thorns and devoured them with the dispatch of a blowtorch turned
on a moth.

What was needed, clearly, was a stern blue eye. After a good
deal of soul-searching and tergiversation, Gladstone turned toward
the steadiest gaze he knew. It belonged to Charles George Gordon,
ascetic, major general of the Royal Engineers, social worker, Bible
student, celibate and authentic hero. Gordon believed that God was
aware of him, that the will must triumph over the flesh, and that
England's cause was a blessing to all. His public image was trite in
its simplicity—the godlike Anglo-Saxon ruling millions with the
wave of a swagger stick and a lick of public-school morality—but
his contemporaries probably knew how much the maintenance of
that façade cost him. His endurance in the burnt chaos of the desert
drew his slight physique to the breaking point; his arrogance toward
superiors came from insecurity; the air of command demanded
such control that he could only relax after hours on his knees in
prayer or days of black despair. His most extraordinary feature was
his reserve. He could be garrulous, a hot temper drove him into
arguments, and he was often indiscreet. But always there was something withheld, something unfathomable behind the luminous eyes
and the delicately plump features. Most thought it was the power
of leadership. It was never analyzed. Gordon reached Khartoum
with Gladstone's orders to evacuate the garrisons from the Sudan.
There the Mahdi shortly immured him, not entirely contrary to
Gordon's wishes; then, in dilatory fashion Gladstone dispatched a
relief expedition under the indispensable Lord Wolseley, dapper

and steely as usual, whose progress was watched feverishly from the
Meinertzhagen nursery.

Enlisting the services of Messrs. Thomas Cook and Sons, the
noted travel agents, Wolseley's sweating army set off for Khartoum.
Two of its steamers eventually reached the city—too late by forty-
eight hours. In the dark of the morning of January 26, 1885, the
Mahdi's spearmen slashed through a breach in the city's defenses
and hacked their way toward the governor's palace. They had been
promised paradise and they were fearless. As the desert dawn rose
pink and purple, they killed Gordon and cut off his head, carrying
it in a white cloth to their master in his city of Omdurman across
the river. It was shown in triumph to Rudolf Carl von Slatin,
formerly governor of Darfur and now chained in the Mahdi's household, then hung in a tree for three days. The hair and short whiskers
had turned white, Slatin noted.

It would take fourteen years for that poor head to be avenged;
nevertheless, the little boy impotently weeping in the nursery for
Charles George Gordon and England's honor would never forget.
Many years later he would stand on the spot where his hero had
fallen, reflecting on greatness and acknowledging his inheritance.
For Gordon, athirst for death in the pursuit of duty, gave imperialism a symbol that gleamed for nearly half a century.*

But in February 1885 Richard Meinertzhagen had more personal
sorrows than that inflicted by the Mahdi. He had, it seemed to him,
lost his brother Dan, who had been sent off to school in Yorkshire,
and he brooded. Dan and Richard were always very close. They
giggled their way through family prayers, ate winkles from a stall
in Kensington High Street with bent pins old Richard Potter kept
in his vest pocket (a habit that disgusted Sarah Peacock because it
was so plebeian), attended with stiff backs and rebellious hearts the

---

* When Khartoum was once more in British hands, a statue of Gordon
—a bronze figure mounted on a racing camel, staring out into the desert—
was erected in a square in front of the Government House. It was a customary
attraction for small children and their nannies. One little boy en route to
England was taken to see Gordon for the last time, "Goodbye, Gordon," he
is said to have murmured. "I'm going to England. And when I come back I do
hope that nasty old man isn't still on your back."

dancing classes of Miss Wordsworth, who sported a glass eye and a bugle for a voice, and raided Hyde Park for wild duck, which they kept in the bathroom after escaping from a park keeper deflected by their ally James, the crossing-sweeper. Though bound to Dan by the secrets of confederacy and crime, and more tightly by simple adoration, there were some pastimes, such as courtship, Richard preferred to pursue alone. At the age of six he discussed marriage with the first of a series of blue-eyed blondes who were to pluck now and then at his heart, but she was two years older and it came to nothing. When forced to act individually, as when drafted to be a page at his Aunt Kate's wedding and forced into the indignity of lace and velveteen, Richard could signify disapproval with fury. In this case he chewed up his mother's best gloves.

Richard and Dan were frequently taken along by Georgina when she visited friends. One afternoon they met Florence Nightingale,* sainted for her work at Scutari; Richard remembered her as rather a stout old lady wearing an old-fashioned lace cap. Appropriately, she asked after his health, which was obviously robust. But Miss Nightingale was too busy to attend to the children, being deep in a discussion about eugenics with Sir Francis Galton, Georgina Meinertzhagen's admirer and friend who lived a few doors away in Rutland Gate. Galton was in his sixties but still sprightly and not above inflaming the boys against a pompous neighbor by implying that he wore stays. His cousin Charles Darwin's book had attracted him to the study of eugenics, a science he pioneered. He had observed that distinction appeared to run in families and concluded that the human race should be selective in its breeding. Coming from a family of rich Quaker gunsmiths and bankers, Galton spent his early manhood exploring parts as outlandish as Walfish Bay in South-West Africa and he had been up the Nile as far as Khartoum. He was a glamorous companion for children walk-

---

* For a great part of her life Florence Nightingale's closest friend was Benjamin Jowett. It was said that he had wanted to marry her. When Margot Asquith was bold enough to ask indirectly, after meeting Miss Nightingale in his company, "What was your lady-love like, dear Master?" he answered, "Violent . . . very violent."

ing in the park, and what made him even more attractive was that he would take their fingerprints, explaining that one day this means of identification would be useful in dealing with the criminal classes.*

It was on a peregrination with his mother that Richard was first encouraged to keep a diary. Georgina took him to tea in St. John's Wood at the home of Thomas Henry Huxley, Darwin's most formidable supporter and a scientific giant in his own right. In this same house Richard had already been captivated by Darwin's serenity and eyebrows, which were of a length so unusual that they brushed his cheekbones. Richard, being dandled in Darwin's lap, had been allowed to tug them. One of Huxley's daughters was a girl of eighteen with blond hair and blue eyes, which prompted Richard, aged five, to propose without delay. He was accepted, but Ethel Huxley's most lasting effect on him was her suggestion that he should keep a journal. He began it on his sixth birthday with a complaint about getting cold feet from riding in Rotten Row. Huxley's eminence and age kept him from a close intimacy with the children; in fact, except for Herbert Spencer, most of the great men Richard encountered in his early years impressed him only because of some peculiarity of appearance, character or behavior. There was one moment, however, when he might have helped to change the course of history by such a contact.

Richard Potter's London home, York House, was a Queen Anne mansion in Church Street, Kensington. There was a rookery in the garden and there was a paddock for cows and a plot set aside for Richard's exclusive use. One afternoon the five-year-old Richard was busily tilling his soil when his Aunt Beatrice and a gentleman with an orchid and a monocle encroached on his property. Another aunt hustled him away, explaining that Aunt Bo and Mr. Joseph

---

* Galton came across fingerprinting as part of his study of means of identification and made use of earlier work by Sir William Herschel and Dr. Henry Faulds, from which emerged the modern police system, first used effectively as prosecution evidence in a capital charge in Buenos Aires in 1892. Galton greatly amused friends by taking their prints but often forgot to supply anything to remove the ink afterward.

Chamberlain were having a serious talk. The gossip in London was that Chamberlain, the great radical and imperialist, was to take her for his third wife, but the gossip was groundless. Aunt Beatrice's refusal might have been influenced by Herbert Spencer's opinion of her suitor as "a man who may mean well but who does, and will do, an incalculable amount of mischief." On the other hand, Chamberlain might have preferred to escape the Potter circle, for he entertained an equally cordial distrust of Herbert Spencer: "Happily, for the majority of the world, his writing is unintelligible, otherwise his life would have been spent in doing harm." Richard was too young to be caught in the crossfire, but he remembered his father's refusing to invite Chamberlain to dinner with enough heat to cause his sister Barbara to write with some alarm to the controversial statesman: "Please do not come here because Father says he will kick you downstairs. Goodbye, your loving Barbara." Few of the Potters' argumentative friends were really welcome in Daniel Meinertzhagen's home.

The Potters rented York House, going there more and more frequently from their main home near Gloucester. They also owned a red sandstone manor house, two hundred years old, called the Argoed. It was in Monmouthshire, overlooking the valley of the River Wye and not far from Tintern Abbey and the woods and cataracts that had so haunted Wordsworth. There were coracles on the river for Dan and Richard to paddle, donkeys to ride, and birds to watch in the woods. The Argoed was run by an old couple who had served the Potters for most of their lives. Old Mills had graduated from being a guard on the Great Western Railway to becoming the butler at Standish House and had married Martha, the family's nurse. They were both Particular Baptists, but while Martha's observances were subdued, her portly husband never missed a chance for a sermon; even a request for a scuttle of coal would bring forth a rambling reference to Holy Writ. He had a small following of bemused Welsh laborers, whom he lured into a deserted chapel for his orotund and interminable vacuities. In times of political stress, such as the general election in which Lord Salisbury unseated Gladstone, Mills slept with a loaded shotgun beside him for fear, he said, of the Whigs. It was true that Liberalism of a sort stalked Wales and Mills's barricading of the house at night confirmed Richard in his dislike of Gladstone and his party. This, with the shocking death of Gordon to lay at their door, left Richard with a heartfelt distrust of Liberalism and its adherents for the rest of his life. The great affairs of the world were reflected in the microcosm of the Argoed in several ways. One day Mills took Dan and Richard to view the body of a large retriever that had been shot for killing sheep. "There's Theebaw," said Mills with satisfaction, "the black devil." His reference was to the alcoholic king of Burma who in November 1885 was deposed by the British and sunk with hardly any record surviving of his bibulous descent toward disaster, save a monotonous series of official telegrams from Rangoon habitually beginning "King still drinking."

In the time he could spare from digging potatoes, chopping wood, fussing around the dame school in a nearby village, and foraging over the Welsh hills, Richard maintained a correspondence which his father touchingly filed. His second letter celebrated the arrival of his sister Beatrice. It was both succinct and concerned: "I am so glad there is another babby and a girl and what will it be caled and does mother know." The children had been taught to read and write by Georgina, assisted by a Miss Kate Shirley, whose placid good nature could only be shaken by Richard's adoration of the ungodly Charles Darwin, whose references to monkeys she abhorred. There was also the less frequent Miss Sophia Mills, so expert in the musical system of tonic sol-fa that she could notate the hissing sound of a burning log. But for Daniel and Richard the true textbook was already the miraculous variety of nature. Their senses and their physiques had grown beyond their intellectual processes. Richard had begun to develop that extraordinary perception of his surroundings that in later years would allow him to react with the unthinking speed of an animal. He was happy, aware, full of life, and in tune with the springing beauty of his land. He was about to discover, as his formal education began, that in addition to love and joy there was in the world a possibility of the most vicious pain.

CHAPTER 3

I Think I Shall Die

It was winter and the rooks hurtled across metal skies like black rags in the wind. The air, when it was still, carried country sounds from far away—from sheep muffled in their pens below the hillside and cattle hot and steamy in the byre, from a boot crunching snow packed hard in the lee of a drystone wall. To the little boy it was an ache in the ears, the stabbing of a fast-caught breath in the cold, brittleness and empty branches, the sharp mew of peewits tumbling on the uplands, the suave and lonely symmetry of a red kite sweeping the valley. Walls of red stone bound him; loneliness oppressed him. There was small comfort in the spicy cakes Martha Mills baked for tea. Old Mills's sanctimonious commentary was an empty rumble, uncomprehending and inappropriate. His mother seemed aloof and uncaring, and all the small treasury of the Argoed had turned to ashes. Richard Meinertzhagen was pining for his brother Dan, who was two hundred miles away at school in Yorkshire. To Richard the distance was meaningless, a day's walk or a month's; what he had to cross was the gulf separating him from the person he loved most fiercely in all the world. So he wrote, "Mother will not let me come to Aysgarth to join you so I think I shall die"; but his practical strain asserted itself, and he ended, "Send me some money so I can come quick at once." Dan, unfortunately, could not finance the expedition, Sarah Peacock would not, and Old Mills and his wife clearly could not be approached; so Richard set off to walk with neither money nor food, was retrieved, and, struggling for his life, was incarcerated once more in the nursery, where like many another seven-year-old he found his anguish deadened as winter softened into spring and Dan came back to him for vacations.

On May 7, 1886, the touch of a world far more complex than that of a small child fell feather-light on Richard, but he was unaware of it. Instead, his ears were full of the hiss of steam and the rumble of porters' carts, and his nose tingled with the acrid smell of oil and smoke and the produce odors of fish and fruit, wet paper and wood. He was standing with his father and Dan on the departure platform of King's Cross Station—cliffs of yellow brick and skies of curving iron and glass, London's terminus for the North. Lewis Cubitt had built it plainly but grandly, with all of a mid-Victorian's confidence that the start of a journey needed no Gothic or Palladian celebration and in the conviction that trains merited individual attention; so there was one platform for a train arriving and one for a train departing. For Richard Meinertzhagen it was the gateway to paradise, full of sweet airs and immeasurable possibilities, and he was not to be disappointed. At Northallerton in Yorkshire the boys were met by a master from the school, George Brooksbank, whose first gesture toward Richard was a spontaneous hug, later recorded by the little boy as "the first demonstration of affection I had ever received." In that instant Richard found a friend he loved for over fifty years.

Georgina Meinertzhagen had chosen Aysgarth for her sons partly because her sister Mary's boy had been there and partly because of its location, since her Potter ancestry looked back to a Yorkshire hill farm and her natural affinity was with the dour and the raw, two qualities that the landscape around Aysgarth very openly exhibited. Her husband liked sheltered valleys, woods and sudden acceptable vistas, but all her life Georgina longed for broad skies, mountains and panoramic views. Aysgarth village huddled at the head of Wensleydale, a green finger of pasture land threaded by the River Ure and thrusting into the mass of the Pennine Range. A couple of miles below the school the river cascaded into Aysgarth Force, a fall as impressive as Niagara to small boys; above the school

it poured down a narrow hill valley between high moors. Wensleydale itself was rich dairy farming country, but the uplands were
forbidding where faults had bared the hard black rock called millstone grit. They were seamed with little gullies where rust-colored
rivulets showed the presence of iron underground. Thin and bitter
grasses grew on the moors, clinging together in clumps and tufts
and seething under the breezes that always blew there. In summer
the slopes showed white for a time with the fluffy bolls of cotton
grass, and in the early fall they were dusted mauve by the heather.
The west winds that had driven across the Atlantic buffeted the
heights, carrying rain (twenty inches a year) and cold to temper
the hardy spirits that walked there, making them stubborn and
sardonic but not unkind. Deep veins of coal and a plenitude of
water had given the Pennine valleys wealth during the Industrial
Revolution. Southwest of Aysgarth lay Lancashire's cotton industry,
southeast the woolen mills and steel foundries of Yorkshire, their
smokestacks of dark red brick trailing black clouds that made the
moorlands grimy and dyed every sheep that wandered there a
gloomy clerical gray.

The valleys were warm places, bustling and bursting with
humanity, purposeful and robust. From them rose not only the
throbbing of the factory engines with their enormous flywheels of
iron that, breaking loose, would tear through walls and tumble
houses in their path; but also the voices of great choral societies,
some exclusively male, that sang Handel's *Messiah* as if their hal-
lelujahs would be heard in heaven itself and judged for tone. This
was the very essence of the North—the steady burden of the bass,
tenors gilding their descants, sopranos and contraltos gentling the
powerful thunder of their menfolk, and above all climbing the
certain trumpet of the Lord, singing deliverance and the love of
God—a deep and beautiful conviction, not showing great passion,
but indestructible and only achieved by a copious expenditure of
sweat.

Though Aysgarth in bucolic Wensleydale was a little removed
from the dynamic life to the south, something of the independence
and endurance of the industrial valleys informed that area too.

Richard Meinertzhagen found it most congenial. Since he was the youngest, he was placed bottom boy in the school, but that was by no means enough to tarnish the joy of being there. Reunited with Dan, he soon made a discovery that brought more pleasure still. Aysgarth was in the middle of a Viking kingdom and the evidence lay all around them in the names of the streams and hills and settlements—Aysgarth itself, Thoralby, Hawes, Beldon Beck and Askrigg—harsh names of a piratical people. Through most of their schooldays their fancy turned always to the Norsemen, sailing their longboats across the North Sea, harrying west and south, and strong enough to rule in Yorkshire for a hundred years. Like the Vikings, they would not brook confinement, loved the wild conversation of the sea, and restlessly sought new shores to conquer. Their imaginations found fuel in William Morris' translations of the Icelandic sagas of Grettir the Strong and the Volsunga, and later in serious study of the history of the Norsemen. The strain, wild and seeking, was something Richard had always carried in his blood, making him love lonely places and cold distances, and turning him briefly, when the occasion forced it, into a berserker.

He was a tempestuous boy. Any hesitancy his new surroundings might have imposed on him soon vanished; before the end of his first month at school he was defying authority on a matter, as was to be expected, of principle. The Reverend C. T. Hales, headmaster of Aysgarth, was a fanatical Jacobite and every year on May 29 would expect all his pupils to observe Royal Oak (or Restoration) Day, a ritual perpetuating the memory of the Stuarts. Each boy was to find a sprig of oak to wear for an emblem of the most hopelessly lost of all causes. Mr. Hales would chastise with a nettle any boy he found leafless, but since, out of ignorance or kindness, his nettle was in flower and therefore innocuous, the persuasion was moral rather than physical. Richard and Dan rejected the whole observance, refusing to stand up after dinner with everyone else when Mr. Hales proposed the toast of the king over the water. Dan was not sanguine about his younger brother's libertarianism and reported to their father the following day, "He is very cheeky to the masters and some of these days he will get into a row," an opinion shortly substantiated by a letter from Richard: "I must get a little bit of paper and the master which is teaching me has to put whether I am good or bad. I am usually not good." He was particularly not good with bullies. There was a bigger boy in the school, known to Richard as "Brown the Cannible," who bit his fellows in the leg; in doing so to Dan one day, he encountered the fury of Richard, who cut open his face at the cost of losing a tooth himself. Richard became very popular at Aysgarth; with the boys, because his bouts with authority made news, and also with the masters, who wisely saw in his troublesome progress more of virtue than of ill.

Hales and his assistants made sure that their boys made the most of the school's surroundings. Richard learned to swim in an icy rock pool below the falls of the Ure and was free on holidays to roam wherever he liked with a friend. Morning and evening prayers were conducted in the open, whatever the weather (though a cloudburst would be considered an act of God), and there were frequent paper-chases with a couple of "hares" laying trails five miles up the fells for the "pack" to follow, urged on by a master with a stick. There was a feeling, unspoken, that the fittest would survive and the Reverend Hales exhorted constantly, "Don't stand there gaping! Do something!" planting in Richard Meinertzhagen a preference for action over words that never left him.

The academic system favored at Aysgarth was learning by rote. Despite this, two of the masters did succeed in interesting Richard in Euclidean geometry; and sometimes the most serious studies would be interrupted when the whole school was called outside to watch an osprey, an eagle or a buzzard soaring across the dale while gray-bearded old Hales, black as a rook in his priestly robe, stared up with love in his eyes. The River Ure carried both salmon and trout, and otters hunted and were hunted there. Curlews cried into the wind on the moors and snipe drummed in the marshland. One wintry day Hales took his boys eight miles to Hawes to look at a great pack of grouse sheltering on the railroad station. The boys lived close to the elements; no window was ever shut at Aysgarth, and since there was no heat they would sometimes wake with drifts of snow covering the bare boards of their dormitories. Their greatest passion was the assuagement of an omnipresent hunger. Breakfast was taken on the run—wholemeal bread and weak coffee—and tea was haphazard. Lunch was the main meal and it followed an unchanging menu, as in every other boarding school in England unto the third and fourth generation. Sundays was roast beef and suet pudding; Mondays was cottage pie, about as appetizing as minced flannel and called "cat pie." Then there were two days of boiled beef, once hot and once cold, and a day of chopped meat after the doldrums of Thursday, which was boiled mutton and suet pudding dotted with raisins. The Thursday pudding was appreciated for its incredible weight, but the mutton was an affliction, since the fat congealed rapidly in Aysgarth's invigorating atmosphere and had to be secreted in pockets because of the rule that nothing must be left on a plate. Once a week there was stewed fruit, but never fresh, and the single vegetable was boiled cabbage. Dan and Richard enjoyed an advantage over their starving friends: being favored, they sat at table on either side of the headmaster and were rewarded for good behavior with pieces of a great Wensleydale cheese he kept in front of him.* Each boy was allowed to spend sixpence a week in the school tuck shop, much of which went on eggs for tea at a penny a time.

Aysgarth's concern was to fashion embryo leaders. It taught endurance, initiative and forethought, and it rewarded energy and competitiveness. It sought, with all other schools of its kind, to mold character, following the mainstream of Victorian educational thought. The proponent of this attitude toward teaching was Thomas Arnold of Rugby School, sometime of Oriel College, Oxford, a Doctor of Divinity and a man of stupendous moral force. He made the chapel the center of school life, preaching there every Sunday evening on his single theme—the quest for Christian

---

* In those days this delectable cheese, nobler than any but the kingly Lancashire, was handmade. On their walks through the dale, the Aysgarth boys were often charged by old ladies riding donkeys with goat skins full of milk bouncing on their flanks. By keeping the donkeys at a trot, the ladies obtained the curds that were then pressed into creamy wheels. The providential result—a rich crumbly ambrosia.

morality—reasserting again and again: "What we must look for here is, first, religious and moral principles; secondly, gentlemanly conduct; thirdly, intellectual ability." Such was his sincerity that the boys would sit rapt in Gothic gloom, the light filtering faintly through the east window and the stained glass of the Magi bearing gifts. It was Arnold's inspiration that heartened men like Hales at Aysgarth, for Arnold was very much a man of his times, and the times demanded seriousness. It was not so much that Arnold made changes; he modernized outlooks and institutions. His second success at Rugby was with the prefectorial system, the day-to-day discipline and administration of the school by a picked handful of senior boys, which he reoriented from its previous anarchical bent by exercising trust and by applying the same ethical principles in detail that he advocated at large. "Work and pray," he admonished. The next generations of England's leaders heard him and obeyed.

Arnold once said, "Our work here would be unbearable if we did not bear in mind that we should look forward as well as backward—if we did not remember that the victory of fallen man lies not in innocence but in tried virtue." It was such thoughts that immortalized him. A generation later, when Richard Meinertzhagen was at Aysgarth, the public schools were still turning out a rich percentage of intolerant clods, but where Arnold's precepts were followed, the percentage was small and the yield of young men capable of meeting their duties, high. Aysgarth, though only a private preparatory school, was one place where Arnold's memory still shone; Richard Meinertzhagen was only ten when he left there, but he had already been taught a way of life—the stern mid-Victorian way of duty before honor.

It was at Aysgarth, too, that Richard's interest in birds crystallized into a passion. He and Dan were first shown how to skin a bird by their uncle Frederick Meinertzhagen, whose own collection stood in two vast cases in his father's home, Belmont, and which was of a quality high enough to be accepted by the Imperial Institute at his death. Their studies were also encouraged by a loan from their father of his five volumes of Gould's *Birds of Great Britain,* which they peered at avidly, absorbing the details so completely that years later Richard could identify a foreign bird at once merely by recalling Gould's plates. Richard acquired one of the early prizes of his collection before he had been at the school a month: he spotted a cock grouse sitting on a wall, and George Brooksbank, the master he was so fond of, bet him he could not hit it with the bow he was carrying. Richard killed it clean at twenty yards and wrote home triumphantly: "I shot a grows with my arrow and it fell dead. Mr. Broksbank is having it stuffed and gave me sixpence but he says I must not shoot any more grows in May because they are breeding and I think I shall shoot a rook." Brooksbank was a great lover of nature, an expert shot and salmon fisherman, and had the remarkable gift of being able to distinguish a male from a female woodcock at a glance. He had shot more than three thousand of them.

Another ally was an assistant keeper of the British Museum, Richard Bowdler Sharpe, with whom Dan and Richard spent much time during their vacations, though they soon found that Sharpe's skinning techniques were less successful than their own, tending toward disintegration. Dan chose to collect hawks, eagles and owls, leaving Richard the crow family, woodpeckers and no feeling of resentment at the preemption. Richard became one of the greatest ornithologists of his day, but in later life he often attracted criticism from less dedicated bird-lovers because he killed his specimens. In 1956, at a dinner party in Nairobi, Kenya, the lady next to him suddenly said with distaste, "I suppose you've been shooting birds again, Colonel Meinertzhagen?" The colonel, by now suffering from a deafness his closest friends believed adjustable, gazed at her silently. The lady began a mime. "You know—bang, bang!" she insisted. The colonel replied, "No, ma'am. Bang!"

The killing was incidental, of course. During most of his life Richard Meinertzhagen hated shooting for sport, but always accepted the need to fill the pot or further science. What he cared for more was the way the kestrel hunted head to the wind, the slow watchful gyres, pinions balancing against the thrust of air, and beyond that the delirious beauty Gerard Manley Hopkins sang in "The Windhover":

I caught this morning morning's minion, kingdom
  of daylight's dauphin, dapple-dawn-drawn
  Falcon, in his riding
Of the rolling level underneath him steady air, and striding
High there, how he rung upon the rein of a wimpling wing
In his ecstasy!

That was the flame and all else was fuel—identification, physiology, habitat, legend. Richard came to know such lore as that the eagles he and Dan kept at home and at Harrow were properly assigned to an emperor. Feeding and keeping the eagles pleased him, but his fascination lay within the golden, cruel eyes and the fierce instinct of that predatory beauty. It was the other side of creation.

It was not necessary for the two boys to collect their specimens personally. Bowdler Sharpe contributed skins, sometimes sadly bedraggled but always well meant, and by now one of their father's gamekeepers could be asked to help. Urgent letters came to sister Barbara asking her to "tell the keeper to shoot as much different birds as he possibly can and get them ready for stuffing." This recruit, or draftee, was a member of the staff of Mottisfont Abbey, the house Daniel Meinertzhagen had rented in 1885. It was not far from his old country house and still near the River Test.

Mottisfont Abbey became Richard's spiritual home. It was named after the font, or spring, that welled up delicious and crystal from the chalk, supplying the family with two hundred gallons of water a minute, their sole source until, in a more hygienic age, analysis found it half full of farmyard organisms. Mottisfont had been first an Augustinian priory and clung still, after nearly nine centuries, to a faintly ascetic air. Subsequent owners coalesced various parts of the old priory and added a pink brick front, which was soon curtained by a thick growth of ivy. The owner was a lively, eccentric woman, not the least of her oddities being the extraordinary terms of a lease that gave Daniel Meinertzhagen and his heirs the house, two thousand acres of Hampshire land, and several miles of the finest trout fishing in England—all for three hundred and twenty pounds a year. Stranger still, the owner could not break the lease but the Meinertzhagens could renew it every seven years in perpetuity, or could quit with a year's notice. She would not allow electric light or central heating, and though the Meinertzhagens installed the latter and laid parquet over the stone paving of the hall, she tore them out when they vacated the house. She would call on them occasionally, amiably dotty and extremely wealthy, wearing her late husband's clothes and boots.

The park had been well planted through the centuries. There was a mourning yew in the churchyard, and horsechestnuts, tulip trees, fine Canadian oaks and three kinds of cedars, including the odorous species from Lebanon, were scattered at random through the grounds. Close to the house stood the finest plane tree in England, thirty feet around and decked with leaves a yard across. The lawns covered nine acres and had to be mowed twice a month and cleared of leaves in the fall. There were seven acres of kitchen gardens and twelve hothouses crammed with flowers, fruit and vegetables all year round: when one of the vines languished, the head gardener buried a dead horse deep under its roots so that thereafter the family enjoyed quantities of luscious grapes. The head gardener commanded twelve assistants, the largest outdoors detail. There were four men in the stables and three gamekeepers living in cottages far off from the Abbey, and for the home farm there was a cowman with a couple of lads when he needed them.

Behind the stables soared the high iron arches of the aviaries Dan designed, within which, their talons gripping thick branches and balks of timber, hunched no fewer than sixteen eagles, one of the largest collections in the whole of England. In more crowded cages there were the smaller raptors—kites, buzzards, hawks and owls—more numerous than the eagles. Two of the latter roamed the valley about Mottisfont feeding on trout, chickens and unwary cats, and at last growing so bold that it was feared they might develop an appetite for young children. Fortunately, the only human to suffer attack was a lone fisherman playing his trout on a peaceful stretch of the Test: blanketed by a swift dark shadow he lost his fish, his line and most of his rod in a fearful explosion of feathers and talons. The pride of Dan's collection was a female white-tailed sea eagle from Lapland with a wingspread of nine feet, the biggest in captivity, but he was fonder of a vociferous sea eagle from Senegal with a bright chestnut belly and a white head, for it was tame enough to be carried on the arm. There was one drawback to this showy relationship, however: it made Jacob very jealous. Jacob was a raven belonging to Dan and Richard. Of unfathomable age, he was set in his ways, not all of which were endearing: in his pitchy soul there burned a raging hatred of the predators, particularly of the kites, which were weaker. If he came upon a kite outside its cage he would drag it down to the river and drown it, yet in his calmer moods he exuded a somewhat eccentric charm, sitting on Richard's shoulder cooing with far from corvine amiability.* Besides Jacob, smaller birds frequented the house, and some made their way there uninvited. One summer two cormorants got into the habit of strolling up the lawn from the river and perching on the drawing-room chairs, but they so depleted Daniel's stock of trout that he caused their banishment from the house, hospitable and spacious as it was.

Mottisfont Abbey had seven guest rooms as well as enough bedrooms for a family of twelve, each with a coal fire and each supplied every morning with great jugs of hot and cold water for the hip baths that supplemented the two bathrooms available. Breakfast, at eight-thirty, was cooked by a kitchen maid while the footmen set the table and the housemaids swept the carpet with wet tea leaves. These indoor servants were ruled by the butler and the cook, who always took their meals with the head housemaid in the servants' room, attended as was proper by the scullery maid. The estate was a microcosm of Victorian society, with principalities and powers at each level and protocol to be observed. When Daniel Meinertzhagen gave a banquet in the stableyard to celebrate the Queen's Golden Jubilee, three hundred people sat down to table, each one a servant or a tenant, recognizing Daniel's authority as well as to some extent assuming his responsibility toward them. Vast

---

* Jacob met a messy end in Mottisfont village. Feeling hungry, he clapped his beak onto the skirts of a passing beldame, his customary signal for attention. The innocent woman turned, assumed him to be the devil, and fell into hysterics. Jacob was blown to smithereens by a rustic coming to the rescue.

as it was, the establishment was no burden to the Meinertzhagens: the head gardener alone stole every year three times what Daniel paid in rent.

Hospitality under these conditions became merely a matter of choosing attractive guests, since there were no economic or administrative difficulties beyond assigning rooms and suggesting menus. Daniel Meinertzhagen preferred business friends whom he could amuse in his coverts or on the river bank and sustain with the excellent clarets in his cellars. Georgina tended to the more esoteric, though what mystery Herbert Spencer (a favored visitor), the great philosopher, might once have enjoyed had been rubbed off by three generations of familiarity. Now this Potter family friend became acquainted with a fourth generation in Dan and Richard. Their grandfather Richard Potter had delighted in his friendship with Spencer, as he had in his acquaintance with T. H. Huxley and in his walks with the irascible but brilliant Thomas Carlyle, but his own humility prevented him from describing any of this as a meeting of minds. He believed that Spencer's cerebration was wearing out his body, murmuring to his daughters, "Poor Spencer, he lacks instinct. You will discover that instinct is as important as intellect." The benevolent head would shake sorrowfully and he would add, "I must see whether I can't arrange another day's fishing with him, poor man." It was significant that his friend was "poor" Spencer to Richard Potter. When the Victorians used that epithet there was less of sympathy in it than of conviction that the subject had taken quite the wrong course and was in grave danger of extinction as a result. It was ominous more than sad. Politically Potter and Spencer had much in common, for the former held that the trusteeship of the country should be left in the hands of the leisured class, men no longer obliged to seek profit on their own account and therefore free to pursue the best interests of the nation. As proof, he often cited the lamentable condition of America caused by the absence of such a hereditary caste. Spencer tended to agree with this affinity for an aristocracy on the grounds that they would have proved themselves fittest to survive, and added a hatred of state interference of any kind.

Long before Darwin published *The Origin of Species,* Spencer had adduced his theory of the survival of the fittest, making it the backbone of the law of progress which it was his life's work to propound and expand. It was a common error, even in Spencer's own time, to attribute the phrase to Darwin, upon whose innocent shoulders fell many slights. Darwin had written: "From the war of nature, from famine and death, the most exalted object of which we are capable of conceiving, namely, the production of the higher animals, directly follows. There is grandeur in this view of life." The stupid and the careless also saw in it belligerence and ruthlessness, and Karl Marx, for one, welcomed Darwin as a fellow revolutionary, a tribute that the old man, had he lived to read *Das Kapital,* would have found inexplicable. To a lesser degree, Spencer's own propositions were also distorted;* he believed, simply, that the universe had been evolving toward greater complexity and greater efficiency by the natural elimination of the inutile and the ineffective. The concept was inspired, and Spencer spent a lifetime collecting data for proof and then applying his findings to contemporary conditions. His vision of the great machine, perpetually in motion and continually self-renewing, aroused by its optimism and essential conservatism more enthusiasm in America, where his works were serialized in *Popular Science Monthly,* than it did in England.

Whatever comfort Americans got from Spencer's works must have been increased by what they revealed of Spencer's passion for individualism. He could not tolerate authority. Any hint of infringement on what he thought of as freedom would make his gray eyes chips of flint, compress his lips into a hard thin line, and cause his tall but slender body to tremble. He even preached ultimate independence in the nursery to nine enraptured Potter girls, driving their governess to such fury that she would snap at them,

---

* The theory of the survival of the fittest suited Marx, of course, and he and Spencer were to find themselves in a bizarre proximity. Spencer had carefully chosen a site for himself at Highgate Cemetery and would go to look at it from time to time, once with Richard Meinertzhagen. He never once noticed that it was right next to the last resting place of the father of Communism. If the misunderstanding ever made them spin in their graves, certainly it must have been in opposite directions.

"You can go out this morning with Mr. Spencer, my dears, and mind you follow his teaching and do exactly what you have a mind to."

Spencer, as might have been expected, had definite views about education, which he communicated to children by example. In spite of his reserve and frequent pedantry, he always got on well with them, though he would withdraw when they got out of hand by inserting some ear plugs he always carried and feigning deafness. Yet he was generous and gentle with children and sought their company. He once said sadly to Richard, "I would sooner have one child of my own than the whole science of philosophy." Practically, Spencer's philosophy meant long walks with Dan and Richard on the chalk downs above Mottisfont or in the woods that cloaked their shoulders. He would repeat when their attention flagged, "Observe, record, explain!" This aphorism, with Spencer's rebellious "Submission not desirable!" joined the Reverend Hales's trumpet calls to action in Richard's young mind and crystallized there hard as rock. Even if these had been the only gifts that Spencer gave they would have made him one of the four or five major influences on Richard, who always remembered his old-fashioned elegance of manner and dress—the silk hat a little too high, the vest a touch too loose, the topcoat with its black retriever collar an inch or so too long—and his slightly obsolete plainness of mind as examples not lightly to be shaken off.

The boys' walks with Spencer round the estate were pacific affairs during which the old philosopher taught them to observe and question, sometimes testing the reactions of living birds to stuffed ones or other stimuli, or finding ways of measuring the speed of flight. The boys' private forays were sometimes more lethally inclined. Though neither was yet allowed a gun, both had bows, Richard's taller than himself and already blooded on his unseasonable grouse. This was the year of Sir Hiram Stevens Maxim's new machine gun, tested at Dulwich by Mr. H. M. Stanley, the explorer, who, having ripped off an estimated three hundred and thirty-three shots in thirty seconds, said, "It is a fine weapon, and will be invaluable for subduing the heathen." Even so, numbers of England's upper classes, especially the ladies, clung to the long-bow that had been England's pride. There were still memories of the whistling hail that had unhorsed the armored chivalry of France at Agincourt and the May-time romance of Robin Hood and his band of philanthropic outlaws. So the Royal Sherwood Archers, the Herefordshire Bowmen and the Royal Toxophilite Society in Regent's Park kept tradition alive, while Victorian ladies in summer dresses graced sunny afternoons at many a country house with arrows flickering white against the shady elms; and Dan and Richard Meinertzhagen stalked the Mottisfont warrens and grew deadly at twenty yards, though the rabbit had to be sitting still. At the end of June 1887 this tendency of the English to look backward through a rosy mist and find there golden assurances to bolster up the present achieved a climactic moment.

It was the fiftieth anniversary of Queen Victoria's accession. The Golden Jubilee ceremonies were designed, not wholly unconsciously, to show Europe who was mistress. London was suddenly full of sovereigns and royal and serene highnesses, including Victoria's sister monarch, the queen of Hawaii, sporting a large number of Hawaiian orders and enjoying precedence over a future empress of Germany. There was a solemn service of thanksgiving at Westminster Abbey, which with a note of reserve before beginning its applause the *Manchester Guardian* described as "more like Cologne Cathedral than the Abbey Englishmen know and love so well." The Germanic air of the proceedings was strong: in addition to the discomfited Prince William and blue-blooded heirs of principalities from the Baltic to the Danube, there were the blind King of Saxony, led up the aisle by the Grand Duchess of Mecklenburg-Strelitz and the Crown Prince of Austria; and, impressing everyone, Prince William's father (and Queen Victoria's son-in-law), the tall, blond Crown Prince Frederick—white and silver from head to toe, the German eagle prideful on his helmet. As all knew, he had been made mute by a cancer of the throat.

In the center of the Abbey, lonely on a red dais, stood the Coronation Chair, newly refurbished from stock with replacements for the bits of carving knocked off through the centuries, a lick of brown paint, and a coat of varnish by the firm of William Banting, undertakers and funeral furnishers of St. James's Street. There was a roar outside, a fanfare from the State trumpeters high up on the Abbey's rood-screen, and then into this glittering and portentous gathering, her rheumatism and backache forgotten, stumped at last with a master stroke of stagecraft—the dumpy widow of Windsor. Wearing the somberest black-and-white bonnet of starched lace, she was the greatest and the plainest of all the majesties there assembled.

The point was not lost on her people as she drove home, having sat through the service and the chorale *Gotha* thinking about her husband, who had written it in five flats. So exuberant and heartfelt was their greeting that she never went back to the seclusion she had practiced since the Prince Consort's death. Throughout the Empire the marks of respect were gratifying. In Sind there was dedicated the Queen Victoria Jubilee Burial and Burning Ground, and the Regency of Gwalior responded to the prevailing mood by deciding to place its savings in the hands of the Indian government. When dug out of their ancient pits, they were found to amount to five million pounds. In Eshowe ten thousand glistening Zulu warriors with three hundred of their chiefs celebrated simultaneously the Jubilee and their formal annexation, and saluted the flag "with apparent enthusiasm." Eight thousand medals were distributed to deserving schoolchildren, and the kindly *Daily Telegraph* issued to every one of the thirty thousand youngsters attending its party in Hyde Park a meat pie, a piece of cake, a bun and an orange apiece, as well as a mug specially made by Messrs. Doulton.

That night great fires were lit the length of England, as they had been to announce the arrival of the Spanish Armada, hilltop to hilltop, and all at Aysgarth school climbed five miles onto the moors to light their fire and to watch others in the chain twinkling far off toward Scotand. Being small, Richard was helped upward by a bigger boy (later editor of *The Times*) and carried down fast asleep by George Brooksbank, though he had recovered enough the next day to record in a letter to his father a quibble about his headmaster: "Mr. Hales says the Queen is a wonderful old lady. I think he ought not to talk like that and how can a queen be an old lady when she is a queen." In spite of his intransigence, in some matters Richard Meinertzhagen had the Victorians' solid respect for Institutions.

Since Aysgarth's rather simple academic curriculum lay only lightly on Richard's intellectual processes, he had time for reflection. His main preoccupation, apart from his concern with collecting birds, was making arrangements for the farm his sister Barbara and he intended to buy in New Zealand. The only eccentricity about the project was its coloring; the chickens were to be white leghorns, the cows white, the ponies white, also the ducks, and if possible the turkeys. Geese and sheep fitted naturally into the decor and their mother had promised them white pigeons. By the beginning of April 1886 Barbara and Richard had accumulated twenty-four shillings to capitalize the venture. Two years later Richard asked his father for a further five shillings, adding, "Please put it in your bank till I return so it will be safe." The idea had been planted by Uncle Frederick Meinertzhagen's tales of his old sheep farm at Waimarima in New Zealand, and nurtured by the enchantment of the open country of the Argoed, Mottisfont and Aysgarth. Not all of the Aysgarth years were spent in the country, however. The rest of the family usually spent a good deal of the winter at 25, Rutland Gate, and once Richard had to be sent to London to have a sprained ankle put right by his uncle William Harrison Cripps, senior surgeon of St. Bartholomew's Hospital and husband of Blanche, most beautiful of the Potter sisters. Richard's disability coincided with Bloody Sunday, November 13, 1887, an occasion marked for the Meinertzhagen children by a line of troops of the Life Guards blocking the Knightsbridge end of Rutland Gate and faced by a crowd of men hooting and jeering. The children, jumping up and down behind the horses, were shepherded into the house by Sarah Peacock, and Coward, the butler, locked all the doors and closed the shutters. Later they watched the mob break a few windows further up the street.

The focus of the riot was Trafalgar Square, mecca of dissent, which the Home Secretary had forbidden as a rallying point to the unemployed and union members who wanted to assemble there to protest working conditions and what they saw as social injustice.

Their inspiration was a contradictory figure, Henry Mayers Hyndman, who had been a conservative journalist and a stockbroker in the City but who, under the influence of Karl Marx, had founded the Social Democratic Federation, among whose members he had counted, briefly, William Morris. Though Hyndman disparaged the trade unions, he was joined on this occasion by John Burns of the Amalgamated Engineers, a powerful open-air speaker, and Tom Mann of the same union, whose experiences in America and England had led him to publish a pamphlet which, while rough in style, was clear of purpose. "The true Unionist policy of *aggression* seems entirely lost sight of," he wrote; "in fact the average unionist of today is a man with a fossilized intellect, either hopelessly apathetic, or supporting a policy that plays directly into the hands of the capitalist exploiter." Thus incited, groups of artisans converged on Trafalgar Square, where they found the police reinforced by squads of special constables hastily enrolled from tradesmen and clerical workers stiffened by a few gentry and later by troops. By the time the fighting ended a hundred people had been injured, of whom two later died. The leaders were arrested and quietly tried, but the police action brought down angry charges of "military high-handedness" and police brutality on the head of the chief commissioner of the Metropolitan Police.

The chief commissioner, Sir Charles Warren, was a friend of Daniel Meinertzhagen. While there was no particle of brutality in his nature, he was swift and ruthless in action. Deeply religious and serious in the best Victorian sense, his career as a soldier had sent him to the Middle East for the Palestine Exploration Fund, to the command of the Diamond Fields Horse during the Ninth Kaffir War and the subsequent administration of Griqualand West, to an expedition against the Transvaal Boers, and to the defense of Suakin against the Mahdi's dervishes. It was not, perhaps, the kind of experience that fitted Sir Charles to deal with London's militant unemployed, fired by radical politicians, and he soon resigned after a refusal to accept the Home Secretary's right to issue orders to the police.

When Richard Meinertzhagen first met him walking down Pall

cause Sir Harry's companion was Sir Richard Burton, whose blazing eyes and raging presence discomforted not only Dan and Richard but the gentle Bowdler Sharpe as well. Not one of the three could bring themselves to speak.

In the spring of 1889 Richard came home from Aysgarth for the last time. He had been ill with measles and chickenpox concurrently. He begged his parents to let him stay at the school, which he loved and where he was appreciated, but they decided to send him to a softer climate, thus unknowingly delivering him into the hands of a maniac. When the move had been arranged, the Reverend Hales wrote a sad and ungrammatical finis in his diary: "I am sorry Dick Meinertzhagen leaves this term, his parents being anxious about his health. He is a most satisfactory boy and with his brother Dan are the most likeable boys I have, even though they are not from the North Country. They are clean-minded, honourable, full of life and have developed a keen interest in natural history. When I said goodbye to Dick this evening he burst into tears. May God be with him all his days." But for the next two years or more it was to seem to Richard that God had utterly forsaken him and that his mother had discarded him. Fonthill, the new preparatory school, was in Sussex downland and in more docile air than that which whistled over Aysgarth. It was owned and run by Walter and Ashton Radcliffe as an inheritance from their father. Both were sadists, but Walter was the more ravenous in his practice; it was no coincidence that Richard, who had been christened "Beauty" by the other boys, not without reprisal, was moved soon after his arrival to a private room without a lock, for Walter was also a homosexual.

The use of corporal punishment was universal in Victorian schools. For the lower classes it tended to be summary and inflicted with a leather strap or a cane; for the elite at the public and preparatory schools there was more ritual and certainly more savagery. There senior boys as well as masters had powers of chastisement, usually accepted with phlegm by the delinquent. While painful, it was not as harmful as softer generations would come to believe. The society of such places was often anarchic and rough, and discipline was correspondingly swift and firm. The sensitive, of course, were in perpetual agony at the mere thought of such usage, and when authority to flog was given to a bullying boy or reserved to a deviate master, all suffered. That circumstance was not uncommon. Winston Churchill, before he was eight, fell into the clutches of the curiously named Reverend H. W. Sneyd-Kynnersley, headmaster of St. George's School at Ascot. The good reverend affected coats of arms all over his establishment, an unctuous respect for High Church observances, and red Dundreary whiskers which he constantly fondled. As a token of love, he served fresh strawberries and cream to his charges. Flogging, however, was his delight. His study held a box draped with black cloth over which the victim was bent and held by the head boy. Sneyd-Kynnersley would then strike with his full force the boy's bare bottom, which would begin to show drops of blood after two or three strokes of the birch rod. After fifteen or twenty strokes the study walls would be spotted red, and then Sneyd-Kynnersley and a favorite would spend some hours washing them down. He died of heart failure at the age of thirty-eight, caused, it is to be hoped, by the ecstasy of one of his orgies. Churchill never complained of this greasy monster to his parents, possibly out of disdain, but equally possibly because he believed his parents would be on the side of authority. In the latter assumption he would have been correct, but Richard Meinertzhagen in a similar predicament still clasped the illusion that the world was a fine place and that his parents would support him. This was very quickly dispelled.

Walter Radcliffe found his first excuse for torment when a sycophant repeated to him a rhyme Richard had picked up at Aysgarth and passed round his new school:

> *Annie Maria, she sat on the fire,*
> *The fire was too hot so she sat on a pot,*
> *The pot was too round so she sat on the ground,*
> *The ground was too flat so she sat on the cat*
> *And the cat ran away with Annie on her back.*

Very cleverly, Radcliffe cleared himself by reporting to Georgina Meinertzhagen that her son had learned "pornographic poetry" and would have to be punished lest "the poison spread to the rest of the school"; then he began his persecution. Within three weeks Richard begged his mother to take him away, to which she replied that he needed a little discipline and that if he behaved Walter Radcliffe would be kind to him. Richard wept but clung to his faith in a mother's love. Every night Radcliffe would come to his room, stealthily, and behave in a fashion Richard could not even understand until years later; when he knelt to pray as his grandfather Potter had taught him, Radcliffe jerked him to his feet. He was beaten three or four times a week, savagely. At the end of the fifth week of term he wrote desperately: "My darling mother, Walter is a devil and is very cruel and he beats me many times a week because he says I am obstinate. I am so frightened I cannot answer sometimes and I think I shall kill him because I hate him so. Do please take me away because last time I was beaten there was lots of blood and I have never done anything wrong here, it is all because he hates me so. Please do come down and talk to Walter. Oh do please help me." Georgina was too busy to do as he asked and was sure, in any case, that he was exaggerating, knowing his reputation for rambunctiousness. When he came home for the summer vacation in 1889, she saw the green and purple bruises all over his back and legs, but she only said that he must have behaved very badly. In that bitterest of moments there was tempered in the little boy a resolution of the coldest metal, but at great cost, for it thrust aside what was warm and loving. All his life Richard Meinertzhagen would find it hard to love, though he never stinted in his efforts.* It was only in old age that he set down what he had not then understood— that his mother had reacted in ignorance and out of a desire to do what was best in following the rigid codes of her time, which did not allow for too much affection. Richard had not told her about Radcliffe's other tastes.

---

* Years later Richard wrote with dreadful pathos: "Was it God who forsook me and the devil who took His place? But whatever left me has never returned, neither have I been able to cast out the evil which entered into me at that moment." This is a sad misjudgment; there was never evil in his character, though anger and ruthlessness lurked there always. What Radcliffe's vicious excesses had done was almost to destroy his trust in himself.

By the end of his first summer vacation Richard had decided not to speak to his mother again about Fonthill, nor did he say much to Dan. But just as Dan was boarding the train to his new school, Harrow, Richard asked him what would happen if he killed Walter Radcliffe. When told he would be hung, he said he would not care; but he had second thoughts when Dan, who knew how serious the little boy was, begged him to remember how such a thing would affect their father. Two weeks into the new term Radcliffe started his practices again, and one October night Richard wrote in the diary Ethel Huxley had taught him to keep: "I feel as though my body were an empty shell wandering about with no desire beyond to kill, my little soul, if I have one left, tucked away somewhere inside, smothered in shame, killed by cruelty, starved and bruised for lack of love. Oh God, release me from this torment and give me back my mother's love." The next day he was deliberately asked a question to which there was no answer. Radcliffe dispatched a boy to fetch his holly stick. The eleven-year-old Richard stood shivering, and suddenly there flashed into his head the voice of Hales thundering "Do something!" He seized the stick and hit Radcliffe across the forehead, saw blood spurt, threw over the desk and hurled the stick through the window. Then in terror he ran to his bedroom and began to pray. Radcliffe beat him that night till he bled.

As soon as he could move, Richard broke out of the school to seek help. A business friend of his father's, Sir Edward Blount, lived at Imberborne Manor close to Fonthill and had given Richard an open invitation to the house. The child arrived weeping and in shock, wealed all over, and with his blood-soaked undershirt sticking to open wounds. The old man swore to himself, made Richard comfortable, and headed for the school. Thereafter there were no more beatings and no one ever mentioned that night, least of all Richard to his mother. His letters were no longer emotional. "I went to Sir Edward Blount's for lunch," he wrote; "he is such an awfully jolly old man, he is eighty-two and I saw him driving a team, whizzing round corners and he is awfully strong, he stops his horses in no time. His home is nearly twice as big as Mottisfont. . . . He has about twenty horses, and such a dinner we had, about a hundred courses but I did not have them all. There was soup, mutton and artichokes, cold pie, ham, open tart, peach tart, all sorts of fruit and cheese, beer, claret, sherry, rossbach and hock. I could not eat them all." But in his diary he recorded: "There are two me's, the outward and visible one, gloomy, argumentative, intolerant and suspicious. The other me is right inside me fighting all these things, longing for a little encouragement and appreciation, hoping that some day and somewhere I shall find love and peace." It was hardly the kind of introspection that might be expected in an eleven-year-old boy. When the Christmas holidays came, he was still shuddering with nightmares about Walter Radcliffe and almost dreaded going home because he felt himself an outcast. Twenty years later he discovered that his mother had received only his first two or three letters about his sadistic treatment; the rest had been destroyed at the school. By then Walter Radcliffe was dead. Forty years later, Richard Minertzhagen revisited Fonthill. The headmaster knew his story and said painfully, "How Walter Radcliffe escaped prosecution is a mystery to us all." He had not seen fit to remove Walter's portrait from its place of honor, however, and when Richard caught sight of it during a last pilgrimage to the school, though he was eighty-four years old, a colonel with many men's blood on his hands and a veteran of close and harsh encounters, he shook like a little boy.

Gradually the horror of Fonthill subsided into mere unpleasantness, which could be mitigated by occasional visits to Sir Edward Blount's lucullan table or to Crabbet Park, the home of Wilfrid Scawen Blunt, another of Daniel Meinertzhagen's friends, though his antithesis in everything but his love of sport. Blunt was an individualist in the grandest of styles, with a wife no less original than himself. They often wore Arab dress on their Sussex estate, the Lady Anne (who was Byron's granddaughter) assuming the woolen head scarf secured with thick ropes of black and gold that were the prerogative of a sheik. Both were orientalists and expert horse-copers, and kept a stud of Arab horses, among the finest in Europe, at Crabbet Park. Blunt loved prizefights and blood sports, brilliant company and the conquest of women, poetry and travel; and directed his energy wholly into the pastime of the moment.

In later years the house became the center of the Crabbet Club, which met for a week each year, when not infrequently its members, a half-dozen men of brilliance, would talk all night, bathe in the lake as the dawn rose, and then play tennis stark naked until breakfast. These glories Richard Meinertzhagen never knew, but Blunt would send a carriage to Fonthill and after lunch pack the boy off to the stables where the high-strung little Arabs would nuzzle him with a silken touch and follow him like dogs when he dismounted. Richard was impressed by Blunt's own thoroughbred air and evident toughness, but not by his love for the Arab tribes,* whom Richard grew to loathe. He was mildly shocked by the language Blunt used when referring to the French, and puzzled by the eminent company of intellectuals and politicians often in the house. He remembered the flash of Oscar Wilde's conversation, without comprehending a word of it, but it did not make up for his conventional antipathy to Wilde's gross appearance. Though their great difference in age prohibited a close understanding, Richard must have sensed in Blunt a rebelliousness not unlike his own, for Blunt opposed all the conventions of his time—even imperialism—as a matter of principle. He believed in a free Egypt, a free Ireland and a free India. Richard could certainly never have agreed with that.

As early as his first Aysgarth days, Richard had expressed his conservative beliefs by denigrating Mr. Gladstone on the school wall, earning a token reproof. By the summer of 1891 he was becoming faintly xenophobic. The new kaiser of Germany, Queen Victoria's grandson William, had taken to visiting the Cowes regatta in his imperial yacht *Hohenzollern*. This bored the Prince of Wales, bothered the Queen, and made her subjects resentful, especially her sea-

---

* When traveling through England in his carriage drawn by Arab horses, Blunt would send his servants ahead to pitch his black Bedouin tent in the grounds of his friends' houses. He had been a close ally of the rebel Egyptian Colonel Arabi and championed his cause of Egyptian nationalism in England against Gladstone's administration. He also welcomed nationalist visitors from Egypt and India. At his death his body, sewn into an Arab carpet, was buried in a great grave near his house, lined with boughs of oak, sweetchestnut, elder and ivy, and thickly spread with potpourri of roses—the attar of Arabia.

farers, to whom the occasion was as sacred as Palm Sunday to the devout. The young patriot Richard wrote to his mother: "It is disgraceful the way we behave to Germany. And the coolness with which Germany receives it. . . . We are at the height of our glory and have a wonderful navy. When the great war comes where shall we be? Does anybody think Germany will help us, no, she will help herself and Russia will take India and we shall lose our Empire if we do not wake up." But his interest in external things could not relieve his grief. The last entry in his diary at Fonthill recorded the comfort of prayers, though he believed they were unheard. He concluded: "I shall never find God because there is none, but I can make my own God out of some little bit of good which still remains with me. And I have also lost mother which is more awful than losing God." He knew as he wrote that his bestial days at Fonthill were over, and that he would soon rejoin Dan, his alter ego, at Harrow. At the beginning of the 1890s that great school was passing the zenith of a golden age that would lead Richard out of his hurtful childhood and soothe his unkindly scars.

CHAPTER 4

The Gatling's Jammed and the Colonel Dead

Sex was never one of Richard Meinertzhagen's main preoccupations, so he was both confused and repelled by a lecture delivered to the new boys by his housemaster at Harrow, the Reverend Done Bushell. Bushell's suspiciousness amounted to a mania that drove him along passages at night in his stockinged feet, listening for whispers never uttered, but his age made him relatively harmless. It was his custom to speak to new arrivals about homosexuality, believing quite without cause that they were longing to practice it. His sermon included personal example. "Cast out the sins of the flesh for they are the Devil himself," he would warn. "When I was a small boy another larger boy said unto me, 'Be unto me as a woman,' and I cast him downstairs and that was my salvation. I ask you all to do unto such a boy as I did unto him." Despite his experiences with Walter Radcliffe, Richard left Bushell's study more puzzled than he had entered it and had to rely on Dan to explain just what the old cleric had been driving at.

This barrier between Bushell and his boys was not unique. For most male Victorian children, except the lower classes, who enjoyed sexual activity and procreated as if it were entirely normal, this kind of knowledge was passed on by pink-faced fathers or by hearty schoolmasters puffing mightily on their manly pipes, if the subject was mentioned at all; for most female Victorian children, with the same reservation, there was almost no theoretical information and practice had to wait until the wedding night. In any case, in the age before Freud made his worrisome discoveries, there was not much to go on. Most parents concerned enough to take up the study relied on a book with a strong claim to be the first read extensively between plain paper covers—Doctor William Acton's *The Functions and Disorders of the Reproductive Organs,* published in 1857. Its unappetizing title did not diminish its popularity and its sales grew for forty years. Though Acton was an originator in his field, his book included Dreadful Warnings that were to cause trouble to the ignorant for half a century. One of these described in terms worthy of a hell-fire sermon the consequences of masturbation, but Acton went even further by condemning too much mental stimulation with the same severity he would have used on the excessive habits of a nautch girl. "For, as one may observe," he wrote, "it is not the strong athletic boy, fond of healthy exercise, who this early shows marks of sexual desires, but your puny exotic, whose intellectual education has been fostered at the expense of physical development." Cold baths and playing fields became the means of perpetuating the purity of the nation's young leaders, with consequent effect upon their attitudes. Much more effort was spent on impressing the necessity and means of avoiding temptation than on describing just what the temptation might be.

For adults, sexual behavior was measured by ethical not, obviously, by psychological or aesthetic standards. The code was strict, simple and puritan: to disregard it meant ostracism, except for members of the fastest and most gilded set or for bohemians, and even they could not play their games too openly. Even that harbinger of a new age, the Prince of Wales, hardened as he was to scandal by his own royal exposure in court, would drop his more brazen friends. It was no accident that the era of the great Queen set woman on a pedestal. What the Victorians saw as the dangers of sexual excess obliged them to pretend that women were ethereal. "Horses sweat," they said, "gentlemen perspire, but ladies only glow," and they regarded going into a decline as almost a hallmark of fine breeding.

Gladstone, the archetypal Liberal, opposed giving women the vote because he believed with all his heart that "it would trespass upon their delicacy, their purity, their refinement, the elevation of their whole nature." The belief had so long been held, with Old Testament authority, that women were intellectually inferior to men that the distinction was fairly generally accepted by both sexes. It was only in the year before Richard Meinertzhagen went to Harrow that an American feminist affronted decency and encouraged a reassessment by shrilling, "Call on God, She will help you!"

The disparity between the world of men and the world of women grew not only from the latter's sheltered status but also from their preoccupation with problems they had not been effectively trained to overcome. A woman like Georgina Meinertzhagen, in spite of the availability of platoons of servants, found that the oversight of ten children, a great house in the country and another in London, and the demands of a rigorous social round was no light occupation. The central emphasis in the Victorian family was less on an exciting sex life for the parents than on the smooth administration of a large and populous microcosm. It must often have taken a great imaginative leap for the Victorian male to perceive, beneath the competent air of his wife and within her fifteen yards of dress material and her fourteen pounds of underwear, the ravishing sylph that fancy bred. Few Victorian men ever saw women as the Elizabethans had—creatures of infinite variety; they counted the fickle will as weakness, the vapors as something to be dealt with by Miss Lydia E. Pinkham's Vegetable Compound (efficacious in every case), and a gleam in a downcast eye as a potential affliction of the flesh. Women at their most feminine were baffling, so it was generally safer to keep them at a distance with other puzzling phenomena like Republicanism, the physical properties of the universe, and visiting Americans.

As a boy Richard was thought a misogynist. In the summer of 1891, at Mottisfont for the vacation before going to Harrow, his mother one day invited him to walk with her to look at the cows on the home farm. Seeking a quick excuse, Richard begged off with "The trouble with your cows is—they're all women." So at the age of thirteen his mother labeled him a woman-hater, which he was far from being. He had learned to distinguish male from female virtues and in common with most of his generation he tended to prefer the former. He admired the virility and strength of the lion and the man in his prime and he sought the understanding and sweetness of the mature woman. It was not a question of a preference for one sex before the other, merely that even as a boy Richard Meinertzhagen recognized and loved distinction wherever he saw it. This made him seem a cold judge, for his single test was quality, and he never temporized. In the summer of 1891, however, his critical faculty had not yet developed the steely temper it would acquire in more mature years and he spent one day of those pleasant weeks in disproof of his mother's opinion by wooing, as tentatively as a thirteen-year-old will, a neighbor's daughter. She was so shy at their only meeting that she spoke hardly a word, but Richard, much taken by her green plush dress and her blond hair, conquered in manly fashion by first complimenting her and then swiftly giving her a Mottisfont peach warm from the sun. He asked his mother to invite the girl again, but it was thirty years before he saw her a second time. She remembered the peach.

Though aloof, the Meinertzhagens could not have escaped their surroundings at Mottisfont even if they had wanted to. Mere occupation of the Abbey set them apart from the life of the villages and hamlets surrounding it, but the pacing of the seasons and the ancient habits of the countryside had their effects within those favored walls. At Christmas came the mummers, masked and fantastic, circling the hall with their curious limping step. The protagonist was St. George, supported by the patron saints of Scotland, Ireland and Wales and confronted as the play wore on by a hodgepodge of enemies led by the Turkish Knight and a rather clumsy dragon. The combat was formal, like a ballet in slow motion, and the dialogue ritualistically intoned, and the effect on the Meinertzhagen children was partly theatrical, partly religious, and wholly cathartic. When the mummers were done in the hall they would withdraw to the servants' quarters for a second performance, which Richard also watched. He noted that it was a little more vigorous but still impenetrably anonymous. No villager would ever reveal the name of a mummer, for a reason which Richard could not have known. Though clearly the play was a reenactment of the Crusades, its meaning held magic. The death and resurrection of the characters signified the recurrent miracle of seed-time and growth, winter turning to spring, and so the mummers, slow-witted plowmen though they might be behind their masks and scarves, were bringers of good luck and therefore taboo. Though Richard asked many times for a copy of their play, he never got one. It had never been written down.

Like all self-respecting great houses, Mottisfont had its residential ghost, an emanation created by a curse pronounced by the last prior of the Abbey before it was dissolved at Henry VIII's command in 1536. The spirit was supposed to reside now in a gilt Buddha, which Richard later bought and had exorcised by the Reverend Welldon, his headmaster at Harrow. From this Oriental camouflage it would wander through Mottisfont's maze of passageways and dark landings, shaking windows, making the stairs creak, and jangling the bells in the servants' quarters. Its meanderings were somewhat confused, however, by Georgina Meinertzhagen's invention of other ghosts, mostly monastic and all lugubriously manacled; her mother had once put Herbert Spencer into a haunted room whence his brother had fled after only one night (though the philosopher slept stoically in it for three weeks and saw nothing), and Georgina inherited a taste for the macabre. Her stories were recorded by Dan in a great folio book every day during the ghost season. Beneath the fantasy, Richard believed, was a strange reality and at last it reached out toward Dan's death. Shortly after their father had rented the house, the two boys asked one of their gardeners, one Smith, about the Mottisfont ghost. The old man told them that ten years before, while standing on the lawn in front of the house, he himself had asked the same question of the then owner, Sir John Barker Mill. Smiling, Sir John told him that the ghost foretold death and that it could assume any shape. He pointed to the hedge. "It might even be that man over there cutting weeds," he said. Smith looked and there was no man there. Sir John was dead within the year. Neither Dan nor Richard took Smith's story seriously.

Smith the gardener was a fertile depository of old country lore. He could remember the ducking stool that once stood beside a pool outside the rectory garden. It was a crude chair fastened to the end of a see-saw plank into which the culprit was bound and then immersed by tipping as many times as his crime warranted. The case Smith remembered was a matter of incest. Though in their time at Mottisfont no trace of the ducking stool remained, the Meinertzhagen children witnessed at least one act of punishment. A single-line railway ran through Mottisfont village and one summer the villagers burned the signalman in effigy, a ritual that represented the ancient sentence of burning at the stake and which took three days to observe. On the first day a ragged procession marched to the signal box headed by a donkey cart in which a young blood was prancing, shouting and clanging together some metal cans. The second day the same assembly circled the church three times. On the last evening a stake was set up in a field next to the signal box and an effigy in the railway's uniform was lashed to it. The signalman was brought to the bonfire, surrounded by everyone in the village (including the Meinertzhagen children in the care of Coward, the butler), and hooted and jeered at until the flames died down. His offense was beating his wife. When the ceremony was over he was received into village society once more and lived there without further incident for many years.

The countryside around Mottisfont and the healing realism of country life did much to repair the savage hurts of Fonthill in Richard. For the villagers of Mottisfont, bound by the weather and the hard disciplines of the land, the last of summer was the climax of the year, a time when diligence and good husbandry came to fruition. On the dry, open shoulders of the downs the sheep, shorn months before, cropped the fragrant grasses to the shortness of a lawn and rubbed themselves idly against warm outcroppings of chalky rock. Below them, in the steep-sided combes luxuriant with beeches and somber here and there with colonies of dark yews, the air murmured with insects dancing in the dappled light. A boy could lie there for hours, thinking of nothing, while the day stood still and the sun slipped along the leaves and the rustle of a tender grass-blade came louder than the wind. The farms were quieter; the plumes of steam and the miasma of dust coughed out by the thresh-ing drums of the new traction engines had settled now that the barns were piled with sacks and the cornfields swept clean like empty rooms. The engines themselves, bold in their liveries of yellow, red and green, their boilers rumbling like volcanoes, had lurched ponder-ously away to an unknown clanking destiny. Work slacked for a spell, the country fairs began. For Mottisfont's inhabitants the biggest fair, and no doubt the world's finest, assembled in the broad irregular main street of nearby Stockbridge. The serious purpose of the fair was animals—"things" as some countrymen still called them —especially the horses. Though slow oxen with brass-tipped horns were still used for plowing, most farms owned at least a pair of draft horses, quicker than the black oxen and easier to turn at the furrow's end. In Hampshire they were Shire horses, tall and massive, swollen with muscle at the shoulder, with proud arching necks that seemed as thick and strong as oaks. As they were led up and down the street at a trot to show their paces, their bright hoofs fell like thunderbolts and the long silky hair bunched on their fetlocks flicked like the plumes of warriors. They had old, gentle names—Dobbin and Darby and Dancer—and their calm, clear eyes betrayed no awareness of the battering weight of their magnificent bodies. For fairs and high days their coats were curried satin-bright, their manes and tails docked and knotted with ribbons and posies and little bells, and the thick strappings of their harnesses were boned like patent leather and heavy with burnished brass so clean it would leave no mark on a white silk glove.

Each area of England championed its own breed or type of stock, fruit, flower or produce from beer to cheese, and in extreme cases village would even be set against village. Country life for the lower classes was so provincial that many villagers had never even visited their county town. Two of Georgina Meinertzhagen's garden-ers had never traveled by train until she sent them with six others to a horticultural exhibition in London. Only one of the men had been to the capital before; though it was only seventy-eight miles from Mottisfont, none of them thought he had gained overmuch from the adventure and London's sophisticated pleasures only accentuated for them the advantages of life at Mottisfont. This parochial stolidity was part of England's strength; over it the tides of great affairs and foreign entanglements flowed like water across some megalithic rock, uncomprehended and unheeded. Though living conditions had improved mightily since the Hungry Forties, a man might labor in the fields six days a week from dawn to dusk for less than forty pounds a year. The gulf between him and a man like Daniel Meinertzhagen was immeasurable in almost any terms, and certainly by the crude standard of income. Richard's Aunt Beatrice once said that none of her sisters married a man with less than twenty thousand pounds a year. That was a sum Daniel's plowman could not even have imagined, while with the best will Daniel could never have conceived an existence in which bacon was something of a luxury.

Such raw comparisons never occurred to the Meinertzhagen children. They were a society to themselves, resenting the intrusion of stray Slocock children from the rectory and, even more, the arrival of cousins, of whom there were more than fifty. The Slococks had arrived in the vicarage shortly after the Meinertzhagens had taken over the Abbey. The families were of the same size and age, but the Meinertzhagens, encouraged by Sarah Peacock, affected a belligerent superiority expressed in sudden yells of "Hurrah for the Meinertzhagens!" The children at the rectory were in no position to press their acquaintance, and Beatrice Meinertzhagen did not encourage them when, at the age of four, she discovered the Reverend Slocock in search of charity in the drawing room of the Abbey and declared gravely, "You're a Slocock you are, and we don't like Slococks here, we don't!" A self-sufficient, articulate mob, the ten Meinertzhagens roamed the dark corridors and twisting staircases of the Abbey in intricate games designed for the general pleasure, settling sometimes like a flock of questing spirits to invent ghost stories for each other, which Dan would record daily in his huge black book. Though their quarrels seldom lasted more than a few minutes, they were always in ferment, particularly in the winter or when rain held them indoors.

It was then that they played a juvenile version of the War Game.*

Each of them owned and commanded a mixed force of tin soldiers, rated according to regiment, with preference naturally given to Life Guards rigid on their horses and then descending through charging Highlanders to "colonial" troops in slouch hats. Their horse artillery, devastating at three feet, could fire either whole or pounded peppercorns; if the latter, used as shrapnel, induced sneezing in the enemy, that whole force was assumed to have capitulated. Much time was given over to parading, reviewing and the arrangement of tentative alliances, which commonly, when war came, were discarded within moments out of panic or sheer self-interest. The only time when all united was to annihilate someone who desperately claimed neutrality. The onset of war was an unpredictable time of high excitement, since no one knew for certain the strength of anyone else, it being permissible to buy troops in peacetime without declaring them. This mercenary habit led to rapid realignments at the beginning of hostilities, and frequently during the opening phases of the battle one or other of the children would hastily saddle a pony and gallop off to Romsey, five miles away, for a shilling's worth of reinforcements. For five shillings the tide of war could be turned by force majeure by the simple expedient of three cannon boxed complete with their crews frozen in the hectic attitudes of loading and firing. For a slightly larger expenditure a wing of fresh cavalry might be hurled into the charge, unsuspected from the cover of a pocket, satisfying victor and vanquished alike as much for its esthetic equine superiority as for its unquestionable tactical aptness.

---

* Most Victorian children of the middle and upper classes owned collections of toy soldiers, built forts with wooden blocks, and evolved a primitive form of tactical exercise. Their parents dignified the hobby with the name of "The War Game," which observed complicated rules and required space for deployment. The Game was often permanently set up in a barn, though Robert Louis Stevenson preferred an attic and H. G. Wells an open yard. By the time Wells had brought out his monograph on the subject in 1913, responsible adult interest had begun to flag and many a child importuning his elders to teach him the Game was told that there was no point in it now because a war was coming that would render obsolete all the good old rules and even change the nationality of the enemy from French or Russian to—of all things—German.

As the nineties began, the horse was challenged as the basic power unit, in war or in peace, only by the steam locomotive. Excursions from Mottisfont, as distinct from an exodus to London, were infrequent, and limited by the distances the horses could comfortably cover in a day on unsurfaced roads. Assuming summer, when the roads were dusty but hard, the distance of a round trip was at most fifteen miles, which let the Meinertzhagens range eastward as far as the Wiltshire border and their furthest neighbor, old Lady Baring of Norman Court. In the fall before he joined his brother Dan at Harrow, Richard paid a visit there under circumstances of such Damoclean gloom that C'lou had arrived from the City already wearing his white wig of grief. The merchant banking firm of Baring Brothers was about to collapse.

Founded like Huth's by a German immigrant, Baring's was the oldest acceptance house in the City and, next to Rothschild's, the biggest. Its fall would precipitate a far greater calamity than the loss of twenty-one million pounds of what was, after all, family money; the failure of a prestigious house like Baring's would call in question the credit strength of the city of London itself. So Richard, his father and C'lou in Cassandra mood drove over to Norman Court, where the princes of the City were to discuss things in the smoking room. Richard was sent out into the garden and amused himself by knocking knots off the cedar trees until the afternoon grew chilly, when the conference concluded and everyone seemed much happier. Richard shook hands with a gently rounded man who seemed to nurse a particular pleasure at the outcome of their deliberations. It was Lord Nathan Rothschild. The irony Lord Natty was enjoying was that some years before Baring's had overextended itself in South America in the process of keeping his own company out of that lucrative field. Now, with a Rothschild guarantee and the solid heft of Rothschild gold to back it, the Bank of England could announce that Baring's was saved. British credit still floated, for all to see, unsinkable.

The ordinary traffic of the Meinertzhagens with their neighbors was usually less spectacular. Custom prohibited casual descents, but there were occasional visits to families like the Dalgetys of Lockerley

Hall, newly built with the fortune Mr. Dalgety had wrung from a remarkable career from penury to great wealth in Australia. Its size, its execution in angry red brick, and the sheer assertiveness of its design forced Georgina Meinertzhagen to the not very reluctant view that it would make a lovely lunatic asylum. Richard was overawed not only by the footmen in plush breeches and brass buttons but by the interior flashing at him when the great front door swung open. Marble walls, velvet, gold candlesticks, mirrors and the general exuberance of the establishment subdued him at the time, but he never lost his admiration for their owner, who, starting from nothing, had built himself this glory, given the village a new church, married his daughters into the aristocracy, and plainly demonstrated the rewards of virtue to be found in a society such as Britain's. He never fully appreciated just how extraordinary Dalgety's achievement really was.

Two or three other local families enjoyed much the same limited degree of intimacy with the Meinertzhagens as the Dalgetys, but most of the visitors to Mottisfont came from London or even further abroad and could be divided sharply into Daniel's friends (fishing and shooting) or Georgina's (literary and philosophical). A few of each group could also be classified as friends of Richard and young Daniel, though the boys' attitudes toward them varied from veneration to terror. The ancient Canon Berthon of Romsey Abbey, inventor of a collapsible lifeboat, fascinated them with his recollections of Queen Victoria's accession. His accounts of the arrival of Nelson's body at Portsmouth after Trafalgar and the battle of Waterloo carried the conviction of an eye witness and the boys' delight in them was only slightly diminished by their calculation that the old innocent was only two years old when the Iron Duke won his golden fame.

Equally fascinating, but for other reasons, was Georgina's friend Henry John Elwes, whose chief peculiarity was the nurture of flocks of curiously primitive sheep. Elwes, a famous collector of plants, ninety-eight species of which he had himself named, had also collected birds, butterflies and moths on his numerous and extensive travels. By the time he first came to Mottisfont he had already

achieved botanical immorality with *Galanthus Elwesis,* a snowdrop
he had picked in Smyrna in 1874. Georgina was amused by his rudeness, Daniel thought him a bore, and the boys feared his temper, but
when the two of them were alone Richard found him an exciting
companion, especially when he talked about the Himalayas.

From time to time the faithful George Brooksbank came down
from Aysgarth, bringing Richard the calm affection he could not
find elsewhere. In the summer of 1891 Richard made the acquaintance of another schoolmaster, more august by far than Brooksbank,
and he was also to become Richard's friend. Returning from his
entrance examination at Harrow School, he wrote in his diary: "I
met Mr. Welldon who was very big but I liked him. He said he
thought I had passed alright but I thought I had not for I could not
answer some of the questions." The Reverend James Edward Cowell
Welldon was in the sixth year of his headmastership and the thirty-
seventh of his life, and the first impression anyone had of him, boy
or man, was of a genial and dignified bulk. His face, open and eager,
could shine with fervor—for cricket or for chapel matters—and
clouded only when there was some mental struggle occupying his
solid mind. Intellectually he was thorough rather than brilliant, but
his conversation was rich and versatile. His devotion to duty was
irreproachable, his talent for administration pronounced and his application prodigious. He resembled, in spirit as in appearance, a
willing, impartial and intelligent bulldog. Everybody but his mother
thought him strikingly ugly. Everyone who knew him loved and
respected him.

The Harrow of Richard Meinertzhagen's day, though still a great
public school, was not what it had been. In the mid-century it had
been revitalized by Dr. Charles John Vaughan, who, as Arnold's
pupil, had brought high precepts and a steely will to bear on the
school's anarchic decay, even (though he had the liberal bias of a
young man) upon the system of fagging, which he defined as "a
daily assertion in a form which makes it palpable and felt of a power
which has been instituted for the good, not of the superior, but of
the inferior of the relation." After fourteen years Vaughan retired
to a second career as a rural saint. His successor, Dr. Henry Montagu

Butler, brother-in-law of Georgina Meinertzhagen's close friend Sir Francis Galton and author of one of General Gordon's epitaphs, was remembered more for his careful husbandry than for his originality; he occasionally betrayed a flicker of puritan passion, however, as when he comforted a prospective assistant master with "I should have liked to have chosen someone whose life had been purified by suffering but failing that I appoint you." By the time Vaughan retired Harrow had born five Prime Ministers for nineteenth-century England; Butler's governance added thirty-three Privy Councillors and sixty-four generals for the commonweal, a supply which reflected the sort of demand the growing Empire was making on the ruling class and those who shaped it.

But neither Butler nor his acolytes burned any longer with the pure fires of Arnold's bosom; nor if they had could their flames have purged the grosser attitudes of those middle-class fathers who expected the public schools to make their sons nothing more nor less than "English gentlemen" and who paid not inconsiderable fees for that purpose. The product they sought was "character." To Arnold the term had meant "that union which I will never consent to think unattainable, between goodness and wisdom; between everything which is manly, sensible and free, and everything which is pure and self-denying, humble and heavenly." Though Arnold's voice was still heard and respected, few discerned the unsentimental, complex meanings hard as iron beneath the apparently simple beatitudes. Arnold had also said, for instance, "I confess that if I were called upon to name what spirit of evil predominantly deserved the name of Anti-Christ, I should name the spirit of chivalry—the more detestable for the very guise of the 'Archangel ruined,' which has made it so seductive to the most generous spirits—but to me so hateful, because it is in direct opposition to the impartial justice of the Gospel, and its comprehensive feeling of equal brotherhood, and because it so fostered a sense of honor rather than a sense of duty." Herein lay the tragic flaw of the later Victorians: with the possibility of excellence before them they chose the merely good.

Richard Meinertzhagen, with his instinct for excellence, realized almost as soon as he arrived at the school that it was passing its zenith. Rendall's—where he joined Dan, since brothers were allowed to share rooms—was one of ten houses, each the fief of a house master and an extension of his character. At Rendall's, under the sway of a querulous and decrepit priest, a number of bullies flourished, always a sign of maladministration. Though they never menaced Richard, he grew tired of them during his second year and in a sudden blaze of social consciousness organized a small commando and beat them to a pulp in less than fifteen minutes. The faults of Rendall's were due largely to the advanced age of its suzerain. It was possible for a master to spend his whole adult life at Harrow, finally flickering out in the same cap and gown he had worn at his graduation.

In Richard's time there was one master who, having been appointed by the formidable Vaughan, had outlived the suave Butler and was still, it seemed, as good as new. He was Edward Ernest Bowen, composer of "Forty Years On," the most famous of all school songs, introducer under Butler of modern subjects and science teaching, inventor of a peculiar form of football, and a great pedestrian on whose wall hung a great map delineating his walking tours, which circumambulated the entire coastline of Great Britain.* Less awesome than Bowen but as warmly loved was the literary Reginald Bosworth Smith,† whose enthusiasm as a naturalist gave him, in Richard's

---

* Bowen must rank among the finest teachers of all time. Solidly Victorian in his sense of duty and the possession of a vigorous physique that allowed him to play his own version of football with his boys at the age of sixty-five, he evolved theories that were far in advance of contemporary pedagogic practice. He insisted that teaching must aim first at interesting the student in his work and at placing him at ease wih his instructor. "Punishments, rewards and marks," he declared, "are the three great drawbacks to education." Believing teaching a gift and a vocation, he deprecated any kind of training. In 1901 he left the bulk of his property to the school he had served for forty years.

† Boz, as he was called, was the official biographer of Lord Lawrence, a paladin of India, whose attitude toward the Russian menace hovering over Afghanistan had been a subject of national debate. The book ran through six editions in two years, enjoying the enthusiastic patronage of the government of the United States, which placed a copy in every public library in the country and aboard every ship in the navy. Bosworth Smith's lectures on Mohammed and Mohammedanism, first delivered at Harrow, were translated into Arabic

eyes, the stature of a god. He would require the boys to name wild flowers he had picked, exhorting, "Nature brings you close to God: study it!" On such occasions Richard bore away the laurels and enjoyed geography and history almost as much. Latin and Greek bored him and when he left Harrow any mathematics beyond simple arithmetic remained for him an odious mystery. As a new boy Richard was placed in the lowest form in the school and there encountered Robert Somervell, who taught Richard, invaluably, how to work and take pride in it. Driven by a longing to catch up with Dan in class, Richard was not long with the diligent Somervell. At the beginning of his second term he next encountered M. C. Kemp and reported home: "he keeps a red and white spaniel in the classroom and she is called Bus and if any boy is naughty Mr. Kemp sends Bus to bite his legs but I have not been naughty yet. If I work hard this term I shall get a double remove and I shall then be only two forms behind Dan." The "remove" was a device common in public schools which enabled boys to find their academic peers by rapid transit through successive forms. In two weeks Richard passed beyond Kemp and his sanguinary pet, and by the end of the year had achieved two double removes in succession and rocketed through six forms, a rate of ascent close to angelic. By some malign arithmetic Dan was still two forms ahead, but Richard's aspiration was undimmed. "I am nearly a year younger than the average of my form," he wrote, "and I am now only two forms behind Dan. It will be lovely when we do our work together but Dan says he is not going to let me catch him up."

Dogged as Richard's pursuit was, it still left him time for his favorite occupation. Bosworth Smith kept a couple of eagle owls in his garden, issued an open invitation to tea, and allowed the boys to wander about looking for birds. Harrow, atop a somewhat abrupt hill (hence its sobriquet "The Hill"), was still surrounded by green fields bouncing with hares. Quail, partridges and corncrakes rattled through the stubble, and the hedges rustled with their population

---

and won him for many years the prayers of the faithful in the mosques of West Africa.

of songbirds. Kingfishers flashed their iridescent path across the lake in the park, past immobile herons and once past a very rare black stork whose demise by gunshot was reported in a precocious letter to *The Field*. His first spring at Harrow Richard went bird's-nesting with a new friend, Harold Cookson; discovering a tree sparrow's nest in a hole in a pollard willow, Richard climbed up and found that by standing on tiptoe he could just reach the eggs and, in the same moment, that he was stuck. Harold ran off to fetch a man with a saw and a chisel, and Richard was able to strike a subsequently thoughtful note in his diary: "My arm is terribly stiff today. Another lesson learned. Never put your hand into a hole unless it goes in easily." It was the last occasion on which Richard Meinertzhagen could have been said to have been totally immobilized.

Harrow's bucolic surroundings, the more remarkable since the center of London was only fifteen miles away, made it seem in leisure hours almost an extension of Mottisfont and allowed Richard to sate the appetite of a born poacher. Richard the amateur soon made the acquaintance of a professional, one George Adams, who kept a sagacious lurcher dog and who for a consideration would loan out his nets, snares and traps. On a good dark night Richard would set thin wire nooses in the hedges and launch the dog on a silent loping tour of the field. As often as not a hare would soon be bucking in a noose, to be dispatched with a swift chop to the back of the skull. Partridges were enmeshed in big, delicate nets that swished down onto the grass with no more sound than a bird's wings. One fall Richard surprised his father with a gift of two brace of partridges, received with a pleasure tinged with suspicion. "I was most grateful for those partridges," Daniel Meinertzhagen wrote, "but however did you come by them as I could not trace any signs of shot and they all had their necks wrung. Have you been poaching?"

Hedgerow and copse, Dan's company in their private room, the discovery of the highly organized society of an old and great school, and the appreciation of men like Welldon and Bosworth Smith began to restore Richard's self-confidence. Besides, he had found a new interest. Perhaps as a natural development of the miniature war games at Mottisfont, he had joined the Volunteer Corps as soon as he arrived at Harrow and had been assigned to the band. He began on the cornet but gave it up because the bandmaster's beery spittle choked up the mouthpiece, was relegated to the cymbals, and finally achieved the big drum. The Corps was not at this time an elite unit. It was woefully under strength and drilled awkwardly and its marching was at best slovenly. Its tactics, as the school magazine had reported shortly before Richard was mustered in, were suicidal. The occasion was an encounter on maneuvers with another school: "The Haileybury Corps, regardless of life, advanced gallantly over a large open space, and would, without doubt, have been annihilated, if it had not been for an unfortunate mistake made by the right flank of Harrow, who mistook a flag supposed to represent a company of a hundred for a detachment of four men. They were obliged to retire in ignominious haste." Richard's first field day was at Hatfield, the gigantic house of the Prime Minister, Lord Salisbury, then at the end of his second administration. The more effective elements of the Corps trooped off toward yet another tactical disaster and the band, including the noncombatant Richard, was allowed to wander where it would through the few square miles of domain.

The seat of Robert Arthur Talbot Gascoyne Cecil, third Marquis of Salisbury, contained a library of ten thousand books, numerous souvenirs of royal favor (including the bloodstained shirt King Charles I had worn to the headsman's block), and trophies of war and sport a Medici might have envied. With such a home only twenty miles from London and another house in the city itself, Lord Salisbury not unnaturally disdained the use of the Prime Minister's official residence at Number 10 Downing Street, since it scarcely bore comparison with one of his own hen houses. He believed with all his considerable heart in the government of the people for the people by the fittest. These latter were, of course, those men of high and gentle birth among whom he moved as a tsar among grand dukes. Salisbury's was the last government by aristocracy outside Russia.

Lord Salisbury on Parnassus cared nothing for popular acclaim. He saw the socialist masses swirling around its foot as perverted by materialism and thus incapable of altruistic action; the liberals on the lower slopes were only slightly less dangerous in their passion for a democracy they could not understand. Only those grouped around the mountain peak should use the power, for they alone carried responsibility and they alone, by heredity, were free of the desire for private gain. In practice the task devolved upon Lord Salisbury himself for, despite his ingenuous view of them, those of his peers who were able were seldom willing and those who were willing were often of the wrong party. Virtually alone, eschewing all passion, he sailed coldly and steadily through the last decades of the nineteenth century, navigating solely by the most brilliant of Victorian stars—a sense of duty to his country. His administration succeeded, particularly in foreign affairs, because Salisbury was superbly competent to rule. In public or in private he existed in a cloud of the most ponderous authority within which there played like lightning a mind unpredictable and agile, deliberately tuned, ruthless when necessary, and swift toward decision. In old age his hunched shoulders and massive head with its round pouched eyes gave him the forbidding look of a bison. He walked carefully and acted deliberately, dependent on no man, and sometimes would escape his guests by taking a book up to the roof, considering some Greek trope among the proliferous chimney pots of Hatfield.

It was before this formidable presence that Richard Meinertzhagen suddenly found himself that summer afternoon in 1892, with a Hatfield rabbit dangling from his belt. The Volunteers had reassembled in front of the great house after their day of martial experiment which, in Richard's case, had been occupied throwing stones among the Hatfield warrens, one of which had proved mortal to the small creature now only too limply obvious at his side. Their host emerged to inspect the parade, paused in front of Richard, and inquired without rancor, "One of mine?" Unfazed, Richard described the manner of its demise, was congratulated, and explained that it would be fed to the eagles he and Dan kept at the school, which led to a rather protracted conversation. Richard noted later: "I was mightily pleased with myself because Lord Salisbury had spoken to me, for I regarded him then as the embodiment of Victorian and Imperialistic Conservatism, a great empire-builder and a symbol of our Empire." In this judgment the boy was absolutely correct. But what was interesting about the exchange between patrician Prime Minister and schoolboy of fourteen was the confidence and ease with which it was conducted on both sides. Richard's Aunt Beatrice once wrote in her diary, "As life unfolded itself I became aware that I belonged to a class of persons who habitually gave orders, but who seldom, if ever, executed the orders of other people." Veteran statesman and young boy had recognized in each other without conscious thought this condition of Victorian life, soon to crumble in the general disruption of their ordered society. It was, of course, the possession of inherited authority which Lord Salisbury had from his family and Richard Meinertzhagen from his class. It was, at least for the time being, as tangible as armor.

Richard's first year at his new school could hardly have ended better. As a reward his father took him and Dan on a trip to Land's End, returning by way of Exmoor, where Daniel had walked as a boy with R. D. Blackmore while the latter was writing *Lorna Doone,* a book Daniel had not yet read. They found the last moss-covered traces of the Doone huts, a bullet embedded in the door of a church, and a Carver Doone still living not far from the valley his outlaw ancestors had terrorized. The boys were delighted by the birds they had seen in the Cornish cliffs and on the tide races sweeping in from the Atlantic, but Daniel had enjoyed only an interlude of fishing for mackerel, though they brought merely vulgar sport compared to his fastidious trout at Mottisfont. The next summer their father gave the boys twenty pounds and sent them off to Ireland on their first expedition for birds. At the end of three weeks they had collected fifty-four skins, not without discomfort, and had run out of money. One evening, Richard recorded, "I wrestled with a cormorant and it smelled horrible and I cannot get the smell out of my clothes so I must go to bed with it." Though broke, the boys were already planning grander adventures: "We must go to Lapland and see waxwings and hawk owls. Dan says he thinks Father will give us enough to go there. And then we must go to the Yenesei and see the grey plover breeding, and our third trip must be to Ladak and Yarkand to find the ground chough. I think we shall be good travellers for we never get tired and we have never yet quarrelled. Dan is splendid at skinning and I can shoot fairly well, better than Dan, but we must both get better at both." Richard's predilections and talents were already firmly set.

This preference for sports above games marked him as slightly old-fashioned, for it was an eighteenth-century taste universal among the hard-riding, hard-bottomed gentry whose fondness for blood— whether spilling from a cornered fox, pumping through the veins of a potential spouse, or oozing from a baron of beef—had made England the most riotous and rumbunctious country in Europe. At Harrow the vogue was games and in winter all boys were daily dragooned onto the football field, where they sank at once into inches of malodorous mud. Summer was given over to the worship of cricket; every afternoon those in the lower forms reported for fielding practice on that part of the Philathletic Grounds reserved to the lordly members of the School XI and rushed about, under the management of three or four older boys called "slave-drivers," until tea-time mercifully arrived and the demigods strolled off, bats held carelessly aslant under their arms and voices drawling asides on this or that young champion's current form. The XI were a kind of priesthood, or more aptly an oligarchy, distinguished from others even in their mode of dress, for cricket had by now become more than a religion. For the public schools of England it was a way of life, so there was nothing even faintly ludicrous when Sir Henry Newbolt preached the imperial mission in terms of that exclusively English pastime:

> *There's a breathless hush in the Close tonight—*
> *Ten to make and the match to win—*
> *A bumping pitch and a blinding light,*
> *An hour to play and the last man in.*

> *And it's not for the sake of a ribboned coat,*
> *Or the selfish hope of a season's fame,*
> *But his Captain's hand on his shoulder smote—*
> *Play up! play up! and play the game!*

> *The sand of the desert is sodden red,—*
> *Red with the wreck of the square that broke;—*

> *The gatling's jammed and the colonel dead,*
> *And the regiment blind with the dust and smoke.*
>
> *The river of death has brimmed its banks*
> *And England's far and honor a name,*
> *But the voice of a schoolboy rallies the ranks:*
> *Play up! play up! and play the game!*

It was very far from Dr. Arnold's creed, but as a philosophy it was to serve its purpose. At the end of World War I, six hundred and forty-four Harrovians had played the game to the bitter twilight, enough, had they lived, to fill the school chapel almost to the door.

Approving in general of Newbolt's patriotic sentiments, Richard was far too logical to worship the same fetish. He was already a fanatic about hard muscle and sound wind's promoting clear thinking, or, as he later put it: "No man can think on sound lines and get the best from the intellectual side of life if he leads a soft sedentary existence. In war I have seen many almost degenerate young men, whose sole conversation had been sex, food, or subversive politics, develop into hard and clear-thinking men when they had purged their bodies of the foul acids and fats which breed vice and gaseous talk." At Harrow Richard took greater pains to develop his body than he did to enlarge his mind, but never through games, partly because he distrusted their exaggerated status and partly because he was not competitive in the accepted way. He hated contests, for the only antagonist he could as yet recognize, because of what had happened at Fonthill and with his mother, was himself. He took up boxing to test his own endurance and lost as often as he won. He swam because, like every boy at Harrow, he was made to, and improved because he liked it. He excelled at track without much practice and learned to shoot well with a rifle. He was energetic in the classroom too, and despite disclaimers showed enough academic skill to achieve the upper school by the end of his second year, thus winning the black swallow-tailed Sunday coat that separated the senior sheep from the younger goats.

Like the wider society for which it was a forcing-house, the little world of Harrow ran day by day on a mechanism of custom, tradition and gradations of privilege. No boy was allowed to wear his overcoat unbuttoned until he had been in the school for three years; no boy spoke of his family, except in the most off-hand way, to another or kept photographs of them in his room; no boy visited anyone in another House other than a master; only monitors or members of the Philathletic Club and the sixth form could sport fancy vests, and the cricket XI alone could wear the distinctive low-crowned straw hat specked black and white. The year's passing was marked by hallowed observances and rituals like Founder's Day, when the whole school assembled to sing Harrow's famous songs with a pure fervor that, remembered, brought tears to the eyes of Old Harrovians as long as they lived. Even as an old man revisiting the school, Richard Meinertzhagen could never join in the singing for the lump that choked his throat, though as a small boy he had been complimented by Welldon himself for the sweetness of his voice. The venue of these concerts was the Speech Room, an amphitheater with steep tiers of seats circling a dais, the scene of one of Richard's minor triumphs. "I was allowed to play God Save the Queen on the Speech Room organ when the Prince of Wales came down yesterday," he wrote to his father. "I pulled out all the loudest stops and thundered it out as loud as I could and I was very proud of it. I shook hands with him after the end of the show. I wish the Queen would come down to Harrow but I suppose she is too old, but if she goes to Eton she might come here for a change." The pleasure Richard took in secular music was not, however, carried over into chapel, which he was required to attend like everybody else in a proper silk hat three times every Sunday. He abhorred all sermons but Welldon's and acquired a marked distaste for church services. In private he still prayed, curled up in his bed, every night as his grandfather Potter had taught him. More sporting occasions such as the yearly cricket match between Old Harrovians and the School XI were far less important to Richard than the sighting of a bird or personal encounters with other boys. Winston Churchill was still a boy at Harrow for two of Richard's years there and had already gained a reputation for determination and truculence; like Richard, he was something of a loner and one day their paths crossed on the street. It was customary, under such conditions, for Harrow boys to contest the right of way, so Richard cannoned into Churchill, trying to force him into the gutter. He hit a body as inflexible as iron and as he bounced off was treated to a glance from Churchill's deep-set eyes that he never forgot. It was neither victorious nor amused, merely a warning to keep off, but of a menacing intensity that Richard recognized again years later in the eyes of a wild boar about to charge him. Neither boy uttered a word.

A confrontation of a different kind led to a friendship begun when Richard made a profit out of a Rothschild. Nathaniel Charles, a younger son of that Lord Natty who had come to the rescue of the Baring family and had greatly relieved C'lou's tattered feelings, was Richard's contemporary at school and shared his love of birds. They launched expeditions together and competed as collectors. One of their sources for skins was a seller of wildfowl called Jones, from whom one day Richard bought a shoveler duck which Charles Rothschild, arriving too late, coveted. It was a magnificent specimen and Richard, beguiled at having a Rothschild in his clutches, equated business with pleasure and made a capital gain of three shillings. Charles became one of those Rothschilds who supported Zionism, but his older brother, Lionel Walter, took a stronger part in it and it was he with whom in later life Richard became more intimate. Though Walter worked, as was required, in the family's bank, he gave all his serious attention to his gigantic museum, which eventually housed a quarter of a million birds (acquired later by the Museum of Natural History in New York) and two million insects, representing an investment of half a million pounds and a lifetime of devotion. Walter's financial insouciance caused Rothschild heads to shake, but his expertise as a naturalist brought him international fame. He was invited to Harrow to lecture and there Richard met him for the first time and was enthralled.

Eminent guests quite frequently arrived to lecture on a catholic range of subjects, among them one day a small, peremptory American with fever in his eyes. When Richard first saw him, Sir Henry Morton Stanley had not long returned from one of the most haz-

ardous journeys of his dangerous career; the privations he had
suffered on it were to bring his death. He had exploded into Africa
to rescue one of General Gordon's lieutenants, Emin Pasha, from
expected immolation by the southward flow of the khalifa's dervishes. Stanley succeeded in doing so, though against Emin's own
wishes, at the end of two years and ten months of disasters that
turned his hair white and rendered the flesh from his delicate frame
as fat is boiled from a chicken. Stanley's account of the journey, *In
Darkest Africa,* an instant best-seller, stoked the controversy about
the expedition that was already blazing. Critics accused him of
abandoning his rearguard in his pursuit of personal glory. Stanley
counterattacked by claiming that the leaders of the doomed party
not only had partially deserved their fate by their cruelty to the
natives but had forfeited all right to sympathy by resorting to can-
nibalism. He arrived at Harrow while the argument was at its
height and told the boys, surrounding him in the dark Speech Room
like a cliff of faces, "Somebody with experience, somebody with
drive, somebody with imagination, somebody with leadership had
to be chosen for that great expedition." He paused. "I was that
man!" His audience roared with delight. In that delirious moment
Africa came alive in Richard Meinertzhagen's heart. Some time
later Richard was able to get a closer look at his hero when Stanley
visited the family, where he immediately antagonized Daniel by
pointing out that he had rescued Livingstone after the British had
abandoned him and then savaged Georgina when she offered him
tea by snapping, "My good woman, tea is an insult to your lunch
and a menace to my dinner." He struck Richard as "an uncommon
little bounder but with immense driving power." In spite of that
reservation, Richard liked him for his talk of Africa and longed to
see more of him. Three years after Richard had left Harrow they
met for the last time when Stanley stayed the night at Mottisfont
and relived for Richard, through approaching paralysis, the sufferings of his march through the forests, hour after hour in the quiet
country night. Finally he gave a piece of advice. "If ever you travel
in Africa," he said, "rule your men with an iron discipline, share
starvation and hardship and never give in."

Nearly half a century later Winston Churchill, at last Prime Minister, enjoying one of his wartime visits to his old school, echoed Stanley's last three words to Richard that evening. They were singularly apt, for the one attribute in which Harrow prided itself was the indomitable qualities of character in its sons. Winchester men might be more mannerly, Etonians probably displayed more poise, but for guts there was no place like Harrow. Not unnaturally this attitude in general summed up Richard's own view of his alma mater. His education there had cost his father fifteen hundred pounds. On the whole, Richard thought at the end of 1895, it had been well worth it. Harrow had not instilled into him the graces of a scholar, but at least he had learned mental discipline and he had warmed, perhaps for the wrong reasons, to history and geography. More than curiosity now drove him to pore over his atlas. He would measure the red flood of Britain's dominance across the globe and covet secretly the wild territories defaced by other colors or as yet unclaimed. Every day in *The Times* sent by his father's subscription, he turned first to the foreign news, which in the mid-nineties was frequently a record of the progress of another of his heroes. Cecil John Rhodes, with the diamond mines of South Africa for collateral, was then buying or blasting his way northward with the intention of bringing the entire world under British sway. Enraptured by such distant odysseys and beguiled by the magic music of the imperial theme, Richard had little time for home affairs. The most pressing of these, at least for Mr. Gladstone and his adherents, was the issue of Home Rule for Ireland. Lord Salisbury, on the other hand, thought the rising waters of democracy and freedom hardly worth the greater part of his attention, since he classed the political maturity of the Irish with that of Hottentots.

One December evening in 1895 Richard walked over to the headmaster's House to say goodbye to Welldon, whose appreciation four years before had wiped out the nightmare of Fonthill. By now Welldon knew Richard well. "He told me," the boy wrote, "there was a tremendous opportunity in the colonies and in science and that I was the type to go abroad for I had leadership in me. He told me to keep in touch with him and that he was always available if I wanted help or advice, which I thought very kind of him. He really is a great man and I hope he is made an Archbishop." Welldon never attained that eminence, but became in succession Metropolitan of the Indian Church, Canon of Westminster, Dean of Manchester and Dean of Durham. He never lost track of any boy he had cared for at Harrow and Richard never forgot the fearlessness of his mind and the warmth of his affection. Walking away from Welldon's through the darkened school that night, Richard thought hard about his friend's advice. He was leaving Harrow with no career decided on and his brain was rocking with the calls that came from the African veldt, from the zoological school at Cambridge, and from his father's office in the City. It seemed to him that there were too many loyalties and he could not measure which was the greatest. But in the meantime it was nearing Christmas and at once his heart leaped for Mottisfont and the river running leaden through the snow, and Dan and the joyous brood of Meinertzhagens united again, and caring for no one. It was Christmas and he could still believe with some semblance of honesty that there was peace on earth and goodwill of a sort among men. Certainly there would be plum puddings dark as night, steaming and aflicker with the blue flames of brandy.

CHAPTER 5

I Would Annex the Planets
If I Could

Africa glowed like a ruby deep in Richard Meinertzhagen's imagination, its fires kindled by Stanley and now nourished by the fierce heat of Cecil John Rhodes, a man whose exuberant dreams were close to mania and whose titanic energy made that immense continent seem no bigger than a paddock. Rhodes had had his first heart attack at the age of nineteen. During his third year at Harrow Richard had begun to follow Rhodes's career northward by means of *The Times,* whose reports he devoured every morning. Not all were hopeful. He wrote in his diary on January 4, 1894, "I fear there has been a ghastly disaster in Matabeleland for I read that the great hunter Selous reports that Allan Wilson's small column has been destroyed by the remnants of Lobengula's impis." When the news was shortly confirmed, Richard determined to go to Matabeleland at once and asked a friend to give him a letter of introduction to Rhodes. But Dan, with whom Richard discussed it, demurred. "If Dan would come too," Richard wrote, "I should go at once, but he thinks it is not in his line and I think he is right. He is not so robust nor so adventurous and impetuous as I am; but he is more able and calculating."

The saga of Major Wilson which had caused Richard such vicarious anguish, though politically and militarily insignificant, brought down the wrath of the British on the Matabele king Lobengula and inspired stories in *The Boys Own Paper* for years to come. The seeds of the gallant major's demise, and incidentally of Lobengula's, had been sown years before by Rhodes. Blue-eyed, fair-haired and tubercular, the son of an obscure vicar, Rhodes had first arrived in South Africa at the age of sixteen. With the pickings he made in the diamond fields of Griqualand West he put himself through Oxford, where he was gloomily welcomed at Oriel, Daniel Meinertzhagen's old college, by its provost with, "All the colleges send me their failures." Books and the academic regimen did not satisfy the hunger Rhodes had come to assuage; though he did not know it, Rhodes had come to Oxford to find a faith. It was provided from an unlikely quarter.

In his early twenties, in the decade in which Richard Meinertzhagen was born, Rhodes attended one of John Ruskin's lectures in which that sinewy aesthete revealed a blazing vision and propounded a startling philosophy. "Will you youths of England," he asked, "make your country again a royal throne of kings, a sceptred isle, for all the world a source of light, a center of peace? This is what England must do, or perish. She must found colonies as fast and as far as she is able, formed of the most energetic and worthiest of men; seizing any piece of fruitful waste ground she can set her foot on, and there teaching her colonists that their chief virtue is to be fidelity to their country, and that their first aim is to advance the power of England by land and sea." Rhodes caught the dream, colored it with some of Winwood Reade's mysticism, and justified its practical application by reference to the theories, as he understood them, of Charles Darwin. He recorded his conclusions: "I contend that we are the first race in the world, and that the more of the world we inhabit, the better it is for the human race. I contend that every acre added to our territory provides for the birth of more of the English race, who otherwise would not be brought into existence. Added to which the absorption of the greater portion of the world under our rule simply means the end of all wars." He dedicated himself to this course and for the rest of his life he strove "for the bringing of the whole civilized world under British rule, for the recovery of the United States, for the making of the Anglo-Saxon race into one Empire! What a dream! But yet it is probable! It is possible!"

Certainly it seemed possible in 1888, when Rhodes was in his prime. His agents, advised by Frederick Courteney Selous,* known as the king of white hunters, struck a bargain with Lobengula, paramount of the Matabele, a warrior race who called themselves the Children of the Stars. At the royal kraal of Bulawayo (the place of killing) Rhodes's men persuaded Lobengula to give them the rights to all metals and minerals in his kingdom, in consideration of which he would receive a royalty of one hundred pounds a month and an outright gift of a thousand rifles with a hundred cartridges apiece and an armed steamer. For such toys Lobengula had virtually given up a land as big as France, Germany, Belgium and Holland put together and the elephant seal of his majesty would soon wind up a trinket at Rhodes's house, Groote Schuur. Within a year the company Rhodes had formed to develop his northern territories had received its royal charter as the British South African Company with Rhodes, also prime minister of the Cape Colony, as its managing director. His next move swung further north still, into Mashonaland, where in the fall of 1891 Selous planted the Union Jack in a piece of red dirt that was to become the city of Salisbury. Lobengula was surrounded.

At the end of 1893 Rhodes's men invaded Matabeleland. His power shattered, Lobengula burned his kraal and, gathering what royalty he could about him, set out for the Zambesi River and what he hoped might be a peaceful anonymity. A flying column of three hundred men set out after him with the indispensable Maxims. They caught up with him on the Shangani River, and a party of fifteen venturesome men under Major Allan Wilson rode forward

---

* Selous' only eccentricity was that when hunting elephant he took off his boots and socks. With a Hottentot called Cigar for a tracker, and armed with a couple of muzzle-loaders, he began at the age of twenty to roam the immense hinterland north of the Cape. Within ten years he was preeminent among the half-dozen hunters who had each killed more than a thousand elephants.

by night to the king's wagons and called out to him to surrender. Hearing only the click of gunlocks in reply, Wilson discreetly withdrew. He was joined before daybreak by another small group, increasing his force to thirty-four men, and at dawn repeated his call to surrender. But Lobengula had fled in the darkness and Wilson's answer was a volley. He sent three men for help and pulled back the rest. The Matabele hemmed them in and began to cut them down. It was said later, without much support, that when only five or six of the Englishmen were left they stood up, took off their hats, and sang the national anthem. When Selous found their bodies they were drawn up in a circle no more than fifteen yards across. Wilson, a kind of inadvertent Custer, might seem to have died somewhat inconclusively, but his departure served its purpose. The British public, like Richard Meinertzhagen, whose diary breathed wrath for a few days, felt both outraged and inspired and quite overlooked in its righteousness the tribulations of the savage Lobengula that had preceded it. No one felt a pang when word came of the king's death of a fever. "And serve him right!" they said.

Before that salutary news had reached England Richard had met Rhodes through Willy Woods, colonel of the local Hampshire Yeomanry. Richard was invited to dine at Woods's London club with a party of ten men honoring Rhodes. While they ate in that leathery, masculine atmosphere Rhodes expounded his plans for a huge federation of Africa, then afterward began to cross-examine Richard about Harrow, in particular about whether he had been taught anything of Africa. Richard told him about Stanley's lectures and how he had pored over his atlas and followed the Matabele War through the columns of *The Times*. Then came the inevitable question: "What does your father do?" Fortunately Richard could return a respectable answer. Rhodes seemed impressed to learn that Daniel was a banker and gratified that he, too, was an alumnus of Oriel College. Suddenly Rhodes said, "You know, you're the type we want out there. Why don't you come? I'll start you off. It's a grand life." It was a magnificent offer and it stunned Richard, but when Rhodes continued to stare at him he recovered enough to say that he would ask his father's permission. Daniel, consulted later that night, was unenthusiastic, though he went so far as to promise to talk to Rhodes when they met in Oxford, where their old college was to hold a celebration. Daniel kept both his promise and his first opinions, so Richard went sadly back to school. There he played his last card. He wrote to Rhodes telling him how disappointed he was and asking if he might come out to South Africa when he left Harrow. If Rhodes would send him passage money he would sail no matter what his parents said. But by that time both Rhodes's fortunes and Richard's had changed.

Late in 1895 Dr. Leander Starr Jameson, Rhodes's principal lieutenant, began to assemble a force of four hundred and seventy mounted men with eight Maxims and three lights field guns in Pitsani, on the border of the Transvaal—a fly-blown jumble of shacks wide open to the sultry oppression of the sun. Jameson's avowed intention was to support a projected rising of certain inhabitants of Johannesburg against the iniquities of the Boer regime of Paul Kruger. Gruff and gross, Kruger had withstood all the efforts of successive administrators in South Africa to bundle him up in the folds of the Union Jack. Ten years before, there had been no Johannesburg, just a stretch of open veldt. But underneath the veldt was gold and soon there was a sprawling mass of iron shanties inhabited by foreigners hungry for fortunes. These were the Uitlanders and they had no vote in the Transvaal. When they protested Kruger and his Boers consulted their oracle, the stern Bible of Calvin, and found nothing there about a franchise for interlopers. There were protests and appeals to Her Majesty and polite letters to Pretoria, but Kruger sat impassively on his stoop in his disreputable black stovepipe hat and baggy frockcoat, looking like a bewhiskered old sea-elephant, offering coffee to visiting burghers (which they drank in their barbarous fashion out of the saucer) and appearing to do nothing. But behind the ugly broad countenance, behind the rheumy eyes with their bags as big as apricots, was an astute and patient brain. Kruger waited.

Jameson's charm lent him a deceptive softness. It hid a nature quixotic and sudden, and a mind as secretive as it was unpredictable. He intended to cover the hundred and eighty miles to Johannesburg by forced marches in three days, reinforce the revolt that would have started there, march on to Pretoria and throw the whiskery old president off his front porch. It seemed an easy matter to Jameson and he could not understand why the order to go did not come from Cape Town. They fretted and the sun's glare became unbearable. On December 29 Jameson's volatile nature boiled over; with a last cable to Cape Town he saddled up, and with a jingle of spurs on stirrups and a last pull at the bottle his doomed cavalry cantered through the wire and into their fool's paradise.

The Boers dogged them all the way, firing desultory shots and riding off until wearily on New Year's Day Jameson's raiders climbed a hilltop aptly close to the little town of Krugersdorp and found themselves blocked by main force. They fought all day but five of their eight Maxims jammed and the Boer commandant brought up his guns. Early in the morning they showed the white flag and by the next day they were safely in Pretoria at last—in jail. Seventeen of their number were dead, thirty-five missing and fifty-five wounded. All of the survivors had totally lost heart for there had been no revolt in Johannesburg after all and Paul Kruger had scarcely stirred in his chair.

When the first news of Jameson's fiasco reached London, many of the English were appalled at what they construed as a piece of madcap banditry. Many would have joined Kruger as he gave thanks to his harsh God, perhaps not by means of the righteous and bloody Sixty-Eighth Psalm with its talk of feet being dipped in the blood of enemies ("and the tongue of thy dogs in the same"), though Richard's uncle Leonard Courtney, the radical Member of Parliament, said he would have been glad to raise his voice with Kruger's. Richard Meinertzhagen called it "a gross piece of aggression" and Wilfrid Blunt, his old protector, wrote gleefully in his diary: "Those blackguards of the Chartered Company in South Africa, under Doctor Jameson, have made a filibustering raid on the Transvaal and have been annihilated by the Boers, Jameson a prisoner. I hope devoutly he may be hanged." However, the liberal national mood changed drastically overnight when it was discovered that Queen Victoria's grandson, Kaiser Wilhelm II of Germany, had sent Kruger a telegram. "I would like to express my sincere congratulations," it read, "that you and your peoples have succeeded, without having to invoke the help of friendly powers, in restoring peace with your own resources in face of armed bands which have broken into your country as disturbers of the peace and have been able to preserve the independence of your country against attacks from outside." Animosity shifted at once to this upstart emperor who could refer to the "independence" of a territory that owed fealty to the Queen. Richard once more reflected the popular mood when he wrote: "The Kruger Telegram is the first act of open rudeness directed against Britain by that conceited and ambitious little Jack-in-the-box the Kaiser. It is no sentimental indiscretion but a deliberate act of policy, the first warning that sooner or later we must fight Germany." In spite of its obvious technical imperfections the poet laureate's* effusion, "Jameson's Ride," printed in *The Times* a week or so after the Telegram, found admirers among the more emotional, with its intrepid interpretation of the sad little shambles at Krugersdorp:

> *Right sweet is the marksman's rattle,*
> *And sweeter the cannon's roar,*
> *But 'tis betterly bad to battle,*
> *Beleaguered, and one to four.*
> *I can tell you it wasn't a trifle*
> *To swarm over Krugersdorp glen,*
> *As they ploughed us with round and rifle,*
> *And ploughed us, again—and again.*

Her Majesty questioned Mr. Austin's sense of proportion but her subjects shared the poet laureate's mood. When Rhodes came to London to face the music he saw nothing but smiling faces in the crowds that greeted him.

Jameson and his men were shipped home in the *Victoria*, transferred to launches in the Thames's mouth, and landed quietly at Waterloo Pier to stand trial before the Lord Chief Justice under the

---

* Alfred Austin had been appointed to the laureateship, inexplicably, by the literate Lord Salisbury. Formerly a right-wing journalist, he never blotted a line of his verse, believing it to be divinely inspired.

Foreign Enlistment Act. They were given light sentences and considerable adulation and their odyssey was translated to the theater as the most popular tableau vivant of the season. But Jameson's action, as Rhodes had himself suspected it would, had put an end to his greater dreams. "I would annex the planets if I could," Rhodes had once declared; now even the Mountains of the Moon were beyond his grasp.

The Raid, with all its implications, did nothing to diminish Richard's admiration for Rhodes. If anything it was increased by Rhodes's remarkable settlement of the rebellion that broke out in Matabeleland a few weeks after Jameson's adventure and long before the Commission of Inquiry sat. In the spring of 1896 the rinderpest swept into Matabeleland from the north, so severely that only five hundred cattle were left out of a hundred thousand. Attempts to stem it by slaughtering herds were interpreted by the Matabele as yet another oppression, so in rage they began to kill the white settlers on the outskirts of Bulawayo. Colonel Robert Stephenson Smyth Baden-Powell* of the 13th Hussars was one of the officers hastily dispatched to assist the local forces in restoring order. The Matabele had been assured by their witch doctors in a pronouncement hallowed by African tradition that they could not be harmed by the white men's bullets, which would turn to water. The fallacy of their promise was quickly demonstrated by an American scout called Burnham, who on the pretext of wishing to profit from this magic had got close enough to one of the three oracles of the Matabele to shoot him dead. Hammered by what Colonel Baden-Powell described as "a hand of iron in a velvet glove," the Matabele retired to their last stronghold, the Matopo Hills, a range of jumbled rock formations strewn with massive boulders and outcroppings riddled with caves, their black slopes offering to the attacker as much foothold as glass.

---

* The colonel is perhaps more widely known as Lord Baden-Powell of Gilwell, author, among other works, of the classic *Pigsticking or Hoghunting,* of *Cavalry Instruction* and *The Downfall of Prempeh,* and as the founder of the Boy Scout movement. Always prepared, he carried on this campaign a soft paintbrush of camel hair for cleaning out wounds.

Cave by cave and peak by peak the Matabele were squeezed into a narrowing perimeter less, as the colonel saw it, by field guns and Maxims than by sheer force of character. He spoke with the true voice of an Old Carthusian: "Your Englishman (and by him I mean his Colonial brother as well) is endowed by nature with the spirit of practical discipline, which is deeper than the surface veneer discipline of the Continental armies. Whether it has been instilled into him by his public-school training, by his football and his 'fagging,' or whether it is inbred from previous generations of stern though kindly parents, one cannot say; but, at any rate, the goodly precepts of the game remain as best of guides: 'Keep in your place,' and 'Play, not for yourself, but for your side.' It is thus that our leaders find themselves backed by their officers playing up to them; not because they are '—well ordered to' (as I heard Tommy express it), nor because it may bring them crosses and rewards, but simply —*because it is the game.*" Rhodes ended this particular game in person by walking unarmed into the Matopos to meet the Matabele chiefs. He promised them justice and they honored him with their royal salute. It was Rhodes's supreme moment. At the end, remembering, he caused his grave to be quarried in that black rock not far from the cave where Mzilikaze, founder of the Matabele nation, sat in skeletal state among the relics of his majesty.

Rhodes died two months before the end of the Boer War, which Jameson's Raid had helped precipitate. Richard met him again when he arrived at Southampton in January 1899. Rhodes greeted him warmly and again offered him a place, but by then Richard was in the army and about to leave for India; even so, Rhodes insisted, all Richard had to do was cable him and come to Cape Town. He wanted to introduce some British birds into South Africa, so when he saw him for the last time Richard presented him with eighteen starlings, eleven chaffinches and seven greenfinches caught at Mottisfont. The dozen or so sparrows Rhodes had wanted escaped when their cage broke. Though he looked old and ill Rhodes had lost none of his glamor for Richard. He was still the Empire Builder, pure and strong of purpose, uncorrupted by great wealth. His two great concepts—the reunion of the English-speaking peoples and the federation of Africa—caught Richard's imaginaton. "Rhodes's vision aimed at the welfare of mankind," Richard wrote, "nothing more nor less, and he believed that the creation of so great a power that war would become impossible was the means to that end. If only others had had the vision of Rhodes, the first half of this century, instead of being a blood-bath of murder, misery and frustration, might have seen the dawn of an era that knew no wars." Such thoughts drove Richard to Groote Schuur, Rhodes's old home, whenever he was in Cape Town, to pay tribute and to reflect on what might have been.

At the age of seventeen, however, Richard had more pressing matters to consider than Rhodes's vision, which he shared. On the whole he had not been sorry to leave Harrow, but now he found himself at Mottisfont with his career still undecided. He had begged his father to let him go to Cambridge to read zoology but he was confronted with two great difficulties. One, he felt, was that his parents misjudged him. "I know that both you and mother think I am no good, but neither of you really knows me or has seen my serious side," he wrote. "You know, Father, I do get things done, I think a lot and am not a complete ass nor have I earned the epithet 'black sheep' which has been bestowed on me." The second obstacle was his father's insistence on a career in the City on the grounds that there he could be of the greatest help, whereas in the scientific world he had no influence at all. When Richard protested, "If I must go into the City I shall run off with a yellow-haired barmaid and have masses of yellow-haired children who will all call you grandpa and you wouldn't like that," Daniel replied, "I think you should give the City a chance for you cannot enjoy life without money and later on when you have all those horrid little yellow-haired imps you will need to be a rich man to bring them up and educate them, and, more-over, barmaids make expensive wives. I have ten brown-haired children and they are expensive but I shudder to think what they would be if they had yellow hair." He added, more to the point, "You have been well educated and enjoy a certain standard of living which is high. You must always try and live up to that standard and keep your place in the world."

Richard enlisted all the friends he could muster, including

Bowdler Sharpe, who promised him a post in the British Museum as soon as he took his degree, and the far more eminent Ray Lankester, foremost zoologist of his day. Sir Edwin Ray Lankester's qualifications were as impressive as his size, which was enormous. He did the best he could in Richard's hour of need. His opinion carried weight, for he was a Fellow of Merton College, held the chair of comparative anatomy at Oxford, and was about to be appointed Director of Natural History and Keeper of Zoology in the British Museum in South Kensington and Fullerian Professor of Physiology and Comparative Anatomy at the Royal Institution.* But even these credentials were not enough, and finally father and son reached an accommodation of a sort when Richard, having stated his case for the last time with "I would sooner be a penniless scientist with successful research to my credit than be a senior partner of Huth's, my soul blighted by gold and ripe to die of cancer in the stomach at the age of fifty-five," agreed to join his father's company provided that if he hated it he would be allowed to quit the day he attained his majority. His father, despite Richard's unflattering picture of the successful banker he himself happened to be, was pleased.

At the end of January 1896 Richard Meinertzhagen sat for the first time at a small desk in a tiny windowless room at 12, Tokenhouse Yard in the City of London and felt himself to be anonymous. His top hat hung on its peg, his striped trousers and black coat were faultless, and his prospects to an outsider would have seemed remarkably good. But Richard gazed with loathing at the papers on his desk and felt stifled. For days no one came near him and though his papers seemed to be changed occasionally nobody troubled to tell

---

* Lankester was an inspiring teacher and a sound scholar with an insatiable curiosity. His famous memoir *Limulus an Arachnid* removed that most succulent of sea creatures the king crab from the class of crustacea and proved its close relationship to the scorpion. Injustice and pretense swiftly aroused his anger. After he had been director of the museum for the better part of nine years his impetuosity led him into direct conflict with the museum's senior trustee, the Archbishop of Canterbury, over the propriety of displaying a nude statue of Eugene Sandow, the world's strongest man. His Grace's delicacy prevailed, Lankester resigned and the statue was consigned to the vaults, where it remains.

him what they meant. They were bills of lading, letters of credit, accounts and checks that seemed to be connected with making loans against coffee crops in Brazil and Costa Rica or on Russian furs or wool from Australia and the Argentine. There was a good deal of correspondence from Hamburg and Bremen relating to shipments from places Richard had never heard of. He amused himself by looking them up in the atlas and making a list of those he would like to visit. Twice he wrote letters to Cecil Rhodes but tore them up for fear of hurting his father. Occasionally he went to a lecture at the Royal Geographical Society, at one of which he and Dan were introduced to the speaker, whose description of the prodigious herds of game in Somaliland and along the Tana River made Richard's mouth water. The lecturer told them that one day East Africa would hold a huge white population. "There's a chance for you boys!" he concluded. "By God," Richard promised himself, "I mean to take it somehow"; then added an odd rider: "What a lot there is in front of me. I only hope I live to see it all." At the end of two months, with the papers undigested still, Richard again begged his father to let him go to the university. Daniel, who believed that Richard was working like a horse, remained adamant but promised in the fall to send him to Germany to learn the other side of the business and pick up the language. It was an escape of a sort.

Dan, still an undergraduate at New College, Oxford, had already spent one summer in Germany, living with, so to speak, an illegitimate daughter of the last King of Hanover. The widowed Baroness von Klenck was supplementing her resources by taking in young English gentlemen at her comfortable home in the university town of Göttingen, a city which the English, judging from the number of them living there, regarded almost as a dependency, perhaps for its early connection with George II (formerly the Elector George Augustus) but more probably because its university was now preeminent for its mathematics and physics. Whatever the Baroness's relationship to the Hanoverian dynasty, the Meinertzhagen connection with it was clear. Deposed by the Prussians in 1866, the king had sent his valuables, among them a group of young ladies, to Richard's grandfather Daniel in London with a request to take care of them. The king suggested that his harem might be accommodated at Belmont, but propriety prevailed, old Daniel was able to make other arrangements, and the king expressed his gratitude with a huge portfolio of atrocious engravings subsequently disposed of by Georgina in an attack of tidiness at Mottisfont. So the baroness and her surroundings did not seem entirely unfamiliar and Richard settled down to enjoy his stay. He spent a couple of hours every day struggling with grammar and the rest talking to a girlfriend he had found, though he admitted to his father that in some ways the liaison was less fruitful than he had hoped because she preferred to talk English.

Dueling was the chief sport at Göttingen at the time. Dan had attended a fight and had been nauseated by the blood flicked over the spectators as they guzzled their beer. There was so much blood that his shoes stained the floor of the carriage he gladly left in. Richard never saw a duel, though he was very soon challenged to one. One summer evening he was sitting idly with a German friend in a beer garden outside the town when a bunch of students appeared. They seemed aggressive but Richard and his friend continued their conversation, laughing now and then at some joke. Suddenly two of the students stamped up to their table and rigidly inquired why they were laughing. They looked so ridiculous that Richard roared with laughter. One of them kicked over the table, spilling the beer, then, before Richard could hit him, smiled sweetly and presented his card. The following day another student called on Richard to demand satisfaction for his friend. In the best German he could command Richard asked him to tell his friend that he had been both a cad and a coward in refusing to fight with his fists there and then in the beer garden. The boy inquired whom Richard's second might be. Richard replied that he was his own second, which must have so upset etiquette that he never heard from the students again. It was perhaps as well, because no man withstood Richard Meinertzhagen's hands for long.

Richard saw very little of the students during his stay in Göttingen, dismissing them as beer-sodden vulgarians who disliked the British. Once a week he accompanied the baroness on her social round in a carriage drawn by two snow-white ponies with cream tails, offspring of the famous Hanoverian strain that drew Queen Victoria in state. They were known in the town as The White Mice. Baroness von Klenck's acquaintance included all the local landowners, so Richard was given a free run of their estates. He shot roe deer and wild pig and collected the Great Black Woodpecker. One of the baroness' visitors that summer was very eminent indeed. Richard hated him instantaneously, discerning something evil behind the pebble spectacles that hid the man's eyes. He sensed hatred. Baron Friedrich von Holstein had in his earlier years been something of a philanderer; whether he still was no one knew, for he drew obscurity over himself like a velvet cloak. To Holstein all men were puppets to be manipulated from the shadowy recesses of the German Foreign Office, which he dominated by extraordinary application and indefatigable intrigue. Everyone feared him, believing that he knew everything, as indeed he did. Moreover, he was delighted to use what he knew to destroy anyone who opposed him. He carried a pistol everywhere with him and practiced his excellent marksmanship several times a week. His hatred for the kaiser was so pathological that there were grounds for believing he had encouraged the dispatch of the Kruger Telegram in order to see his master humiliated. His only pleasure was revenge. He was remembered after his demise in 1909 for the purity of his rancor and for the superimposition of an egg upon the humble schnitzel. His influence upon Richard was negligible, for Richard refused to say a word to him, so immediate and intense was his antipathy.

By November Richard was thought to have mastered enough German to be placed in the Bremen firm of H. H. Meyer, an importer of tobacco and cement. He lodged in a cosmopolitan boarding house full of young men from various countries, with whom he committed the classic youthful misdemeanor of stealing a policeman's helmet and with whom he paid the classic forfeit of a night in jail. Since there was a family connection with the city, Richard spent some time looking for kinfolk. One evening he was invited to dinner with seven old ladies, one of whom, a very distant relative, told him that the Meinertzhagens had come to Bremen and Cologne from

Schleswig and that the emblem on the family crest was the hagen-berry, common in Denmark, a bush of which she promised to send him for planting at Mottisfont. Riding home through the old part of the city one day through a snowstorm, Richard found the crest itself carved on a stone in the outer wall of an old church. When the church was demolished in 1898 Georgina bought the stone from the pastor and had it installed in Mottisfont church, where it was to remain worn and gray against the pure white of the lime-washed wall. But for the rest, social life in Bremen was both formal and dull, Herr Meyer's office was every bit as oppressive as Tokenhouse Yard, and the only consolation was vacations at Mottisfont.

Year by year Daniel Meinertzhagen had improved the shooting on his modest estate until it had some of the best partridge ground in the county. In a good season his guests would bring down as many as six hundred brace. He also reared up to three thousand pheasants a year, arranging his coverts to provide high difficult birds and beg-ging the guns strung out on the crisp stubble to let the low flyers pass by. His concern, being as fastidious in his pleasures as in all his duties, was to provide challenging sport in preference to the gigantic bags popular with many of the more vulgar landowners, who posed their late-Victorian and Edwardian house parties behind feathery walls high enough to have assuaged a famine. On one famous ac-casion a party killed nearly four thousand birds in a single day. It was the paradisal age of the crack shot, whose expertise alone guaranteed him entrée to some of the great country houses. It was by no means uncommon for such a man to have three birds dead in the air as he loosed his fourth barrel; he would fire thirty thou-sand cartridges a year and bring down a bird with most of them. One of the last of these nonpareils of marksmen was King George V, who always used three hammer guns, on his best day killing thirty-nine birds with thirty-nine successive shots. Few men, including George V, really relished slaughter on this gargantuan scale and as the First World War approached the taste for the gigantic battue was in decline.

Driven game was not greatly to the Meinertzhagens' taste. Daniel much preferred to beat along the hedgerows with Richard and a good working dog. They took all kinds of game from duck to woodcock and even tried for some wily white-fronted geese, but had to content themselves with the sound of their flighting, for the big birds chose a different feeding ground every evening. By now Richard and Dan knew every coppice and field corner, every chalk-pit and reedbrake. They even had private names for individual trees and were the only ones who could penetrate the swampy wilderness of the duck ground's center. In 1942 Richard found a saucepan, a couple of cans of sardines, and a pot of jam under a maple on an island in the morass—exactly where he and Dan had left them forty-five years before. They knew where the big trout lazed by the riverweeds and where the lean pike lurked. The nests of Mottis-font's two kingfishers were familiar entertainment. They had seen an osprey haul a fish glittering from the Test and watched falcons swinging in hard weather, retrieving three of their kills in a single evening. On a stormy fall night with the river in spate and the eels heading for the sea, they would let down their nets below the weir until the long black shapes writhed like Medusa's hair in the rushing water. Their best catch was a hundred and sixty-four pounds of eels in two hours. Sometimes, if the day was sultry with thunder, they could spear eels from a punt as they lay under lily pads basking in the sun. Richard always loved eels, frequently serving them at dinner in his London home but never identifying them when his guests re-marked on the delicious flavor of his fish. The streams that fed the Test also held crawfish, but it was cold work to catch them, turning over stones in three or four feet of water, but they made excellent salad and soup. For sheer bulk killing, however, the boys relied on copper wire, an art they had been taught by one of their father's water-keepers. The thinner and brighter the wire noose, lashed to the end of a twenty-foot pole, the better; so the boys polished theirs every day. They were even expert enough to catch trout.

One day, certain of his skill as a master craftsman, Daniel chal-lenged his two eldest sons to catch some fish. They said they would take more than he would. Knowing his own prowess, Daniel thought that ridiculous and promised them a sovereign for every pound of fish they got beyond his own catch. The mayfly were up and under such conditions on his own water Daniel was one of the best fishermen in England. He knew that Richard and Dan could wire pike, but he never dreamed that they could wire trout. Off went Daniel with the precision of a surgeon and off went his sons with the stealth of otters. They had been checking where the big fish lay for weeks. By teatime Daniel had caught four fish weighing eleven pounds. The boys had caught seven weighing sixteen pounds, so they demanded and got their five pounds of reward. Then, as something of a consolation, they offered to take their father out that night to initiate him into the mysteries of fishing with torch and spear. Dan impaled a trout with his first thrust, at which his father exclaimed in horror, "Atrocious sport!" and left in anguish and at once.

In addition to enjoying the free run of Mottisfont, Richard and Dan leased some dilapidated acreage from an amenable old neighbor called Dutton for a kind of peppercorn rent. They first approached Mr. Dutton in 1892 (when Richard was all of thirteen) and offered him ten shillings a year for the shooting rights to a property they had christened "Naboth's Vineyard" because they coveted it so hard. Mr. Dutton accepted the money, said they could go there whenever they liked, and presented them with a pound for cartridges. It was a sedgy marsh of ponds and tussocks, the habitation of almost every creature but rabbits and particularly of duck. The boys spent hours there, silent as animals themselves. Another haunt was a jigsaw of ponds a mile upriver, inaccessible enough to attract the rarest of birds and offering as many as a hundred duck on the water at a time. Richard would wait for their morning flight an hour before dawn while the ice tinkled in the cold and widgeon whistled up and down the valley or geese came creaking in, white and powerful in the waning moonlight. Once he watched an otter glide over the ice and many times bitterns as slow as bishops stalked from one dense bed of reeds to another.

As they grew older the boys were able to hunt farther afield, an activity which their generous uncle Ernest happily facilitated. The idea had been Richard's. When his uncle and aunt asked what he and Dan would like for Christmas, he wrote in high excitement to his brother: "Don't you think we might ask for that punt and a nice Holland swivel gun with a hundred rounds? Think of the geese and duck and smew and curlew on a still frosty morning with a white fog and nice little gabble on the water and we both in nightshirts all frozen! Shall I ask for it? How much does it cost? We don't want to stick the old dears for a fortune. Let me know at once before they change their minds." Dan replied that the cost would be around two hundred pounds, but it was worth trying as a joke. Their uncle was serious. He attached only one string to his gift—that he should be supplied with a duck or two from time to time. They berthed the punt where the Test flowed into Southampton Water within handy reach of Mottisfont and engaged a professional wild-fowler to show them how to paddle and stalk. The gun was a breechloader mounted on a swivel and projecting over the square bows of the punt, which had to be propelled from a prone position. Since only one shot was possible, the art lay in the approach. Their first day out the boys never came within range, but on the second they paddled stealthily up to a flock of teal bobbing in the estuary. The huge gun went off like a thunderclap. Seven birds were ex-tinguished, rocketing the boys into such a state of excitement that they shipped enough water almost to sink the boat. By the end of the week they had killed seven geese, thirty-four widgeon, twenty eight teal, four mallard, a smew and a curlew. A dozen widgeon were sent off posthaste to Uncle Ernest.

Wildfowling was a craft rather than an art, but it demanded skill and great concentration. What the boys liked was the hard-ship, the exposure and the need to strain muscle and brain, and the occasional danger. The cold was sometimes so bitter that they could not open the breech of the gun, but the reward was the feeling of being alone and wild, dependent on the senses only as the salt tide slapped their low gunwales and the brass barrel, pearled with the damp of dawn, thrust through the eddies of mist. They loved the smell, cold and slightly acrid in the lungs, and the dry whisper of reeds and the mudbanks glistening as they slid by. They lusted for the far-off calling of their prey so plump and immaculate and unaware. It was not all killing, though. Sometimes Dan would make his elegant sketches of a pintail or a brent and give them to his brother. Aesthetics apart, they were not above showing a profit from their exertions and sold over seventy pounds' worth of game to a dealer in Southampton. They became so proficient that on their last day out, early in 1898, Dan killed forty-eight duck with a single shot.

As well as the spiritual regeneration of Mottisfont Richard's vacations from Germany included a day or two in London. Early in 1897 Dr. Fridtjof Nansen arrived there from Norway and found himself accorded one of the liveliest welcomes ever given to a foreigner. His exploits were so popular and so pervasive a topic of conservation that after a few days the great egocentric and actor-manager Sir Henry Irving burst out in pique, "Nansen? Oh, yes. The fellow who stands the cold so well . . ." Nansen's plan was to reach the North Pole by drifting with the uncharted currents that circled northward from Siberia in a wooden ship designed to lift when the ice gripped her. He spent eighteen months in the *Fram* with a crew of thirteen, then set out on foot knowing that the polar currents would bring her back. He never found the Pole but when after three years he emerged from among the floes he was famous.

Richard met him at the Royal Geographical Society by simply walking up to him, introducing himself, and inviting Nansen to dinner at Rutland Gate. Something in this forthright approach must have appealed to Nansen because he began to talk in the friendliest way. Richard thought him charming, though he noticed at once with his usual penetration that while Nansen's pale blue eyes might smile, his thoughts were sad. That night at Rutland Gate Nansen spoke shyly about the white beauty of the Arctic and the birds he had seen there, and delivered himself of such tid-bits as his epicurean discovery that the raw skin of the white whale combined the merits of a nut and an oyster. Daniel went to bed but Nansen stayed on, becoming more at ease, until early morning. When he left he had offered to take Richard with him to the Arctic some day. Overwhelmed by the kindness of Nansen's attentions, Richard wrote, "I have seldom met a man I feel I could trust more. He sounded so strong, sincere and genuine." He heard Nansen lecture to a huge audience in the Albert Hall, including the Prince of Wales, the Duke of York and the most sparkling of London's society, and decided to accept Nansen's offer if ever it became definite. The Arctic was a popular subject in 1897, for the year that had begun with Nansen ended with Robert Edwin Peary lecturing about his discoveries in Greenland at the Royal Geographical Society, which by now was a kind of home from home for Richard and Dan. In his wanderings in Northern Greenland, Peary had found a mountainous fertile area not covered by the icecap. He exhibited some of the huge meteorites he had found there and explained his plans for reaching the Pole.

These encounters, though they might sweeten Richard's dreams, did not affect the flow of his mercantile existence. His daily occupation was unutterably dull and his environment sterile. At the age of nineteen he was already suspicious of Germany's aims and apprehensive about the hysteria that seemed to transform the Germans in moments of crisis from kind, responsible individuals into an insensate mob. "They regard war as a magnificent climax," he wrote, "and indeed the natural climax of policy instead of as the result of a deplorable failure of diplomacy. In peace the German is neither brutal nor cruel, but when roused by passion a streak of beastliness surges up transforming them from normal, kindly humans to wild beasts of the jungle where force is their sole weapon. I have often seen it in the streets and in the cafes. And yet there is nothing fundamentally wrong with the Germans." This sanguine view was not modified by Richard's impression of the kaiser during an imperial visit to Bremen in his blue and yellow train. Richard thought "he looked terribly artificial, arrogant and conceited, seeming to treat everyone as dirt." The first time Richard had seen the emperor had been six years before after a review of Volunteers on Wimbledon Common in London. His aunts' house on the Common, probably because of their friendship with Princess Beatrice, had been commandeered for the comfort of the All Highest at lunch. He was imposing in his white uniform and his helmet with a silver eagle on top, though to a schoolboy his fiercely upswept moustache rather spoiled the effect. When Richard was introduced to him by Aunt

Tal, all smiles and curtsies, for she dearly loved royal blood even if tainted by foreign strains, he noticed that the kaiser seemed unduly affable. Meditating later on why the great man should have been so pleased with himself, he concluded that the condition of the Volunteers, every man a hero but trained for the antique warfare of the Crimea, must have encouraged him. As Richard put it, "I have often wondered whether the Kaiser was not really roaring with laughter at our obsolete army and looking forward with relish to the day when he could eat them up with his highly trained and efficient battalions."

Still preoccupied with the possibility of escaping from the drabbest of all futures, Richard had written to his father from Germany suggesting a military career. Daniel had thought the army a repository for incompetents. Altering his tack slightly, Richard asked if he might join the county yeomanry, a regiment of volunteer cavalry, thinking that if there were a war at least that would get him out of the City. When his father agreed, Richard wrote ecstatically: "The excitement of battle must be a marvellous tonic. You never get anything like that in the City unless you've invested all your money in some rotten company which looks like going phut." Never one to miss a moral, he added: "How can I justify my life to the Almighty if I have frittered away my time trying to make money, whereas if I can say I have done something to benefit humanity, I might get a good mark. But perhaps a soldier's job is war and might not be included in benefiting humanity."

Three weeks after his nineteenth birthday, Her Majesty was pleased to grant her liege subject Richard Meinertzhagen a commission as second lieutenant in her regiment of Hampshire Yeomanry. His travails in the German wilderness at an end, Richard was back in London and so blithely able to spend his evenings in Knightsbridge Barracks, not far from Rutland Gate, learning sword drill and horse-mastership, jingling forth with his troop for mounted drill in Hyde Park and fluttering the heart of an occasional nursemaid. Tall, broad-shouldered, erect, his hardness softened by grace of movement, he looked magnificent in full-dress uniform of modified hussar jacket snug at the waist and slim overalls striped with white. His serious young face stared out from a burnished cavalry helmet from which swung a plume of white horsehair, and his dark blue serge was barred and striped with heavy ropes and knots of gold lace. He felt glorious.

That Christmas of 1897 promised to be the best Richard Meinertzhagen had ever had. He and Dan had sawed down a twenty-foot spruce and set it up in the hall, topped by a fairy dressed in lace and bearing two hundred candles on its dark branches. The Mottisfont larder was full of delicacies sent by Daniel's business friends—gray caviar from St. Petersburg, turon from Madrid and marzipan from Bremen, a turkey from Amsterdam, a huge box of candy from Riga. Richard loved the preparation, the ritual, the feeling of being surrounded by a big family in a season of love. There were presents for everyone except Richard. "Poor me," he wrote in his diary, "forgotten by both Father and Mother. I suppose each thought the other was going to give me a present. However, I don't really want anything beyond Mother's love." It was a remark far beyond vanity but he kept his hurt private, as the years had taught him. It did not mar his appetite on Christmas Day, when the Meinertzhagens, fine trenchermen always, extended themselves to the limit with a meal that in size and content was a family tradition. It was based on a turkey at each end of the table, one boiled and one roasted and each weighing over twenty pounds, followed by one plum pudding for each child varying in richness and size according to age and an enormous one for the adults, with a bowl of clotted Devonshire cream, dishes of mince pies, and a box of chocolates for makeweights. Near death, Richard and Dan staggered away from the dining room and out to the duck ground to see if fresh air would prevent their expiry. Huddled against an east wind blowing up for snow, their hair damp with drizzle, they talked over their plans for the future. By evening Dan had plumped for a trip to Siberia; Richard had determined on Africa.

Two days later they were out stalking a flock of white-fronted geese and watching the duck sailing down onto their favorite pond. The sky was clear and still, but darkness was falling when they reached home. Stepping onto the lawn, Dan suddenly whispered,

"Who's that walking across the lawn?" Richard, whose sight was keener, saw nothing. "There he goes!" Dan said and ran toward the end of the garden. They reached a sunken ditch and stopped. "You're seeing things," Richard told Dan. In that instant they both thought of the old gardener Smith and his stories of the Mottisfont ghost. Dan laughed, but later that night he was uneasy enough to ask Richard not to repeat the incident to Georgina. Next morning both of them went back to the ditch. There were no footprints, though the earth was soaking wet, and Dan showed his disquiet. Six weeks later he was dead.

Dan had gone to Bremen to perfect his German before joining his father at Huth's, the expected course and the prerogative of an eldest son. He was living happily at Richard's old lodgings when suddenly he developed appendicitis. Dreading the almost certain onset of peritonitis, Daniel hired the best surgeon he could find and left at once, but Dan died before they could reach him. Daniel was so stricken that he could not even bring himself to see the boy's doctor. Richard went to Dover to meet his mother, who had been in Naples when the blow struck. There was nothing they could say, but Richard wrote, "Her pluck in facing such a tragedy has always been a lesson to me." Neither she nor Daniel ever completely recovered from it and it meant the end of Mottisfont as they had known it for all of them.

After the funeral the snow came. Richard walked away from the little churchyard and up the narrow lane to the Abbey gates. He took his horse from the stable, called Dan's dog, and trudged aimlessly across the park through the thick white flakes, too sad for tears. After dinner Georgina went to her room and Daniel sat hunched and brooding by the fire. Richard tried miserably to speak with love, but the reserve that had been forced on him locked his tongue. He sat silently until his father went at last to bed. The wind had risen when he left the house again. Glancing back he saw it looking more beautiful than he had ever seen it, its windows soft with lamplight and the snow pure as a blessing along the roof. The grave was mantled as Richard knelt by it and prayed and found comfort in that wild night. In his bedroom he wrote: "I cannot believe that I shall never see Dan again. I must try and perpetuate his memory by trying to mold my character on his and give my sorrowing father and mother some of the love which they always received from Dan." He did not expect comfort for his own grief, for it did not occur to him that he had lost more than a brother. He had lost the only person who could sound the depths of affection yearning beneath that self-sufficient mask. And with Dan had vanished his own youth.

CHAPTER 6

Grant Him a Nice
Little War

London was a mass of lights. Thousands of gas flares threw their flickering glare on the crowds that still walked the streets, bathing in the reflected glory of that day of Jubilee. It was June 22, 1897. At Buckingham Palace a state banquet was in progress with a mountainous centerpiece of orchids dominating the high table and exceeding in opulence even the Queen's Diamond Jubilee bouquet, which had included one exotic bloom valued at over a thousand guineas. The whole length of Britain bonfires burned, twenty-five hundred of them twinkling from hilltop to hilltop. Every town was rejoicing with lights and banners. Even trade shared the national mood: the makers of a famous extract of beef, whose new electric signs illuminated some strategic heights in London, had arranged that the first two and last two letters of their brand name Bovril should switch off intermittently, thus celebrating the cypher of Her Majesty.

Through this fairyland Richard Meinertzhagen trudged in misery. His mother's action that morning—her irrational slap when he had quenched the burning flag—had been the last in a long series of what he saw, with reason, as injustices. He reviewed all the times he had been checked or scolded, all the cold rejections, back to his days at Fonthill. Georgina was recognized by all who knew her as the most critical of all the Potter sisters, most of whom were not best known for the sweetness of their tongues.

Time after time, Richard discovered from relatives, his mother had maligned him in her letters, calling him bad-tempered, ill-mannered and rude to women. There was a cruelly insensitive streak in Georgina. It was her humor to order every year two roast geese for dinner on her wedding anniversary, a sour joke that Daniel did not share. She persisted, even on their silver wedding anniversary, but Daniel's distress was so evident, and Richard's resentment so hot, that she never perpetrated her solecism again. Richard's adoration of his father and his pain at hearing criticism of him, which Georgina would level in front of guests and servants even in Daniel's absence, widened the division between him and his mother. The root cause of it all was pride, a quality that Georgina seemed to have been born with and which certainly she passed on to her son. It was this that drove them to extremes; Georgina to defend her own self-respect by attacking others, Richard to hide his needs behind clenched teeth and a face of stone. It was only years later, after his father's death, that Richard began to recognize the cause of the rift. He had always loved her. As an old man he wrote: "She influenced my life for good more than did any other person; I held her in greater respect and love than any human being with whom I have come into contact." Toward the end of his life he pointed to the bitter record in his diaries as the impressions of a moment, adding, "I do not doubt now that my mother loved me as much as she loved the rest of us." Then he recognized that his own difficulties might have blinded him to his mother's problems. But now, at the age of nineteen, all he could think of was the insult of that angry blow, the dull insistence of his memories and the sad truth that, whatever her virtues, each one of his brothers and sisters avoided being left alone with their mother. Next morning she tried an apology. It was meaningless.

The end of the Jubilee day was only the start of the festivities. Before retiring, the Queen, quite recovered from the tears she had shed earlier, had written in her journal, "The cheering was quite deafening and every face seemed to be filled with real joy." The cheering continued to support that emotional old heart for days of visits and inspections. There were fire brigades to be inspected, visiting dignitaries and schoolchildren to be interrogated, chieftains to be received, statues to be unveiled. Driving back from a function in Kensington Gardens, a grandchild asked her, "Grandmama, doesn't all this make you very proud?" The pale eyes, veiled with cataracts and tears, gazed at her. The little rosebud lips pursed. "No, dear child," said the Queen, "very humble." Humility had not thus far been the chief characteristic of this great anniversary, but on the morning following the procession Her Majesty's sentiment was stated in more enduring fashion in the columns of *The Times*. To everyone's astonishment there appeared what could only be an Awful Warning. It carried weight not only by virtue of its intrinsic excellence as verse and the stern music of its message, but also because it bore the signature of Mr. Rudyard Kipling. It was called "Recessional" and its tone was elementally mid-Victorian:

> *God of our fathers, known of old—*
> *Lord of our far-flung battle-line—*
> *Beneath whose awful Hand we hold*
> *Dominion over palm and pine—*
> *Lord God of Hosts, be with us yet,*
> *Lest we forget, lest we forget!*
>
> *The tumult and the shouting dies—*
> *The captains and the kings depart—*
> *Still stands Thine ancient sacrifice,*
> *An humble and a contrite heart.*
> *Lord God of Hosts, be with us yet,*
> *Lest we forget, lest we forget!*

Mr. Kipling's thoughts, continuing as they did with talk of navies melting away, were not perhaps the kindest for a morning after but they had some effect. In their light the remaining events of the Jubilee took on a more sober significance, at least for some.

Richard Meinertzhagen had drunk deep of Empire. What he had seen in the marching files was his own future, for he had decided barely a month before the Jubilee that he would be a soldier. It had happened one afternoon as he sat his horse on a Hampshire hillside warm with summer at the end of his first maneuvers. Shortly after he joined them the Hampshire Yeomanry had gathered at Winchester for the two weeks of field training they were required to undergo every year. Their headquarters were at the George Hotel and their inclinations bent more toward a stag party than toward an exercise of war. Richard rode his hunter Melksham, already one of the most striking personalities at Mottisfont. Richard had acquired him as a boy of twelve, partly because when he arrived in Mottisfont's stables as a five-year-old, Melksham's most prominent feature was his teeth, which he used on everybody. Richard appealed to his stomach and charmed him into tractability with oats and brown sugar. Melksham would do anything for him, though he reserved the right of comment: Richard liked to practice tent-pegging and one day missed a peg three times in succession. When on the fourth try he carried the peg with his lance, Melksham gave a friendly kick and emitted a celebratory and extremely rude noise.

Both horse and master knew the country picked for the maneuvers through years of hunting and wandering. The training seemed like a rather casual game until the last three days, when the pace became warmer and more challenging. The Yeomanry was to oppose the regular cavalry brigade from Aldershot, commanded by General French. John Denton Pinkstone French of the 19th Hussars already enjoyed a reputation as a comer in the army and his appointment to this particular command was confirmation of it. A moustache as fierce as a saber, glowering eyes, cheeks that darkened from pink to purple in an instant, a small but compact and powerful body, a dandy's love of uniforms, and a disposition to charge headlong at the foe and, it was whispered, the ladies, made French the very picture of a cavalryman.

In the early summer of 1897 French became much impressed by Richard Meinertzhagen. Richard and the Hampshire Yeomanry had been positioned on the shoulder of a hill overlooking Colonel Willy Woods's ugly manor at Warnford, not far from Mottisfont. Woods sent Richard with ten men to block the road along which French's brigade of regulars must advance. Richard raided his colonel's outbuildings for farm carts, dragged them onto the Warnford road, and then took off their wheels. Woods was none too pleased to see his property commandeered but the roadblock held up the regulars for half an hour, time enough for the Yeomanry to take them in the flank. That evening at the de-briefing French singled out Richard for praise and honored him by inviting him to act as his galloper next day, in effect giving Richard professional status. Richard careered over the countryside for twelve hours, prompting French to ask him to join the regulars for a further three days as they continued their campaign.

Richard's Viking blood was roused. French's cavalry brigade had camped just outside Winchester, and the "enemy" (Richard's erstwhile comrades of the Yeomanry) was known to be lying in the open country east of the River Test. To Richard it was like playing soldiers in his own backyard; he knew every spinney and track from years of riding Melksham home from the hunt or a dinner. He was told to take out a patrol by night to locate the enemy. He found them, a regiment of yeomanry with a section of horse artillery, above the beechwoods on a ridge scratchy with gorse and bramble. In the darkness Richard and his party came up to them unobserved. Unfamiliar with the military etiquette proper to such a circumstance, Richard simply drew his sword and charged, with the rest of the patrol tumbling after him. The enemy's horses stampeded and were lost among the bushes. The patrol hurtled right through the bivouac, providentially leaping over numbers of officers inert in their sleeping bags, and were swallowed by the night before the first oaths could catch them. Back in camp, Richard reported to French, who at once issued orders for a full attack. They reached the down at six o'clock on a bright morning but abandoned their plan because the hillside was still dotted with angry men searching for their mounts. The enemy was more enraged at Richard's lack of manners than at its ignominious defeat, but French took his side. By lunchtime decorum had returned. Two staff officers who had been attached to the enemy as observers walked across to Richard. One of them smiled and introduced himself. "My boy, you jumped over me last night!" The other added, "Yes, and you jumped over me too. Not too pleasant on peaceful maneuvers!" The first remembered Richard twenty-one years later when Richard, meeting him for the second time, brought him the terms of the armistice on November 11, 1918; by then he was Field Marshal Sir Douglas Haig, victorious commander of an army of nearly two million men. The second was Edmund Allenby, on whose staff Richard would later ride out of Sinai to the conquest of Palestine and the destruction of the army of Turkey.

That evening Richard took his leave of French. Kindly, French asked him what he was going to take up as a profession. When Richard told him, French grunted, "Good God! What a waste! You should come into the army." Richard's parting salute was in the nature of a promise. French had entered the army by way of the militia, a course Richard determined to follow. Guessing at his father's probable reaction to such a notion, he decided to say nothing for the moment. Daniel had now placed him with a firm of stock-brokers in Threadneedle Street, much revered in the legend and romance of high finance but no more alluring than Tokenhouse Yard. Richard wandered about as an honorary clerk on the Stock Exchange, making money he did not really want by means he did not understand, unaware that Daniel's plan was to set him up with a friend's son for a partner and forty thousand pounds for capital. His father's friends asked Richard to call on them, chatted pleasantly and went through the pretense of asking his advice, thanked him and gave him commissions. He wrote: "These attempts to persuade me to sell my soul for money I regarded as bribery and, though meant kindly, they had precisely the opposite effect to what was intended. They disgusted me."

The day after Dan's funeral Daniel offered Richard the place Dan was to have had at Huth's. It was no time for temporizing and father and son both knew it. Daniel admitted that it was no longer possible to make really big money in his calling and revealed that in any case Georgina wanted Louis to succeed Dan, believing Richard unfitted for the City. Richard told his father for the first time that he was secretly working toward the army entrance ex-amination. Honesty brought them both relief. Daniel finally recon-ciled himself to the idea and even began to catch some of his son's enthusiasm. At first some of his old doubts about Richard's capacity still showed through. On the eve of Richard's first examination he wrote to his daughter Margaret: "It seems that they are rather hard up for officers and are letting them in rather easier than usual, so I hope there is no doubt about his getting through. He looks very well and happy." When Richard passed this preliminary test nineteenth out of more than a hundred, Daniel came as close to exultation as he could: "Did you see how well Dick did in his examination? I think it's wonderful and does him great credit." Aunts, uncles and friends sent their congratulations, but Georgina Meinertzhagen said nothing.

Richard had already resigned his commission in the Hampshire Yeomanry because of his decision to enter the regular army through the militia. He was gazetted second lieutenant in the 3rd Battalion of the West Yorkshire Regiment, a militia unit, in February 1898. In June he reported at York for a month's training over territory not unlike that he had roamed as a boy at Aysgarth. The voices of exhortation, though they did not sound at all like old Hales's, said much the same thing: "Don't just stand there! Do something!" Richard settled into a routine that began at half-past five with two hours' drill before breakfast, with such ease and verve that he was soon recognized as the smartest of the subalterns (known as "warts" because they were excrescences) and appointed orderly officer for Lord Wolseley's visit of inspection. He courted disaster by dressing up in his lordship's cloak and hat while he was at dinner.

Richard's next month was spent with a regular battalion of the Welch Regiment at Barrosa Barracks in Aldershot. His first morning there he was late for parade and was accorded a lengthy and violent reprimand by the adjutant, who happened also to be his cousin. It was the last time Richard was late for anything in his entire service. At the end of the month Richard was placed second among the subalterns on attachment and sent to London to join the Guards at Wellington Barracks, conveniently close to the place where he would take the last part of his examination. One morning at the end of October 1898, Richard rode in a hansom to the solemn portico of Burlington House, the place of interrogation for young men wishing to serve the Queen, slipped through the fashionable ladies parading toward the elegant shops of the Burlington Arcade and Bond Street, and began to answer the questions in the order set. Daniel wrote to a daughter: "Dick has just finished his Army Entrance Examination and as he seems very pleased with himself I hope he has done well. But as it is competitive one can never be certain. However, if we are to have war with France, which looks rather likely, I suppose they will take any officers they can get."

The threat of war with France had come out of a papyrus swamp on the upper Nile and a confrontation, moustache to moustache, of two fiercely intrepid men. The name of the place was Fashoda; the antagonist was Captain Jean-Baptiste Marchand of the Army of France and his protagonist a general nominally in the Egyptian service, one Horatio Herbert Kitchener. Kitchener's savage temperament made slaves of his friends and mincemeat of his enemies. On September 2, 1898, outside Omdurman, he had killed eleven thousand dervishes before lunch and sealed the reoccupation of the Sudan at a cost of twenty-seven British dead. It had been an economical affair: Kitchener had even checked any waste of ammunition personally by stopping the shooting of the dervish wounded. To counter the British move south the French government, with a certain insouciance, had given Marchand twelve officers and a hundred Senegalese. It was magnificent but it was not war. Kitchener chugged up the Nile in one of Gordon's old steamers wearing, by a masterstroke of tact, the red tarboosh and Turkish insignia of a general in the Egyptian army.

Marchand had a bony look, the eyes small and sunken but alert, and the nose thin and sharp as a spinster's. He was not much to look at, despite his ramrod back; all his strength was in his pride. Kitchener dwarfed him. Marchand saw crescent and star, but there was no Union Jack, no reminder of the British army, anywhere. Though Kitchener's face was burned purple from the sun, there was no sign of choler suffusing it; thin folds of flesh above his eyelids gave his wide-set, staring eyes the look of a hawk, but there was no animosity in them. They forbade intimacy but for once they were bland. Marchand was no threat to Kitchener: an inclination of the head, a cold glare at an aide de camp, and Marchand could be wiped out. But there was more at stake and Kitchener went carefully, for the balance of Europe swung for a moment on this tiny steamer's deck. Kitchener spoke good French and poured forth charm and professional respect, and after lunch, over coffee and liqueurs, arranged the demise of the French power in the second most important part of Africa. He and Marchand agreed to await the decision of their distant governments. As politely as he had come, Kitchener sailed away, leaving the Egyptian flag flying beside the Tricolor, a detachment nearby to ensure that it continued to do so, and Captain Marchand (who had refused his offer of a luxurious trip home via Khartoum and Cairo) wondering how long it would take him to return to Paris, if it should come to that, by way of Ethiopia. It did and he had to.

In London Kitchener was given a state banquet by the Lord Mayor at which the only foreign diplomat, significantly, was the American charge d'affairs. Lord Salisbury, proposing Lord Kitchener's health, reviewed his great victory over the forces of oppression, commended his economy, and announced incidentally that the French ambassador to the Court of St. James had that very afternoon conveyed his government's conclusion that its occupation of Fashoda would be terminated in view of its expense and inutility. The applause was prolonged.

It had been a year of some anxiety for Lord Salisbury's administration: once already during the year he had delivered an important statement of policy before the Primrose League at the Albert Hall, known afterward as his "Dying Nations Speech." He had been referring specifically to the disintegration of the Chinese empire and the acquisition of bases along its decrepit periphery by the Powers. He adduced from this that nations might be roughly divided into the living and the dying, the weak growing weaker and the strong, stronger. He continued: "The living nations will gradually encroach on the territory of the dying, and the seed and causes of conflict amongst civilized nations will speedily appear. Of course, it is not to be supposed that any one nation of the living nations will be allowed to have the profitable monopoly of curing or cutting up these unfortunate patients, and the controversy is as to who shall have the privilege of doing so, and in what measure he shall do it."

Now, as the year drew toward its close, Salisbury pursued his theme, illustrating it by the remarkable emergence of America at the expense of Spain. "It is the first year," he said, "in which the mighty force of the American Republic has been introduced among the nations whose dominion is expanding, and whose instruments to a certain extent are war. I am not implying the slightest blame. Far from it. I am not refusing sympathy to the American Republic in the difficulties through which it has passed, but no-one can deny that their appearance among the factors of Asiatic, and possibly of European diplomacy is a grave and serious event, which may not conduce to the interests of peace, though I think, in any event, it is likely to conduce to the interests of Great Britain." Alone among European nations, the British public agreed with the Prime Minister. At the year's end a popular summary was able to consign the event to history with a somewhat complacent, "One remarkable result of the war was the change of American feeling towards the mother country."

One fact that may have endeared the American adventure in the Philippines and Cuba to British hearts was the very British way in which the Americans had muddled through. Dewey had been unleashed by a fast cable from Colonel Theodore Roosevelt one afternoon when his chief, Secretary of the Navy John D. Long, had gone home early, leaving Roosevelt in charge of the office. Dewey had had to suspend his bombardment in Manila Bay to check his ammunition, having started with only a little more than half of his requirements. The troops came back from Santiago and even Florida to their camps on Long Island, New York, racked by typhoid and dysentery they had caught before embarking. The British, from long familiarity with such things, immediately recognized these inadequacies as the marks of greatness.*

---

* The aftermath of Dewey's cannonade caused Rudyard Kipling to publish yet another of his great thoughts, this time addressed directly to the United States on their new relationship with the island tribesmen of the Philippines. He gave them cold comfort:

Richard Meinertzhagen had followed these events in a distracted frame of mind: the settlement of Fashoda might have lessened the odds on his acceptance, so he had viewed Kitchener's victories with apprehension as well as admiration. But at last the word came: he had qualified third on the list. All that remained was to wait for the War Office to grind through the ritual of gazetting him to a regular regiment. Telegrams came from Meinertzhagens, Huths and Potters but not from the one person whose respect he most craved. Hearing the news, Georgina made no comment. Never dreaming that her silence might have come from the fear that she was losing another son, Richard was wounded yet again. And again he determined to prove himself: "I shall be free now and able to live my own life and I'm going to show them all that I'm not such a black sheep as they imagine."

He had asked for a commission in the Royal Fusiliers partly because they were also known as The City of London Regiment and so symbolically provided a farewell salute to his father's way of life. He requested an immediate posting abroad. Like every other young officer of his generation, he repeated from time to time an irreverent little prayer, "Thou seest, Dear Heavenly Father, the sad plight of Thy servant Dick; grant him a nice little war, that he may better

---

Take up the White Man's burden—
Send forth the best ye breed—
Go bind your sons to exile
To serve your captives' need;
To wait in heavy harness
On fluttered folk and wild—
Your new-caught, sullen peoples,
Half devil and half child.

Take up the White Man's burden—
The savage wars of peace—
Fill full the mouth of Famine
And bid the sickness cease;
And when your goal is nearest
The end for others sought,
Watch Sloth and heathen Folly
Bring all your hopes to nought.

his condition and continue to praise Thy Name." There was every reason to believe, as the end of 1898 approached, that his plea would be answered on one continent or another.

On January 18, 1899, *The London Gazette* announced Her Majesty's appointment of Richard Meinertzhagen to a commission in the Royal Fusiliers, seventh in seniority of the regiments of infantry of the line. Richard concluded: "So everything in the garden is rosy except that I would give everything to be more intimate with Mother and share some of the love and affection she shows my brothers and sisters. It's probably all my fault and that makes it worse to bear." He had spent his last family Christmas at Mottisfont, a sad affair without Dan. For the first time there had been no Christmas tree and after dinner Richard had walked unhappily to the duck ground and prayed in the sanctuary he and Dan had kept there. As darkness fell, a brown owl hooted near him and a few widgeon whistled on their way through the valley, which cheered him a little. But it had been decided that Mottisfont would be given up because every part of it cast up memories of Dan; Daniel and Richard wanted to stay because of that, but Georgina, for the same reason, wanted to quit at once. Richard elected to stay at Mottisfont until his orders arrived.

He packed up the skins he and Dan had collected and sent most of them to the Liverpool Museum. The eggs were to be housed by the kindly Bowdler Sharpe among the acres he had amassed at the Natural History Museum. For company Richard had the Slococks, grown at last after the antipathies of childhood into friends, and he spent occasional hours with Colonel Lenthall, a neighbor who kept up the sort of poaching shoot that Richard loved. Lenthall was a close friend of Daniel's, but his habit of referring to spades as bloody shovels made Georgina discourage his visits to the Abbey. He had introduced Richard to the art of truffle-hunting with a dog. He had trained the animal as a puppy by giving it a tennis ball stuffed with truffles, then burying it and rewarding the puppy for retrieving it. The dog could finally detect truffles as deep as two feet down. Sunday was the colonel's day for truffling. He took Richard with him into a beech wood and the dog soon filled a basket for them, one of the truffles weighing almost a pound. Lenthall gave them all to Richard, advising him to boil them for ten minutes in milk, then slice them and fry them in butter with a few drops of lemon juice. For himself, he always bottled them and used them in sandwiches whenever he was out shooting.

Lenthall had always been fond of Richard, no doubt seeing in him some of the qualities of his younger self, and he was anxious to pass on what he could of his own experiences as a soldier. His best advice was to avoid the rut of regimental soldiering by volunteering as often as possible for service away from the tedium of the average infantry battalion. He thought that Richard should work for the Staff College, but admonished him never to lose touch with the troops. Very sincerely he spoke his simple creed: "Remember that you serve the troops and it is the troops who matter. Take care of your men and they will never let you down." Then he presented Richard with a saddle and a rifle, bade him a gruff goodbye, and left him close to tears. "I only hope," Richard wrote, "I shall live up to his expectations." The day before he left Mottisfont Richard toured all the sanctuaries of his childhood, conscious that he was saying goodbye not only to the scenes of his childhood and the memory of Dan but to all the joys and confinement of his past life. He was conscious of making a new start. He called on his friends in the village and they wished him well. At last, reluctantly, with everything disposed in order he walked out of the Abbey gates, down over the little bridge that squeezed the river momentarily into a torrent, and up toward the signal box bright with paint, where he would catch his train to London and his new life. At a gap in the high hedge he looked back. So familiar, so unchanged, the Abbey's stone lay silent among the light green budding of the great trees, placid and timeless and, for all the memories it held, unmoved. It belonged already to his past and he turned. "I knew," he said, "that I could never recapture the irresponsibility and joy of childhood."

Nevertheless, it seemed to Richard at this watershed of his life that the world was a glorious place. It was still called, in the moments of euphoria that it frequently engendered, the Century of Hope. As Adam Smith had predicted more than a century before, industrialization was producing more and more goods at smaller and smaller cost. But in doing so it had stolen something away. Herbert Henry Asquith, later to be Prime Minister, had stood one noontime outside a factory in Lancashire and seen an awful dearth. "The great gates opened," he wrote, "and there burst out an ocean of men, a long procession of wan-faced, grimy, tired, silent figures. They get an average of eighteen shillings a week and work, with intervals for meals, from six to six. Civilization and religion have done something for them—given them paved streets, watertight houses, board-schools, chapels and even an art gallery. But life in its real sense they have never known, and to their dying day they will never know." The mills had claimed their prisoners and the one statesman who by his vision and force of spirit might have rescued them was dead, for William Ewart Gladstone, after the long agony of a cancer in the throat, had come to his last stillness. A quarter of a million people had filed past his bier in Westminster Hall at the end of May in 1898, not one of whom but knew that with Gladstone had passed a purity and a strength. Richard's Aunt Beatrice and her Fabian Society were already at work with their massive research and their diligent pamphlets to alleviate the problems now facing by far the greater part of society. Their well-meant but intellectual exercises flickered encouragingly and, when George Bernard Shaw was involved in them, amusingly; but they were a candle when a great flame was needed. The tragic fact was, as the century spun out, that the late Victorians—at least as far as dealing with their new kind of society was concerned—suffered a total failure of imagination. The tales of high adventure from mountain and veldt brought the clash of sword and bayonet ringing through oily workshop and dusty counting-house, lending a spurious glamour to thousands of uninspired lives; trade had followed the flag into continent after continent; yet no man pointed the true moral of the tales or preached a viable philosophy for the aftermath of conquest. The late Victorians made a virtue of expediency and sought to excuse it with a bogus thesis. "The Latin and other races are beginning to see," a speaker declared on November 13, 1898, "that the world-wide supremacy of the Anglo-Saxon race is imminent, if it has not already arrived." The subject of his address was "Labor and the Empire" and he was no conservative despite his tone. His name was John Burns, for years a fighting leader of the longshoremen's union.

The idea of Anglo-Saxon supremacy had been given some intellectual respectability quite innocently by the Oxford historical activity of the seventies and eighties that sent the collective mind of the nation to reflect upon the island's historic roots and succeeded in creating a sense of the homogeneity of English history, from which must come the implication that what had passed must be preparation for some future purpose. If not for fitness to lead, then for what had their long experience molded them? Before long "Anglo-Saxon" had become a catchword applied to numerous theories, but in general it was taken up by the new imperialists, of whom by far the most forceful, loquacious and persuasive was Joseph Chamberlain. Chamberlain accepted the office of Secretary of State for the Colonies in Lord Salisbury's cabinet of 1895 and made his statement of principle with vigor. "I believe in this race," he announced, "the greatest governing race the world has ever seen; in this Anglo-Saxon race, so proud, tenacious, self-confident and determined, this race which neither climate nor change can degenerate, which will infallibly be the dominant force of future history and universal civilization." Mixed with a pinch of Christian morality, this was strong stuff indeed to fuel a nation.

These principles and ideas were the currency of the books Richard had read at Harrow; they echoed in the columns of *The Times* and they had been the bones of conversations with guests at Mottisfont and Rutland Gate. Their complexities he did not and could not then explore; for him the business of Empire was entirely a matter of duty made pleasant by exotic surroundings and every possibility of action, lethal or sporting. His affinity was with the sensuous and the physical, his mind not much more than a mechanism for coordinating movement and reaction. It would be fifteen years before he began to realize how the high principles he had learned from his family and followed in the best manner he could were often translated in the expedient world of diplomacy and politics into compromise, deceit and lies. But that was toward the middle of his journey. At its start he was all innocence and fire.

Only one thing remained, the day before his departure, that Richard knew he must do. He had to wipe clean the unhappy years of childhood finally by making his mother know how much he loved her, black sheep or not. The last evening at Rutland Gate the family had dinner together. It might be years before they could do so again. Richard knew that Georgina would speak to him that evening and he was ready to throw himself into her arms. She did. She told him that now he was going out into this new world he must learn to control his temper, watch his manners, and try not to sulk. Whatever insecurity or misplaced sense of duty prompted so tragic an error was unimportant. Richard froze into ice. His mother had not touched him or put an arm round him, and her words made him rigid as a dead man. They were alone in the room with a terrible silence between them, gripped in their own horror. At last, her face drawn, Georgina said in a voice made hard by the control her pride forced her to use, "Well, I suppose there's nothing more to be said." His face masked with tears Richard ran out of the room and stumbled upstairs. He lay awake knowing that his mother must be in equal pain, but not daring to go down to her room. Pride had reached its bitter climax.

Around midnight, for the last time, he made an entry in the diary of his youth. He set down what had passed that evening in simple pathetic words. "And now," he said, "I shall have to go to India and I don't know when I shall ever see Mother again." The closing of the diary took him a long time, but eventually, having written, "I feel like a sponge, dried up and devoid of all feeling beyond a desire to get out of England," he pursued his thought. His pain had made him untypically philosophical and he ended, "Life is rather like a sponge, starting at birth a small shrivelled object, slowly absorbing moisture in the shape of knowledge and experience, but all the time not altering the general character. Then, on reaching a maximum size from absorption, it commences to give out, first in drops and then in streams of digested experience and knowledge, so that smaller sponges can absorb what the bigger sponges exude. But whilst giving out, the old sponges still absorb until a state is reached where the power of absorption ceases. Then should man stop work. The sponge then shrinks back to its original small shrivelled form. Then should man die."

With these words as conclusion Richard Meinertzhagen completed the seven notebooks he had filled with conversation, speculation, hopes, matters of record and memories of sorrow. He had made the first entry when he was six years old. When he was sixty-four he burned all the notebooks, having copied what he thought was relevant. When he was eighty-six he summed up what they had held, and in particular how they had ended, with "Thus ended my Genesis and commenced my Exodus." That Exodus began with the high tide of Thursday, March 23, 1899, when he sailed on the Peninsula and Oriental Line's vessel *Rome,* bound for Port Said, Aden and points beyond. He was so excited that, scenting the sea air at Spithead, with the Queen's residence of Osborne hidden on the starboard beam, he could almost smell the East.

CHAPTER 7

Let Dusky Indians Whine and Kneel

The consciousness of India lay over England at the turn of the century like a vast velvet canopy sprinkled with jewels, but beyond the luxurious myth lay realities whose magnificence and squalor could never be communicated to the British public going about the mundane business of a nation of shopkeepers. The English public was sinking into a mindless lethargy that could be stirred only by the cheap excitements offered by a meretricious press and politicians interested only in expedients. The age of sensationalism and opportunism had begun to dawn and in its lurid light not many retained an older vision and a more pressing sense of duty. Of these few, unwittingly, Richard Meinertzhagen was one.

What Richard had picked up at Harrow from Bosworth Smith, biographer of Lord Lawrence the great viceroy, or casually from acquaintances, furnished him with no more than rags and tatters to clothe his dream of India. Like all his contemporaries he carried with him an unconscious load of principles, prejudices and predispositions forming a reality that would make his life in India different only in degree from his life in England. It was from this invisible baggage that the British had built, decade after decade, the superstructure that was known as British India, which began to all intents and purposes almost as soon as the India steamer left Tilbury. The first of the imperial entrepreneurs, the servants of the East India Company, had been expected to be tradesmen one minute and rulers the next. They were paid very little by the Company but a little initiative brought them fortunes; one of the more successful was said to have received more than a million pounds in bribes from a single native prince. These nabobs gave way, after reforms, to a generation of whom Macauley wrote, "They are men who after ruling millions of subjects, after commanding victorious armies, after dictating terms of peace at the gates of hostile capitals, after administering the revenues of great provinces, after judging the causes of wealthy Zemindars, after residing at the courts of tributary Kings, return to their native land with no more than a decent competence." Following these came the generation who were to settle the Punjab and live through the Mutiny of 1857–58, among them Sir Henry Lawrence, an old-fashioned believer in government through the native leaders, for which view he was retired to Rajputana when the viceroy decided on direct rule and "modern" ideas. The Mutiny washed over Lawrence in Lucknow, which he defended and where he died having composed his own epitaph: "Here lies Henry Lawrence who tried to do his duty. May God have mercy on him." Lawrence and his like were proud men, sensitive and courageous, but even while they followed their duty, the pressures of a new time were molding men of a different stamp. These men were more numerous, less austere and of a coarser stock. Their way of life produced as close a facsimile of Surrey or Kent as they could contrive and they agreed with the old Persian couplet often quoted by the Moguls:

> *If there is a Paradise on earth*
> *It is this, it is this, it is this!*

But in many ways it was an island paradise, no part of the main, in which they sported and toward which Richard's ship was steaming.

After twelve days of the spacious routine afforded by a Victorian voyage, Richard's vessel put in as was usual at Port Said and there the East hit him like a sledgehammer. He went ashore while the passenger list rearranged itself and found himself plunged into "a sink of immoral filth." Wandering away from the docks, he was drawn by a sort of revolting fascination deeper and deeper into the old quarter of the town, following narrow streets with gutters that doubled as latrines and fetching up in an area that seemed to contain nothing but drink shops, gambling dens and brothels. Assaulted by the stench of an Egyptian afternoon, he was just passing a doorway when a little fair-haired girl of twelve called out to him in English. As he turned, the child was snatched back into the darkness by a fierce old hag protected by a couple of brutal-looking Egyptians. Richard hurried to the British consul and with difficulty persuaded him to call the police. Back at the house with an escort, Richard found the girl cowering in a sordid room and weeping. As soon as she saw him she clung to him and begged him to help her. Leaving the police to argue the case, Richard took her to the consul and announced that he was going to leave her in the care of the consul's wife. The consul, his afternoon becoming more and more irregular, said that that of course was an impossible notion. Richard then announced that he would take the child to India with him. Thus made to seem the instrument of an abduction, the consul surrendered and his wife promised to find a Mission home for Richard's protégée. Richard insisted on being given a receipt for her, kissed her abstractedly, and returned to the sanity of his ship. Before it sailed he wrote a report of his knight errantry, attached the receipt to it, and mailed it to Lord Cromer, the august ruler of Egypt, whom he did not know but who he felt sure would put things right. Lord Cromer's reputation for omniscience and plain dealing was a byword in England.

Richard had plenty of time to reflect on the unexpected appearance of the East as his ship sailed steadily toward the sunrise. At Aden he had his first glimpse of Africans when the ship coaled: strings of them humped the great sacks off the wharf and up the gangways, the sweat channeling the black dust on their black skins as the sun struck on the rocks of that barren cauldron. Eastward again the flying fish began to play, flecks of silver splashing back into the blue like a handful of thrown pebbles. At sunset the sky glowed a deep, pure cobalt and the bow-wave began to glimmer with the sheen of phosphorescence. When the night came up it was soft and sparkling with stars ice-clear and brilliant. This was the magic road to India, but India's gateway was less romantic.

Richard's first impression of the subcontinent was a blue-gray line on the horizon, the low flat coast of Bombay. Drawing closer he could pick out a darker hill behind the white huddle of the city but no great building loomed as a symbol. There were palms and cluttered wharves, a couple of towers, and a few factory chimneys, but most significant of all was the odor borne on a whisper of an offshore breeze. In fact, Richard was lucky to encounter the smell of India first at Bombay, for as Rudyard Kipling had put it: "Bombay cloaks her stenches with a veneer of assafoetida and tobacco; Calcutta is above pretense. There is no tracing back the Calcutta plague to any one source. It is faint, it is sickly, and it is indescribable. It is certainly not an Indian smell. It resembles the essence of corruption that has rotted for the second time—the clammy odor of blue slime. And there is no escape from it." The air was warm and slightly humid but by no means debilitating as Richard stepped ashore onto the Apollo Bunder Quay and entered the needle's eye through which all who came to Bombay must pass. This was a big iron shed in which the air throbbed with heat and tumult, roofed with a structure meant to simulate a Mongol tent. It was not the least of the architectural curiosities of the city.

Above all else rose Sir Gilbert Scott's clock tower at the University Library, a statement in pure fourteenth-century Gothic except that in its niches fidgeted twenty-four Oriental figures representing the castes of western India. Nearby bulked University Hall, made possible by the munificence of one Sir Cowarjee Jehangir Readymoney and executed in the French Decorated style of the fifteenth century. The Town Hall was Doric without and Corinthian within, a classic hedging of bets, but the High Court's pinnacles and groined corridor indicated a return to Early English, while the Government Secretariat building presented an uncompromising Venetian Gothic with the arms of Sir Bartle Frere stamping approval over its entrance; it was difficult to escape the shade of Sir Bartle in Bombay. The Telegraph Office lasped into Romanesque but the new municipal buildings returned to the Gothic norm, though by a freak of creative inspiration their towers had been stoppered with bulbous masonry domes like the tops of perfume bottles. All of these buildings were, of course, Victorian and the traveler might stand before more than one vista and think himself in an only slightly distorted Manchester. Elsewhere the illusion was more difficult to maintain. The eye fell on painted Hindu temples and the thin minarets of mosques, and, ominous on the western skyline, upon the stark gray Towers of Silence where the Parsees disposed of their dead. As worshipers of Zoroaster the Parsees could not, unlike the Hindus, defile their sacred fire with corpses, so they bore their loved ones to the tops of the Towers, to be consumed by vultures and kites and then tipped the skeletons into deep wells within the Towers. This vulturine undertaking impressed itself upon the more affluent British residents, whose estates spread along Malabar Hill under the flight paths of the scavengers, when from time to time an accidental bird would let fall a morsel of anatomy in the midst of a garden party. For all its superficial appearance of Victorian corporate solidity, Bombay's rich essence was a brew of the essential India.

The great homes on Malabar Hill, outside the city proper, were a luxurious version of the British cantonments and civil lines all over the subcontinent, always removed at least a mile beyond the limits of the Indian towns. Government House itself lay at the seaward tip, isolated among green lawns and greener trees. The old Government House was now during the current epidemic a plague hospital. In little more than two years the plague had killed over a quarter of a million people and it had hardly begun; at its height it was to account for two thousand deaths a week in Bombay alone in spite of the vaccine prepared in the research laboratory at Government House. During 1902 more than half a million died of it. The number of European casualties was small because of their seclusion and superior hygiene, but they suffered other ills, of which the most feared was cholera. Richard, like every Englishman entering India, encased his stomach day and night, on his doctor's orders, in a cholera belt made of flannel. Since the cause of cholera was not yet known and since its first symptom was intense intestinal pain, the doctors hoped for the best by keeping that area warm. More frightened of cholera than of anything else in India, the British troops believed it was carried in an invisible cloud that floated through their barrack rooms by night. Once a man was struck he was almost certain to die within twelve hours. Within another twelve at the most he would be in his grave with the regimental band playing a doleful tune over it but quickly changing to something more sprightly like "The Girl I Left Behind Me" as it marched away.

The compendium of Indian diseases was as exotic as the variations of its peoples. A Charitable Dispensary in one of the princely states of Rajputana offered cures for "Asthama, Numonia, Catrack, Skindiseas, Dabality and Loin-Bite," this last affliction fairly common to the locality, famous for its tigers.* Not a few young empire builders succumbed to enteric fever; others were overcome by "heat apoplexy," though warned to wear topees whenever they stepped off their verandas, and it was not uncommon for a British community to be shocked by the suicide by shooting of one of its members, his private problems grown monstrous in the savage climate. It was impossible to escape mortality in India, where day and night the smoke rose endlessly from the burning grounds, and the rivers bore away from their banks onto the flood the small corpses of infants garlanded on funeral rafts.

Richard's early impressions of India, however, were of seething life. His route to Watson's Hotel lay through a press of people, multitudes, it seemed, of pedlars, beggars, clerks and merchants, mostly anonymous in white robes of one design or another, among whom soldiers from the native regiments or occasional Pathan money-lenders in dazzling embroidered vests stood out like carnival figures. In this hubbub Watson's Hotel was an oasis of long, shaded balconies, soft-footed servants, and tables on the lawn under the mango trees. The next day the bustle began again when Richard took his train from Victoria station, where there seemed to be at least ten

---

* Tigers, leopards or panthers, and *Panthera leo persica* were all lumped together in the vulger vocabulary as "lions." The Indian lion proper, once common all over northern India, had been almost exterminated by the mid-eighties by English trophy hunters.

times as many people intending to travel as the Great Indian Peninsula Railway could possibly convey. He was still six hundred and
twenty-five miles away from his regiment. The train took him north,
cooled by a block of ice dripping in a zinc tray in the middle of his
compartment, across a spur of the Aravalli Hills. Gradually the
terrain began to change. He had been traveling through belts of jungle between which lay mile after mile of flat, cultivated country; but
now, with more than half a day still to go, the land grew rockier and
drier until finally the track began to climb into the blue of the northern hills. The little stations it passed were domed like mosques, as
if this arid area bred a sparer taste, a desert flavor. At Ajmer Richard
changed trains. Standing on the platform with his uniform and gun
cases and trunks piled beside him, he smelled the dust of Rajputana
and gazed at the fort built by the Mogul emperor Akbar three and
a half centuries before as a stronghold from which to rule the whole
north of India. The City, walled with stone at the foot of a mountain,
was a place of pilgrimage for Hindu and Muslim alike, but it would
be some time before Richard could explore it.

A branch line took him the fourteen miles to Nasirabad, running south through flat brown country in which green cultivated
fields blazed suddenly. He saw spiky hedges of cactus everywhere
and here and there thickets of sugar cane, but for the most part
there was only hard-baked earth. At Nasirabad an orderly was waiting, a courtesy Richard welcomed if only for the comfort of the
Fusilier badge shining on his white sun helmet. The mountain of
baggage was manhandled into a bullock cart and Richard was led
off to Nasirabad's prime public transportation—a low-slung, two-
wheeled carriage whose proprietor seemed more powerful than the
pony he was driving. Ram Baksh was a local tycoon whose optimism
could weather any perversity of clients, geography or climate; a man
of means and ingenuity, whose eight tongas and twenty pairs of
horses were at the service of the garrison for projects great and small,
Ram Baksh approached with the same equanimity a trip to the station or a shikari into tiger country which might take days of negotia-
ting rocky tracks. He brought Richard down the straight military
road to the cantonment at a stately pace and, as satisfied as a conjurer

accomplishing his finest maneuver, drew up outside the adjutant's office. Captain Allen Victor Johnson looked up without surprise as Richard came to attention in front of his desk. "Ah, Montezuma!" he said, "Had a good trip?" Richard Meinertzhagen had acquired a nickname and found a new home.

The 1st Battalion of the Royal Fusiliers (City of London Regiment) had already been stationed in India for twenty years when Richard was born. Arriving too late for the major campaigning of the Mutiny, they had been in time to witness reprisals against the mutineers, marching into their garrison along roads lined with gibbets. They had fought on the Northwest Frontier in a forgotten raid, had held Kandahar until Lord Roberts marched to relieve them, and carried as their latest battle honor on their colors "Afghanistan 1878–9." The bloody names on those colors did not, however, tell the regiment's full story. Formed by a royal charter under the hand of James II, it had fought for William of Orange in the Low Countries while Marlborough was learning his trade. It had served aboard ship as an impromptu force of marines, and for over a century as a reminder its band played "Rule Britannia" before beginning the national anthem. Another curiosity cherished by the regiment was that its officers did not drink the Loyal Toast after dinner, having been excused the duty by William IV in person. At the beginning of the War of the Revolution, the fusiliers lost their colors almost immediately to Montgomery's raiders; after a winter of comfort in Philadelphia they lost them for the second time at Cowpens. In the Peninsula under Wellington they were cut to pieces time after time but won no fewer than eight battle honors. Back in America for the War of 1812 they were just in time to help lose the Battle of New Orleans two weeks after the peace treaty had been signed. They fought throughout the Crimean War with the same sullen gallantry they had shown against the French and five of them won the Victoria Cross. Like all regiments they felt that their victories overshadowed their defeats; they had never known dishonor and they were jealous of the small distinctions that made them, as they thought, singular. The tone of the 1st Battalion, as Richard was to find, was stolidly conservative in military behavior as well as in social matters. It was also a trifle snobbish. The Royal Fusiliers were quick to point out to newcomers that the regiment, though infantry, played polo.

Renegade as ever, Richard first bought not polo ponies, but an elephant. Just before he had sailed, Uncle Ernest's generosity had shone forth once again with a promise to buy his godson anything he liked for use in India. Richard cabled for twelve hundred rupees (eighty pounds) and invested in Archibald, a highly trained beast experienced enough to be taken out after wild pig or even tiger. But Archibald's massive calm hid a whimsical will, for Archibald was a cow. Richard tested her professional qualifications by shooting a chinkara, the delicate, chestnut-brown common gazelle of India. Archibald behaved perfectly, even going so far as to pick up the chinkara with her trunk and pass it back over her shoulder to Richard, standing in her howdah. He was enchanted. But he was beguiled.

As was customary in military cantonments the officers' quarters were bungalows with their own small gardens, grouped in an enclave about three-quarters of a mile from the regimental parade ground and the men's barracks. The senior officers lived in splendid isolation, but subalterns almost always shared quarters, an arrangement Richard found disagreeable at first because he was assigned a house with the senior lieutenant, whom he loathed. Richard discovered one morning that unless he hurried he would be late for the first parade of the day, a sin abhorrent to God. Archibald was standing in the drive, as monumentally impassive as usual. It was Richard's habit to ride her as far as the guard room, where he could dismount out of sight of the battalion. His own pleasure in Archibald was not felt by his brother officers, who thought her an improper possession for a newly joined subaltern, so he was careful not to give offense by vulgar display. Shoving his brilliant white topee firmly on his head with one hand and holding his sword off the ground with the other, Richard rushed out of his bungalow shouting to Archibald's mahout to make all haste and scrambled up the waiting ladder onto the elephant's broad back. Archibald was capable, when pressed, of seven miles an hour, but on this particular morning she was still accelerating past her maximum when she reached the guard room. The mahout's cries only drove her faster. She burst from behind the guard room at a near gallop. In front of her the battalion was just forming into line. The adjutant, supervising this peaceful maneuver from his charger, caught sight of Archibald and spurred gallantly forward in an attempt to head her off. So hectic was Archibald's locomotion, however, that Richard could do nothing about acknowledging the adjutant, being fully occupied in merely staying aboard his mount. Unfortunately Archibald's demeanor so upset the adjutant's horse that it reared and unseated its rider, who only just avoided the great pounding feet. Richard caught a glimpse of him as he swept loftily by and in the same instant heard the regimental sergeant major's mighty voice roaring at the men to stand firm. Archibald hit the line and dissolved it without injury to the fusiliers, who had wisely scattered, and came ponderously to a halt. Nothing quite like it had been seen since the dervishes broke a British square.

At nine o'clock Richard presented himself at the Orderly Room, where he was not encouraged by the regimental sergeant major's icy civilities. He was marched before his colonel. "What," asked the colonel, "is the Army coming to?" Richard found himself at a loss for an answer. The colonel mentioned his own thirty years of loyal service to the Crown, enlarged on the regiment's unsullied honor during its four decades in India, then returned to his original line of inquiry. "What is the Army coming to," he demanded, "if subalterns can charge a battalion on parade with a bloody elephant?" Richard said he was sorry. The colonel stared at him. Finally he said, "You must dispose of it at once." Later, however, he relented. Richard was allowed to keep Archibald so long as he never rode her while in uniform. His routine thereafter sank into a more normal pattern.

He had arrived at Nasirabad as the hot weather began, so the daily schedule was at its lightest. It began with the bugle singing from the Guard Room while the morning was still relatively cool. After the assembly, all in the white drill of summer, the battalion enjoyed a leisurely breakfast. The men could buy eggs, pats of butter, or steaks to supplement their rations from the little groups of native tradesmen outside their quarters. The officers would clank over to the Mess for kedgeree or deviled chops or more familiar dishes. The rest of the morning was spent in company training of a subdued kind until it could be assumed that the colonel had gone home. In some stations, particularly in the Punjab, the excessive heat made even such a leisurely day impossible. Then there would be a parade at seven in the morning and occasionally a brief one after sunset; the men spent the day in torpor while the temperature climbed past a hundred and twenty degrees. Some of them dozed all night in zinc hipbaths of tepid water. Everyone itched from head to toe with the pink rash of prickly heat, which turned to boils or to huge blisters that peeled off at a touch. Nasirabad, though uncomfortable, was never unbearable. Lunch was followed by a siesta, then at four the officers gulped down their tea and cantered off to the polo ground or for a couple of hours' shooting. On their way home to change for dinner they might stop off at the Club for a chota peg of whisky and soda and half an hour with the newspapers from Home.

Late as they were, Richard was for the time being anxious to scan the stories they were carrying about the Dreyfus scandal, a passion he shared with Georgina. Captain Alfred Dreyfus, an artillery officer serving on the French general staff, had been found guilty of espionage in behalf of Germany in 1894, degraded and imprisoned for life on Devil's Island. By 1898 enough indication of an official conspiracy against Dreyfus had accumulated for Émile Zola to publish his article "*J'Accuse*," charging the French army with suppression of the truth and worse.

On the first day of July 1899, the cruiser *Sfax* stole into Quiberon Bay with Dreyfus aboard; by the time Richard was reading this news in India the second Dreyfus trial had opened at Rennes. It was an international issue, because aside from the division of French opinion into two impassioned groups, there now lay over the affair the stench of anti-Semitism, exemplified by Princess Lobanoff's remark when Dreyfus emerged as a luncheon topic at Windsor: "Jews! What are they? Little heaps of dirt and rags. How can anyone speak to them?" Once more Dreyfus was condemned by the military court, but this time to a mere ten years on the Ile du

154 DUTY, HONOR, EMPIRE

Diable. It was a travesty. The whole world railed against the intransigent French and was scarcely mollified when two weeks later the President of the Republic granted Dreyfus a pardon. For once in complete sympathy with his mother, Richard commented, "It exposed the rottenness of the French, the injustice which pervaded the whole national structure, and the corrupt morals of a people governed by a still more corrupt gang of treacherous and decadent politicians." Georgina wrote to Dreyfus as soon as he was released inviting him to recuperate at Mottisfont, but much to Daniel's relief the silent, ill-used Frenchman declined. Richard applauded his mother's enthusiasm for the oppressed from afar, ignored the newspapers again, and returned to the study of his men, who briefly dismissed the whole affair as just another mad caper of "those bloody Froggies."

The troops had their own pursuits. Many of them kept dogs with which they coursed hares or wild cats brought into the camp in wooden cages and sold for a few pence. For eightpence they could buy a jackal and then they would pit two or three dogs against it for money in a handball alley. Some men raised gamecocks and held mains where the flashing little birds fought to the death in a flurry of blood-stained feathers. The mongoose made an affectionate pet but it was less profitable than a minah bird, which could easily be captured and with a little patience taught to talk, an education often accelerated by lowering the bird down a well and yelling at it. A few men caught cobras or collected butterflies, but many more marked the crows that flapped everywhere like convocations of tattered and starving clerics. They would trap a crow, slide a filament through the two holes in its upper beak and tie on a bell or a metal disk bearing the company's mark. The troops' canteens were open for an hour at lunchtime and for several in the evening for the cheap and copious consumption of rather watery beer. One curious effect of the heat was that the beer never seemed to stimulate the bladder however much was drunk. For abstainers the Army Temperance Association ran coffee bars and reading rooms stocked with improving literature.

In the larger military establishments there were billiard rooms and libraries, and brothels in the native bazaars supervised with care by the regimental police and staffed by girls in a proportion of about one to forty. Light duties gave the men a great deal of time to themselves: even their personal hygiene could be accomplished without personal exertion. Every morning before dawn an Indian barber circulated among his regular customers so circumspectly that he could shave a man without fully waking him. His services were available for twopence a week, while for a penny the nail-wallah would clip a man's fingernails, pare his corns, cut ingrowing toenails, scrape the tartar from his teeth, and pick the wax from his ears. All less intimate chores in the barracks were performed by natives. Some cleaned the rooms, others the latrines, some—the dhobi-wallahs—did the washing, some cleaned equipment and boots, some tugged day and night at ropes that propelled the ceiling fans to induce a suspicion of a breeze, and others spent their day damping down the straw screens that cooled the air passing through the doorways. All that was left for a British soldier to do was to clean his rifle.

It was a gentleman's life for all ranks, though the men still sang when the bugles sounded the Officers' Mess Call at dusk:

> *Officers' wives have puddings and pies*
> *And sergeants' wives have skilly,*
> *But privates' wives have nothing at all*
> *To fill their poor little bellies.*

There was less of antipathy in it than recognition of the gulf between the two classes. Richard very soon came to terms with his own men across the divide, but in idiosyncratic fashion. One evening he was riding home from the polo grounds when one of a group of fusiliers walking by called out derisively, "What ho, Tod Sloane!" Recognizing the man as one of the battalion's noted toughs, Richard reined in his pony and announced that he would now punch the man's head. He had not even considered the meaning of the remark: the fact that the man had had the temerity to speak to an officer without being spoken to was enough, without the mocking tone he had used. It was still possible for a man to be tied to the wheel of a gun carriage all day for "dumb insolence," the mere intractable flicker of an eye. So Richard began to swing out of his saddle, but before he could give battle a sergeant major had appeared. Next day the man was confined to barracks for a week and Richard was lectured for threatening private soldiers. But Richard, still feeling that justice had not been done, summoned the man to his bungalow. In the privacy of its backyard they squared off, Richard with the advantage of his boxing coaching at Harrow. At the end of two minutes he knocked the man off his feet. Then he helped him up, gave him five rupees to celebrate with, and shook his hand. The man grinned at him, called him a sport, and left with an amiable salute. Richard had consolidated his reputation as an original.

It was just as well that his companion in the bungalow had not been at home at the time, or Richard would have been in serious trouble. The companion stood on his dignity as the battalion's senior lieutenant without, in Richard's opinion, much cause. It was the custom in all British regiments that no officer was allowed to leave the Mess after dinner until the last guest had gone. One night, having been out shooting since dawn, Richard ignored the rule and went home to sleep. He was wakened much later when his companion rudely tipped him out of bed and began to deliver a pompous speech about gentlemanly conduct. Shivering with a rage, Richard loaded his revolver and forced him at gun point to remake the bed and then, alone again, began to wonder with anguish whether he had gone too far. It was the first time he had lost his temper as an adult and the blind power of his anger had scared him. But the lieutenant never reported the incident and before long Richard was able to move to another bungalow with a more congenial spirit. Richard's new friend, Neville Gardner, shared the same provocative sense of humor but not Richard's physique, a combination of characteristics that almost cost him his life. There was an eccentric officer in the battalion called Hare, nicknamed in token of his nervous disposition "March Hare." Without thinking, Gardner called Hare by his nickname, whereupon Hare seized a hog spear and lunged at him. Gardner yelled and fled as fast as his tubbiness would allow, with

Hare behind him and gaining, silent and murderous, and he only just managed to reach Richard and safety.

The regiment's young officers were all boisterous and for the most part keen to learn their calling. They were constantly put in their place on both counts by their elders and betters, for the army's mood was still conservative, preferring by far the amateur over the professional.* Richard was soon at odds with his colonel again, this time over a domestic matter. His and Gardner's compound surrounding their bungalow seemed to support little but various kinds of thorns, except for a solitary and rather feeble little tree. After breakfast one morning Richard discovered a camel eating its leaves in the supercilious fashion of its kind; he drove it away, only to see it led back immediately by its keeper. When Richard told the man to remove his offensive beast, there ensued an argument which Richard terminated by kicking the man and the camel indiscriminately until both left. Later in the day the colonel took Richard formally to task for assaulting his (the colonel's) camel man and his (the colonel's) camel, and set him to reflect bitterly on the vagaries of a justice that could prefer a commander's servant to a subaltern's only tree. It was believed throughout the army that subalterns had no manners, so every Mess had its inflexible rules and practices, any breach of which would bring down censure. Richard was told that gentlemen did not smoke pipes in the anteroom to the Mess but might do so in the billiard room. He was found reading a training manual in the anteroom and declared a bounder for not knowing that shop talk or study was indecent in the Mess. As another young officer wrote at the time, "It is difficult not to deteriorate mentally in this atmosphere." But Richard had too many interests and too much free time in which to pursue them to be bored.

He could shoot sandgrouse, chinkara and blackbuck any afternoon, he played polo almost daily, and he occasionally went out pig-sticking. For many of the British in India this was a sport next to

---

* It was said of one chic cavalryman that he kept a notice pinned on his Orderly Room door announcing "The Adjutant will attend at this office on alternate Fridays," but not specifying which Friday might be which.

godliness, and no less an authority than Lieutenant General Sir Robert Baden-Powell (lately the hammer of Matabeleland and soon to be defender of Mafeking against the boorish Boers) had provided its sacred tablets with his *Pigsticking or Hoghunting*. The sport made great demands on the skill and nerve of its devotees, and offered advantages that not everyone had noticed until Sir Robert pointed them out. "At the same time," he wrote, "the horse without a doubt enjoys it almost as much as its rider, and the pig, too, being endowed with a fighting and blood-thirsty nature as well as a particularly tough and unfeeling nervous system, seems to revel in the fight up to the bitter end."* The technique was to beat patches of jungle or scrub to force sounders of pig into the open. Sows and under-sized grunters could not be hunted, but once a boar of rideable size was sighted two or three horsemen would take off after him in an attempt to get first spear. Whoever speared the pig first claimed him whether or not the wound was fatal, but the great danger lay at the end when the pig, tired of running, turned and made its charge, for it had the strength and weight to topple a horse and the ferocity to disembowel even a tiger. The country hunted by the Nasirabad Tent Club was too barren to nourish giant pig and the rocky slopes of Sendolia hill were dangerous taken at the full-blooded gallop that was the essence of the sport. Richard was horseman enough to account for three boars during his stay there, all creditable and one weighing out at over three hundred pounds.

The hard, sandy near-desert of Nasirabad's environs offered

---

* Things did not always go the pigsticker's way. One noted authority from Eastern Bengal records how he approached a seemingly moribund pig on foot and was immediately bowled over by its charge. He fought it off while it tried to expose his vitals with its tusks. It bit off the end of his thumb, but it was eventually subdued by some natives and the bold sportsman's thumb tip was picked up by his assistant with the suggestion that it might be reattached by a process recently perfected at Oxford. The sportsman, bleeding in various places, rather pettishly told him not to talk such nonsense. "However," the sportsman reported, "he put the bit of thumb down, and it was at once carried off by a crow (*Corvus splendens*), and that was the end of the end of my thumb."

only a small selection of game but birds proliferated and Richard rapidly added to his collection. A couple of hours away by tonga, just to the north of the city of Ajmer, there was a sanctuary, an artificial lake formed by damming the River Luni, which provided a haven for varieties of waterfowl, duck, fish-eagles and occasional flamingoes and which incidentally contributed to the excessive aridity of the Rann of Kutch. The cool waters of the Ana Sagar were delightful, troubled only by the gentle wakes of swimming birds, and reflecting lustrous white the five marble pavilions ranged on the bank by the Mogul emperor Shah Jehan and just now being restored at the express direction of Lord Curzon, the new viceroy. Six miles or so west of the Ana Sagar was the most sacred lake in India, Pushkar, in the fall the site of the devotions of a hundred thousand pilgrim Hindus and the venue for a magnificent fair where bullocks and horses were sold and where camels competed in jumping races. Muslims were drawn to the city of Ajmer itself, to the Dargah shrine within the wall. On his first visit to the Dargah a rich man was expected to fill one of two vast iron cauldrons in its courtyard with a mixture of rice, ghee, sugar, almonds, raisins and spices to feed the poor, an act of contrition and generosity it would be difficult to diminish, since each pot had a capacity of ten thousand pounds of food. The city was astonishingly colorful. Its houses were plastered white and decorated with formal paintings of animals, people and flowers mostly blue and yellow. Its inhabitants were fine, fierce Rajputs, the men in floppy turbans of scarlet or ocher and boldly printed gowns, carrying curved swords with a military air intensified by the magnificent sweep of beards parted in the center and brushed upward to meet the ends of curling moustaches. Women passed with a jingle of jewelry—bangles at the wrist and gold and silver belts at the waist, nose rings, a pendant on the forehead, and even a ring or two gleaming on the toes. They wore primary reds and yellows or bright greens, and carried themselves like the nobility they felt themselves to be. They were brilliant strangers to Richard.

Like his compatriots, Richard found his acquaintance among the Indians limited, though one day he and Neville Gardner were invited to lunch by a local rajah. But the only detail Richard remembered later was that after the meal everybody belched loudly and politely as a compliment. The household servants he came across, from humble sweepers to water-carriers to lordly kitmutgars standing immaculately in the background at dinner, might have been so many automata. Though he never treated them unkindly he never became in any way familiar with their individuality. His attitude, benevolent but aloof, was the standard one, unconsciously expressed by a friendly cavalry officer who found himself seated over the mulligatawny soup next to a colonel of native infantry, and kindly inquired, "Colonel, I take a great interest in your branch of the service and I have always wondered what you do when the trumpet sounds the trot—do your blacks run?" Queen Victoria herself showered benefits on her personal Indian servant, the Munshi, whose leech-like attachment she took for innocent devotion, and announced that the whole British endeavor in India must be "to protect the poor natives and advance civilization." In practice the attitude of her white subjects toward her brown liegemen was more ambivalent and had already been best expressed by a private of infantry asked for diplomacy's sake to abase himself before a native prince. "Let dusky Indians whine and kneel," he had said stoutly. The old rumbustious days of the East India Company's freer habits with the local population, freest of all with the docile Indian women upon whom they laid the firm foundations of the Eurasian population, had long since passed. In their place grew an imported civilization hedged about by a color bar made necessary, as it seemed, by wives and daughters joining their menfolk now that the practice of retiring to the hills in the hot season had become established. The fact that the voyage home now took only days instead of months induced a more British outlook in the expatriate, who felt it less necessary to get to grips with the realities of Indian life since he was no longer quite so cut off from the more wholesome atmosphere of his own country.

This attitude breathed from every page of Mrs. Flora Annie Steel's *The Complete Indian Housekeeper,* a work which included one and a half pages on "Native Cookery." The Mrs. Beeton of Asia, its author was a true daughter of her time who expressed profound convictions in plain language. "We do not advocate an unholy haughtiness," she wrote, "but an Indian household can no more be governed without dignity and prestige than an Indian Empire." Though in general sympathetic, Mrs. Steel preached a rough justice for the stupid or careless servant. A dose of castor oil, she had found, would expose him to great ridicule from his fellow servants. Her book ran to thirty editions, less for the originality of its content than for the confirmation it afforded of what everyone had really thought all along. Men who had spent their lifetimes in the country grumbled about the passing of the old days: then a man riding along any road would expect to see an Indian stop his own carriage and get out until the sahib had passed. Certainly civilities were no longer ostentatious, but the British were too tight-lipped and too complacent to recognize a shift in the wind, so bound by their iron codes of conduct that the ladies and gentlemen watching a tennis tournament in Peshawar while Sir Bindon Blood's guns boomed in the mountain passes of the northwest frontier could know that wounded sepoys were passing on bloodstained stretchers right behind their wicker armchairs and yet not look round. None of them could have realized how fast the Indians themselves were changing.

The change was radical. The system of castes, which had evaluated individuals according to their hereditary functions in society, had operated as a divisive force for centuries. What had begun to erode it, paradoxically, was the extraordinary European notion imported by the British (though plainly not extended very far in practice) that a nation was comprised of equal citizens. Naturally it was a long time before the idea took root at all. Ram Mohan Roy was the first to identify it with the mainstream of Hindu thought; it had been one of the sparks that lit the flame of the Mutiny and by 1900 it was beginning to glow all over India. Its chief supporters were the Indian middle class the British themselves had created. Given a common tongue by the adoption of English as the official language, economic stability through mercantile appointments and minor employment in government, and access to more knowledge in schools and universities—the new class found its self-respect in the books, popular at the time, in which British authors rediscovered with admiration, and no little bombast, the glories that had been ancient India. This diet, far from satisfying Indian dreams, created new appetites for distinction and power. To such men the British in their cantonments, so concerned with the rituals of bridge, the gossip in the social columns mailed from England, and the arts of dressing for dinner or sport or the act of government, were hypocrites whose public speeches professed the noble ends of imperialism but whose day-to-day conduct was a brutal reminder that there were those who ruled and those who obeyed. To the new class it was bad enough to be governed by a foreign power, but to be told that it was for their own good was almost insupportable. However, the British seemed to have one saving grace: at least they believed that freedom encompassed the right to oppose and the right to protest. The opposition grew more stubborn, the protests louder, and the majority of the British regarded this untoward development with a raised eyebrow. The first confrontation between the old order and the new bourgeois sensibility of the Indian middle class had come in 1883 with the proposal of the Ilbert Bill by Gladstone's viceroy, Lord Ripon, a practitioner of the liberalism his mentor trumpeted from Olympus. Superficially the bill was merely a measure to recognize the services of Indian judges in the Bengal presidency by according them the same powers as their European brothers-in-law. It soon dawned on the British that in practice a white man could be tried by an Indian without a jury. They threatened to kidnap the viceroy rather than submit to such an inequity. Caught between the racial wrath of his countrymen and the injured susceptibilities of his native charges, Ripon sought a compromise and precipitated intensified political action by the Indians. Two years later they formed their Indian National Congress, which spread steadily throughout the subcontinent and by the turn of the century achieved enough support to have some claim to form a responsible opposition to the government. But still, though the Indians hungered for a larger portion of the joint, they had no teeth with which to bite it off.

These powerful political aspirations flowed over Richard Meinertzhagen. He was preoccupied with the difficulties of learning his profession. When he had joined the army a mottled major had bellowed at him, "Are you a Wolseleyite or a Robertsite?" Not having met either general, Richard had been lost for a choice, but the major had quickly set his thinking right with "By God, sir, the sooner you know the better. Wolseley's the man to follow—don't you forget it! Roberts is only a Sepoy general. He knows nothing about modern warfare. So you're a Wolseleyite, young fellah!" Such conclusions formed the pure product of the military philosophy of the majority of the British army's officers. Lulled by nearly half a century of comparative peace, they had not yet fully recovered from their last experience of modern warfare on the rain-swept redoubts of the Crimea. Roberts, they thought, was a good enough chap for chasing about the frontier with his crowds of sepoys fighting riff-raff, but when it came to the real thing Wolseley's efficiency and the snappy attributes of a modern major-general would do the trick. Neither commander in fact had the experience or the accomplishments the war of the future would require, and Second Lieutenant Richard Meinertzhagen was astute enough to see that.

Richard had read enough to realize that what had brought victory of a sort in the Crimea was the determination of the fighting men, the regimental officers and soldiers. That expedition had had no intelligence service, no trained staff officers, and hardly any administrative organization at all, a condition of such romantic inefficiency that it was a marvel the Russians could be less competent still. He had seen enough in his first months in India to realize that the 1st Battalion of the Royal Fusiliers was no fitter now for modern battle than it had been then. Toward the end of the monsoon season the battalion was able to begin more rigorous training as the days grew cooler. In Richard's opinion the battalion's second-in-command had learned nothing since Agincourt. They were taught to assault an enemy position by advancing in sections of twenty men each, shoulder to shoulder in perfect alignment, until within a couple of hundred yards of the enemy. At this vulnerable stage the groups coalesced, dressed by the right, and formed battalion line before essaying the charge. Its precision was glorious but as serious tactics it was burlesque. Venturing further afield, always in solid column of route for neatness, the battalion next learned the proper method of forming square against attack by cavalry, performing the maneuver with enough precision of drill and smartness of appearance to draw warm approval from the senior officers, who had quite ignored the fact that the hilly country in which it was executed was so thick with woods and sown with rocks that no cavalry could have achieved more than a canter without breaking the legs of all its horses. More significantly, they had not yet realized that the most recent charge of cavalry upon infantry—that of the Lancers into the gully at Omdurman—had come within an ace of annihilation. These symptoms of professional turpitude in his superiors worried Richard enough for him to bring up the subject with his young peers in the Mess. Fortunately his lapse of taste and subversive attitudes passed undetected and at the appropriate time his colonel made out Richard's annual confidential report with approval: "Promising officer. Plenty of common sense and takes an interest in his work. Is keen on and well informed on natural history. A keen sportsman and polo player. He is well qualified for promotion."

When Richard read it, as he was obliged to, he was relieved by this effusion, particularly since he had just antagonized the station commander, an irascible old man who though he lived within the cantonment had never visited the regiment nor spoken to one of its officers. Richard had made his acquaintance somewhat abruptly one afternoon when some terriers started a fox from a ditch near his bungalow. Wearing the rumpled shirt and slacks in which he had been dozing, Richard grabbed his hog spear and without saddling up flung himself onto a polo pony. The fox bolted straight across the series of compounds with Richard pounding behind oblivious of his neighbors' privacy. He leaped a mud wall and managed to spear the fox as it headed for the dark haven beneath a rather spacious veranda. No sooner had Richard killed the fox than a pack of nondescript dogs drawn from the most disreputable quarters of the barracks flooded over the wall and began to mangle the poor limp thing. Glory in the chase vanished when Richard heard a rich port-wine voice thunder, "I will not have half-naked young subalterns spearing foxes in my garden! Take your dogs away!" It was the station commander, furious as a bonfire. Richard left with his mongrel pack while the commander rumbled on. "What on earth," he was demanding rhetorically, "is the Army coming to?" Later Richard noted mildly in his diary, "What fussy old things colonels are."

He had also noted earlier, "If we have to fight the Boers in South Africa, if the rest of our army is anything like this battalion, we shall suffer disaster after disaster." Not many thought so clearly in that heady year, begun by Joseph Chamberlain with "We are all Imperialists now. We realize, but we do not flinch from, the responsibilities and the obligations which Imperialism brings." The Boer War began when, on October 11, 1899, the British pinned their best hopes on lyddite, coolness under fire, and regimental tradition, and squared up to an enemy who placed his on the Bible, mobility, Mauser magazine rifles, and new field guns from Alfred Krupp of Essen. In England and India the armorers' grindstones growled and sparked, putting an edge on the cold steel of bayonets and sabers that would soon have Kruger's hobbledehoys on the run. Along the roads to the quays where the troopships lay, the air reverberated with a song last heard from American voices bound for Cuba. "Hark!" they sang, "I hear the bugle calling! Good-bye Dolly Gray." For many of them it was goodbye to more than the girls they left behind them, and for their nation it was a farewell to the Century of Hope. Disillusion came when the war was only a little more than two months old. Despite the best efforts of twenty-two thousand regulars and the country's heavyweight general Sir Redvers Buller, three towns—Kimberley, Ladysmith and Mafeking—were invested by the Boers, three major battles had been lost, and military reputations were shattering like defective glassware. The tidings of this Black Week struck England with such force that for the first time women began to buy newspapers from street vendors. It intensified the soul-searching of intellectuals like Richard's uncle Leonard Courtney, the left-wing Liberal who continued, nevertheless, to oppose the war, and Richard's Aunt Beatrice, who wrote sadly, "The cleavage of opinion about the war separates persons hitherto united and unites those who by temperament and training have hitherto been divorced." But the Queen, as usual, expressed the popular mind when she told Lord Salisbury's rather hesitant nephew, "Please understand that there is no one depressed in this house; we are not interested in the possibilities of defeat. They do not exist." She sent as immediate comfort to her "dear brave soldiers" one hundred thousand tins of chocolate.

As a further sweetener Lord Roberts of Kandahar was appointed to command with Kitchener of Khartoum as his chief of staff. The country rallied, if indeed it had ever been really shaken, and began the campaign of attrition that was bound to wrest victory from a smaller and far poorer foe. Dapper little Lord Roberts left England deafened by cheering and uplifted by a letter from Admiral Mahan in Quogue, Long Island, which said in part: "I am persuaded that your noble people will come out of it purified and nobler, to resume its beneficent work in the world. With my prayers for the success of yourself and your cause, which I believe the most and best of my countrymen recognize to be that of equal rights and human welfare." He could hardly have put it better if he had been an Englishman.

Massively reinforced and monumentally popular, Roberts broke up the Boers' positions and slowly forced them back toward their capital. The relief of Mafeking, last of the garrisons under siege and for two hundred and seventeen days virtually the private domain of Colonel Baden-Powell, propelled England into two nights and a day of delirious celebration during which London was choked with crowds carrying peacock feathers and exuding the fumes of too much liquor. Roberts handed over command to Kitchener under the impression that his duty was accomplished. In fact by far the grimmest part of the war lay ahead, for Lord Roberts, so fondly remembered for his warm feeling for the troops in his charge, had in effect been killing them with kindness. The battles they had expensively won for him had neither quenched the burghers' ardor nor walled in their commandos.

Left to fight a guerrilla war, Kitchener, as a general must, immediately demanded more troops. He fenced in the veldt with a line of blockhouses and swept it with infantry extended like beaters driving partridges. He pressed the families of campaigning Boers into concentration camps without proper administration, where they died in impressive numbers through hunger and from disease. Richard's nagging aunt Kate joined her Quaker sister-in-law Emily Hobhouse in agitation against the monstrous inadequacy of the camps, calling forth the comment from Richard that he did not mind her reviling the government, whose cause he thought unjust, but found her attack on the army as slanderous as those of the "unbalanced" Emily. Miss Hobhouse's discoveries pushed the government into action, though when she landed at Cape Town for a second visit, Lord Kitchener gave orders for "that bloody woman" to be deported by force. Twenty thousand died in the camps, mostly women and children, out of the total Boer losses of twenty-four thousand. Against this the British lost twenty-two thousand, a third of them dead of disease. But at the end Kitchener's mills ground out a peace; after nearly thirty-two months of war the Boers signed a treaty acknowledging the paramountcy of the British, and Kitchener was able to shake them firmly by the hand and assure them, "We are good friends now."

By then there was a new century and a new sovereign. The Queen had died at Osborne on the evening of January 22, 1901. Her body was ferried to the mainland aboard the royal yacht *Alberta* in a coffin draped in white satin embroidered with gold and surmounted by the orb and scepter and the imperial crown. *Alberta's* paddles churned a wintry sea through an avenue of anchored men-of-war, British battleships to the north, and foreign vessels southward. She was preceded by eight lean torpedo boats and followed by the white *Hohenzollern* with the German emperor aboard; a band repeated over and over Chopin's Funeral March, a melancholy air taken up by the band of each stationary ship as the coffin passed, while the guns thudded their last salutes. It was a gray sky and gray ships slid on a leaden sea, but as the cortege drew into Portsmouth

Harbor the sun appeared in a last funerary gesture of Queen's Weather, gleaming a living red and striking from the crown a final golden fire. Richard wrote: "So that ends the Victorian age of peace, prosperity and contentment. We shall never again see an age quite like that presided over by that dear old lady."

His mood was matched by all those in the nation sensitive to the new currents stirring over Europe and across the Atlantic. Even *The Times*'s self-important corpus was racked by a pang of doubt, betrayed in a leader on January 23, 1901. "At the close of the reign we are finding ourselves somewhat less secure of our position than we could desire, and somewhat less abreast of the problems of the age than we ought to be, considering the initial advantages we secured," it admitted. "The command of natural forces that made us great and rich has been superseded by newer discoveries and methods, and we have to open what may be called a new chapter." Richard's diary was more specific. "Of one thing I am certain," he wrote, "there will be a great change during the next twenty-five years, possibly due to war with Germany, possibly due to social changes at home."

Richard had never trusted the German emperor since he had met him as a child in his aunts' garden and it was beginning to seem as if he might be right not to. The kaiser's attendance at Osborne during his grandmother's last hours and the revelation that she had practically died in his arms temporarily softened the harsh image the kaiser's arrogance had been creating over the last few years. In 1898 he had made his second visit to the Middle East and announced in Damascus that three hundred million Muslims could look on him as a friend. Later he confided to the Brandenburg Provincial Diet that he had stood on the Mount of Olives and renewed "his military oath of service to Heaven." At the end of 1900 he laid the foundation stone of a museum near Homburg amid scenes recalling the glory that was Germania, where "Roman warriors mingled with friendly German chieftains clad in the skins of bears," which moved the kaiser to predict that in future *Civis Romanus sum* would be overshadowed by "I am a German citizen." Pride, some thought, was riding for a fall. But early in July 1900

Wilhelm vaulted higher still. He was at Bremerhaven to review his troops bound for Peking, where the Boxer Rising* had done enough damage to give the Powers a pretext for pushing deeper into China without showing either the energy or the savagery that might have brought victory to its cause. Booted, belted and helmeted, the kaiser had stood by the waiting ships and harangued his grenadiers. "When you meet the foe you will defeat him," he had ordered. "No quarter will be given, no prisoners will be taken. Let all who fall into your hands be at your mercy. Just as the Huns, a thousand years ago, under the leadership of Attila, gained a reputation in virtue of which they still live in historical tradition, so may the name of Germany become known in such a manner in China that no Chinaman will ever again even dare to look askance at a German." Such bombast was frightfulness itself, causing even the kaiser's men to shift in embarrassment, for they were decent burghers at heart. In any event it was the Russians who were worst behaved, as many had suspected they might be. The British minister in Peking wrote to Her Majesty after the Legations had been relieved: "The Russians are behaving like wild beasts, ravishing women and plundering and murdering on each side and the Sikhs were heard to say 'These brutes shall never cross our frontier nor have a chance of invading India!'"

The news of Queen Victoria's death came to Richard at Aden, as he was on his way to rejoin his battalion after six months' sick leave at home recovering from enteric fever. He had found his

---

* More properly the "Righteous Harmony Fists," the Boxers had begun as a secret organization favored by the Chinese government and pledged to extirpate all foreigners. They proclaimed: "Telegraphs and railways have been established, foreign cannon and rifles manufactured; railway engines and electric lights the foreign devils delight in. Though they ride in sedan chairs unbefitting their rank, China still regards them as barbarians of whom Heaven disapproves; and it is for their destruction that Spirits and Genii are now sent down on earth." The Boxers believed, of course, that they were impervious to bullet and sword, but their Spirits and Genii proved no match for German generalship and Japanese infantry. Those who were still alive joined that real revolutionary, Sun Yat-sen.

father as affectionate and undemonstrative as ever and his mother friendly but still withdrawn. But his old horse Melksham had come galloping up with tail streaming and ears pricked and had nuzzled him vigorously all over the face. When Richard had lain down on the sweet, familiar grass, glad to be home, Melksham, collapsing beside him, had dropped his not very handsome head on Richard's lap. While Richard had been recuperating the Royal Fusiliers had been moved to Mandalay in Burma, governed as a province of British India. A vessel of the Royal Indian Marine took Richard from Calcutta to Rangoon to join his regiment but no sooner had he begun to settle back into the routine than he was returned to India. The hot season was approaching, so the battalion intended to send its sick and convalescent to a hill station, as was the practice. The subaltern who was to have been in charge had been badly reported on that year and so was sentenced to swelter in the jungle for expiation. His place was taken by Richard, whose report had read: "A good worker, quiet, clear-headed and will do well. Very keen on sport and an authority on ornithology, of which he has made a special study," and whose health was now excellent. Richard arrived with his suffering command at Wellington in the Nilgiri Hills of southern India in April 1901.

Wellington was the military equivalent of a civilian resort nearby, so embedded in the affections of generations of British that many preferred to live out their lives there instead of going home. So delightful a facsimile of Home was Ootacamund, indeed, that it might have been a blessed plot of English earth preserved forever like the magic scenes in Victorian parlors sealed under glass domes. Lord Lytton had written of it in rapture to his wife: "Imagine Hertfordshire lanes, Devonshire downs, Westmoreland lakes, Scotch trout streams. Such beautiful *English* rain, such delicious *English* mud." These insular delights thrilled Richard less than they did the men who had spent their lives on the searing plains of Madras or among the baking valleys on the Frontier, but he was pleased to discover new varieties of birds not yet in his collection and an abundance of butterflies of astonishing beauty awaiting only the consummation of the killing-bottle. There was a smaller resort closer to the barracks than Ooty but its tennis courts and race course could not outweigh its more convalescent atmosphere. Coonoor was favored by those of delicate health, who could be seen approaching their lodgings among the eucalyptus and the mimosa drawn by teams of trotting bullocks whose horns were capped with silver. From Wellington's barracks, spreading like a white barrier halfway up the hillside that overshadowed the town, it was three miles to Coonoor and a mere nine to Ooty.

The difference in distance was compensated for by the presence in Ooty of a Hunt. Duties at Wellington were light, so it was easy for Richard to put in a day here and there with the Ootacamund Hunt's foxhounds brought from England, whose belling chimed through the English gorse scattered over the Nilgiri downlands like an echo from an English shire. The pack hunted jackals which were not, it had to be admitted, in the same class as good Leicestershire foxes; nor, it had to be confessed, was protocol quite so strict, for the pack sometimes followed a second jackal when the scent of the first crossed his. In really thick country, however, the nostalgic English image would shatter occasionally when a quick strangled yelp and a suddenly depleted pack following the line announced a fatal encounter with a panther.

Much of the area around Ooty and Wellington was preserved, but there was still game in the more remote hills and in Mysore at the northern foot of the Nilgiris. A hunting trip, or *shikari,* even of the modest kind suited to a subaltern's station, was no spur-of-the-moment enterprise: much preliminary planning and correspondence were needed before the best locations and times could be chosen, a string of porters and specialists assembled, stores bought, and for tiger an elephant or two hired, for the habit of sitting in a tree waiting for a beast to come to tethered bait was not yet popular. Besides *shikari* clothes, which in Richard's case always included shorts, to everyone's horror, ordinary suits and perhaps an evening jacket were de rigueur for social occasions that were quite likely to occur in the remotest spots. A folding bath, a table and chairs, lanterns, cooking pots, tools and bedding were divided into loads for the porters, not forgetting a medicine chest in which the wise man packed plenty of ointment, castor oil, permanganate of potash and quinine for the villagers who were bound to come to the camp in patient droves as soon as they saw a white man. In these spacious days a man could find himself comfortably ensconced high in the Himalayas with as many of his household goods about him as usual and nothing to mar his pleasure but the temperature of his bath water.

The indispensable member of the expedition was the *shikari* himself, usually a wiry, elderly fellow who knew the country and had informants dotted all over it to tell him where the game currently lay. The *shikari* led the hunter to the quarry and when it was slain attended to the preservation of whatever was to be taken as a trophy. The great cats were always skinned, of course, in the more luxurious ventures by specialists, but more often by the *shikari* and the hunter himself. The inside of the pelt would be rubbed hard with arsenical soap, rolled into a wet bundle with the head or skull inside it and given to a runner for delivery to the nearest taxidermist. When a tiger was shot the *shikari* was careful to preserve two small bones that were called the wing bones and were believed to have survived the tiger's transmogrification from his original form as a griffin. At night, lying in his tent beneath a mosquito net, Richard would hear the voices talking of such marvels and wish himself no finer life. Before he left the Nilgiris Richard was able to enter in his game book two tigers, both male and one measuring ten feet four inches from muzzle to tip of tail, two leopards, one of each sex, and three Indian bison, one a superb bull standing seventy-one inches at the shoulder. These additions to Richard's tally cost him a total of seven shots.

His daily routine in the convalescent depot had its minor irritations. The other subalterns there were equally energetic and devoted to their profession, but they were damped by the senior officers, among whom was an adjutant too pompous for safety. One morning at breakfast, finding a medium-sized black beetle in his coffee, Richard complained quite dispassionately, "I have a beetle in my coffee." The adjutant grunted, "You ought to be thankful you get any coffee at all!" and continued to read his antique copy of *The Times*. Scenting mischief, Richard said slowly, "But we don't *like* black beetles in our coffee." It was too much. The adjutant rose to the bait in morning wrath, screaming about insubordination. In one swift flowing movement Richard got up, tugged the cloth from the table, and deposited butter, coffee, marmalade and some rather sorry toast into the adjutant's lap, and left at a run.

He was also put out by the commanding officer's refusal to let him train his detachment in the open country, but after four months in Wellington the men were well enough to work and Richard defied orders. He took his troops some distance from the cantonment on an exercise demonstrating the best way to ambush a convoy. In his unconventional fashion he made every man wreath his helmet with ferns for camouflage before getting into position along the road by which his imaginary convoy was to pass. Unfortunately the camp commander was just returning from his morning canter by the same route. When a hundred and fifty infantrymen suddenly opened up with a joyful fusillade, his horse threw him and galloped home. Purple and spluttering, he ordered the men to remove their "vegetable gardens" and return at once to the decency of the barracks. Next morning in the Orderly Room he addressed Richard on the subject of defacing the King's uniform. "Fancy placing a man like that in charge of troops!" Richard wrote in his diary.

The only regrets Richard felt on leaving Wellington were for its superior facilities for diversion. He had been there long enough to sample most of the delights of the season, including the famous Flower Show on the sloping lawns of Government House in Ooty between the bandstand melodious with the very latest London hits and the classic pillars of authority's seat. As with every one of Ooty's affairs the effort that went into the show was prodigious. Blooms of every kind and color scented that decorous air, while even the competition for decorating "infantile carriages" brought forth such endeavors as a palanquin fashioned of white blossoms with a V picked out in violets on its canopy and with six resplendent little Indian boys as blackamoors to carry it. With memories of his childhood sufferings at the dancing class still painful, Richard tended to partake of Ooty's more sophisticated fare only lightly.

He felt uncomfortable in formal clothes, found conversation artificial, and suspected hostesses of planting him next to the dullest wits. He wrote with conviction: "I despise the overfed, overdressed, empty-brained, amusement-loving creatures who constitute but a small minority of society women; but I am never so content as I am when in company with the healthier and more sensible type." He had once run away from Mottisfont to avoid one of his mother's dances, excusing himself with "I only make myself ridiculous and no girl can possibly derive any pleasure from dancing with me." His dance programs at Ooty remained blank because he could recall the big ball at Mottisfont when he had claimed as partner a young heiress whose wealth was great enough to outweigh her undeniable plumpness. At the end of the dance, pencil poised on the end of the silken cord that attached it to the program, Richard had felt bound to ask in spite of having bumped into every couple in the room, "May I have the last dance with you?" The girl had been crushing. "You've had it!" she said. Richard took to the floor only once again in his whole life, in a ship bound from Bombay to Suez. He was then forty-five years old and his partner was the immortal *ballerina assoluta* Pavlova. She had no command of ballroom dancing and Richard repeatedly trod on her toes.

The more decadent joys of the Nilgiri Hills did not soften Richard but the gay inconsequent atmosphere of the place caught even his austere inclinations. It was unreal, a lotus land, but when orders came for him to return to his battalion in Burma he left it with at least partial regret. The Royal Fusiliers had undergone some changes during his absence, the most important of which was the formation of a mounted infantry company. This organization was the army's very latest innovation, currently thought to be the most important lesson learned from the Boer War, and an attempt to lend great mobility to the infantry ready for the next conflict, which must surely be a war of movement. Richard embraced his new task with enthusiasm. With his troops on horseback he could easily get them away from the cantonment and out of sight of his creaking superiors. He gave them riding drill until they ached, he hid in his bungalow to study forbidden manuals of tactics, still an unpopular pastime with his seniors, and then poured his new knowledge over his company until they groaned. But they took it and they liked him. They sensed a professional. In a couple of months he brought them to such a pitch that the brigadier remarked on their efficiency.

But Richard was having trouble with his new colonel. Stanley Bird was a little unusual for an officer of his rank at that time in that he had graduated from Staff College. But his temper was uncertain at best, and when he surrendered to his frequently liverish mood his language was violent and vile. One Sunday in January 1902 Colonel Bird joined Richard for a snipe shoot that Richard had arranged at his request, buying the lunch and hiring the beaters. The colonel insisted on a two-hour siesta after lunch, to Richard's annoyance. Next morning Richard was astonished when the colonel called him to the Orderly Room to ask what the devil he meant by absenting himself from Sunday morning Church Parade. Confused by so illogical an attack, Richard explained that he obviously had not requested leave because the colonel had invited him to shoot. This loosed a tirade, ending in a threat to place Richard under arrest. That night Richard wrote a formal letter to the colonel asking to be transferred to another unit, preferably in Africa. The colonel replied blandly, hoping that Richard would forget the whole thing, which had been merely a fit of temper. But Richard was determined. He threatened to resign his commission unless his original request was forwarded.

Not long afterward his chance came: volunteers were needed to officer the local forces being raised in East Africa and Richard applied at once on the appropriate form. By now his reputation had spread beyond the battalion, engaging the interest of powerful men. Sir Hector Archibald Macdonald was an authentic national hero who, born the son of a Scottish crofter, had risen by gallantry and brilliance from private in the Gordon Highlanders to major general, Knight of the Most Honorable Order of the Bath and Aide-de-Camp to the late Queen. He was known throughout the army as "Fighting Mac." He had fought with Roberts' vanguard all the way to Kandahar, against the Boers at the fatal hill of Majuba, and with

Kitchener from the Egyptian frontier as far as Omdurman, where his coolness and skill in turning his brigade to meet the dervishes' unexpected charge had saved Kitchener's reputation. He had received the thanks of both Houses of Parliament. Later he had led the Highland Brigade in action after action against the Boers. He was a little above average height and his shoulders were so packed with muscle that they seemed stooped; he wore his hair close-cropped and his style was spare, deliberate and open. As far as the troops were concerned he was the most popular soldier in the army. At the end of April 1902 Sir Hector wrote to Richard Meinertzhagen offering him an appointment as aide-de-camp at his headquarters in Ceylon, where he was commander. It was a brilliant recognition, but Richard at once cabled his refusal, which as things turned out was perhaps as well,* partly on the grounds that he would never enjoy such a sedentary and social appointment. But his principal reason was that three days before he had received new orders. He was required to embark at once from the Port of Rangoon and report at the earliest possible date at Mombasa on the east coast of Africa. He was on the edge of a lyric period of his life, the happiest years he had yet known. They would be filled with blood.

---

* A year later what a contemporary account called "an opprobrious accusation" was leveled against Sir Hector. He traveled to London to consult the War Office. An inquiry was ordered. Setting out for Ceylon to face it, Macdonald stopped off in Paris, took a room at the Hotel Regina, and there shot himself, leaving a widow and a son. He was memorialized by a hundred-foot stone tower at Dingwall in Scotland.

CHAPTER 8

The Black Man Will Benefit and Cooperate

At the beginning of the twenti-
eth century East Africa was a country raw as the carcass of a zebra
newly flayed. It was a land without fat, and without mercy, sun-
beaten, dry and sanguine. Its rivers sloughed a red silt into the sea as
if the earth were bleeding; its mountains were touched at sunset with
a pale red fire and whatever moved inland toward them became
powdered with a dull red dust; over the fort at its entrance, the port
of Mombasa, flew the flag of the sultan of Zanzibar, the color of
blood. Everything in the land spoke stridently of blood, of the stark
division between bubbling life and the sudden blankness of death.
Pain was mute, for suffering and deprivation had washed over the
land for centuries. The strong survived, the weak were left to die; all
else was vanity. It could have been a country made expressly for
Richard Meinertzhagen.

He arrived off Mombasa on May 12, 1902, in the German
freighter *Safari,* sliding below the buff blank walls of Fort Jesus,
where the Portuguese had prayed to the Virgin to deliver them
from the Arabs, and into the harbor packed with dhows, their
high poops carved and set with false windows in the manner learned
from Vasco da Gama's galleons. In the cool of the late afternoon
their masters lay indolently, lean and dangerous, on Persian rugs,

waiting for the last of their cargoes before they lumbered on the monsoon to Aden, Muscat, Kutch or Bombay. They had brought camels, dates and rugs, and they carried back cloves and sharks' fins, mangrove poles, sacks of frankincense and myrrh from Somaliland, and perhaps illicit ivory and rhinoceros horn. Two hundred or more dhows would arrive in the season, each a hundred and fifty tons of Malabar teak shining a dull gold from its fish-oil dressing, their lateen sails slicing toward the languorous islands of Lamu and Pemba and Zanzibar, a reminder of the power that once held the coast for the desert lords of Oman.

At first glance Mombasa was an Arab town, all white and green and jasmine-scented. Richard was absorbed at once. He went ashore in darkness, knowing no one and speaking no word of any useful language. His heaps of baggage were claimed by the customs officials—it seemed in perpetuity—but a porter, jabbering Swahili, took the initiative and one essential bag and led Richard through a narrow alley perfect for a murder and into the grounds of a building where loud, cheerful English voices were ordering drinks. It was the Mombasa Club, pride of East Africa, and not at all unlike the clubs Richard had known in India and Burma, the chief difference lying in the size, numbers and variety of the snarling heads and curling horns along its walls. He was given a room and dined with two other officers just arrived to join his new regiment. But Richard's mind was traveling far beyond his trade; that night he wrote in his diary, "the Dark Continent has me firmly in her grip." The immense land mass on which he now had a foothold was in fact a lot darker than he could possibly have imagined. A stygian ignorance pressed upon its peoples and lapped even over those who had come to rule and to enlighten them. The indigenous cultures of the savannas, forests and deserts of East Africa knew no means of writing or of counting except on the fingers or by notching sticks. Time was measured by the alternation of light and darkness, by the seasonal migration of game, or by the flowering of trees. When the British East Africa Company had received its Royal Charter in 1887, the year of Queen Victoria's Golden Jubilee (celebrated by Richard at the Aysgarth School bonfire), its inhabitants had been far more primitive than had the woad-painted Britons when the first Roman galleys had arrived. By 1902 the tribesmen of the interior had taken a preliminary step toward the rudiments of civilization: they had learned that the rifle was more powerful than the spear. Many of them, however, still chose to ignore that lesson.

The reasons for the British incursion into East Africa were complex and to some extent involuntary. When Richard Meinertzhagen was born the area was known only from the journals of a handful of explorers and missionaries, who reported it given over to barbarism, swept by Arab slavers, and blessed with extraordinary natural beauty. The principal catalysts of the change were two Scots. Sir William Mackinnon of the British India Steam Navigation Company saw possibilities of trade, though these must have been long-term indeed since the natives survived by subsistence farming or on the milk of cattle, practiced no commerce more advanced than barter, and used cowrie shells as occasional currency. Sir John Kirk, agent and consul at Zanzibar, saw the territory as a target for British political interest and a field for pioneer work in the abolition of slavery. Kirk had trudged with Livingstone along the Zambesi, had stood beside him when that saintly man first set eyes on Lake Nyasa, and had helped carry him to his grave in Westminster Abbey. Patient and tenacious, Kirk had at length persuaded the sultan Barghash, whose accession had been secured over other contenders, as he himself put it, by the length of his sword, to close the slave market in Zanzibar in 1873.

At its height the trade had dealt annually with between eighty and a hundred thousand bodies brought eastward from the edges of the Congo and southward from the Ethiopian border and consigned to Arabia, Persia and even India. The bare feet of this human traffic had beaten flat the only roads in Africa. It had been a singularly economic and efficient business, affording the single instance of an industry in which transportation produced a greater profit than the goods carried, even though those goods were ivory and rhinoceros horn.* The sultan's governors controlled a strip of the coast ten miles deep and six hundred long. Beyond that the slavers roamed as masters.

Gradually the Victorians, out of conscience, suppressed the trade, but not at once; even after Kirk's efforts with the sultan the yoked caravans still clanked toward Mombasa and clandestine markets. In 1886 Britain and Germany defined their spheres of influence in the sultan's East African dominions, the former to the north and the latter to the south. By then two necessities were emerging for the British: slaving could not be abolished without administration far inland, which meant a railroad; and the Germans and the French (expanding to the northwest) must be prevented from acquiring the headwaters of the Nile, Egypt's lifeline. This too meant a railroad. Before much longer it also became clear that the Imperial British East Africa Company could not by itself develop or even administer its vast domains, so in March 1895 the British Treasury paid into the Company's coffers a quarter of a million pounds. The Company was wound up, still with a huge deficit, and the territory became a Protectorate of the Crown. The East Africa Protectorate was then governed by a commissioner with a hierarchy of sub-commissioners and district officers, these latter with functions approaching omnipotence, for each of them was charged with duties embracing practical administration, justice and finance over an area as big as an English county. For muscle the government relied on police recruited from the native population and in times of serious trouble the military could be called in.

---

* The horn was greatly valued in the Orient and particularly in China for its aphrodisiac powers when powdered and mixed with other stimulants. In Arabia it was used for the hafts of daggers to which it lent the magical ability to turn aside any ordinary blade. Princes favored it for cups, for it could also indicate the presence of poison in a drink or nullify its effects; the one prized by the khalifa Abdullahi may still be seen in his house in Omdurman. Though in fact a conglomeration of hair, the horn could be carved like bone and when finished displayed a pleasant, light brown translucence. Its popularity has not diminished with the years; an advertisement seeking it was still appearing regularly in the personal column of *The Times* in the 1960s.

At the end of 1901, six months before Richard Meinertzhagen joined the military forces of the protectorate, the last spike of the railroad had been driven home on the shore of Lake Victoria Nyanza. Each of its five hundred and eighty-two miles from Mombasa on the coast had cost the British taxpayer nine thousand five hundred pounds, and the construction gangs who worked on it a few Indian coolies. It had taken less than five and a half years to push it through rock and swamp, across waterless plains and over the shoulders of mountains, its bridges menaced by flash floods, its track by shifting mud, and its personnel by man-eating lions. Now at last it was open for business—if there was any business. So far the main activity along it had been troop movements, and to the officers of the King's African Rifles, of whom Richard was now one, it seemed as though the railway was merely a romantic notion they would spend the rest of their lives protecting. To the natives it was a source of ornaments for their women and steel for their weapons. They included a tribe as fierce as any in Africa.

Richard's first day in Africa was a delight. Immediately after breakfast he extricated his belongings from the Mombasa customs and installed himself in a house with his two new acquaintances. The rest of the day he spent marveling, propelled by two coolies through Mombasa township in a trolley. The miniature track ran along the principal street and branched away at numbers of offices and private houses whose residents, of course, maintained private trolleys. Richard thought it a novel way of traveling that compensated for the deficiency in any new kinds of birds. He had to be satisfied with some tropical swifts and a great number of butterflies. Outside the town the countryside was spread with dense bush with a small forest of banyan trees to the south shading the ruins of some Portuguese forts. During the afternoon Richard came to a gathering of baobabs, the grotesque trees that from the gnarled entanglement of their branches seemed to have been uprooted and turned over, and found there some gigantic snails the size of baseballs. They were sought after as a delicacy, having the flavor of kidney but the consistency of rubber. The next day Richard took the train for a two-day journey into the immense hinterland.

His new regiment had recently moved its headquarters inland to Nairobi after a thorough reorganization. The 3rd Battalion of the King's African Rifles had been brought up to a full strength of twenty-five white officers for its seven rifle companies and one camel company of black askaris drawn from various tribes. Though its command remained in Nairobi the battalion was spread across great distances in company or smaller groups that filled their days with patrols and occasional minor wars. The battalion's camel company was far away across the Tana River, operating in the dry wastes where the Somali nomads wandered. Three hundred and fifty of the battalion's men were even further off in Jubaland and three hundred more had just been sent to Fort Ternan to assist its garrison in patrolling the railroad.

The first thing Richard saw from his carriage window when he awoke was seven cock ostriches quietly feeding right outside. Opening the window he caught sight of Kilimanjaro shining in the sun, and mile upon mile of open plain across which were slowly grazing enormous herds of hartebeest and zebra, one of which alone he estimated at several thousand head. As was the custom, the train had stopped for the night, but now in the early morning it set off again toward Nairobi. Soon there were falcons flying over it like heralds. Their purpose was practical. The train flushed doves from the telegraph wires beside the track and the falcons swooped on them as they scattered. At Athi River station, twenty-five miles out of Nairobi, Richard began to count the game on the south side of the track. His tally came to five rhino, eighteen giraffe, seven hundred and sixty wildebeest, four thousand and six zebra, nearly nine hundred hartebeest, more than five hundred gazelle, twenty-four ostrich and sixteen baboon.

The adjutant was waiting at Nairobi station. He had won his commision from the ranks at Omdurman and retained the brisk manner of a sergeant major, but Richard took to him. It was a cool, fresh day and they drove pleasantly away from the station westward toward some higher ground. In the distance Richard could see a scattering of unfinished corrugated-iron huts and lines of tents below them. They were the new barracks, begun two months before when bubonic plague had broken out in the old mud and wattle huts and most of the town had been burned to the ground. It was no loss. The railroad had reached Nairobi from Mombasa three years before; then it had been a windswept papyrus swamp without a single tree, christened by the Masai "place of cold water" and pock-marked with pits dug for the game that came to drink there. The railroad brought workshops, store dumps and Indian construction gangs and the gangs brought filth and disease. They crowded together in labyrinths of tumbledown shacks without design and without any kind of sanitation; the ground in the slippery alleys gave underfoot like a noxious crust, and those who walked there were the dregs of the coast and human refuse cast out by the local tribes. Within months the slum was razed by fire one crazy night by a strange martinet colonel of engineers who left the country shortly afterward. His name was J. D. Patterson and he had been the nemesis of the man-eating lions of Tsavo.*

Much of this now ancient history the adjutant recounted as he drove Richard past Wood's Hotel and the new Club and Jevanjee the Parsee's soda water factory. There were few enough comforts in Nairobi but already one or two long, low roofs on the higher ground indicated the more luxurious homes of senior officials. By the time they got to the Mess, where Richard met the two other officers then at headquarters, all the others being on some far-flung duty or other, he had been briefed on the military situation. He summarized it with, "We should have six companies here but most of them are

---

* During the building of the railroad at Tsavo, hundreds of Indian rail-road coolies had been petrified into complete inactivity by these particularly cunning and ferocious beasts, probably the only animals ever to frustrate an Imperial design. What gave the affair its peculiar quality of nightmare was the extraordinary sagacity of the man-eaters in avoiding traps while maintaining a horrible frequency of kills, and the discovery that they appeared to be suck-ing the blood from their victims. This latter aberration was in fact not at all strange. A lion always licks its prey; the thin skin of humanity offered slight resistance to tongues abrasive as files, so the man-eaters were tempted to lick a little longer. Scores of lions were killed near Tsavo but it was generally accepted than the two shot by Colonel Patterson after months of spiritual anguish were the man-eaters. They may still be seen, far from svelte and not at all terrifying, in the Museum of Natural History in Chicago, Illinois.

up the line protecting the railway coolies from a tribe called the Nandi." As he closed his diary and climbed into bed the demented howl of a hyena rose into the night. No trumpet could have sounded sweeter. Next morning he was assigned to Number 8 Company and got his first hint of trouble. Two askaris, as the black rank and file were called, were being sentenced at the Orderly Room, one for having saluted so smartly that the officer to whom the courtesy had been addressed had been thrown by his horse, and the other for having been found in bed with the sergeant major's wife. The former was given ten, and the latter twenty-five, lashes on the bare backside with a whip made of rhinoceros hide. Richard was revolted by this injustice but when he took a look at his new company he was even more shocked. Walking along the ranks, he lifted the tarboosh from the head of one of his askaris. Underneath was a seething mass of lice. Rifles were corroded, uniforms greasy with dirt, and, worst of all, the men were sullen. It was clear that the Meinertzhagen command would have to be given a rough time, but not by flogging. When Richard reported one of his men for insubordination, in that he had called his sergeant's mother and father a crocodile and a hyena respectively, he was appalled when the senior officer awarded twenty-five lashes. Richard had to witness the punishment, which was extremely bloody. Sickened and angry, he went back to the Orderly Room and declared that flogging should only be used against crimes of violence and that in any case the prisoner should be discharged from the regiment afterward in view of the degradation it involved. He announced that no man in his company would be flogged in the future as long as he served with it. Richard's brother officers lacked the moral courage to refute him or to confront him directly, but only the adjutant spoke to him again in a way at all friendly. In his new ocean Richard Meinertzhagen had begun once more to swim against the tide.

The effort did not tax him for, as he put it in his diary:

> *They say I'm a quarrelsome fellow.*
> *God rot it, how can that be?*
> *For I never quarrel with any—*
> *The whole world quarrels with me.*

Discipline was not the only matter of controversy. Richard was disgusted by the behavior of all his colleagues but the adjutant. One drank himself into a stupor every evening, another "prefers boys to women and is not ashamed," others brought native concubines into the Mess, all talked smut, and most were heavily in debt. His popularity was not increased by his rather priggish announcement that unless they reformed he would submit a formal complaint. Fortunately he found some social life outside the regiment among men of a different stature. The deputy commissioner for Ukamba Province, of which Nairobi was the administrative center, was Frederick Jackson,* a forthright and experienced man whom Richard had first met in Bowdler Sharpe's sociable Bird Room at the Natural History Museum just before leaving Harrow. Jackson's writ ran through the Province, but he was charming enough to make a young captain feel welcome. They soon found a common interest beyond ornithology and fell into a vigorous discussion of the merits of small against large bore rifles for stopping power. Jackson had already written the Africa section of the standard work on big game shooting, and Richard thus far in Africa had shot one Thompson's gazelle but he did not allow the discrepancy to diminish the vigor of his argument. He had, after all, two tigers in his game book.

The topic had arisen from the bedraggled arrival that day in Nairobi of one Roberts, one of the first sportsmen to come to the territory after big game. Big game, unhappily, had come to him. He had hit a lion in the belly with his first shot, then, changing rifles, had hit him again, this time with a .450 bullet from a cordite

---

* Sir Frederick John Jackson (1860–1929), as he became, joined the Imperial East Africa Company in 1888 when the independent means that had supported his hunting and collecting expeditions around Lahu and Kilimanjaro suddenly vanished. He was sent to explore the hinterland, make friends with chiefs, and if possible find Stanley returning with the rescued Emin Pasha. He was chiefly responsible for foiling the plans of the sadistic German agent Dr. Karl Peters to annex Uganda. Jackson eventually entered the government service there. He helped quench a Sudanese mutiny in the Eldama Ravine in 1897 and a Nandi uprising in 1900. From 1911 to 1917 he was governor of Uganda. His collection of birds numbered over twelve thousand specimens of seven hundred and forty-four species.

cartridge. Thereupon the lion had charged at Roberts' gunbearer. Roberts socked the lion again with the .450, once in the lower jaw and once in the shoulder. The lion sustained another bullet in the jaw and one in the chest en route to Roberts, and toppled him like a doll. "With great presence of mind," Richard reported, "Roberts gave him his arm to maul while he got another cartridge into his rifle." Roberts then blew out the lion's brains. "That," Richard concluded, "is just the type of real good game lion I want to meet."

Richard's discussion with Jackson hardly touched on the sufferings of poor Roberts or on his chances of recovery, but rather on the doubtful killing power of the new cordite rifles. Richard's feeling was that Roberts would have been better off with a twelve-bore Paradox, a weapon that was rifled only near the muzzle to combine some of the accuracy of the rifle with the blasting power of the gun. Jackson believed in large bores, producing for proof the analogy of the fist and the skewer. If, he maintained, a man were hit in the chest by a fist with sufficient force he would be knocked down, but a skewer striking with the same force, though it penetrated, would not knock him down. Moreover, the harder the blow from the skewer the less it would be felt. Richard opposed this with the argument that a small-bore rifle was handier and more accurate and that a man should never fire unless he was properly placed for a killing shot. With all the assurance of his two weeks in East Africa he pointed out that he *always* relied on his first shot at dangerous game to put them completely out of action. This emphasis on technical matters in preference to human sympathy was due less to insensitivity than to the fact that Roberts' adventure had come dangerously close to cliché. The first six graves in Nairobi's new European cemetery were occupied by men who had died from the teeth and claws of lions, and every week there came news of another unfortunate mauled.*

---

* Few of the survivors, however, described their experience with the verve of the Major Williams who was with Theodore Roosevelt and Selous on the Uasin Gishu plateau in 1909. Williams had hit a charging lion in the shoulder without effect and just had time to club the beast on the head with his rifle barrel before it sank its teeth into his leg and grumpily began to shake him from side to side. It then dragged Williams through the bush but found its

So far Richard had not even seen a lion. He had to spend his mornings going about his military duties, but most afternoons and evenings he was free to wander the plains. One afternoon he came across a lot of skeletons, all that was left of a group of Masai killed by the famine of the previous year. Instinctively the collector Richard picked out two or three of the most attractive ones. Some while later, with skulls from some other tribes, he presented them to the Royal College of Surgeons. Living Masai he found less easy to categorize and file away; when one came loping up to him on the plain south of Nairobi he committed something of a social gaffe. The Masai came up with a grin, hefted his spear across to his left hand, and spat into the palm of his right, which he then extended to Richard with every evidence of affability. Richard could not bring himself to shake hands. What he should have done, of course, was spit into the herdsman's palm with as much velocity and volume as he could muster.

There were no more than fifty thousand Masai in the whole territory at that time but they had already attracted strong feelings, both for and against them, among the white men. Their partisans saw them as the epitome of the noble savage, tall and lean and haughty, living in austerity on their dry plains and calling no man master. They had a reputation for ferocity not wholly warranted but certainly accentuated by the headdresses of lions' manes they affected on occasion. Lord Delamere, the leader of the white settlers, adored the Masai for their bravery, but Lord Delamere's judgment in such matters tended to the standards of a Captain of Cricket.

---

way stopped by a mass of thorns. "Suddenly," Williams recounted, "he seemed to become more angry, changing his direction, and in so doing pulled my leg out of joint from the hip, the noise from which alarmed me. The chosen corner found, he settled down and lay three-quarters across me with the claws of his front paws securing me by the thighs and back, and his teeth never relaxed. I had made up my mind, when he had finished with my leg, and tried elsewhere, I would try to jam my rifle barrels down his throat, though I really doubt if I should have succeeded." Williams was not to be put to this desperate expedient, for his bearer drove the lion off and Williams, firing from the hip, shot it dead. He recovered, carrying away with him "the very happiest recollections of that little hospital right away in the heart of Africa."

Frederick Jackson had long since been struck by the notion that their truculence had been exaggerated by traders wishing to keep the doors of commerce closed. The commissioner, Sir Charles Eliot, whose views certainly mattered, put his own attitude toward the Masai in writing with: "Their habits may be interesting to anthropologists but they are socially and politically abominable. Their love of raiding is a danger to the public peace, and the arrangement by which the warriors do not marry, but live in separate villages with the immature girls, is a moral scandal and physically disastrous for the race."

None could deny the Masai their arrogant red beauty but few knew enough about them to assess their real worth. They themselves were vague about their origins but they were probably Nilo-Hamites. The whole center of their existence was their cattle and they ranged with them, in their separate divisions, as far as the Tana River and the outposts of the Nandi, for whom as warriors they were no match. They had a standing army but its chief purpose was the protection and acquisition of cattle; it was for this purpose that the warriors were segregated. They were the young men in their prime, cloistered and forbidden beer, tobacco and marriage. Their sweethearts (those "immature girls" deplored by Sir Charles Eliot) camped with them but under a chaperonage by the warriors' mothers and aunts both ferocious and efficient. The Masai ate no fish nor fowl, killed no game but eland, and seldom indulged in meat. They grew nothing, since agriculture was beneath their dignity. They were renowned as drinkers of blood—much of their glamour relied on it—but they only did so in times of drought. Mostly they drank milk, preferably curdled, out of gourds flavored by plunging smoking slivers of wild olive wood into them. Their herds were enormous and it was their conviction, based on the legend of their birth, that all the cattle in the world belonged to them. None of this, however, made the Masai a threat to good government. Richard never found himself making punitive expeditions against them but only against other tribes with Masai irregulars to help him.

Throughout his first month in Nairobi Richard was still

overwhelmed by the game that clotted the outskirts of the town. Every day he made his count of animals, even of the Masai cattle, and he had begun to sit outside in the darkness after dinner, just listening. Almost always there were lion roaring. He wrote, "This is certainly a wonderful place and exceeds my wildest dreams of Africa's big game; I fear I am developing a blood lust, but I must improve my rifle shooting if I am to do any good."

As a result of his meticulous attentions during working hours, his company had begun to look like soldiers. Richard himself thought he looked very smart in his King's African Rifles uniform of khaki drill tunic high at the neck and trousers bound below the knee with dark blue puttees, the whole crowned by a red tarboosh with tassel. He had himself photographed sitting on the steps of his iron-walled cabin, swagger stick in one hand and black local cigar between the fingers of the other. He was long-legged, big-boned and supple, and his shoulders sloped with power. His hair was cropped short at the sides, making his face seem too plump for one of such burning energy. His lips were slightly parted in a half-unwilling smile and the eyes were dark, friendly and direct.

At the end of the second week in June 1902 Richard embarked on his first journey into the bush. It was not Homeric. He had with him twelve askaris and twenty-three native porters each with a load of fifty pounds and food for four days. He was headed for Fort Hall, some fifty miles from Nairobi, in Kikuyu country, where he was to take charge of the KAR detachment and preserve the King's peace. He made eleven miles on the first day out and saw his first lion as he camped, but he was growing angry at sighting so many birds that he could not identify for lack of a handbook. He met his first Kikuyu at Punde Milia (Zebra Camp), an elder who brought a hen as a present. The old man was anxious to talk and chanced to mention, finding a good listener, that all the fingers of his right hand had recently been chopped off in a fight. Though Richard showed no sign of disbelief he insisted on supporting his tale by shaking out the fingers from a small tobacco can. Beyond Punde Milia the Kikuyu farms began and soon after dawn the next morning the small column began to pass by plantations of bananas, cassava and yams and scattered fields of maize, beans and millet. It was rolling country rising up to the cold forests of the Aberdares, whose eastern slopes formed one boundary of the Kikuyus' land, the other being the southwestern slopes of Mount Kenya, home of their god Ngai and named by them "cock ostrich" for the blackness of its jagged peaks and the pure white of the snows between them.

The Kikuyu were a comfortable people, for their red land was rich enough to give them two crops a year, but as a nation they were fragmented. They lived in families and small groups of families and thought of their tribe as a ramification of their own circle, so they had never developed a means, political or social, of operating the tribe as a single unit. Not even those close to the Kikuyu in these early days understood their society or the history of their development. They were Bantu, part of a slow and massive migration eastward from the Congo basin that had eventually reached the East African coast. At some time in the sixteenth century the Kikuyu had headed northeast and had settled the area they called Metumi, which Richard Meinertzhagen knew as Fort Hall. The land was heavy forest, dark and cold. A more primitive people, the Dorobo, flitted through it hunting with poisoned arrows and collecting the honey of wild bees, berries and edible roots. Reaching an accommodation with the Dorobo, the Kikuyu painfully hacked out farms for themselves, each owned by one man or by a group of men in the same clan. Kikuyu culture was based firmly on the ownership of land, a condition which was to cause a good deal of trouble; in the first place the Kikuyu had as they thought bought the land from the Dorobo by a payment of goats. Goats were the Kikuyus' chief currency, not a source of food, and when the Dorobo ate the payment and asked for more the Kikuyu were hard pressed to explain the difference between a freehold and a leasehold. Gradually the distinction became irrelevant when the Kikuyu made it plain, sometimes by force, that they were there to stay. When the white man in turn began to take the land from the Kikuyu, its true ownership became once more controversial.

Long before Richard's arrival in the country the Kikuyu had

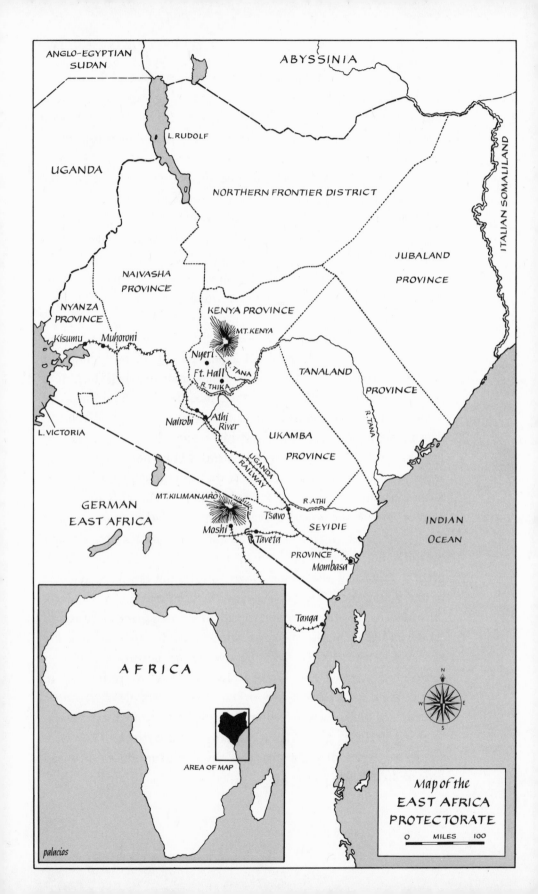

come to believe that they had originated at Fort Hall as the issue of Gikuyu and his wife Muumbi. The nine daughters of these first ancestors had been given the land thereabouts by their god Ngai and from them had descended the nine clans into which the nation was divided. A man's clan was less important socially, however, than his age-group: all men circumcised within a certain span of years belonged to the same set and it was the set which assumed what little general leadership there was of the tribe. The transfer of power from one generation to another involved everybody in a series of rituals taking years to complete and introducing a degree of tension into the reasonably bucolic existence of the tribe. One such transition was nearing its end when Richard Meinertzhagen first came to Fort Hall.

The Kikuyu arranged a dance to celebrate. Twenty young men and twenty maidens dressed, as Richard put it, "in everything but clothes," faced each other in two lines, moving their feet in a single monotonous step, swaying their shoulders back and forth and revolving their pelvises in a very amateur bump-and-grind routine. The men's heads were smeared with a pomade of red earth and mutton fat, and their legs and forearms were patterned with clay and ringed with circlets made from the government's good copper telegraph wire or the fur of colobus monkeys. The girls wore mob caps of cowrie shells and a few bandoliers of the same currency slung over their shoulders. Despite the inadequacies of its choreography the dance worked up to a fine heat, concluding with a general exodus of the young ladies toward the darkness, pursued by the young men. Richard's review of the dance that night read, "It was essentially barbaric, and lacked all sense of grace or decency." At the end of the performance he was presented with a rather sickly zorilla, a creature rarely seen because of its nocturnal habits. It looked like a skunk and Richard did not grow overly fond of it. One of the district officers at Fort Hall owned a couple of creatures more to his liking, tawny yellow and elegantly spotted with black, their big oval ears giving their cat faces a chubby look. They were servals and since they got plenty of meat with no effort they had little to do but look suave.

The two district officers at the station, the civilian overlords of the area, shared one grass hut for living quarters and another as an office, next to which a stone house was being built for the sub-commissioner. This unassuming seat of government was surrounded by a stone wall on the inside of a ditch. The police and military lines did not enjoy the wall's protection, so Richard settled in a grass hut set slightly apart from those of his men. It squatted on the edge of a bare field that served for a parade ground, much visited by crows. When they got drunk the local Kikuyu would ring the whole area shouting rude remarks and loosing off blunted arrows in its general direction, but they were always contrite the following morning.

It was not long before there was more serious trouble. A young man strolled into the fort with the news that a mail party had been attacked while making for Nairobi along the Thika River to the south. Confirmation and details came by runner at noon. A police-man and three porters had been murdered at a spot twenty-nine miles from Fort Hall. Richard set off at once, setting such a pace that his porters and askaris began to drop back one by one until he was left with only four men. It was raining and when night fell they were in thick bush country terrorized by man-eating lions. They could hear a lion tracking parallel with them and grunting so ominously that they fixed bayonets, but they arrived safely at the scene of the attack just before three o'clock in the morning. The Kikuyu had rushed the mail party's camp at night, wounding nine men and a couple of women as well as killing four, but not carrying away any loot.

One of the district officers had arrived before Richard, having been closer. Richard sent him to Fort Hall for medical supplies and dispatched a runner to Nairobi for a doctor. The district officer had not been able to face what had to be done for some of the wounded, of whom the worst afflicted were the two women. One was transfixed by a spear entering her right armpit and protruding from her left. Using a good deal of force Richard pulled it out. The other woman had taken a thrust in the stomach; maggots had already infested it and a part of the entrails had burst out. Richard cut off this inconvenient protuberance with a pair of scissors, stuffed permanganate into the wound and sewed it up. Having thus done what little he could, Richard set his men to strengthening the camp fence with more thorn bushes for protection against both Kikuyu and lion. The campfires of the former glimmered on the far side of the river but it was the latter that attacked. Richard was sleeping in the open. In the darkness a man suddenly screamed nearby. Richard rolled to his feet, revolver in hand, and saw by the fire's flicker a lion just leaping the thorn boma. It had seized one man by the buttocks, released him when he cried out, caught his neighbor by the throat and carried him off. Only the skull was left by the time it was light enough to follow the lion's pug marks. A doctor arrived the next day and Richard was able to set off for Nairobi to renew his wardrobe.

The rigors of the bush had left him with only a dirty shirt and a pair of shorts, the remainder of his clothing still lying at Fort Hall or adorning the limbs of the wounded he had left at the Thika. It was decent enough dress to visit the Masai *laibon* Lenana,* in his village just outside Nairobi, but an embarrassing condition to be caught in when a dinner invitation arrived from the residence of the commissioner. Sir Charles had discovered that Richard was the nephew of Mrs. Beatrice Webb, a lady he worshiped from afar. Priding himself on his lack of formality (a commissioner stooping to a junior officer), he insisted that Richard join him, hoping no doubt for some illuminating tid-bits about that famous and formidable woman but ignorant of his guest's violent views of Aunt Beatrice's public pronouncements. Eliot was a tall man, fair-haired and heavily built and not yet forty. A graduate of Jowett's Balliol, he had left Oxford glittering with honors and with his grounding in the classics ornamented by a knowledge of San-

---

* Lenana was the senior *laibon* of the Masai, an office having to do with medicine and ritual but not with politics. His authority led the government to consider him a chief and present him with a malacca staff embossed at the top with the Royal Arms to establish his importance. Richard innocently admired it, thus forcing Lenana, out of Masai courtesy, to hand it over. Fifty-four years later he gave Lenana's staff to Sir Evelyn Baring, then governor of Kenya.

skrit, Pali, Hebrew and Syriac, to which he later added Hindustani
and Chinese. During his first two months in the foreign service in
St. Petersburg he mastered Russian and published shortly afterward
a standard Finnish grammar; transferred to the Middle East, he
had been obliged to spend three months in Tangier to learn Arabic,
which enabled him while on duty in Constantinople to add Turkish
to his vocabulary and to write the most authoritative work on the
history and philosophy of the Ottoman Empire yet seen. As was to
be expected he spoke with fluency a number of European languages.
Richard thought he looked like a university don or a priest.

Sir Charles's diffident personal manner did not carry over into
his official correspondence. His opinions were elucidated with
force and his objectives sharply defined. "The main object of our
policy and legislation," he wrote that year, "should be to found a
white colony." He saw the function of the European influx as
"simply introducing order into black, uninteresting, brutal barbarism." There was some justification for his proposals in that two-
thirds of the native population, with a culture plainly primitive, had
crowded themselves into only two major areas—the Kikuyu in the
shadow of Mount Kenya, and the Kavirondo beside the north-
eastern shore of Lake Victoria Nyanza—which left an area almost
the size of France with scarcely a habitation of note to be seen.
But when Sir Charles revealed his vision Richard was appalled.
Forgetting his insignificant rank and innocence of the country, he
suggested to the commissioner that after all the land did belong
to the Africans. Eliot insisted on the "paramount" claims of the
Europeans. When Richard countered with the idea that some day
the Africans would be educated and armed, which would bring about
a clash, Eliot overrode him with the conclusion that by that time
the Europeans would be strong enough to look after themselves.
Half a century later Sir Charles's and Richard's opinions were to
be put to the test in the damp bamboo forests of the Aberdares,
where the Mau Mau terrorists were suppressed by the white men,
making Sir Charles's point, but which very shortly thereafter, together with the rest of Kenya, the Africans took over as their own,
vindicating Richard. The argument had been vigorous but not

acrimonious, and although Sir Charles's familarity with Aunt Beatrice had not been much advanced he had formed a bond of sorts with her nephew, for he had discovered Richard's interest in nature. Sir Charles was one of the world's leading experts on nudibranchiate molluscs. His passion, in short, was sea slugs.

Eliot's policies were of course heartily supported by the settlers, personified by Lord Delamere, some of whose interests were of a downright material kind. Yet Eliot and many of the settlers would have been quick to point out the morality of their position. They were convinced that it was right to bring "civilization" to the savage; in this Lord Delamere was a crusader and Eliot a prophet. Tribalism to them was an institution that suppressed the individual, so they naturally proposed the disintegration of the tribe, the education of each member of it as an individual, and the eventual emergence of something they could not define but no doubt vaguely thought of as a democracy.*

The finer points of this philosophy escaped Richard Meinertz-hagen. When it produced arguments for the settling of the natives in reserves, or in favor of the agricultural development of the high-lands, he clung stubbornly to his simple black-and-white view that the land belonged to those who were there first. It was ingenuous but at least it had some durability. Besides, his own duty was plain. He was a soldier, with all the heavy responsibilities that entailed, and a sportsman, which also demanded a lot of time. The friendly neigh-borhood of Fort Hall had begun to turn a little disgruntled, enough at least to alarm the senior of the district officers, who was inclined to send for more troops at once. "Here we are," Richard admitted,

---

* The whole idea, as events would show, was based on ignorance of the real nature of tribalism. The African was happy to think of himself as a small unit in the mass of complicated relationships that made up the tribe. It was his one sure lifeline in a world of malignant and powerful forces both natural and supernatural. Moreover, few Europeans recognized at that time how complex was the system the Africans had evolved for their own well-being and how satisfactorily it answered their needs. The Europeans superimposed on it an administrative system which neither supplanted tribalism nor quenched the dark enmities between tribes but they thought they were bringing some order into chaos. This misapprehension was the root of their failure.

"three white men in the heart of Africa, with twenty nigger soldiers and fifty nigger police, sixty-eight miles from doctors or re-inforcements, administering and policing a district inhabited by half a million well-armed savages who have only quite recently come into touch with the white man, and we are responsible for the security in an area the size of Yorkshire. The position is most humorous to my mind." He guaranteed in the event of trouble to burn every village within a five-mile radius of the boma in less than twenty-four hours, quite mollifying the district officer with his confidence. He so restored morale that neither of the civilians thought to ask how he intended to honor his promise when he was spending most of his time miles away from the station building a bridge across the Tana River, hunting, and beginning a survey of the river and the road to the Aberdares. His first bearing on the snowy summit of Mount Kenya forty miles away revealed that the War Office map was incorrect. Any further measurements were interrupted when, returning briefly to Fort Hall, he learned that his promise of force must be honored.

A new district officer had arrived at the station and begun badly. He had requested the headman of a Kikuyu village a mile from the station to come to the Fort to confer about some minor thefts. When the elder did not arrive the district officer sent a Swahili policeman to arrest him. The policeman arrived at the village in the middle of a ceremony of some sort; not understanding and unable to speak Kikuyu, the policeman loaded his rifle and threatened the headman, whereupon the celebrants, egged on by two witch doctors, fell upon him and killed him. The district officer was faced with the choice of punishing the village that same night or handling the offense through the council of elders. Richard pressed for immediate action on the grounds that delay might be taken as weakness and, his view prevailing, sent out a spy at midnight. At three o'clock in the morning the spy reported that the populations of neighboring villages were now joining in an orgiastic celebration round the body of the policeman, which had been mutilated, and intended to attack the Fort. Half an hour before dawn Richard surrounded the village with twenty soldiers and twenty policemen, the latter a questionable asset since they had not yet learned how to fire their rifles. Bonfires were blazing in the center of the village and by their light Richard could see warriors in full war paint dancing themselves into the state of exhilaration that would explode them into action as soon as it was light enough. One of the warriors stumbled into Richard's cordon. The shot that killed him sent the rest of the warriors scrambling for the bush, but the volley that followed threw seventeen of them sprawling. Richard began to comb the valley in which the village lay. He rounded up the sheep and goats, burned the huts, and killed the few Kikuyu who showed fight. By early afternoon about thirty warriors were dead and the valley was sweet with the smoke of burning thatch. He had lost six of his own men. "So," Richard wrote in his diary that night, "order once more reigns in Kenya District." Inquiries showed that the trouble had been instigated by Kikuyu medicine men, a fact which prompted Richard to add a somewhat more penetrating footnote a couple of months later. "The Kikuyu are ripe for trouble," he wrote, "and when they get educated and medicine men are replaced by political agitators there will be a general rising." It would be half a century before his prescience was generally acknowledged in Kenya.

On the first day of September 1902 Richard set out on a more serious survey of the Aberdares, accompanied by some of his troops and a district officer from Fort Hall. Their intention was to locate the headwaters of the Thika and Chania rivers somewhere near the chilly peak of Kinangop. The track had almost vanished under a tangle of fallen trees and new creepers but they forced their way uphill through the forest sprinkled at every step with cold droplets, unable to see more than a few yards ahead and little comforted by the occasional sound—like the boiling of a gigantic kettle—of elephants digesting the damp bamboos among which they were ruminating. At seven thousand feet, having traveled at the rate of a mile an hour, they emerged into a garden of begonias, blackberries, red and yellow gladioli, violets, pansies and wild roses and many kinds of delicate ferns and mosses. It was cold and clouds still hid Kinangop some six thousand feet above them. The following day they reached the alpine zone. Catching mountain fever Richard accelerated and reached the peak alone, threading his way up a slope dotted with huge boulders shining with damp. As the first white man to climb Kinangop he built a cairn six feet high and left in it a bottle of beer with a request to the finder to drink his health and write to him care of 25 Rutland Gate. Richard and his companion tasted the crystal spring where the Thika River first bubbled out of the ground, camped that night at the source of the Chania, and headed back for the plains. On their way through the forest at dusk Richard caught sight of a huge red antelope striped with white and a gigantic black pig. The former, though he did not then know it, was a bongo and the latter a beast that would be named after him as its discoverer. There were elephant about as usual, one an old tusker carrying ivory worth at least a hundred pounds that Richard might have shot with ease. He resisted the temptation, having reached the conclusion that it was a pity to kill so wise a beast "in order that creatures not much more intelligent may play billiards with balls made from its teeth."

Clearing the thickest forest, but still trekking down the mountain, Richard suddenly heard firing and saw flames leaping from the villages below and ahead of him. Soon a runner reached him with the news that a small expedition had been sent out from Nairobi to punish the section of the Kikuyu that had ambushed the mail party he had aided some weeks before. It was this force that was burning the Kikuyu farmsteads and Richard was ordered to cooperate. Almost immediately Richard and his party became embroiled as groups of Kikuyu fleeing from the punitive force came across this unexpected obstacle in their path. The fighting was spasmodic but fierce, concluding with seventeen Kikuyu dead for two of Richard's men. That night the officer from Nairobi told him that the Kikuyu had caught a settler on his way to buy sheep, had pegged him spread-eagled on the ground and drowned him by wedging open his mouth and urinating into it one by one. It would be Richard's task to deal with the village. He cordoned it in the darkness, watching the Kikuyu dancing round the corpse. He had ordered his men to kill everything but children and when it was light enough they began, finishing off with the bayonet even the wounded. There were no children or young women as it happened, but some of the dead were grandmothers. Richard took the white settler's body, disemboweled and mutilated, and washed it in a stream before burying it. But his anger and horror at such a sight could not force back the recurrent feeling that his own ruthlessness had been monstrous. He was never sure he had been right. But what was certain was that he had re-acted naturally in the manner toward which all the training and ex-perience drilled into him thus far had directed him. He had become a killing machine; but he was beginning to develop some scruples.

But before they had time to grow painful, however, he was called out into the hills again. Another branch of the Kikuyu, the Tetu, had seized an Indian caravan passing along the edge of the Aberdares, murdered its conductors, and refused to pay the fine demanded by the administration. One column was to attack these Tetu from Fort Hall and Richard was to take another circling over the mountains in a primitive pincer movement. He had a hundred and fifty Masai spearmen as auxiliaries to support his company of askaris. Coming down through the high bamboo, he was shivering with malarial fever, but fifty grains of quinine set him to rights before he reached the Tetu. The paths out of the forest leading to the Tetu settlements had been blocked with trees and pitted with holes about five feet deep and three feet round, lined with sharpened stakes. Their presence was revealed when an askari fell into one and screamed as the stakes caught him in the side. Fortunately they were not poisoned and no Kikuyu lay unseen in ambush nearby, but they slowed up Richard's Masai scouts, who began to prod the paths with apprehension and respect. Reaching the first Tetu settle-ment, Richard's men drove off the handful of Kikuyu who showed fight and sequestered nearly seven hundred cattle and a sea of sheep and goats. These they impounded, then set up an oval boma of thorns around them with a Maxim gun at each end for safety. The Kikuyu tried to rescue their possessions by a night attack but Richard dispatched his Masai at them, pouring them through a gap in the boma—a red stream of warriors glinting with steel and grunting their guttural, rhythmic warcry like the coughing of hunting lion. By morning Richard's dead amounted to ten and he had thirty-two wounded, evidence that the Kikuyu were fighting much harder than he had expected.

He found the Fort Hall column camped below a small sugarloaf hill and held a council of war. Neighboring tribes were beginning to join the one with which Richard had been involved, and it was decided to send to Nairobi for reinforcements. It was also decided, after a good deal of argument, to call the site of their camp Nyeri.* The period of waiting that followed was enlivened by the great abundance of rhino in the environs. Richard met one of them face to face while taking his evening stroll around the camp and shot him in the chest at twenty yards. The rhino staggered but made off. Richard hit him again, a raking shot, and the beast accelerated toward the camp, where he was pursued by all the askaris and a hundred Masai. In the melee Richard shot the rhino yet again but it caught one of the Masai and tossed him ten feet in the air. In the end Richard killed it with a neck shot but by that time there were thirty-seven Masai spears in its hide and twenty bullets in various parts of its body. Richard took one of its feet for an inkstand.

By chance a patrol had captured a prominent elder of the Tetu Kikuyu and it occurred to Richard that the insurrection might now be terminated by diplomacy. When he suggested this to the civilian political officer with the expedition, he was overruled in favor of more severe punishment, though Richard suspected that the real reason was the prospect of more looted stock which could then be sold to pay for a new government station at Nyeri. So when forty askaris and two hundred Masai arrived from Nairobi, Richard had to resume operations. He succeeded by a ruse. He had noticed that the Kikuyu had a habit of entering his overnight camps as soon as he left them. One morning he sent off his main body but himself stayed behind with fifteen Masai in the boma they had been occupying for the night. As soon as the column was out of sight

---

* Nyeri in due course became a pleasant township but only acquired international fame when a hotel was built there in a fig tree that commanded a salt lick to which at night came all manner of game. Treetops Hotel is the best-organized tourist attraction in East Africa, offering a closeup of elephant and other beasts without having to move far from a bathroom or a bar.

Kikuyu warriors began to flock into the camp, just as Richard had predicted, without discovering him hiding with his Masai behind some piles of brushwood. When fifty Kikuyu had packed into the boma Richard shot the nearest one and rushed to the entrance, which he blocked with a Masai shielding him on each side. He bayonetted every Kikuyu who tried to escape his main body of Masai spearmen. His shirt was ripped by a spear thrust he never felt. "I was surprised at the ease with which a bayonet goes into a man's body," he wrote that night. "One scarcely feels it unless it goes in to the hilt. But one frequently has to make a desperate tug to get it out." After that morning's slaughter, it was felt, the people of Tetu would acknowledge a stronger hand. The punishment was called off and the expedition left for Nairobi.

On the way Richard spent a dismal Christmas at Fort Hall under a depression he did not recognize as a reaction to the killing. But the closer he got to Nairobi the higher his spirits rose, helped by his meeting on the road a party bringing up the English mail and a Christmas pudding from his mother only four days late. On the first days of 1903 he dined in the Mess off a white tablecloth, a luxury he had not enjoyed for eight months. He had missed a visit by his Aunt Beatrice's old suitor Joseph Chamberlain, who had made a most enthusiastic speech to the officers about the future of the colony but without revealing a plan just beginning to form in his complex mind to settle large numbers of Russian Jews there. When Richard had first arrived in Kenya he could have counted the settlers on the fringes of the Kikuyu country on his fingers, but now a land office had been opened and by the middle of 1903 more than a hundred adventurers would have arrived to try their fortunes. A Crown Lands Ordinance allowed them a hundred and sixty acres; if they were successful they could expand by stages until they were farming a whole square mile. Men with enough capital could buy a thousand acres freehold. As a government official Richard was allowed only ten acres and he chose a tract close to the military lines well supplied with fat guinea fowl, duiker and steinbock. As a private citizen he also took a six-month option to buy forty-five thousand acres between the Ithanga Hills and the Tana River, an area he had first heard of at Harrow when the American Donaldson Smith had described it as a paradise for game. He was hoping that his father would loan him five thousand pounds to develop it, build a cottage, and turn it into a game sanctuary. But Daniel Meinertzhagen, the banker, would have nothing to do with such romanticism.

It seeemed to the new settlers that their major problem was what not to grow. Everything they put into the ground luxuriated and produced such alarming visions as brussels sprouts as high as a man. They had yet to discover that a thunderstorm could strip every blossom from a fruit orchard in minutes, that acres of wheat could fall under strange blights and rot in a day or two under the smiling sun, that sheep on apparently immaculate highlands could die in hundreds of liver fluke or from huge grubs battening in the sinus, and that migrations of siafu, the dreadful soldier ants of Africa, could come out in millions after the rains in seemingly solid columns that moved with an almost inaudible hissing to devour whatever poultry or young stock could not escape their swarming, agonizing pincers. The first settlers in Kenya were men of the boldest character, prepared to gamble everything on virgin land without knowing where they might find a market for their produce or even if they could overcome the natural hazards that had kept this vast country from human exploitation for scores of centuries.

Their leader, morally and materially, had just arrived in Kenya for the third time when Richard met him, a man of thirty-two with red hair he wore as long as a girl's to hide a neck permanently twisted by a riding accident. He also wore a blocked boot to correct the limp a lion had given him, and he was shortly to sustain a fall that would break his neck a second time and put him in plaster of paris for months. He was Hugh Cholmondeley, third Baron Delamere of Vale Royal, and his pig-headed, courageous,* romantic

---

* When the lion took him in Somaliland, Delamere was saved by his gunbearer's making the classic riposte in seizing and twisting the lion's tongue. This distracted the lion and Delamere shot it. He lay where he had fallen under a shelter of leaves for five days, believing that the poison from the lion's fangs would not mount his leg if he stayed absolutely immobile. He lanced the wound himself periodically with a knife.

spirit was the beacon that guided all other settlers for nearly thirty years. Always in financial difficulty, he met failure and success with indifference, being preoccupied with what was unquestionably a vision of the purest sort. He expressed it succinctly to Richard when they met at the races in Nairobi. "I am going to prove to you," he said, "that this is a white man's country." When Richard, mindful of his conversations with Sir Charles Eliot, asked, "But it is a black man's country. How are you going to superimpose the white over the black?" Delamere brushed him aside with a touch of temper. "The black man will benefit and cooperate!"

The January race-meeting was already one of the great social events of Nairobi's year. Richard attended with a fellow officer who distinguished himself by entangling a spur in his horse's bridle, while Richard won modest fame by coming in third out of a field of five. But what the meeting lacked in honors it made up for in raw comedy. The second race was just ending when a rhino appeared on the course, cantering counter to the riders. The latter returned to the starting gate much faster than they had left it, and the rhino amused the crowd for half an hour by making little demonstration charges here and there before trotting off with his tail in the air and a feeling of superiority in his tiny brain.

A few days after the meeting Richard broke three ribs in a fall from his pony and was allowed a short furlough in Zanzibar to recuperate. Richard fell while he was pigsticking, a sport he and his brother officers introduced into Kenya. They had begun with bayonets lashed to bamboo poles but soon imported proper hog spears from India. Their prey was the warthog, the fat, dusty red variety of pig that ran with its little tail high in the air, topped with a disreputable tuft of hair like a worn paintbrush. It was the warthog's habit to head straight for its hole and disappear into it bottom first, so that the sport in Africa differed greatly from that in India, there being less danger from the pig but more from the terrain, which was riddled with holes and pits. Another difference lay in the variety of game that could be hunted; if pigs palled there were wild dogs with great bat ears, or troops of baboon, but these were spared the spear. Once there was a cheetah that ran for two miles before he stopped and lay down, so spent that Richard could get off his horse to stroke him. Beyond these lay the greater challenge that Richard knew would one day have to be accepted. The finest prey of all was lion, but a spear was a feeble thing against that tawny power and Richard dreaded such a contest. One afternoon Richard and a friend sighted a lion on the Athi Plain. It was too great a temptation for the friend, and honor sent Richard after him despite his better judgment. Disturbed by their headlong gallop, the lion got up and began to lope away. However, the friend's pony was faster and the lion decided to fight, turned and crouched. The pony swerved in panic and threw his rider about ten feet away from the lion, where he sat trying to get his pistol out of its holster. Richard forced his horse up to the lion and was in the act of spearing it when he heard his friend's pistol fire and the lion jerked away from him, dead. The two skinned it and rode home in silence but that night they drank champagne to celebrate and admitted to each other that though they had been terrified they had been even more afraid to show it.

Sport occupied at least as much of Richard's time as his military duties, and other kinds of social life came a poor third. He met Burnham, the American scout, who had been charged with buying land for a syndicate. He began to see a good deal of John Ainsworth, the taciturn sub-commissioner of Ukamba Province, whose new white house significantly commanded the path formerly used by both Masai and Kikuyu raiding parties. Ainsworth and his wife, Ina, were always entertaining visitors like Sandbach Baker, to whom Sir Charles Eliot had given five thousand acres in return for supplying Nairobi with meat. Richard often rode out to Baker's farm for fresh butter, a luxury he loved. The food elsewhere was deplorable; when he gave a lady-friend lunch at the hotel he called it "a miserable dirty place—tinned salmon, rancid butter, high meat and maggotty cheese, the whole garbage costing me eight rupees." Such occasional intimacies were far from central to Richard's existence. He busied himself refitting and training his company and improving their shooting. They were mostly Manyema tribesmen from the Congo and Richard had made one of them, a large fellow called Simba, his gun bearer, having been attracted by the man's silence, fearless nature and apparent devotion, as much as for his reputation as a cannibal. Richard's drilling improved his men's soldierly appearance and bearing, but on maneuvers they tended to revert to a sort of anarchy during which they were carried quite beyond primitive tactics into the fervor of real fighting. The battalion's membership was drawn from an assortment of tribes, among them some Masai who one day were chosen to act as "enemy" for a company of Sudanese. These latter were partly remnants of Emin Pasha's small force and partly refugees from the khalifa's army who had seeped into Uganda to avoid Kitchener's ire. They were a somewhat be-mused lot at the best of times: catching sight of a new Sudanese officer wearing the medal ribbon of the Sudan campaign, the khalifa's veterans had demanded the distinction for themselves on the grounds that—as the losers—they had suffered more than any. On this particular day the Sudanese approached the Masai with a pleasure quickly mounting to excitement. Oblivious to orders they fixed bayonets and charged. The Masai had perspicaciously secreted a few rounds of ball ammunition about themselves, which they now began to use. The historic dervish élan prevailed, however, when the Sudanese proved themselves upon the Masai by bayoneting three of them to death and freely puncturing a number of others. The Masai fled, but they were not rescued until Richard interposed his company of black cannibals.

During most of 1903 there was little employment for Richard's company, though in August he moved them out to garrison Fort Hall and Nyeri, his old killing grounds. Passing fairly frequently between the two stations, Richard often camped near a Kikuyu village and became friendly with its chief elder, one Wambogo, who affected elegant earrings and a necklace, a bracelet over each bicep and a heavy wire ornament on his right wrist, and a bangle round his left ankle. Since Wambogo's people were disaffected it took some time to establish comfortable communication, but there began a bond Wambogo still felt after more than forty years. When Richard visited him after the Second World War, Wambogo held his hand for more than ten minutes, protesting the Kikuyu's grievances against the white men and sadly preferring a return to the old barbarism instead of facing the armed clash he clearly foresaw. Game abounded in the area, staggering by their numbers even Richard, who was accustomed to counting herds by the hundred and thought nothing of seeing five rhino within a mile of his hut. At dawn one morning one of his men woke him with screams of "Elephant! Many elephant!" The mass of Mount Kenya was still a black silhouette in the morning sky as Richard stared at the stream of animals plodding north and stretching as far as he could see. It was a migration. Though Richard could not count accurately, he guessed there were about seven hundred elephant in the column, which ended at last with a cow and her very small calf. All the rhino in the area were disturbed enough to spend the day frisking about with their tails in the air to display their resentment.

At Nyeri Richard got word of the plan to settle Jews on the Uasin Gishu plateau, and soon his copies of *The Times* for late August 1903 arrived full of acrimonious correspondence about it. In the summer of 1902 a Royal Commission had been appointed in London to inquire into the dangers of unlimited Alien Immigration in response to stirrings of displeasure among the English at the number of Eastern Jews crowding into Whitechapel. Nathan Mayer, Lord Rothschild, the first of his race to enter the House of Lords, was a member of the Commission and, not unnaturally, it seemed politic to him to have some preliminary discussions with a fanatical Austrian Jew who had been called to give evidence before it. His lordship was nervous about what conclusions Theodore Herzl's aggressive mind might force upon his subtle colleagues on the Commission, so he was the more charmed to find that Herzl was prepared to bend. Lord Nathan suggested Africa and Joseph Chamberlain supported him warmly with the information, gathered on his recent tour, that a Jewish colony in East Africa would soon grow fat on cotton and sugar. Herzl preferred, nonetheless, a settlement under British protection at El Arish in Sinai, so Chamberlain arranged a meeting for him with Lord Lansdowne, the Foreign Secretary. Lansdowne in due course consulted his proconsul Cromer, who turned the proposal down on the grounds that the Wadi El Arish could not be irrigated, but probably with the unspoken and deeper feeling that a Jewish settlement subject to Egyptian law in an area still technically a part of Turkey would constitute a political mixture he would much prefer to avoid. Before Cromer's grave negatives were received, a Russian mob had completed a pogrom in Kishineff within the Pale of Settlement, killing forty-five Jews, severely wounding six hundred more, and pillaging some fifteen hundred houses. Herzl felt himself under pressure and proposed the British offer of approximately five thousand square miles of East Africa to the Sixth Zionist Congress in Basle, Switzerland, in 1903.

The area had been outlined by Sir Charles Eliot. It lay to the east of the Rift Valley and north of the Nandi escarpment, a high grassy plateau watered by the Nzoia River and grazed sporadically by the Masai. Sir Charles thought it "sufficiently isolated to protect the Jews from any hostile demonstrations of other races." Sir Charles's tongue must have been in his inscrutable cheek, for one race that was becoming hotly hostile was his friends the Kenyan settlers. After the Zionist Congress had half-heartedly decided at least to investigate the British offer, a group of settlers had asked Sir Charles's permission to accompany the expected Jewish commission. Eliot agreed: "I am sure, gentlemen, that you will be able to show members of the commission many things that they would not otherwise see." Indeed they were. All innocence, the Jews were marched into the wilderness until their soft feet blistered, woke one morning to find lions' pug marks circling their tents, and were told in full the horrid saga of the man-eaters of Tsavo; then they were surrounded by a prancing war party of Masai, ochered and malevolent, whom miraculously the settlers were able to pacify with a few words. The Commission's report that the Uasin Gishu was no place for a national home disappointed few Jews, for by the time it was made Herzl was dead and the Zionists were straining once more toward Palestine. That solution, in Richard's view, would be much the best. He had been against the Uasin Gishu scheme from the first, with a severe entry in his diary: "The scheme would only add to political confusion, and God knows there will be enough trouble here in fifty years when the natives get educated. Also, the Jews are not good mixers—never have been; they have their own religion, customs and habits and would constitute a most indigestible element in East Africa if they came in any numbers. Why not persuade the Turks to give them Palestine? The Arabs are doing nothing with it, and the Jews with their brains and dynamic force would be a tremendous asset to Turkey." A waspish judgment of national character, the entry owned a certain political logic. It was one of Richard's first thoughts on the matter.

Richard's third year with the King's African Rifles began with another punitive expedition, this time visited upon the Iraini section of the Kikuyu inhabiting the slopes of Mount Kenya. They had been refusing passage to caravans trying to cross their country, replying to objections from Fort Hall with insulting messages and even murdering a few policemen sent to expostulate. The plan was the familiar double-prong thrusting from Nyeri and Fort Hall, where Richard had prepared a force of sixty askaris and two hundred and fifty Masai levies. He marched at night, taking the Iraini by surprise and capturing nearly nine hundred head of stock without bloodshed on either side. Then the fighting started. Richard had split his force into small parties to comb the bush. Coming to a stream spread with great patches of reeds, Richard's own patrol was fired on by Iraini bowmen invisible in the thick growth. Thinking that the arrows had come from a reed bed, Richard fired into it, but as he did so twelve warriors came charging in from a different direction as a lion simultaneously burst out of the other side of the reeds. The medical officer, standing beside Richard, fired at the lion and wounded it. Richard had already shot four of the Iraini and killed a fifth in the act of spearing the sporting medical officer. The askaris finished off the rest of the attackers while Richard swore at the doctor for his asinine behavior, but vainly, for the man insisted on following his lion.

The two of them had only just begun to force their way through the reeds when a warrior, spear poised, jumped up in front of the doctor. Richard shot him dead. In the same moment the lion reared up five yards away from the doctor. Richard killed it with a neck shot. The doctor, waving his rifle about, had not even taken aim during these rather hectic seconds so Richard grabbed him by the shoulders and threw him backward out of his way. Setting fire to the reeds as a precaution against further alarms, he recovered the charred bodies of the warrior and the lion, whereupon the medical officer objected loudly to the spoiling of his trophy. Pressing forward, the party now came under fire from a thick stand of trees which Richard raked with his two Maxim guns without disposing of all of the Iraini. The doctor glimpsed one of them on a high branch and fired, with Richard's permission, bringing the man toppling down almost at their feet. He was still alive and clutching his short sword, so the doctor shot him again. "And so close to me was his head," Richard wrote, "that a hot fid of human brain hit me in the eye as the head was split open. It was very disgusting."

Richard had made it plain to askaris and Masai alike that any of them killing women or children would be shot. They came upon a cluster of Kikuyu huts, rushed in, killed four warriors and dispersed the rest. As Richard was re-forming his men on the other side of the village, he heard a woman scream. He ran back. Two of his men and three Masai were just dragging a woman out of one of the huts, another Masai was pulling his spear out of the body of a little boy, and a fifth Masai was about to club a little girl. Richard shouted but the Masai smashed the child's head and one of the askaris bayoneted the woman. Richard dropped both of the soldiers and three of the Masai as they ran. Then he paraded his men, offered to deal with any of them who sympathized with the murderers, and when no one moved, ordered them to bury the woman and the children. He left the dead askaris and the Masai for the hyenas. He knew that what he had done was contrary to military law and he did not report it officially, though in private he told the civilian political officer who was with the column about it because he felt he had acted rightly. Certainly he had curbed the brutal dispositions that seethed beneath the military correctness of his men; he felt that his harshness might be criticized but not his motive.

After a week of small but bloody encounters the Iraini appeared still full of fight, though they had lost nearly eight hundred warriors and over nine thousand head of stock. Nevertheless their elders

The "perfect little animal." Richard, aged five.

The Meinertzhagen family at Mottisfont in the Golden Age. *Standing (l. to r.):* Frederick, Margaret, Dan, Barbara, Richard, Lawrencina, Beatrice. *Seated (l. to r.):* Georgina with Betty; Daniel with Mary, Louis. The dog is Dan's.

"Grant him a nice little war." Richard as a
Hampshire Yeoman, 1897.

"There she was, coming straight at him, so
small and so awe-inspiring." Queen Victoria's
Diamond Jubilee Parade, 1897.

"I have felt the magnetic power of the African climate drawing me lower and lower to the level of a savage." Richard in East Africa, 1905.

East Africa could have been a country made expressly for Richard Meinertzhagen. Richard in Nairobi, 1903.

The semiprofessional spy. Richard in Mesopotamia, 1914.

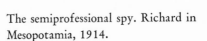

The homemade cabaret at Richard's house in
Nandi Fort. *Left to right:* Scraggie, Baggie
and Maggy, sisters three.

Allenby enters Jerusalem in the guise of a
prophet and as its first Christian overlord
since the Middle Ages.

"My eyes are sore with the falling scales of disillusion." Richard *(seated, left)* at the Paris Peace Conference, 1919.

Lawrence of Arabia in campaign dress. One night he came to Richard's room with a strange confession.

"He had been honest and he was not ashamed."
Richard in his eighty-fifth year.

came into Fort Hall to submit to the government and to offer their services against their neighbors, the Embu, who had just taken up arms and against whom they had a grudge. The Embu were of common stock with the Kikuyu but spoke another language and practiced slightly different customs. As fighting men they were brave to a degree, twice charging right up to Richard's bayonets. But spears and arrows could only delay their end, which came when Richard fell upon their massed herds grazing on the open plain and crushed the warriors who were protecting them. He marched back to Fort Hall with five hundred cattle and fifteen hundred sheep and goats, leaving two hundred and fifty Embu dead in the bamboo thickets and scattered over their pleasant pastures.

It was the end of his assignment at Fort Hall and he was sorry, for he admired the Kikuyu among whom, despite the execution he had wrought, he had made friends. He liked their gaiety, the respect the young showed for the old, and the love they spent on their children. "I found them honest and truthful," he said, "but behaving quite differently to some of the European administrators, who treated them as 'bloody niggers.' The same cheerful young men or girls who visited me would become unscrupulous, dishonest and treacherous to the man who behaved badly to them." Above all he sympathized with the difficulty of their position. "They are the most intelligent of the African tribes I have met; therefore they will be the most progressive under European guidance and will be more susceptible to subversive activities. They will be one of the first tribes to demand freedom from European influence and in the end cause a lot of trouble. And if white settlement really takes hold in this country it is bound to do so at the expense of the Kikuyu, who own the best land, and I can foresee much trouble."

Propounding his view yet again over dinner with Sir Charles Eliot in Nairobi, Richard was once more snubbed, partly because Sir Charles's sense of decency had been discommoded by the figures of Iraini and Embu dead exactly reported by Richard and suppressed by the administration out of humanity and for appearance's sake. Sir Charles was anxious as usual to talk about Richard's Aunt Beatrice; could he have known that her husband, Sidney Webb, would share Richard's sympathy with African rights and as Colonial Secretary declare their interests paramount, he might have been less enthusiastic. He applauded Aunt Beatrice's Fabian gospels and was crushed when Richard defined her aims as the dictatorship of the lower classes through trade unions, and categorized Marxian socialism as a foul, infectious disease. After these undiplomatic exchanges Richard introduced a subject that was beginning to concern him. Fearing that the incursion of thousands of European settlers would mean the disappearance of all the game he loved, he had suggested to Blayney Percival, the solitary game warden in East Africa, that a reserve should be set aside and made the direct responsibility of the British Parliament. The best area, he thought, would be the territories grazed by the Masai. Sir Charles thought him sentimental but bent far enough to ask Richard for a memorandum on the subject, though it was clear that in his mind farming and game preservation did not mix. It was not until the same idea occurred to Lord Delamere that Masai and game were put together and Kenya's tourist industry of half a century later was thus rescued from stillbirth. Sir Charles, Richard noted, still could not bring himself to like the Masai; it particularly offended him that they wore their short togas slung over their shoulders with such careless grace that they might just have well gone about stark naked.*

Richard was nearing the end of his tour of duty in Kenya, but he was suddenly sent up-country to take over the garrison at Muhoroni and charged with guarding the railway from the depredations of the Nandi. These were a people of audacity and vigor who worshiped the sun and raided in broad daylight wherever they pleased, quick to snap up such unconsidered trifles as mail runners or stragglers from those caravans bold or stupid enough to

---

* Early in 1968 the government of Tanzania announced measures against the "uncivilized habits of dressing" of their Masai citizens. Mr. S. S. Oloitiptip, a Masai member of the Kenya Parliament, immediately held a press conference during which he thundered, "If Almighty God could stomach to see the entire anatomies of Adam and Eve in their complete nudity, is it not a little prudish for an African government to have fits merely by viewing a casually exhibited Masai buttock?"

pass within range of their fleet warriors. They had always been particularly attracted to the railroad and the telegraph line that ran alongside it. The latter gave them copper wire by the scores of miles for their handsome women to wear as ornament; and the former, bolts, plates and even sections of rail to beat into weapons or to fashion into jewelry, causing Sir Charles Eliot to complain to London, "The male sex are attracted by a particular kind of bolt which forms an ideal instrument for braining your enemy." The Nandi disliked the Indian coolies of the construction and maintenance gangs for trying to procure their women, and they would sometimes kill one or two or mutilate them or bury them alive; they left one poor telegraph lineman hanging on his pole so bristling with arrows he looked like a porcupine. A force of the Uganda Rifles sent against them in 1900 had been cut to bits. Another expedition two years later had been more fortunate but equally ineffectual.

At the beginning of 1903 the collector of Nandi District, one Walter Mayes, a junior civilian official, had been ordered to establish the government's authority with the Kamelilo, believed to be a tribe of the Nandi people but in fact an age-group or regiment. Two days after Mayes's descent on them they not only made a daylight excursion to the railroad for fishplates but were impertinent enough en route to try an attack on the regimental garden and the cattle boma of the King's African Rifles. In April 1903 the Nandi were suddenly assailed by six hundred soldiers with five Maxim guns and a Hotchkiss quick-firer. It was too much even for these bold savages and they sued for peace after five weeks. As soon as the troops withdrew, however, they resumed their predatory habits with the satisfaction of men settling into a familiar routine after a period of distraction and Mayes was unable to control them.

The crisis that precipitated Richard's dispatch to Nandi was the murder of a guest at the American mission at Kaimosi, twenty-three miles beyond Kisumu, the terminus of the Uganda Railway on the Kavirondo Gulf of Lake Victoria Nyanza. Richard marched through the heavily cultivated country of the Kavirondo, his passage marked by groups of stark-naked agriculturists squatting in groups on the immense boulders dotted all over their meager farms.

The three American missionaries at Kaimosi—Hole, Blackburne and Chilson—welcomed Richard with an excellent dinner accompanied, to Richard's disgust, with drafts of tea. At breakfast Hole stunned Richard by announcing that his wife had just given birth; Richard had spent a pleasant evening in her company without once noticing her interesting condition. The Americans told Richard that Dr. Wenthe, their deceased guest, had arrived two weeks before, professing himself a Quaker missionary and satisfying all his needs by begging. Just as the others at the mission were beginning to hope he would have the charity to move on, he was killed. Mayes had been close to the mission skirmishing with the Nandi and confiscating stock, though without proper authority to do so. Hearing cattle lowing in the forest, one of the missionaries had rounded them up, thinking that by so doing he would be helping the government. In fact they were cattle the Nandi were trying quite legally to hide from Mayes. When Wenthe strolled forth a little later to investigate gunfire and bumped into some Nandi, they not unnaturally visited their wrath on him with a multiplicity of spear thrusts.

In view of these circumstances, which led him to suspect Mayes's intentions, Richard was reluctant to move against the Nandi, a feeling that was reinforced when he met Mayes for the first time and disliked him on sight. Mayes, the roughest of diamonds, had been a seaman, a gold prospector in Madagascar, and a transport man in Uganda. He had married a Creole girl, which Richard thought vulgar, and deserted her immediately, which Richard thought unforgivable. He told Mayes at once very coldly that he considered him to blame for the whole business of Dr. Wenthe's departure for more heavenly, but perhaps premature, pastures. As things turned out Mayes settled the affair after a fashion without further intervention from Richard by persuading his superiors in the administration to fine the Nandi forty-eight head of cattle which he had appropriated before they speared the Quaker.

The night air at Kisumu sang with mosquitoes and men died with tedious regularity of blackwater fever. Richard's tents and bedding were sodden by the incessant rain and he was prevented from leaving his camp except in force because the high matted grass surrounding it hid Nandi on the watch for lonesome strangers. He welcomed any chance of a brief safari or a liaison mission to some less bedraggled station. On one of these he made a new friend. E. S. "Grogs" Grogan was already a minor legend in Kenya. He had been the first man to walk from the Cape to Cairo in a perambulatory realization of Cecil Rhodes's dream of an all-British route from top to bottom of Africa and, it was rumored, in order to prove his worth to a father who had refused his daughter's hand to him. Grogan's sense of humor was superb if painful; one night he pegged out a claim to the whole of Nairobi, causing the administration to write and publish overnight a new ordinance altering the law and preventing him from swallowing up every township in Kenya; Grogan was not at all angered.* Richard accepted Grogan for his whimsical charm, the clarity of his brain, and the obvious strength of his character as well as for his friendship with benevolent Uncle Ernest. Grogan had heard of Richard, too, and repeated some flattering reports. "He is a great man," Richard concluded, "and will be even greater some day."

Throughout his tour Richard had been pondering the mystery of the black pig he had first seen in the Aberdares. From time to time his askaris had brought in pieces of hairy skin they had found while searching native huts and Richard had sent them to Ray Lankester at the British Museum. Everywhere he went Richard sought news of his pig; then one of the Americans at Kaimosi Mission sent him a skull. But still Richard's only impression was of a forest animal about the size of a small buffalo. In the middle of June he shot one, a young sow. The skull and complete skin went to Lankester and in due course there returned the good news that

---

* Grogan's jokes were too honest to attract anger. He attended the first speech made by the first African member of the legislature, a historic moment certainly. He had known the new member's parents and probably his grandparents too. When the speech was over Grogan rose, delivered a pretty minute of sincere congratulatory prose, then added, it is said, "I could not help wondering, however, while the honorable member was on his feet, whether he was debating which of the honorable members opposite he might have for dinner." Everyone screamed with laughter, not least the African. He and Grogan both knew that he came from a long and respectable line of cannibals.

a newly discovered species of pig, the Giant Forest Hog, had been officially named *Hylochoerus meinertzhageni.**

At about the same time a letter arrived from his mother telling him that the battalion of the Royal Fusiliers he had left in India had been assigned to an expedition into Tibet. The pretext for this burlesque of an Imperial enterprise had been the failure of the Dalai Lama to observe the provisions of a Convention and a schedule of Trade Regulations signed, respectively, thirteen and ten years before. Behind the pretext lay the viceroy Lord Curzon's suspicion that the Russians were coming to Lhasa. It was just the kind of nice little war Richard had been looking for, so he cabled at once to his regiment asking permission to spend his forthcoming leave with them fighting the unspeakable Tibetans. His cable was never answered, which was perhaps a pity, for when the Royal Fusiliers prepared to storm the breach at Gyantse Fort, there was an "unfortunate incident" and the honors went to a battalion of Ghurkas. The Royal Fusiliers returned to more satisfactory soldiering in peaceful India and eventually to a triumphal parade through the City of London, exercising their right to march with bayonets fixed and dragging with them as a mascot a Tibetan wild ass that had been lassoed by the expedition's gunners.

Disappointed but far from dejected by the Fusiliers' conclusion that they could conquer Tibet without his help, Richard left the searing humidity of Kisumu with the memory of an old gray parrot chattering to himself in the equally gray dawn, and the bitter entry in his diary, "The incessant rain, the lack of anything to do and being absolutely by myself would have forced me to some vice or other if I had remained there much longer." He was hungry for an English sky, all cold metal, and a blustering northeast wind. He left Mombasa with falcons swooping over the old fort for bats on the wing, and at Zanzibar, pervaded by a heavy scent from the pink

---

* *A Field Guide to the National Parks of Kenya* identifies *Hylochoerus meinertzhageni* as from forty-eight to fifty inches in length and thirty-two inches high at the shoulder. The best specimen Richard shot was a boar seventy-seven inches long and thirty-seven and three-quarter inches high at the shoulder. It weighed three hundred and twenty-nine pounds.

waxen buds of its cloves, he took the Messageries Maritimes mail steamer *Djemnah*. All but one of the passengers were French officers and their wives. "A pretty moth-eaten lot they are, too," Richard recorded sourly. "They all come from Madagascar and they all look broken down either with fever, drink, or some form of vice." They ignored him and he did not approach them.

He had time to reflect, homeward bound, on what he had accomplished and where, since he was Richard Meinertzhagen, he had failed. He had killed a tremendous amount of game, from little dik-dik, tiniest of antelopes that flickered through the grass like hares, to bull rhino weighing over twenty-five hundred pounds. Thus far his total of rhino came to nine—five bulls and four cows. Of the other members of the "big five" he had taken eight lion, one of them from the hip as it charged, two of them man-eaters, and the best of them measuring nine feet four inches; two leopard, one of which was bigger than the best he had bagged in India; and two buffalo bulls with inferior heads, for one of which (since he was licensed only for a single specimen) he had to pay a fine of seventy-five rupees. He had not killed an elephant, and never would, on principle. Few days had passed on which he had not killed some species of animal. He had shot for the pot—his own and his soldiers' —anything from thick-set waterbuck to bull hippo providing five thousand pounds or more of succulent meat. He had brought down Thomson's gazelle smartly striped with black along the ribs, klipspringer bouncing a-tiptoe over rocks, bohor reedbuck, hartebeest with lugubrious faces perpetually turning in stupidity, bull eland as hefty as steers, shiny red topi, ostriches with legs that tasted of roast beef, impala, once in necessity a bull giraffe, warthog and oribi and oryx, and, out of gourmandise, fat guineafowl, francolin, bustard and sandgrouse. He never had to look for a target; even Nairobi was roamed by leopard and lion, one of which killed a zebra not a hundred yards from the Mess. A zebra once foaled on the parade ground and an elephant trampled John Ainsworth's new garden until he discouraged it. Richard did not seek to excuse himself for what he had shot. "I am not proud of it," he wrote, "neither am I ashamed of it. When I arrived in the country I was obsessed by blood-lust. Hunting is man's primitive instinct, and I indulged it and enjoyed it to the full. The hunting of big game gave me good healthy exercise when many of my brother-officers were drinking rot-gut or running about with somebody else's wife; it taught me bushcraft and how to shoot straight."

It taught Richard Meinertzhagen, in short, the trade for which he was paid—the hunting of men—and when the war came he was grateful for the lessons Kenya had taught him. As to the human deaths for which he had been responsible, by his own hand and indirectly, he felt no guilt. He professed to hold no belief in the sanctity of human life because he knew of no age that had held it so, nor in the essential dignity of man. He added, "To do nothing in an emergency is to do something definitely wrong." His hundred soldiers had sometimes been an island in a sea of three hundred thousand savages; inaction would have meant annihilation. Richard himself had little fear of dying, for he could not imagine that the death of his body meant the end of everything. It was a kind of hazy faith in an afterlife not securely connected to any orthodox religious belief. He had been required one day in Nairobi to fill out an official form and, when asked to what religion he belonged, had written, "To all religions which recognize the Unknown God," whereupon he was stuffily informed that he had better put down something that made more sense.

It made a good deal of sense to Richard and he refused. At Harrow he had begun to question the doctrines of the Church of England he had followed slavishly and in fear at Fonthill. He concluded that ritual and ceremony mattered less than an immutable faith in God, Whom he saw as an influence for good, and less than staunchly Christian behavior based on the moral pronouncements of the Bible. He believed, as he always had, in the efficacy of prayer. But it was private prayer in which he answered to his God, sought comfort, and asked for guidance or accepted reproof. One of the words often used in those austere and halting dialogues must have been an echoing and reechoing "Duty!" But now, sailing north and west, his prayers were for a full sweet homecoming and for a welcome from those he loved. They were not to be answered.

CHAPTER 9

This Is the Gentleman Who Shot Your Grandfather

King Edward VII had assumed the imperial crown amid a pomp of blue and gold to the strains of an anthem—"Be Strong and Play the Man"—especially composed by the Master of the King's Musick, and had at once shown the humanity that was to distinguish his reign by extending a strong and portly arm to assist to his feet the aged Primate of All England kneeling in obeisance and decrepitude before his throne. The deeper note of this act of dedication and celebration (the actual details of which had been difficult to determine, since none of King Edward's courtiers had been alive long enough to recall the protocol for a coronation) was sounded outside the Abbey: by the King's wish Edward Elgar, the first British composer of any consequence since the Elizabethans, had adapted a fine martial part of his "Pomp and Circumstance" to form a Coronation Ode. Having fashioned his brazen melody, Elgar asked one A. C. Benson, a rather diffident housemaster at Eton, to provide some words. Benson began thoughtfully with:

> *Land of Hope and Glory*
> *Mother of the free,*
> *How shall we extol thee,*
> *Who art born of thee?*

but confessed, "I don't think I quite have the popular ring." However, it was not long before he conceived his thunderous—and popular—final verse:

> *Wider still and wider*
>   *Shall thy bounds be set;*
> *God, who made thee mighty,*
>   *Make thee mightier yet!*

At its first performance the ode had to be repeated five times, leaving its audience, secure among diamonds and correct in starched white shirtfronts, convinced that as a work of art it displayed not only beauty but a certain amount of truth. "Land of Hope and Glory" was much to the King's taste, too, with its solid and stately rhythm and its simple aspiration toward what after all was only right. Might was what had sustained the peace of Europe for so long and in the proper hands it would continue to do so; there was no question as to whose those hands should be.

Richard Meinertzhagen had celebrated King Edward's coronation two years before at Fort Hall by marching his black detachment around the boma for half an hour, stopping occasionally to fire a ragged *feu de joie* or to present arms to the Union Jack, hanging somewhat limply on its pole under the African sun. King Edward's loyal subjects among the Kikuyu had been invited to witness the martial display and had been rewarded with a feast of hartebeest meat and a roasted ox. In gratitude they had reciprocated with a dance that came to a climax which, as Richard wrote, "can best be imagined. It certainly could not be introduced into Belgravia, though modern dancing in England is sometimes little better than the savage displays of tropical Africa." At the end of August 1904, taking his first home leave from Africa, Richard found himself in a London for which the dance and its attendant etiquette formed the high-water mark of gracious living. To all intents and purposes the social arts had become the consummation of western civilization, with His Majesty himself as arbiter. A summer warmth, opulent as gold, laved the endless afternoon that was Edwardian England and the hey-day of the upper middle class to which Richard

Meinertzhagen undeniably belonged. As regards sport, renewed friendships with some of his contemporaries, a change of climate, and the comfort of familiar scenes—Richard's furlough was enjoyable. But his mother was as reserved as ever and his father, though kind, unable to show his true affection. Richard felt his ties with his family looser than ever before. Nor could he lose himself in the London society that saw in *The Arcadians* the reflection of its own ideal:

> *In Arcady life flows along*
> *As careless as the shepherd's song,*
> *But Strephon pipes along the lea*
> *In Arcady, in Arcady . . .*

He could not delight in the dishes of delicate pink salmon dressed with a jelly of claret on tables cloyed with the scent of tuberoses, the platters of peaches and grapes perfect from the hothouses, the exquisite ladies with gloves to the armpit that required eighteen buttons, or the languid, clever gentlemen faintly redolent of Floris's essential oils. All the elegance and grace of that pearly time were lost on him. "I prefer Africa and the savage to England and the over-civilized society which lives there," he wrote flatly in his diary and turned his back on the affectations of his class and attitudes which, at the age of twenty-six, he was too old-fashioned to admire.

It was not so much that the Edwardians were devious* but merely that they thought appearances important. Their rules—whether for croquet or for a weekend house party—were set and understood; but they were rules, as everyone knew, that could be adjusted so long as decorum was preserved. Richard always distrusted the quality Edwardians esteemed quite as much as any other. This was charm, which oiled what might otherwise have appeared rather troubled waters.

---

* They were frequently refreshingly blunt. King Edward himself insisted on one royal occasion that a King Kalakua of the Cannibal Islands should take precedence, as a ruling monarch, over the Crown Prince of Germany with the argument, "Either the brute is a king or else he is an ordinary black nigger, and if he is not a king why is he here?"

At the beginning of Richard's leave the newspapers were pre-occupied with a distant conflict in which for the moment England's interest was academic. In 1903 King Edward, on a visit to Paris that had begun with sullen jeers and ended with cheers of approval, had charmed the French into considering a liaison with the British. This was the seed of that "Cordial Understanding" that consisted in diplomatic language of one Convention and two Declarations, which had the principal effect of leaving Egypt to the British and Morocco to the French. Concluded on April 8, 1904, the agreement was at once tested as the Russo-Japanese War began to escalate after the Russians (France's allies) crossed the Yalu River and the Japanese (Britain's allies) had sunk the battleships of the Port Arthur squadron. The British, Richard among them, were not displeased at the apparent superiority of the Japanese. On October 21 this urbane partisanship almost turned to belligerence. Richard opened his newspaper and found his long suspicion of the Russians confirmed. Incensed, he read that the Baltic Fleet under Admiral Rozhdesvensky, called to the other side of the world, had emerged into the North Sea and, bearing down upon the Hull fishing fleet by night, had opened fire with its secondary armament under the impression that it was already beset by Japanese torpedo boats. The Russians in their might sank the steam trawler *Crane,* beheading its captain and a third hand, riddled two other vessels, and wounded sixteen fishermen. At this intelligence the Admiralty signaled the Home, Channel and Mediterranean fleets to stand by. Had things gone further the Russians might have been caught at something of a disadvantage, since they had left Kronstadt so laden with coal and stores that they could not have worked their upper deck guns. An apology and indemnities prevented any further hostility, however, and the Russians sailed slowly on, tending to harbor in French possessions en route. After a month in Cam Ranh Bay they attempted finally to reach Vladivostok, but steaming through the Straits of Tsu Shima they were battered to pieces in the most decisive naval engagement of modern times.

By then Richard was back in Africa. Landing in Mombasa, he felt as though he had never left the country. The plain, homely stench of open gutters and the lunatic welcoming grins of the Swahili porters were a comfort. He went to bed early, so as to be ready for the morrow, when he would be busy buying stores and hiring servants. In his absence Richard had been promoted and it did not much matter that it was to a run-down company slated for disbandment. It was based in country far away from Nairobi on the other side of the Rift Valley. On March 24, 1905, he arrived at Nandi Fort and took over his command. The only other white man at the station was Walter Mayes, whose commerce with the local population Richard already mistrusted, though there were two Boer families apprehensively encamped four miles away. Before the week was out Richard and Mayes had come to their first confrontation. Mayes kept a herd of cattle in his own boma; one night two head were stolen, so Mayes took out his police and surrounded the village they had been taken to. He shot one man and captured another, retrieved his own cattle and exacted a fine of ten more. The next night, hearing that the Nandi had been raiding their neighbors, he took by force eighty-two cattle and two hundred sheep and goats in the name of justice. Richard was disgusted by this travesty, more so because Mayes neither reported his actions to his superiors nor credited the fines to the government's account. He took ninety per cent of the proceeds himself, as Richard knew from the station books. "These rough-and-ready methods may be successful in keeping a tribe down by brute force," he noted, "but they savor too much of Congo atrocities."* He told Mayes that in future all police actions must be properly reported and honest records kept. Mayes promised to do so and begged Richard not to do anything that might harm his career. Richard agreed. Fortunately

---

* In 1903 Roger Casement, a colonial official, had been charged with the investigation of the means used by agents of Leopold, king of the Belgians, to increase the output of their labor force in the Congo Free State, King Leopold's private domain. Casement revealed that quotas for collecting rubber had been set. The Congolese impressed to the task were virtually unpaid. Those who failed to meet the quota were shot or mutilated in the genitals or lost a foot or a hand by casual amputation. It was not uncommon for severed hands to be smoked and retained by the overseers in baskets as evidence of their zeal.

there was plenty of game in the area for Richard to pursue and study, so the two men were not thrown too much together.

Richard had known for some time that the escarpment north of the railroad was supposed the home of a fabulous creature, and he now began to question his local acquaintances about it in the hope of repeating his success with *Hylochoerus meinertzhageni*. By popular account the Nandi Bear was a ferocious, tawny beast capable of scrabbling its way through any boma and killing cattle, pigs or people indiscriminately in the grip of its long claws. Its cry, half roar, half scream, had been heard in the night by Europeans but none had ever set eyes on it. The Nandi themselves were a little vague about it. They gave it the name "chemosit," maintaining that it had been common when they first came to their country longer ago than anyone could calculate. But they used the same name for a devil with one leg, nine buttocks and a mouth of flame that came out at nightfall to eat small children. They said "chemosit" was hairy, stood on two legs, and still lived in the forest: which of the two creatures they were referring to was difficult to distinguish. It occurred to Richard, not one to take up too rapidly with a folk myth, that the animal, if it ever existed at all, must be some kind of anthropoid ape that had become extinct through a serious decrease in the rainfall. His theory was reinforced in a conversation with his native officer, Massud Effendi. Five men of the King's African Rifles, of whom Massud had been one, had been in London representing the regiment at the coronation of King Edward VII. As a treat they had been taken to the zoo in Regent's Park, where one of the men, a Nandi, had suddenly begun to jump up and down in delight in front of one of the cages. "There's the Nandi Bear!" he was shouting. He was looking at a rather startled chimpanzee.

Communication with the Nandi was not easy, partly because their way of life, both spiritual and temporal, was so different that a European could comprehend it only by a strenuous exercise of his imagination, partly because the official interpreters were unofficial spies for one side or the other, and partly because the Nandi were great liars, either to achieve their own ends or to please the questioner by giving him the answers they thought he wanted. Like the

Masai, the Nandi were Nilo-Hamites. They had settled in their present territory at some time in the seventeenth century and begun the style of life they still enjoyed. The Swahili of the coast, who had always regarded them with apprehension, christened them "cormorants," perhaps from their elegance of bearing but more likely for the voracity of their appetite for other people's goods. Their economy was centered on cattle but they also grew grain and other crops. They were not concentrated in villages but scattered their round mud huts at their pleasure over the countryside, though never in absolute seclusion. The Nandi would not suffer the rule of a chief, which the British could never bring themselves to realize. Instead they recognized the authority of a council of elders. There were numbers of these councils, one for each group of huts whose inhabitants acknowledged themselves part of the same *koret,* a kind of parish. The elders' eminence came from their proximity to that part of the tribe no one could see: being men of advanced age, they must obviously be closer to the spirits of the dead who, though they dwelt underground now, were still undeniably part of the community. The old men sat in the shade of a fig tree when one was available, and deliberated all matters but war. This was the affair of the young men and though they would refer their plans to the elders, with the respect due to age, the warriors made their own decisions.

Like the Masai, the Nandi were a tall, lean people, affecting much the same style of dress, a cloak of leather or cloth thrown over one shoulder and draped where the wind blew, but less given to the use of red clay for decoration. Their warriors were spare, muscular and determined, having been trained in the use of spear and shield from the moment as children they could lift them from the ground. Before the white men came they had roamed where they would, never knowing defeat and never expecting it. They acknowledged none as equals, let alone superiors, including Europeans. The Nandi called Richard "Kipkoror," the ostrich, from his habit of wearing ostrich feathers in his sun helmet for camouflage. He very soon began to make friends among them when they brought him gifts of milk, honey and eggs, for which he returned presents of a few rupees. He like them and loved their country but found some of their customs deplorable. When they killed some sheep for his men by simply squeezing their nostrils until the animals suffocated, he forbade a repetition. The Nandi began to tell Richard about the injustices Walter Mayes had been practicing on them, and gradually, as their confidence increased, they added scraps of information that Richard could piece together into a crude but useful picture of the way they lived and thought. This was the beginning of the intelligence work that was the love of his professional life.

For a while Richard was busy installing himself in his new station. He had brought with him from England a guinea box of Sutton's seeds, mainly vegetables, and they grew luxuriously. The main difficulty was to protect them from purely local hazards. Soon Richard's nights were disturbed by the loud cries of a hyena and a jackal that had developed a taste for his tomatoes and were not too fastidious to ignore his cabbages. By sitting up over a bait of rotting meat Richard succeeded in shooting both one night and was gratified to have his suspicions confirmed by the tomatoes undigested in the jackal's stomach. The same bait attracted a serval cat two nights later; its death removed the threat to the garrison's chickens. But the jackal was replaced by others of his kind and Richard was forced to stand guard yet again in the moonlight. That night he shot a duiker helping himself to the lettuce and severely frightened a huge forest pig that he could not quite bring himself, in view of its cognomen, to kill. The countryside round about the boma was no less a garden, where Richard could take his ease on crisp sweet grass and demolish for lunch with hunting knife and dripping fingers one whole and luscious pineapple sent up by a friend in Nairobi. On the open downlands of the plateau, edged by primeval forest, grew gladioli, forget-me-nots, red-hot pokers, yellow broom and blackberries, belladonna lilies striped magenta and white, and plants that had no English names—little blue flowers like petunias, creepers that bloomed a gaudy orange, and one strange scarlet fruit swelling leafless out of the ground that tasted like an orange though smelling of apples. On the side of the escarpment leading down to the railroad blazed among the other trees the brilliant spathodea, called from the bloody red of its flowers the "Nandi flame." One tree there sported yellow blossoms, so Richard sent some of its seeds to Uncle Ernie for presentation to the Royal Botanical Gardens at Kew.

Less than six weeks after Richard's arrival at Nandi the Boers came into the boma complaining that the warriors were stealing their stock. Since he had warned them that they were squatters with few rights, Richard was astonished when they insisted that he provide guards for them on the grounds that they were paying Mayes a rent of sixty rupees a month. Richard had just completed a short safari with Mayes during which Mayes's boasts of his sharp practice at the government's expense had not encouraged Richard to think better of him. But before Richard could present this new charge the heavens fell on Mayes. He rushed into Richard's house yelling, "A terrible thing has happened! My wife has arrived!" and made straight for the Scotch. All dignity and savoir faire, Richard walked across the compound. In Mayes's quarters he found a weeping, bedraggled woman not in the least attractive but clearly determined to stay after tracing her husband all the way from Mauritius. Richard could see no solution. "It is all a bit difficult," he wrote, "as Mayes has half a dozen Nandi concubines in the house. I left them to fight it out among themselves." He later taxed Mayes with the Boers' allegations and Mayes once more begged him not to disclose what he knew because he was a poor man to whom this was the only livelihood open. So many grievances were being brought to Richard by the Nandi themselves, however, that at last he felt bound to report the situation to Mayes's superior, the sub-commissioner of the province. Richard sent a copy of his report to Mayes, who countered by dispatching his interpreter on a tour of Richard's Nandi friends with instructions to boycott him. These orders were ignored.

By now Richard's information about Nandi affairs was growing in volume and accuracy. His agents were mostly Masai from a settlement near his house whom the Nandi allowed to circulate fairly freely, but he also picked up tid-bits from neighboring Nandi, partly by guile. Nandi Fort had received orders, like every out station in the territory, to build permanent defenses. Richard inveigled a Nandi friend into demonstrating the ranges of his weapons; the warrior's arrow flew a hundred and thirty-five yards and he could throw his knobkerrie sixty-eight yards and his long-bladed spear forty-two. Richard accordingly drew his plans for two bastions with ditches and parapets, Maxim gun stands and a barbed wire entanglement, had them rapidly carried out and cleared the bush all around to a distance of a hundred and fifty yards. At the same time he sent out spies to locate Koitalel, the *orkoiyot,* whom he had been told was a great man among the Nandi. This *orkoiyot* (whom the British called by the Masai title of *laibon*), or witch doctor, was the most powerful individual in the tribe. The *orkoiyot* carried no political weight, for the Nandi had no political machinery, and though feared he was not liked. His function, however, was vital. He was a rainmaker, with powers both of attracting and of dispersing rain. He could cast spells and seek out those who caused afflictions not of his prescription. He could ensure success in battle and some said he had the ability to detach his head at will so that it could witness the fighting and note down the cowardly. He was naturally accorded certain privileges in the shape of goats or calves as gifts, quantities of beer, free labor for his crops, and the proximity of a kind of bodyguard sometimes more than a hundred strong. In Richard's time at Nandi Fort there were three such individuals, though one was living with an off-shoot of the Nandi, the Kipsikis, in self-imposed exile. The Nandi's own relations with their *orkoiyot* were troubled. They had clubbed one Kimnyole to death after he had shown himself incapable of averting several natural disasters. In dying Kimyole had prophesied that foreigners would overrun the land. He had been succeeded by his son Koitalel and six years later the British had arrived, an event that tended to make the Nandi treat Koitalel with more deference than they had shown his father. What Richard wanted if possible to discover was what plans Koitalel might have to meet an expedition sent against him by the government, a likelihood that seemed to be growing more imminent. One source of the brewing discontent was now removed, however.

Mayes was transferred to another station and replaced by a political officer more to Richard's liking. In Mayes's mind when he left was the determination to avenge himself. He was soon to find the opportunity.

For some weeks Richard had been conducting a survey from the escarpment northward. Shortly after Mayes's departure he combined this business with pleasure by a seventy-mile march to Kitale, which had been described to him by an old man he had befriended, one Mbarak, a Sudanese who had deserted Emin Pasha and taken his rifle with him into the service of Tippu Tib the slaver, whose writ had once lain over the entire center of the continent. Richard had met Tippu on a visit to Zanzibar. He was immensely wealthy and his house was stuffed with treasures, one of which, a beautiful old silver coffee pot, he had surrendered according to the rules of Arab hospitality when Richard admired it. But he would not give Richard any account of his slaving days, during which he had supplied Stanley with porters for the rescue of Emin Pasha and when his stations had been the only dots of civilization, brutal though they were, between the Congo and the Indian Ocean. Mbarak's tales of Kitale whetted Richard's curiosity so sharply that he resolved to take the old man with him though his feeble legs could only totter ten miles a day. Kitale had been the concentration point before the caravans set out on the terrible march to the coast. On the way there Richard encountered more giraffe than he had ever seen and had difficulty preventing his cannibal corporal, the redoubtable Simba Manyema, shooting one for meat. At Kitale Mbarak shook with excitement, pointing out his old sleeping quarters, the place where the boys were castrated and that where the men were shackled to logs in groups of eight, and where the girls were held for the pleasure of the guards. The main gate of the wooden stockade was still standing, though partially burned. Under Richard's questioning Mbarak's mind went back, but he could only dredge up a few details. He remembered that the young eunuchs were the most valuable slaves and so the best treated but that every other one of them died on the walk to the sea and the waiting dhows, that the girls were raped day and night whenever the caravan halted, and that any man who seemed exhausted was shot. He could not recall the exact route but when Richard asked him how he had liked his work he smiled. "Plenty food, plenty women; very lovely," he said through his yellow stumps of teeth.

Back in his armed camp Richard found more news of the Nandi's restlessness. Koitalel had begun to make medicine against the government; it was his custom, among other practices, to smear a club with a magic paste which, touched to the forehead and chest of each warrior, would confer impregnability. The section commanders were waiting to carry the clubs into battle. One night in June they came patrolling and attacked the Masai manyatta outside the fort. A month later one of Richard's askaris went absent without leave to buy a Kavirondo wife. On his lonesome way down the escarpment the Nandi speared him and carried off his rifle, an offense serious enough to bring the commissioner himself all the way from Nairobi.

Sir Donald Stewart had replaced Sir Charles Eliot the year before. He had none of Eliot's talent for diplomacy nor was he blessed with Eliot's brains. His advocacy of the policy of standing no nonsense from the natives had won him the affection of the settlers, as had his loyal support of the East Africa Turf Club, where conventionality and conviviality were mandatory. Sir Donald's downright manner was everywhere as admired as his addiction to alcohol was politely ignored. The Nandi elders were summoned down the escarpment and into Sir Donald's presence, where they explained that one of their young men had quarreled with his fiancée, had thus attracted the wrath of his prospective mother-in-law, and had become so inflamed by the whole situation that he had gone off to relieve his feelings, understandably, by killing the first man he met, who by chance had been Richard's lovelorn askari. As Richard knew, this was a pack of lies. Accordingly, and taking into account other indiscretions committed recently by the Nandi, Sir Donald warned them that peace must descend at once. The elders replied that their hot-headed young warriors were clamoring for war and that their *orkoiyot* was promising that the government's bullets would turn to water. Nevertheless, Sir Donald repeated, there must be an end to their depredations and a beginning to the payment of hut tax or he would send an army against them. It was an ultimatum of a sort but Koitalel, pleading sickness, had not been there to receive it and it was, Richard thought, inconclusive. That disturbed him. "I should dearly like to take on the young men of Nandi and smash them up," he wrote, "as they are becoming too full of themselves, but the old men and the girls who live round me at Nandi are the most charming type of savages I have met and I should be sorry to molest them."

At this warlike moment the company that Richard had so painfully restored to efficiency was taken away from him and replaced with another that depressed him with its filthy equipment and apathetic mood. He did not see in this repeated assignment of troops needing his talent for training and discipline the evidence of his superiors' regard. They considered him an outstanding young officer, zealous in his profession and not afraid of responsibility, and said so in their reports, but never directly to his face. So he merely felt oppressed by the monotony of it. He was also unhappy about the policies he could not persuade anyone to change. In conversations with the sub-commissioner he expressed the view, in which he was alone, that the political officers were not trying hard enough to avert war while the soldiers were longing for it and the medal it would bring. The sub-commissioner agreed that the government's procrastination was construed by the Nandi as weakness and that Koitalel was at the core of the problem, but when Richard suggested capturing him and bringing him to the commissioner for a good talking-to he was ignored. He felt frustrated. Evidence of the accuracy of his interpretation of the situation was all around him. The Nandi frequently set ambushes for him on his way up and down the escarpment, always discovered and always dispersed, once with bloodshed. One night a rain of stones, arrows and knobkerries rattled down on the iron roof of his house, causing annoyance but no injury. The following night Richard caught the culprits, five young boys and a girl, whom he locked up in the Guard Room before having the boys spanked by his sergeant and impressing the whole group for a day's hard labor in his garden. He dismissed them with a rupee apiece and they left converted, having been under the impression that they would all be slain out of hand.

In addition to Richard's there were now four companies of askaris in the district, not nearly enough to subdue the Nandi and too many to withdraw without seeming to confirm the white man's awe of their prowess. Sitting behind his depressing barbed wire, Richard could find no relief from his woes. He began to ponder things that would not leave his mind; they led him, inevitably, to the source of his despair. "What worries me most," he wrote late one night, "is disappointment and bitterness that my own family seem to regard me as a black sheep." The love that was not returned was turning him in upon himself and he felt alone. So he sat in the hut that was his world and struggled for a glimpse of happiness. Fortunately he realized that his isolation in this barbaric country accentuated his mood: "It is hard to resist the savagery of Africa when one falls under its spell. I have felt the magnetic power of the African climate drawing me lower and lower to the level of a savage." His horror of losing the veneer of western civilization was real and legitimate; he could see plenty of evidence of deterioration in those around him. What he did not recognize was the superior strength of his own character which at least led him to analyze his despondency. He ended the records of these thoughts that night with a feeling of relief. "It does me good to commit them to paper," he concluded. "It is only by frequently reviewing my own acts and by recognizing the dangerous influences which constantly beset me that I am able to realize in time how far I have sunk and how fast is the process. It enables me once again to set myself up on the pedestal of English tradition." What Richard Meinertzhagen really needed was some action, and he was soon to get it.

The commissioner had issued to the Nandi elders a formal ultimatum imposing a fine of three hundred cattle to be paid within three weeks. The Nandi response was hilarity. At the end of September 1905 the government faced the inevitable and authorized a full-scale expedition against the Nandi. Twelve full companies of the King's African Rifles and two hundred armed police were to be employed under command of Lieutenant-Colonel E. C. Harrison.

On the same day that he received notice of this mobilization Richard's spies brought him word that Koitalel had advised a convention of the Nandi that, since no expedition was in sight, they should wipe out all the white intruders right away, beginning modestly with Richard and the political officer in his boma. Koitalel required of his warriors the acquisition of such parts of Richard's anatomy—the brains, heart, eyes, liver and the palms of the hands—as he would need to make the medicine that would turn the white men's bullets into water. As Richard saw it the contest was resolving itself into a personal confrontation and Koitalel seemed to agree. As yet, however, the latter was at a disadvantage, for Richard's intelligence was so accurate that on the one hand he knew about Koitalel's plans long before they matured and on the other he could feed false information to Koitalel through one of the *orkoiyot's* few agents, the official interpreter at the fort, whose perfidy Richard had discovered but not revealed. Richard awaited with amusement Koitalel's gambit which, the spies whispered, would be the presentation of a beautiful young virgin whose mission it would be first to seduce and then to poison him. But for Richard there was something beyond the personal enmity. He still believed that Koitalel could be persuaded or forced to avoid fighting and he strove to impress this upon his senior officers, mainly because he suspected that at the root of the government's policy lay the intention to clear the country of the Nandi, only to fill it with settlers as part of the new concept of the White Highlands. The fear that he might be the tool of such a design nagged at him.

The mobilization orders were detailed. The expedition was to be split into four mobile columns, one of them comprised of Richard's company and a company of Sudanese. The strategy was to wrest all their stock from the Nandi and in so doing draw their warriors onto the guns of the columns, thus eventually breaking their will to fight. The orders even included some notes by the medical officer recommending the use of strychnine in cases of wounds by poisoned arrows but not explaining how to distinguish between an arrow that had been poisoned and one that had not, so it seemed likely that the antidote might be as fatal as the disease. As the columns assembled along the railroad Richard begged permission for an attempt to capture Koitalel or at worst kill him. The answer came in a guarded telegram written in abominable French for secrecy's sake: if he was sure of his dispositions and if his plans would not interfere with the advance of his column he might try to capture the *orkoiyot* on October 19, two days before the start of operations proper. Richard recognized in the telegram's ambiguous tone his superiors' intention to avoid taking responsibility if he should fail. He determined to act.

His spies had given him a map of Koitalel's quarters about nine miles from Nandi Fort, a cluster of some twenty huts guarded by three hundred spearmen. Koitalel slept in a different hut each night. On a stake in front of one of them had been impaled the head of the askari who had provided something of a casus belli. Dances concentrated round it and Koitalel had promised to place Richard's head beside it before much longer. His plan was simple. He intended to invite Richard to a parley at a place surrounded by hidden warriors. When Richard shook hands Koitalel would pull him toward him so that one of his retinue could make the fatal spear thrust with Richard off balance. Of all this Richard had been apprised. In the meantime Koitalel launched his secret weapon. "The poor girl arrived this evening," Richard wrote, "very bashful, very young and quite attractive. She had nothing on except a small leather flap in front and behind to cover her private parts." The girl was carrying a small package of dark powder inside her diminutive apron which was pronounced poison by a Masai agent. With no heart to punish her Richard sent her back to the *orkoiyot*. Koitalel now saw the extent of the expedition being mounted against him and suggested a meeting. Richard, unable to surprise Koitalel by night, sent the interpreter to arrange everything for next morning. The interpreter returned with the stipulation that Richard must bring with him only five men. That night the final sentence in Richard's diary read, "During the next twenty-four hours I suspect that Koitalel or I will have said goodbye to this world; I do not really very much care which of us it is." That admission made Captain Meinertzhagen a very dangerous antagonist indeed.

At five o'clock on the morning of October 19 Richard marched out of the boma with a junior officer called Butler, eighty men, and a machine gun. Richard's hope was still that he could discover from Koitalel his whereabouts for the night so that he could be captured by stealth without bloodshed. En route the party encountered fully armed warriors in twos and threes who seemed reasonably friendly. Close to the rendezvous the interpreter, also fully armed with spear, shield, club and short sword, joined the column. They all halted as agreed on the summit of Ketparak Hill, eight miles from Nandi Fort, and Richard sent the interpreter to ask if Koitalel were ready. He then rehearsed his plan with Butler and sited the machine gun. With their binoculars he and Butler swept the slope opposite the little hollow in the hillside designated by Koitalel as the meeting place. There was a spear glinting behind every bush. Below them the *orkoiyot* moved into the open with an escort of twenty-two men, a breach of the agreement. But Richard walked down the hill as he had promised with only five. These were the native officer Mbaruk Effendi, Corporal Simba Manyema the gun bearer, and three askaris picked for their speed with weapons. They carried their rifles at full cock with bayonets fixed.

When Richard got to the edge of the little piece of level ground in the hollow he saw that there were now fifty armed men with the *orkoiyot,* one next to him with an arrow already nocked in his bow. Others were crouching in the scrub, too arrogant even to hide themselves properly. Koitalel was a tall spare man of about forty with a long intelligent face and pierced earlobes that brushed his shoulders. His eyes were bloodshot and wary. He was wearing a black cloak of monkey fur that glistened in the sun and he held a spear upright in his right hand. Richard walked toward him across the clearing slightly ahead of Mbaruk and Simba and stopped about six feet away. Through the interpreter, standing slightly forward to his right, Richard asked Koitalel to come and shake hands. "The sun is too hot," Koitalel said and did not move. Everything was very still. "Very well," Richard said, "We will conduct our conversation at this distance. Shall we sit down?" The interpreter spoke.

The moment he had finished Koitalel made an imperative, impatient gesture with his spear. An arrow whacked into the sleeve of Richard's shirt and the interpreter pivoted and drew back his spear for a thrust at Richard. Simba shot him. Richard took three steps forward, seized Koitalel and dragged him forward, feeling the *orkoiyot's* spear glance along his side. An arrow knocked off his helmet. Koitalel wrenched free. As he straightened, both Mbaruk and Richard shot him. Those closest to Koitalel were already dead and others of his bodyguard were pulling back. Richard snatched two stone-headed clubs from Koitalel's side and withdrew toward Butler, racing down the hill with the main body. They fought a running battle all the way back to the fort and reached it just before they had exhausted their ammunition.

Half an hour later Richard was recording the whole affair in his diary. He was jubilant. "So may all the King's enemies perish," he wrote grandly. "As both Koitalel and all his successors male were gathered today, I much regret that the dynasty must stop from today." As to sentiment, Richard's elation would be modified when his blood cooled; as to fact, he was misinformed. He afterward visited Ketparak Hill several times, fascinated by what he had done there, but with feelings more confused than those that now rushed forth. Fifty-one years later, in 1956, he was to come to Nandi for the last time. By then Koitalel's second son, Parserion, raised by his mother to hate the British, had threatened his own rebellion and been banished by the government. Parserion's son was one of those Richard, an old man now, met on that visit. Richard went to his old house in the boma, noting that the blue gum trees he had planted as mere sprigs now towered gigantically high with trunks sixteen feet around. The house was occupied by one Elijah, a local dignitary, whom Richard had known as a child. Elijah invited Richard to a parish council meeting and there proudly presented him to a score or so of Africans all smartly dressed in European clothes. Gently Elijah guided him round the circle, murmuring appropriate introductions; "This is the gentleman whose house I now live in . . . This is the gentleman we knew as Kipkoror . . . This is the gentleman who lived in Nandi before you were born." At last they came to a very handsome young man with the bearing of a chief, to whom

Elijah whispered politely, "This is the gentleman who shot your grandfather." The council burst into applause. Stunned, Richard stammered, "I hope you will forgive an act of war." The young man smiled and the applause redoubled.

Before Richard could complete his official report congratulatory telegrams arrived from Frederick Jackson (acting commissioner after the death a few days previously of Sir Donald Stewart), Colonel Harrison and others in authority. Three of his fellow officers, including Butler as eyewitness, had recommended him for the Victoria Cross, which Richard thought exaggerated. He had expected none of this, but neither did he see the consequences the *coup de main* would have on his career or the small effect it would have upon the Nandi. Momentarily astounded by Richard's audacity, they had completely recovered by the time the columns moved out and even had a new *orkoiyot* in the person of Kipeles, the late Koitalel's cousin. They had driven most of their cattle into the forest out of harm's way. On its third night out Richard's column was attacked in the darkness by a large force of warriors. At the alarm the camp stood to arms. One of the machine-gunners suddenly slumped sideways with an arrow in his chest. Moving him aside to take over the gun, Richard too was hit. The arrow had cut right through the fleshy part of his thumb and behind its barbs along the shaft gleamed a sticky black paste. It was time for the strychnine injection. The Nandi did not press in to the zariba but they left one porter dead and seven askaris wounded. If one of their arrows hit in the arm or leg it could be pushed right through, elsewhere its barbs had to be cut out. Richard pushed through three and cut out four from his wounded men, giving them all strychnine injections. Within an hour two of them had died from either cure or cause. Richard's own hand had turned black as jet, but by morning it was less swollen.

The column marched daily deeper into Nandi territory, sending out patrols in search of cattle and warriors. Skirmishes were frequent, brief and inconclusive but always ended in the soldiers' favor. Corporal Simba Manyema returned from one of them with a pleased expression. As Simba shouldered his rifle for the customary inspection, Richard saw with horror that in addition to the hand clasping the rifle butt at waist level five more were sticking out of Simba's belt. Richard demanded an explanation. Simba gladly gave it. They were for his supper, he said, adding that where he came from the fingers were considered the tenderest part of a man. Richard hastily ordered him to bury his supper and warned him to expect retribution. A hasty search through the Manual of Military Law did not disclose any offense with which the corporal might properly be charged, other than the catch-all of conduct prejudicial to good order and military discipline, so Richard was limited to a reprimand in general terms and instructions to avoid mutilating enemies in future. Afterward he could not resist asking Simba for more information about his tastes. Simba repeated his preference for fingers but concluded amiably, "The best of all is the buttocks of a young girl."

It took three weeks to convince the Nandi that they had met their masters. The lesson cost them some six hundred young men, upward of ten thousand cattle, and a total of sheep and goats estimated at anywhere between eighteen and seventy thousand. They agreed to move into a reserve and Richard was ordered out to complete his survey so that the area could be delineated. Just before he left camp he heard that somebody was spreading rumors that he had invited Koitalel to a friendly conference, shot him when he shook hands, and then killed the interpreter to silence him. Suspecting Mayes, who had been assigned to one of the columns during operations, Richard asked for a military court of inquiry to set the record straight. The court convened at Nandi Fort as soon as he returned from his safari. It read Richard's official report on the death of Koitalel and then heard Butler's evidence which, since Butler had been the only other white man present, was crucial. He had watched Richard walk down into the hollow to meet Koitalel but then had lost sight of everything but the top of Richard's helmet. He had heard a shot, quickly followed by others, but got no clear view of what was happening until he dashed down to Richard's assistance. Though not specific, Butler's evidence in general substantiated Richard's and certainly did not contradict anything Richard had reported. The court did not invite any native troops to give their accounts, nor any of the Nandi to offer theirs, and set down as its conclusion, "The court is of the opinion that the Laibon Koitalel was killed by a native officer (Mbaruk Effendi) of the 3rd King's African Rifles during a fight, which was the result of treacherous conduct on the Laibon's part, at a meeting which had previously been arranged between him and Captain Meinertzhagen." Richard invited the president of the court and some brother officers to a dinner and a homemade cabaret, performed stark naked except for some red and white paint by three young Nandi girls dressed as warriors. They had been left in his care by their father before the expedition began; Richard had trained them to do his housework and now they would not go home. He called them Maggie, Scraggie and Baggie and they were so fond of him he was almost embarrassed. But the celebration was premature, for Mayes's hearsay allegations had not been directly challenged at the inquiry. The rumors gained wider currency.

In the middle of December 1905 the Nandi elders were met and given final terms by the new commissioner, Lieutenant Colonel James Hayes Sadler,* and Brigadier General William Manning, the inspector-general of the King's African Rifles. They must move into the reserve within a month. At the meeting Richard discovered that two of his fellow officers had written to their superiors complaining about the court of inquiry's suppression of native evidence and demanding therefore a new inquiry at which Mayes could also appear. Manning deplored the letters and assured Richard that he himself was entirely satisfied. Nevertheless a second court was held while Richard was sketching a route through the Kabwuren forest and being exploited, to his delight, by a honey-guide.† The outcome of

---

* Colonel Sadler's plump features were customarily arranged in an expression reflecting his inner expectation that he was about to be surprised, as indeed he frequently was. As governor of the British East Africa Protectorate, he practiced white man's magic by taking a gramophone with an enormous horn into native villages, an imposition the inhabitants bore with commendable politeness. He was better known as "Flannelfoot."

†The greater or black-throated honey-guide (*Indicator indicator*), a bird of somewhat undistinguished appearance save for its bright pink bill, is unique in its remarkable habit of employing agents, sometimes human beings,

the second inquiry was the same as at the first, but Mayes had not appeared before it and its findings did not kill the rumors, so Richard requested yet a third inquiry. It assembled in the waiting room of the railroad station at Muhoroni. Part of the evidence was the report Mayes had sent to the sub-commissioner of Nandi embodying complaints made to him by Nandi prisoners of Richard's treachery toward Koitalel. When closely questioned and rebutted Mayes offered to withdraw his charges and apologize; when this was declined he refused to take any further part in the proceedings. Once more the court cleared Richard, recommending that Mayes be dismissed from government service.*

Vindicated once more, Richard was further pleased to be congratulated again on his conduct by General Manning himself. But Manning said one thing in public and wrote another in private. The mills of government trundled all the papers in the case on their way to the Colonial Office and Manning in his covering letter had not only written that Richard had arranged to meet Koitalel on his own responsibility (which was untrue) but had added his opinion that Richard's behavior had been "discreditable." This enabled a civil servant in the Colonial Office to make the sort of long-distance judgment, flavored with irony, for which civil servants believed themselves created. The man wrote in clerkly hand: "There was never such an unsuccessful ambuscade in the history of warfare. Five men who are taken in the ambuscade escape without a scratch, while

---

to get its food. It hungers after the larvae and wax of bees and will excite attention to a nest of wild bees with a repetitive chattering cry and by short rapid flights in the direction of the prize. Three of these astute birds captivated Richard in the forest and led him to the nest they had found, settling nearby and uttering low chirrups of satisfaction as it was broken open and the comb spread on the ground. The Nandi maintained that if the honey-guide were denied the fruits of its discovery it would lead its persecutor next time to a poisonous snake or some other nemesis.

* Subsequently Mayes was transferred to a junior post on the coast which he soon resigned. He then operated a plantation with so little success that by the time Richard returned to East Africa at the outbreak of the First World War he was almost destitute. Richard recruited him into his intelligence organization but within a month Mayes was embezzling funds. He went back to his plantation and died.

the fifty or more ambuscaders lose twenty-three killed. These facts appear to testify stronger than any evidence that treachery was not intended by the Laibon." Thus, by ignorance and pretentiousness, was Richard Meinertzhagen damned.* However, in Richard's routine confidential report for the year, which Richard by military etiquette had to see, the ambivalent Manning had written: "This officer has good professional qualifications. His action in the matter of the death of the Laibon during the late Nandi Expedition showed him on that occasion as wanting in judgment though prepared to accept responsibility. He is a hard-working and painstaking officer." This followed Lieutenant Colonel Harrison's "Would make a good intelligence officer in the field. The best company commander in the battalion." Richard was refreshed by these apparently golden opinions.

Out of incomprehension or stubborn arrogance the Nandi had not complied with the commissioner's orders to enter the reserve by the time stated. Some eleven hundred men, including Richard's company, were therefore extended in a line forty miles long to drive them in like sheep. It was a fairly leisurely proceeding not much assisted by the departure of the expedition's headquarters personnel to Nairobi for the week's races. The soldiers hated the work of evicting families and burning villages and they tried to avoid clashes. But when the war parties attacked, as they did infrequently, their losses amounted to about fifty per cent. Meeting two Nandi girls in the forest one afternoon, Richard challenged them. They said they were heading for the reserve, a design for which Richard commended them. He issued a pass and they gave him a present of some honey which he was greedy enough to eat at once. Within ten minutes the sweat had started out of him in rivulets and his head was reeling. His men gazed at him in consternation, clicking their tongues in concern and giving it as their opinion that he was

---

* Fifty-three years later, when a reluctant bureaucracy let him see all the papers that, by law, should have been available after fifty years, he realized for the first time how he had been betrayed. He had been caught between the upper millstone of high government policy, oiled with a certain hypocrisy, and the nether of necessity.

certain to die of the poison. He took a huge emetic of salt and water, vomited for an hour though scarcely conscious, then dosed himself with big drafts of castor oil and chlorodyne, that sovereign remedy by Dr. J. Collis Browne. Though he had to exert a prodigious effort of the will to stay awake, by morning the agony in his belly had abated.

The more obstinate Nandi were still hiding in the forest but encounters with them were brief. It was a beautiful place with deep, dark gullies at its heart, where Richard found orchids pink as salmon with centers of lambent orange; as soon as he brought them out into the sunlight they faded and withered so quickly he had no time even to press them. At last the dreary business came to an end. During the drive Richard's company had burned more than nine hundred huts, scores of granaries and cattle compounds, and a hundred and forty-five acres of standing crops, and had had to kill fifty-one Nandi in the process. Heartsore and tired, Richard was relieved when orders came for the driving line to coagulate into groups ringing the reserve in entrenched camps. In sixty-two days he had marched nine hundred and twenty-six miles and he was sick of the sight of elegant, powerful black bodies laid out in rows like trophies. He made camp on the spur of a hill frequented by a leopard; roused by a sentry, Richard killed the beast with a shoulder shot, a feat he was surprised to hear being cheered by a bunch of Nandi spearmen watching from the edge of the forest. He put his second bullet just over their heads. "Really these Nandi have the cheek of the Devil," he wrote.

Back at the fort he found the first evidence of the scheme he had suspected months before in the shape of two prospective settlers. They had come to look at the Uasin Gishu with its rolling grassland bountiful with game, where the francolin when flushed whirred away like English partridges; two million acres without a barrier of any sort, natural or manmade. Richard had first seen it when it was still an Eden and he was among the last to do so. Before long the Boers would come with long spans of oxen dragging their creaking carts over virgin earth to places where only the impala had set her delicate hoof. Within two years they would be thinking it a home from home, another high veldt, plotting it into farms and breaking it beneath the plow. When Richard had started his second African tour at the beginning of 1905 the white population of the East Africa Protectorate amounted to no more than seventeen hundred, of whom more than two hundred were functionaries of various kinds.

Before very long it would be possible for a noblewoman to pen notes of advice to "any girl who determines to try the life of a settler in the Protectorate." Such a girl had better acquaint herself with cooking, gardening, stable management and the more basic rules of farming. "I would add house management," her ladyship continued, "were it not that the supervision of native servants is an art in itself, and one in which the qualities which make success or failure seem ingrained. One could not, for instance, learn by experience in England when is the right time to have a servant beaten for rubbing silver plate on the gravel path to clean it, and that after several previous warnings." The unmistakable accent of the middle class was beginning to sound over Africa.

In East Africa the words of Lugard,* the first man to practice on that continent the art of indirect rule, were lost in a babel of acquisitive voices. He had said: "For two or three generations we can show the Negro what we are: then we shall be asked to go away. Then we shall leave the land to those it belongs to, with the feeling that they have better business friends in us than in other white men."

Richard Meinertzhagen disliked the change in climate. Sitting atop Ketparak Hill, he began to feel he had had enough of the

---

* Frederick John Dealtry Lugard, first Baron of Abinger, was the most selfless, modest and energetic servant by whom any backward people had the good fortune to be governed. His beginnings were humble enough to force him, in order to buy a good rifle, to hunt down a man-eating tiger with a bounty on its head. All his great endeavors, from his fight with the slave-traders of Lake Nyasa in 1888 to his amalgamation of Nigeria in 1914, were impelled by the purest altruism. His conclusion that the only justification for one nation to exercise control over another less developed must be the will and ability to produce benefit for both remains a classic declaration. No one since has discovered how to provide this benefit without the control.

country. It had given him certain advantages: he had arrived with nothing but his father's modest allowance and he would leave with three thousand pounds in the bank; he had seen a lot of active service and gained immeasurably in professional experience; he had learned to face violence without being overwhelmed but never without a sense of shock after the action ended; he had reveled in luxurious years of sport and the study of nature. But he sensed that a time of decision was coming and he suspected the eternal sorcery of Africa that would seduce him forever away from his British regiment if he allowed it to. Besides, the climate was beginning to sap even his brute vitality, the natives were growing more and more irritating to him, and though he had made friends he had found no boon companion. He was beginning to dread the long periods of solitude in stations like Nandi Fort. Though he entertained visitors there, some more welcome than others, he missed what Kipling called "The loveliest sound in the world—deep-voiced men laughing together over dinner," the token of what for Richard's generation was one of the most precious kinds of human communion. If ever they referred to it directly they called it "mannishness." They regarded it as next to godliness. It was a fusion of idealism and sensitivity, with the common background of public school and the imperial theme for catalyst, and while to a post-Freudian world it might seem effeminate it was powerfully and exclusively masculine. It was the impulse, rarely rationalized and seldom described, that made men sacrifice their lives for others without visible hesitation. It was a subtle, delicate and vital relationship in which the emotions were deeply committed, and it was, of course, quite incomprehensible to those who had no need of it. Cecil Rhodes had been one of its personifications: his last will and testament, published in 1902, gave evidence of that when it stipulated that a candidate seeking election to a Rhodes Scholarship must be investigated for "his qualities of manhood, truth, courage, devotion to duty, sympathy for and protection of the weak, kindliness, unselfishness and fellowship."

Like all aspirants in this strangely spiritual, quasi-monastic rule Richard was scarcely aware that it existed. He felt yearnings but he could not give them voice. He was more directly concerned with the next practical step in his career, so he was glad to receive orders that would at least get him away from Nandi and give him fresh surroundings in which to debate his future. In 1905 *Regulations for The King's African Rifles* had appeared for the first time with a warning, partially obscured by schedules and directives about boots, that battalions could be called on to serve anywhere and might even encounter a foe "able to use arms of precision in open country." In the spring of 1906 it was still unclear just who this external enemy might be, though the Colonial Office began to issue memoranda with titles like *Defense of Colonial Ports* and *Notification of Preparation for War*. It was all the more confusing when at the same time the Colonial Office announced, "With regard to Germany, it seems probable that they will have enough to do for some time to come to keep their own natives in German East Africa in order, but in any case, with the troops in Uganda, the East Africa Protectorate, the British Central Africa Protectorate and Zanzibar, and with our white settlers and the railway, we ought to be able to dispose of any force which the Germans could send from their Protectorate." No member of this array of might shared the Colonial Office's confidence that such a feat could be accomplished without reinforcement from elsewhere in the Empire. Colonel Harrison wisely decided to send Richard to the German frontier to find out what was happening and to guess what might. Richard fully agreed with his commander's reasoning. "Sooner or later we are bound to have a war with the Germans," he wrote, "and what I do now may be of great value to any force of ours advancing from Voi toward Kilimanjaro."

Southeast of Kilimanjaro, that mountain of light which lay within German East Africa, the frontier thrust a salient into German territory like a derisory and unwelcome finger. On the British side lay Taveta and the railroad station at Voi and on the German side Moshi, some seventy miles as the crow flies from Voi. These were the towns named in the the directions for Richard's reconnaissance. Passing through Nairobi on his mission, Richard was astonished at how the place had been transformed. Two years before he had known every resident but now he scarcely recognized a face.

There were new buildings everywhere. It was even said that there was to be a new Government House and Richard was amused to be told that the projected site for it was an empty plot of ten acres or so. It was the land he had bought when he first came to the country; no one had asked his permission to build so he kept his peace, scenting a delicious tangle for the future. At Voi he dropped off the train and began to trek in a downpour across the Serengeti Plains, stopping for a day or so at various points to sketch the country. It was so densely wooded that infiltration would be simple and water was plentiful, so the best defensive position would lie forward, causing the Germans to cross as much waterless desert as possible from Kilimanjaro before they attacked. "It is gorgeous country for ambushes," Richard noted with relish. Crossing the Bura River he met a Maltese trader who imparted the uncomfortable news that the Germans had settled two thousand five hundred vengeful Boers on the slopes of Kilimanjaro. Richard decided to be careful.

There were giraffe on the road of an unusual three-horned variety. Richard shot a bull weighing half a ton for meat for his men; he himself dined off its marrow bones and a roast partridge, salting its prehensible tongue for future consideration. Every night he heard lions roaring and saw their fresh spoor in the morning when he struck camp. At one of his camps one evening two German askaris arrived, having passed through Taveta on their way from Moshi to mail letters at Voi, a practice he was surprised to learn was commonplace. Since they were going armed in British territory Richard forced them to surrender their equipment but allowed them to deliver their letters. He was glad of an excuse to examine their rifles and ammunition. On the fifth day of his safari Richard came through the rain to Taveta, a township the finest weather would not have much enhanced. He decided that at least a brigade would be needed to hold a position there and reflected that in case of war the choice must be between defending Taveta in strength with the desert behind and concentrating at Voi for a slow advance across it later, assuming always that any advance might well be unnecessary when the decisions of such war would be reached in Europe. From Taveta to the frontier was a short step and Richard crossed it under a German post striped red, white and black. Ten years later, passing that way again with General Smuts and an army, he removed the post and sent it home.

The first white man Richard met was a German trader in camp on the the bank of the Shalo River in the shade of some magnificent baobabs. From him Richard learned that there were no Boers on Kilimanjaro after all but that four hundred of them had settled near Arusha, where they were not taking too kindly to the rigors of German rule. Next day Richard marched into Moshi Fort with no sense of indelicacy since he had been introduced to its commander in Nairobi. Oberleutnant Abel of the Imperial German Army was a pleasant enough fellow and certainly enough of a gentleman to show Richard his finest hospitality. Aware nevertheless that they were probably nursing a viper to their bosoms, Abel and his colleagues bombarded Richard with questions of a friendly but military nature. Supposing the torrent of questions to be a means of inhibiting his own, Richard answered as innocently as he could. While his hosts were playing tennis in the cool of the late afternoon Richard strolled about the fort admiring the view, noting the location of its water supply and mentally mapping the best routes for attacking it. He fell in with three noncommissioned officers also taking the air who, supposing him from the excellence of his German accent either one of themselves or a Boer, obligingly described the strengths and weaknesses of their askaris and the location and composition of their garrisons, and revealed that though there was then no reserve in the country, the hundred and forty or so Europeans now living there after serving in the German army would shortly form one. Next day Abel insisted that Richard take the salute as his company marched past and then took him round to watch their training.

Richard left Moshi with a sense of achievement not unmixed with surprise. The euphoria had not quite worn off when a second triumph came his way. He was camping near the Maktau waterhole on the road back cross the Serengeti Plains when his men brought in an African they had casually met. The man admitted that he was a German askari. He was carrying a letter to one Count Cudenhove which he was to deliver, on Oberleutnant Abel's orders, without passing near Richard's camp. He was delighted to accept Richard's offer of a night's protection from the lions so abundantly audible in the approaching darkness. While the man slept his letter was privily removed from his keeping. It required Cudenhove, who was on the Bura River, to discover by stealth what notes of military value Richard might recently have made. The letter was resealed and replaced and Richard marched happily toward Bura and the unsuspecting Count.

According to a local planter Cudenhove had been reconnoitering the Voi-Taveta road in the guise of a geologist and prospective settler of Austrian nationality and was now ensconced with seven servants in a cluster of tents and grass huts. Richard had made plans. Cudenhove was to receive an invitation to the planter's house and his servants were then to be called to the local administrative office to fill out some forms. In the middle of the afternoon Richard and one of the planter's assistants walked into Cudenhove's deserted refuge, removed two dispatch cases and some maps from a tin box under Cudenhove's bed, sprinkled some kerosene around, put a match to it and left. Seeing the smoke, Richard's men innocently rushed down from their camp to help, "but," as Richard sadly recorded, "it was no good. Grass huts burn very quickly." Cudenhove was forced to accept Richard's hospitality for the night and Richard was careful not to disturb what equanimity Cudenhove might have left by disclosing that he knew the count was an officer of engineers in the German army. Cudenhove left, composed but not wholly unsuspicious, for Moshi Fort and Richard celebrated by plunging into the Voi River. He was sitting contently on a mossy rock enjoying his glory and his utter nakedness when there trotted into view on a white donkey a very beautiful woman in the white habit of a nun. She was so ravishing that Richard in awe could not move a muscle. The apparition broke the silence by wishing him good morning in French. Richard regretted, also in French, that he could not stand up. It transpired that the lady's name was Cecilia and her rank, Mother Superior. "She looked perfectly heavenly as she sat on her white donkey in midstream," Richard remembered, "but I was thankful when with a smile she wished me goodbye."

Cudenhove's maps were exquisitely drawn and lavishly detailed and covered exactly the same terrain as Richard's. His notes were comprehensive and Richard was flattered to find that their conclusions agreed with his own. Determining to attach this independent but expert opinion to his own report he bore away for Nairobi with the air of a privateer captain bringing home to port a particularly lavish treasure ship. Marching smartly and expectantly into Colonel Harrison's Orderly Room, he was given the bad news. The Colonial Office, having considered all the papers relating to the recent Nandi Expedition, regarded it as undesirable that Captain Meinertzhagen should continue to serve in East Africa. He was to be sent home as soon as possible.

CHAPTER 10

All of Us Russians
Are Armed

Richard Meinertzhagen's leave-taking had been painful. Tears had stood in the soft dark eyes of his askaris as he walked down their ranks before quitting Nandi Fort for the last time. In Nairobi Colonel Hayes Sadler, the commissioner, had agreed reluctantly to grant an audience but could not bring himself to discuss the reports on the Nandi Expedition or to meet Richard's steady gaze. In his smaller office Frederick Jackson, friendly as ever, had risked his superior's grave displeasure by telling Richard that Hayes Sadler had refused to countenance the recommendation by the battalion commander, Colonel Harrison, of a high award for valor for Richard. Jackson advised Richard to put his case, on reaching London, to the War Office. The officers of the King's African Rifles gave Richard a farewell dinner in the Mess consisting almost wholly of champagne and nostalgia and followed, as was customary, by a roughhouse. Two officers who bore grudges against Richard took advantage of the melee to set upon him in earnest; both were heavier but neither was sober or fit and each in turn retired with a nose broken by Richard's knee. Next morning Richard called on them and, finding them abed, left them a note apiece extolling the virtues of the sound mind in the sound body. His train pulled out for Mombasa with the regimental band struggling tunelessly but passionately with "Auld Lang Syne."

Richard sailed home in the French steamer *Natal* with some misgivings, unaware that Harrison and a brother colonel had both written to his father explaining the circumstances of his return, commending his conduct and promising their support. He knew he could count on his father who, having read with horror in *The Times* the report of his wound from the poisoned arrow, had at once hurried to the War Office for more information and had not rested until he had got it. His letter of sympathy had warmed Richard's heart then, as had the telegrams from uncles and aunts. From his mother had come only silence and he feared that she would take this latest episode as merely another proof of her conviction that he was the black sheep of the family. She did. Her reception of him was not unkind, but it was cool.

The Meinertzhagen family was not without influence; shortly after his return Richard received two replies to a request he had made to the War Office for a chance to present his case in person. The first assured him formally that the Army Council had virtually ignored the charges against him. The second invited him to an interview with the Secretary of State for War himself. Richard Burdon Haldane was, as it happened, a very great friend and something of a disciple of Aunt Beatrice's small but permeative husband, Sidney Webb. A large man with a pudding of a nose, Haldane presented to the unwary the padded symmetry and the melting gaze of a big seal, yet his eyes shone with the hard evidence of a gigantic intellect and his fancy tripped along within that well-groomed mass on the feet of an unpredictable and slightly demoniac elf. A friend, idly inquiring what kind of an army Haldane proposed to build, had been told "Hegelian." Though repeated across a score of dinner tables this gnomic answer defied analysis and was never amplified by its author. Whatever was at play in the labyrinth of Haldane's mind, the fact was that he found in the War Office little promise of profitable conflict. When his generals guardedly assembled to inquire what might be his plans Haldane charmed them with a metaphor. Sitting solid as a dragoon he bent on them the most serene of looks. He was, he explained, a blushing virgin barely united to a masterful god of war; none in the country could expect issue of the match before nine months had passed. Apart from reorganizing the dessicated command network of the army through its new general staff, Haldane's chief concern was the formation of an expeditionary force for service on the continent of Europe of six infantry divisions and one of cavalry backed by the mass of a territorial force founded on the age-old prides of the country militia and the yeomanry. Many, including Lord Kitchener, scorned his plan but it would be Haldane's professionals who held the line against the German hook at Paris in 1914, the impeccable and deadly rhythm of their musketry drumming a diapason in the twilight of an older order.

Haldane was not the man, as Richard well knew, to allow friendship to distort fact. Richard was greatly relieved therefore when Haldane allowed him to present his version of the encounter with Koitalel and clearly believed it. He promised Richard that his military career would not be affected in any way in spite of the Colonial Office's antipathy. With this lesson in bureaucratic lubrication for study Richard went home to await orders and promptly forgot it.

The next military communication Richard received required and requested him to rejoin the battalion he had last seen in Burma five years before, now returned to its native soil and still commanded by the irascible man whose bad manners had helped drive Richard to Africa. Joining the battalion at Bordon, some ten miles from the great military complex of Aldershot, Richard was amazed at the improvement in its professional standards. It was even permissible to discuss training or to read a military textbook in the Mess, though the social climate there had not altered much even though ladies were sometimes present. At supper one evening Colonel Bird sportively flipped a piece of bread at one of his female guests. She, replying more accurately with a morsel of ham, Bird now fired a chicken leg which, through an error in trajectory, hit Richard. Not wishing to join the bombardment, Richard took a plate of cold soup and contrived accidentally to tilt it down the colonel's overheated neck. On the best of days Bird's offensive language in his passages of temper were no easier to bear than before and Richard was glad to receive orders to embark for South Africa. Though his time in England had been brief Richard was delighted. It was a chance to see a new country but beyond that, and deeper, lay his unhappiness at home where, partly through his own uncommunicative habits, he felt himself a stranger. Moreover he sensed running through the country currents of change that he did not like and only partially understood.

The voices of radicals were rasping louder and louder from those parts of Britain that industrialization had laid under a black pall. Early in 1906 a general election had brought these voices, shouting in the triumph of a Liberal landslide, into the House of Commons. One of them, more melodious and more savage than most, sounded the note of revolution. "All down history nine-tenths of mankind have been grinding corn for the remaining tenth," David Lloyd George declared, "and been paid with the husks and bidden to thank God they had the husks." It was a bitter and an ominous cry and it raised echoes everywhere in the raw, red-brick sprawl of an England growing proletarian.

In 1906 an orchid could be sold at auction in Cheapside for eleven hundred and fifty guineas, a sum that represented three times the yearly wages of ninety-nine Englishmen out of every hundred. At a time when tax was paid on incomes of over a hundred and sixty pounds a year, fewer than a million had to pay it out of a total in England and Wales of seven million households; half the national income was taken by one-ninth of the population and a half of the nation's capital sat comfortably in the pockets of one-seventh. But the efforts of the Liberals to reduce this alarming inequity were bedeviled by forces that within a decade would engulf the western world.

The first intimation of this passed relatively unremarked for what it signified, when in February 1906 there slid into the chilly waters of the Tyne a line-of-battle ship whose new turbine engines gave her a speed of twenty-one knots and whose ten twelve-inch guns could hurl an unanswerable broadside. She had been named *Dreadnought* and she was acclaimed, as was right, a revolutionary weapon of war. What was less obvious was that in immediately rendering obsolete every other capital fighting ship in every other fleet in the world, at the same time she had reduced the potential of the Royal Navy far below tolerance. Her begetter, Admiral Sir John Arbuthnot Fisher, had launched not only the first all-big-gun ship but also an arms race. Fisher's sea-beaten countenance, circular and seamed, was habitually arranged in the pugnacious challenge, accentuated by his round, hooded eyes, of a samurai. Exuberant, impelled by the purest of motives, and as ruthless within the Admiralty as outside it, he built a new navy, realigned the fleets to face the threat from Germany, and gave his country the weapon without which she might not have been able to enter the First World War, and certainly could not have won it. Fisher's advocacy of oil fuel was as passionate as any of his policies and was to have unforeseen results. In 1904 he had been told by Lord Selborne, First Lord of the Admiralty, "The substitution of oil for coal is impossible, because the oil does not exist in this world in sufficient quantities." Nevertheless, the following year an oil concession was obtained in Persia which, though not at first productive, was later with Admiralty help to turn into an Imperial asset and affect the whole attitude of the Powers toward the Middle East. The first evidence of this in Europe was Fisher's launching in 1906 of the torpedo boats known as "oily-wads" that were the precursors of the oil-fired navy.

Presently, however, Britain's interest in the lands that since the Crusades had been little more than an exotic wilderness, ground for poets and eccentrics, was much more concerned with her prerogatives in trade, traffic and matters of defense than in the production of petroleum. The Persian Gulf itself was recognized by all as within the sphere of the government of India, a reality Lord Curzon, then viceroy, had asserted late in 1903 with a stately perambulation of cruisers off the desolate shores of those petty princedoms that existed by pearl fishing, piracy and brigandage, and a hand-to-mouth commerce by dhow with India and Africa. Within Persia the Russian domination of five northern provinces was accepted equably, as was Britain's primacy in the south. For the rest, all was rock and sand and cities set in ancient ways; as yet there was no realization of the great turgid reservoirs of power that lay below.

It was not an area in which Britain felt the need for much activity, since without it her possessions and dependencies already covered more than a fifth of the land surface of the entire earth and counted a population of some four hundred millions.

A speck in this vast Empire, but destined to play no small part in its fortunes in the Middle East, Richard Meinertzhagen arrived uneventfully in the long sweep of Table Bay at dawn on February 3, 1907. The cloud clothing the flat top of Table Mountain lifted with the sun and Richard went ashore into Cape Town, to be packed at once onto an overcrowded train for a journey of two days and two nights. He slept in a lavatory with four other officers and arrived at Middelberg in the Transvaal without having seen much of the majestic scenery of South Africa. The 3rd Battalion of the Royal Fusiliers was under the temporary command of Major Guy du Maurier, whose abundant charm captivated Richard at once and whose opinion of this new company commander read, "His self-reliance is unusual and I think justified." Richard's old acquaintance from India, Hare, was there; still, in Richard's opinion, "as mad as his March namesake." He thought the adjutant "outrageously punc-tilious," humorless and unimaginative, but admired his industry. Militarily the battalion was more efficient and socially a pleasanter home than the 1st Battalion had been when Richard had first joined it at Nasirabad, but it was put to some ludicrous extremes by higher authority, such as a sudden preparation in the middle of the night for immediate war against the far-off Zulus, all the result of a garbled rumor picked up from the local station-master by a hysteri-cal staff officer.

Middelberg, the Fusiliers' current base, lay east of the long escarpment of the Drakensberg, noticeably hotter and more humid than the puritanical Boer townships on the high veldt. In December 1907 the battalion moved to Pretoria, in time for Richard to eat lunch on Christmas Eve at the Union Club, in its way as notable a building as the simple house where Paul Kruger had lived and the State Model Schools whence Churchill had famously escaped one day before his repatriation was due. The Club extended its facilities to the Fusilier officers as guests and Richard had been wondering if he might become a member. A slim man sitting at the next table with a heavier, deep-chested companion overheard him talking about it and came over. His name was Jan Smuts and he introduced Richard to the muscular man. He was General Louis Botha, then premier of the Transvaal and within three years to become first prime minister of the Union of South Africa. Botha spoke English haltingly and he seemed rather sullen and tired, but his manner obscured the moderation and sagacity that made him a statesman of rank. Smuts had recognized Richard's name at once, having met his mother at Aunt Kate's house in Cheyne Walk, a haven of a sort for Smuts since Aunt Kate (now Lady Courtney through the elevation of her husband, the radical Leonard, to the dignity of Lord Courtney of Penwith) had vigorously supported the cause for which he had fought in the Boer War, reviling the British army and antagonizing her nephew Richard. The more Smuts talked that lunchtime, the more Richard liked him.

Richard's standing in the regiment continued to grow. At the end of 1907 the new battalion commander, Colonel Shipley, reported: "Good temper and pleasant companion. Keen on sport. Is at present on leave shooting in Central Africa." Richard added two buffalo bulls, a huge eland and a variety of antelope to his total of trophies. The next year's summary read: "An excellent officer. Great capacity for command and leadership and power of instructing. Exceptionally self-reliant. Tact, temper and judgment all good. Good eye for country. Influence with officers and men is good. Very active, energetic and fond of sport. Good rider and polo player. Very temperate. Is particularly good and enterprising in the field." Colonel Shipley's confidence prompted him to assign Richard to a difficult but familiar duty, the command of a company of mounted infantry that had been allowed to run badly to seed. The men were sullen and dirty and Richard began by sending two-thirds of them back to riding school. Shortly after his arrival two of his fusiliers deserted. They were located by some natives, so Richard surrounded their hiding place in the hills with the rest of his company, each man with his rifle loaded since the deserters were armed and presumably desperate. Richard called out to them to surrender and began to walk toward them. One of the men shouted to him that he would shoot if he came closer. An easy target, Richard turned cold with fear, "but," he said, "from a pure sense of duty I had to go on." His resolution was the stronger. Both deserters laid down their rifles when he was only a few feet away. Richard saved them from a court-martial that would certainly have sent them to prison, delivered a searing homily, appointed one his groom and the other his horse-holder, and thus made two devoted friends. "I consider him quite the best Company Commander in the battalion," wrote Colonel Shipley approvingly. "He has a particularly good influence with the men and his company is always in good order."

On top of his regimental work Richard had been reading military history and whatever books he could find on the arts of war with the intention, not wholly in the front of his mind, of preparing himself for Staff College. Since he was due for home leave he determined to spend part of it touring the field of Waterloo and the more extensive battlegrounds of the Crimea. At the latter he had a double purpose. Not long after arriving in London he called at the War Office, impeccable in the silk hat and long morning coat that were de rigueur, to inquire of the Russian Section if he could perform any service for them while on his academic vacation. He could. The Russians were building a fort above the north entrance to Sevastopol Harbor; he might reconnoiter it. He might also assist the Admiralty by taking soundings in the harbor. And further, he might proceed to the Caucasus to check reports from an agent there. He must not, of course, be identified in any way with the War Office, the Admiralty, or if possible even the army, though since the Foreign Office insisted on writing his rank and regiment in his passport this last affiliation would have been difficult to disown. Richard therefore traveled as a military student.

He had prepared thoroughly. He had practiced memorizing a landscape or a building so accurately that he could sketch it later in detail. The War Office had given him entrée to the forts at Dover and Portsmouth so that he could familiarize himself with the art of the engineer and the shape of cannon shrouded by tarpaulins. He had even held a private dress-rehearsal by stealing into the fort at

Tilbury in the mouth of the Thames by night, making a sketch and retiring without having disturbed the garrison that was supposed to be alert against such rude intrusion. He knew that he would never be able to retain a mass of figures in his head and making notes would be dangerous so he decided to transfer his observations and measurements onto maps that were already crammed with detail. Accordingly he bought Baedecker's *Russia* and Kinglake's *Atlas to the Crimea*, hoping they would perform a double service.

Richard arrived in the Crimea looking the complete tourist, though his pieces of baggage were sealed with bits of khaki thread almost invisible to anyone but a professional. At the gentlemanly hour of eleven on the third day of his stay in Sevastopol he hailed a carriage and directed its driver toward the Alma, a location most fruitful to the military scholar. There, on September 20, 1854, the British army had advanced to the seizure of Sevastopol at seven o'clock in the morning; Lord Raglan's unassuming plan of a frontal assault in parade-ground formation through vineyards, across a river, up a hill, and into the Russian redoubts and trenches was simpler to comprehend than to execute, but the bloodied remnants of the Light Division, the Duke of Cambridge's Guards, and Sir Colin Campbell's Highlanders had scrambled at last onto the heights. It was thus, if only in a negative sense, a place of instruction. It was also the site of the new Russian fort. A few hundred yards away from it Richard stopped his carriage and began to approach it on foot. He could not see a single sentry but as he neared the edge of the ditch two soldiers came out of the main gate on the double. Calmly Richard dropped his trousers and squatted. The soldiers halted at a respectful distance. Seeing that he could postpone but not prevent a confrontation, after a few minutes Richard stood up and adjusted his dress. The Russians questioned him in their own language, but getting no answers merely shrugged and trudged off back to the fort. Richard reentered his conveyance and drove leisurely on to another part of the river.

That night after dark he slipped out of his hotel and headed at a fast walk back to the fort. It took him three hours. He spent another three inside the fort, which he had found it easy to enter, and got back to his hotel just as a raw dawn was breaking, his head packed with figures. He was a little disconcerted, therefore, when an elderly gentleman blocked his way through the foyer and asked point-blank where he had spent the night. Fortunately, Richard was ready for that. He said he had slept in a brothel. The gentleman asked for its address. At this indelicacy Richard became irritated, told the old man to mind his own business, and pushed past him to his room. Once there he began to think. At least his boxes were intact, but this surveillance at night was unexpected. He decided to contact the Admiralty's agent in the city. The agent turned out to be a middle-aged Dutchman running a small business; when Richard described his adversary in the hotel the agent immediately identified him as one of the most dangerous officers of counter-intelligence in the area. Less than comforted, Richard determined nevertheless to persevere and the Dutchman offered him the services of his son, a boy of four-teen, for his next reconnaissance. Back in the hotel Richard discovered that his boxes had been opened by knocking the pins out of their locks.

Two days later Richard enjoyed a prolonged lunch with the governor of Sevastopol. While he was doing so his boxes were searched again. Undeterred, he made a final excursion to the fort in daylight with the Dutch boy for company. Richard was carrying a flower press which they began to fill with crocuses and any other spring plants they could discover, slowly working their way up the slope toward the blank walls of their objective. Nearing the ditch they sat down to await events. After a while two Russian soldiers debouched and requested their company. At the entrance Richard and the boy were searched, then marched to the Commandant's office, attended by their captors with the flower press. Finding his own language unintelligible the commandant asked Richard in French what he was doing on forbidden ground. Richard explained that he was collecting plants, the press was presented as evidence, and the commandant launched into an enthusiastic account of his own botanical interests. The conversation moved from that to birds and thence to the Crimean War, after which vodka was offered and coffee brought in. Apologizing for its incomplete state the commandant insisted on conducting Richard over his fort. As an engineer there was much he could illuminate. They strode here and there with the commandant eulogizing and Richard memorizing until after half an hour the commandant was called away. Sitting in the sunshine Richard hastily unloaded his aching brain by scribbling notes on a scrap of paper. There was no denying, however, that he had most seriously abused the commandant's hospitality; he recalled his similar lapse at Moshi. He left the fort with a pleasant sense of achievement and gratitude but he felt also the prickings of reproach.

Next morning Richard was up early for a last saunter along the promenade circling the harbor. He had been followed, he noticed, by a stocky, nondescript man. Richard stopped. The man approached, quite relaxed, and politely raised his hat. In perfect English he asked if Richard were a photographer. Richard said he was and moreover had a permit from the governor allowing him to be. The man offered to develop his film at a reasonable price but Richard declined with the excuse that he was about to leave for Odessa. They began to walk and the man then started to talk about the Crimean War so interestingly that Richard did not notice that they had drifted away from what little traffic there was. Suddenly they were quite alone. Richard had not yet had time to transfer the previous day's harvest of figures from the fort to his guidebooks and the incriminating scrap of paper was still in his pocket. As calmly as he could he offered the man a cigarette. As the man took one Richard suddenly asked for a match and patted the man's pockets. There was a revolver in the righthand one. "Why are you armed?" Richard demanded. A little discomposed, the man said, "All of us Russians are armed." Bluntness now his best defense, Richard told him that if on their way back to the promenade the man moved his hand to his pocket he would club him. Meanwhile he surreptitiously crumpled up his notes and flipped them unseen into a bush. When the man had left he retrieved them and was able to leave their information with the rest in the hands of the British consul in Sevastopol, who had kindly offered to carry them to the British embassy in Constantinople to await Richard's arrival. Boarding the steamer for Odessa, Richard was annoyed to find his companion of the morning already gazing keenly over the rail and anxious to resume converse. As they were passing out of the harbor in the shadow of the fort the man borrowed Richard's binoculars. He returned them as soon as they had rounded the headland.

Warned by Richard's fellow-traveler, the customs officials at Odessa made a thorough search of his luggage and his person but finding nothing were forced to apologize so abjectly that Richard's irritation turned to amusement. The next day, his thirty-second birthday, he received one of the worst shocks of his life, more revolting and more lasting in its effect even than the scenes of blood he had lived through in East Africa. He was having dinner with the British consul-general when they heard a running in the street outside and the faint babble of terror in the distance. People were milling about hysterically in front of the consulate. "It's a pogrom," the consul-general said. The house stood on one side of a small square so well lit that the two Englishmen could clearly see what was happening. Russians waving clubs, knives and axes were breaking down doors and flushing frantic Jews into the street and looting stores. They clubbed or knifed their quarry among the broken glass. One old man's head was cloven by an ax in front of the consulate; a young woman twisted through the gate and flung herself inside gibbering with fear just as her Russian pursuer was about to fasten on her; a youth was beaten, robbed and dumped mangled in the gutter. The consul was having difficulty in restraining Richard from action. Richard was now as angry as he had ever been, through a sense of impotence and because he had realized with horror that from their expressions the Russians were relishing this calculated brutality. "For God's sake don't provoke them! They're mad!" the consul was saying. Richard heard old Hales's voice, echoing from his Aysgarth years: "Don't just stand there! *Do* something!" A thick-set ruffian lurched past the doorway dragging a twelve-year-old girl by her hair through the gutter, shouting in his lust above the girl's screams. Richard could not help himself. He launched into the attack, so unhesitating and swift, that made him such a dangerous fighting man. He kicked the Russian low in the belly, hit him with all his strength as he crumpled screaming, and gathered the child in his arms. "I am deeply moved by these terrible deeds," he wrote that night, "and have resolved that whenever or wherever I can help the Jews, I shall do so to the best of my ability. There is no word in the British language to describe such vile and bestial behavior."

His introduction to espionage had been exciting work, Richard concluded, but dirty, and he decided never to undertake another mission of the kind. "The risks are not worth it," he wrote, "and it involves too much mental strain. I feel a perfect wreck, tired out both morally and physically. It also requires too great a memory capacity for men of my caliber. My advice to others doing such work is to be British and sociable, two rather paradoxical qualities. Avoid acting. It adds to one's difficulties, and one forgetful moment may ruin one's whole work." It was advice of dubious utility to a professional. His mission accomplished, Richard chose to go home by way of Greece. About an hour away from Patras his train suddenly began to buck like a wild horse. Realizing that they were off the track, Richard peered out of the window. A hundred feet below yawned the jagged rocks of the Gulf of Corinth. Richard was pondering the likelihood of the whole train's plunging onto them when he was entombed under the monstrous weight of a German woman who had been sitting opposite. He partially freed himself but was slammed to the floor again by falling baggage. The carriage stopped, tilting toward the sea. When Richard had succeeded in struggling from beneath the stunned fat lady he helped evacuate those too frightened or too hurt to move. Screams of terror were coming from the seaward side of the carriage, so he climbed back inside and saw a teenage girl dangling in mid-air. Edging along the overhanging footboard Richard caught her by the waist and yelled to her to let go her grip on the handrail. She was too hysterical to respond. Richard felt the carriage begin to slide. He hammered at her fingers until her hand opened and threw her onto the track. The carriage went over the edge as he jumped and they heard it shatter thunderously on the rocks below. He walked back along the track. There was a horse lying across it, cut almost in two, and bits of human flesh were scattered around it. He was sick. Eventually another train was brought up and everyone crowded aboard. This time there was an

American woman, a Mrs. Dennison, among Richard's companions. He learned that her brother was now in one of the hospital carriages and he noticed that she was growing more and more uncomfortable. She was pregnant and Richard, as he delicately put it, "feared the worst." Before long the worst happened and Mrs. Dennison, asking her fellow passengers kindly to look the other way, collapsed with a groan to the floor.

Richard enlisted a quiet man who struck him as respectable and asked the other gentlemen to leave the compartment. Richard and his assistant delivered the baby without incident, cutting the umbilical cord with a providential penknife. After a quarter of an hour that neither man had greatly relished, Richard "took the slimy brat to the lavatory where I washed him with cold water, put my finger in his mouth which was closed and gave him a good spanking on the bottom; he yelled blue murder and started breathing." Richard wrapped him in one of his own undershirts and presented him to his mother, who through her sobs said she would call the boy Richard. Mother and child left the train at Patras and that was the last Richard saw of his namesake though he often wondered what sort of a person he had turned out to be. Watching the lady join her astonished husband Richard's assistant turned to him and said, "*Das ist gut!*" Feeling that their ordeal excused a slight breach of manners, Richard then introduced himself and asked the name of his colleague in obstetrics. "I am the King of Saxony," the man said. The king was on his way to Corfu, whither he now invited Richard for a couple of days. They stayed at the Villa Achilleion, the stately pleasure-dome decreed by Empress Elizabeth of Austria and now the property of Kaiser Wilhelm.* "If it was not for my broken rib,"

---

* The kaiser had bought the palace from Emperor Franz Joseph as much for the treasures he hoped might lie beneath it as for its baroque splendor. In 1911 his imperial archaeologist dug up, aptly enough, the head of a Gorgon dating from the seventh century B.C. The kaiser grew extraordinarily fond of it. A quarter of a century later, during his retirement at Doorn, he made it the subject of a scholarly paper which rambled through a thicket of theories to a conclusion dealing with the significance of the swastika. This followed his earlier work of 1934, *The History and Meaning of the Chinese Monad*, his first and most extensive study of the history of that Nazi emblem.

Richard wrote in the midst of luxury, "I should roar with laughter."

As soon as he got back to London Richard delivered his loaded guidebooks to the War Office. A few days later he was summoned to the Directorate of Naval Intelligence, warmly congratulated, and asked if he would now repair in the guise of an ornithologist to the island of Heligoland, famous for its sea birds and its German naval installations. Richard declined, not wishing in part to lose his amateur status as a spy.

As spring was burgeoning into early summer Richard's leave drew to an end while, with the sweet promise of the young leaves outside, Daniel Meinertzhagen lay in a still room on his death bed. Richard was under orders for Mauritius as his father lingered on the edge of darkness. It was time to go; the carriage stood by the door. For the last time Richard walked into his father's room where the limp body lay unconscious and barely alive. He stood by the bed thinking of the generosity and simplicity of that gentle man, and of his silences. The eyes were closed, the beard dull, the breath so faint. Richard bent and kissed his father, whispered "goodbye," and knelt for a final prayer.

Kneeling there he heard the door open and the rustle of a dress. It was his mother. In utter quiet, side by side but each alone, they thought of what might have been. They got up together to leave. Then, as Richard walked toward the door without looking back, Georgina put her arms around him, a thing she had never done before. In that instant the barrier between them broke, Georgina sobbing as Richard held her, all pride sundered, pouring out her sadness and recalling her old love for Daniel. It was the first time Richard had ever seen tears in her eyes. He recognized in a flash of insight how she yearned for love as he did, and how by a sort of impotence it had been denied. "At last we understood each other," he wrote in his diary. "From that moment my mother was indeed my mother." He was to know her fully for four more years, during most of which he was far away.

Richard mailed his first letter to his mother after that agonized farewell from Port Said. It reached her two days after Daniel's death; she took it into Daniel's room, kissed him for Richard, and called out Richard's name. "I kissed him too for his early love, and for his worn old wife," she wrote; then continued, "I do not think you children can ever understand what a tragedy my married life has been. It may have been my fault or at any rate the fault of my character in being unsuited to the character of the one I loved best in the world through my early life, and one whom I have always admired for his uprightness, generosity and great charm of person. But there it is—I have failed—and our lives have gradually drifted apart till we were absolute strangers to each other." In a second letter Georgina wrote: "He had his happiness in life to a very full degree, but not through me. I sometimes wish I could try again, but then my heart fails me. It is one of the ironies of fate that sometimes the more we try, the less we succeed." Daniel was buried in the lea of the thick old hedgerow sheltering Mottisfont churchyard beside his eldest son, and not too far from his beloved river to miss its babble through the weir borne faintly on a country wind.

Georgina's letters reached her son in Mauritius, where he had arrived in June 1910 to join his battalion, which had moved during his leave. The broad veldt of South Africa had made a perfect training ground but Mauritius was mountainous and so forested and planted with sugar cane that it was difficult enough to deploy even a section. The Royal Fusiliers grew a little frustrated with work thus limited and with the society of the island, thrown together in such small compass, a brew of the most volatile kind. With Réunion and Rodriguez, the other islands of the Mascarene group, three green pimples in a waste of waters, Mauritius had become a colony of the British Crown almost as an afterthought, though armchair imperialists were fond of calling it the key to the Indian Ocean. The Portuguese had been the first to come there but the Dutch after them had settled more heavily, finding ebony trees and indigenous birds with hard, greasy flesh they called "walgvogel."* The Dutch left the

---

* Translated, walgvogel is "disgusting fowl." This maligned creature was the dodo, a bald bird with a portly, spherical body made ridiculous by vestigial wings and a ludicrously sparse tail. It lived in the woods, cracking the pericarps of pandanus nuts with its heavy beak and incapable alike of self-defense or flight. Its customary expression, not surprisingly, was reported

island as inconsequentially as they had arrived and it was eventually picked up by the French and renamed Ile de France. After nearly a century it passed as part of the booty of war in 1810 to the British, who were content to retain its by now predominantly French culture for its inhabitants, but did not feel obliged to adopt it themselves. Under the successive overlords the original inhabitants of Mauritius had been outnumbered by imported Malagasis, Africans and Indians both Hindu and Muslim. The result was a racial mixture volatile enough to make the presence of British troops advisable.

Outside the British circle trouble on Mauritius tended to be political. Though the island could boast only two townships of any size, no fewer than fifteen newspapers blossomed there, nearly all scurrilous. They battened on a strong diet of invective which they partially imported from England, producing at the time a lush crop under the husbandry of Lloyd George, who, following the text "Blessed is he that considereth the poor," was stumping about setting class against class and attracting opprobrium from all but the underprivileged.* In Mauritius the factions were divided into the Oligarchs (the old French families, many of whom had been touched with the tar brush, and the wealthier Creoles) and the Democrats (comprising the Indians, Chinese and, according to Richard, "The other scum of the island"). Polling days generated an excess of excitement that the

---

to be lugubrious. A specimen was exhibited in London in 1638 by an impresario who insisted that visitors feed it only on pebbles, but the species was extinct by the beginning of the eighteenth century. Quantities of curious bones were found in a Mauritian marsh in 1865 and the dodo achieved a fame in death it had never enjoyed in life. It was best memoralized in *Alice's Adventures in Wonderland*, published in the same year, and it is both significant and touching that when Lewis Carroll's Dodo arranged things everybody got a prize.

* Lloyd George's most famous speech in this vein was delivered in Limehouse, a seedy quarter of London, on July 30, 1909, during which he pointed out, "A fully equipped Duke costs as much to keep up as two Dreadnoughts, and Dukes are just as great a terror and they last longer." He later added injury to insult by referring to the current vogue for ducal marriages to American heiresses and declaring that many a noble house had been underpinned by American dollars.

Fusiliers were required to cool. One night Richard's dinner was interrupted by a demand for his company in Curepipe, where a riot was reported. He covered the mile from the barracks to the town at a run; hearing shots from the direction of the Town Hall, he changed course in the pitch darkness and bumped into a mob of Frenchmen and Creoles firing off pistols like cowboys on Saturday night. He circled the crowd with a ring of bayonets and the atmosphere grew more reasonable. In the confusion a Frenchman fired his revolver and wounded a Creole. Richard hit the Frenchman in the face with the hilt of his sword with a good deal of power and the Frenchman shortly accompanied the Creole to the hospital. At that, peace reigned once more.

This sort of patchwork duty was not to any soldier's taste. There were few diversions on the island—tennis courts and a golf course at the Club, and a polo ground but no ponies—and even its agreeable climate and astonishing natural beauty, all vivid greens and flashing blues and mountain peaks fantastically hewn like rhino horns or jagged molars, could not compensate for the feeling that they were isolated and confined. There was rejoicing when word came that the battalion was for the red dust of India. There Richard joined them after a leave at home, spent most diligently in study for the Staff College.

The old system of summer in the hills and winter on the plains was still in operation; by April 1912 the Royal Fusiliers had already settled down at Chakrata seven thousand feet up in the Himalayas. One of the older military stations, Chakrata was perched on one of the series of ridges that swept up toward the awesome glistening mass of Everest. Big bungalows for the troops and smaller ones for the officers clung to the hillsides with no pretensions to proper military alignment. It was pure joy to Richard to see from his house the mountains northward, pearly and pink at dawn and sunset, and to hear the harsh challenge of eagles riding the air currents of the gorges, their breasts silvered like mail in the clear light. Some of the hillsides were bare rock pile on pile but most were thick-sown with oaks and rhododendrons of a deep mourning green or scented marches of firs. Ingenuity had contrived two small parade grounds for the station, so drill was possible, but apart from that the only martial exercise attempted at Chakrata was an amateur species of mountain warfare. Richard used the leisure these light duties gave him solidly at his books. In October 1912 he took the entrance examination for the Staff College at Quetta and passed in top.

"Work at the Staff College," Richard was soon writing, "makes me realize what a ghastly business the next war is going to be." He was at the watershed: all that had so far passed had belonged to the sense and native wit; what was coming belonged to reason and the brain. What he had learned as a regimental officer seemed to have little immediate bearing on what he now studied of the dispassionate sciences of strategy and logistics. Under Haldane's rule a new spirit had been born in the army: a consciousness that efficiency was a truer road to victory than camaraderie, and a new orientation that saw the likely battleground as the continent of Europe instead of some barbarous mountain range on the periphery of Empire. The philosophy provoked change. In 1913 the old structure of the infantry battalion of eight companies, suitable for small wars and for police actions when small units might be detached for independent missions, was superseded by a new organization based on a battalion of four rifle companies. Richard approved of the smaller, more manageable battalion, but deplored its lack of automatic fire power. "The power of machine guns has not yet been appreciated in our Army," he wrote.

Students at the Staff College were encouraged to interest themselves in all matters affecting military thinking. One lecture, called "Preparation for War," raised among others the subject of railroads in Persia and from that passed to Russia's hopes of a port on, or preferably outside, the Persian Gulf, and a discussion of the disastrous consequences to India's isolation from a hypothetical conjunction of a British and a Russian railroad in Persia. However, the plan which then threatened to alter the status quo in the Middle East originated neither in London nor in St. Petersburg but in Berlin. The Anatolian Railway Company, controlled by the Deutsche Bank, had long been an instrument of German policy as well as a source of profit, and had enjoyed a series of concessions from the sultan and his ministers in the Sublime Porte. Ever since the departure in 1890 of Bismarck, who had restrained himself from dabbling in the Ottoman Empire for fear of offending Russia, Kaiser Wilhelm had dreamed of an iron road beginning in Berlin and ending on the Persian Gulf, and he was not above proclaiming himself while his vision hardened into reality the champion of Muslims everywhere. In 1898 on a visit to the Holy Land, known then as the Sanjaq of Jerusalem, he had chosen to renew his military oath of service to heaven, standing, of all places, on the Mount of Olives. By 1913 this dedication was bearing a steely fruit. It was partly to investigate the progress made on the Baghdad Railway, the latest projection of the *Drang nach Osten,* that Richard Meinertzhagen was allowed leave in December 1913 to travel in Mesopotamia, the land of Tigris and Euphrates and Adam and Eve. He was also to compile a report on transportation of all kinds by land and water, for the government of India believed with reason that the area might soon become a theater of war and was making plans to occupy Basra in that event.

Richard took with him a fellow student, Captain G. R. Maitland of the 14th Regiment of Bengal Lancers (Murray's Jats). They came to Baghdad on the second day of January 1914 to the Grand Tigris, a hotel they had been assured was clean and fairly comfortable. According to Richard, "It was a dirty little hovel in an insanitary lane," and after one night of ticks, lice, fleas, beetles, rats, mangy cats and stray dogs, and the coming and goings of an enormous brothel, they moved to the Grand Babylon Hotel, their only alternative. The local manager of Lynch Brothers, a British company that maintained a monopoly of steam traffic on the river, was able to provide a lot of information about the Baghdad Railway. It now reached seven miles north of the city and all necessary earthworks and embankments had been completed as far as Samarra, eighty miles away. Despite their vaunted efficiency the Germans seemed to have got themselves boxed in; all tugs on the Tigris belonged to Lynch's, who were not overanxious to expedite shipments and who in any case were not allowed by the Turks to put more than five vessels on the river at the same time. Richard was encouraged by these byzantine difficulties.

The peacock and gold City of the Caliphs was a disappointment. Though Haroun al Rashid had ruled there in magnificence, it had been sacked first by the Mongols of Hulagu, who turned the river into ink with the ashes of its mighty libraries, and later by Tamurlaine. Since then Baghdad had merely progressed from ruin to squalor. Its streets were too narrow for one horse comfortably to pass another; its mud-cored walls were losing their facings of soft brick, and the great river itself was more like a sewer than an artery. Outside the city the land stretched desolate where once had lain the Garden of Eden and the fertile crescent, now so impregnated with salt that nothing grew.

From Baghdad Maitland and Richard traveled three hundred miles north and slightly west to Mosul. It was a penance. Their conveyance was a painted cart hardly big enough to take their baggage, roofed over and draped at the side against the sun with smelly curtains. It was drawn by four skeletal mules harnessed all abreast and its four wooden wheels seemed to seek out every bump in the interminable road. Mosul was a city of some interest, with a large Christian quarter of Syrians and Chaldeans and a shifting population of brutal-looking Kurds, but from a historical point of view it was merely an adjunct to Nineveh across the river. Richard and Maitland had decided to return to Baghdad by raft, and while this was preparing they spent an afternoon at the supposed tomb of that worst of shipmates Jonah, the Nebi Yunus. They approached it wearing fezzes so as not to appear too conspicuous. The tomb itself crowned a mound from which rose a mosque and a minaret. Taking them for Turks, an old Arab led them about the place until they came to a mud sarcophagus of doubtful provenance, recounting the while the story of the prophet. Unfortunately his version of the tale was that Jonah had swallowed the whale, which sent the two Englishmen into helpless giggles. They left among curses which Richard did not at the time take seriously.

The raft slid downstream from Mosul in a hurricane and a wall of rain with the river in flood. On the second morning it went hard aground on a sandbank, where waves breaking over it finished what the rain had started. Everything was drenched, including their firewood, so they found an Arab village and begged refuge from the headman. For discretion's sake Maitland and Richard had assumed the coarse burnous and loose turban of the region; while Richard wore his with a certain panache, heightened by a new beard that would not have disgraced a sheikh, the total effect was less than perfect whenever he squatted cross-legged in Arab fashion, for there peeped from under his robe the gleaming hobnails of a British army boot. Undeceived, the headman gave the two infidels a room and a cooking fire and they ate in the company of an Arab mare and her foal that strolled in out of the rain.

At midnight the wind ceased. The river had risen, so the raft rode the crest all night under a sky of stars. When the raft reached Baghdad on the third day the river was seventeen feet above any previously recorded level. The Tigris narrowed as it cut through the center of Baghdad, so the raft was hurled downstream whirling and lurching absolutely out of control right through the city. Emerging at dizzy speed, it crunched into the iron bows of one of Messrs. Lynch's steamers and held there long enough for everything to be transferred to a lucky flotilla of the round boats like washtubs that plied the river. The last Richard saw of the raft was two pieces of wreckage tumbling rapidly downstream toward Basra. Maitland and Richard followed them by steamer in more leisurely style, passing through Basra, by now practically inundated by flood waters, and coming ashore at Muhammerah, a village of much greater importance than its appearance suggested.

The sheikh of Muhammerah presided over a modest establishment at the juncture of the Karun River with the Shatt-al-Arab, where the waters of Tigris and Euphrates mingled. Nominally a subject of the shah of Persia, the sheikh in practice was an ally of the British, whose pipeline carrying oil from Masjid-i-Suleiman happily ran through his principality. In 1909 Doctor M. Y. Young, following both his vocation and a political career in Muhammerah, had signed with the sheikh an agreement that included the use by the Anglo-Persian Oil Company of one square mile of a disgusting and quite useless mud flat called Abadan Island, halfway between Basra and the Persian Gulf. The British built a refinery on it. By the time

Richard saw it, it was capable of handling more than a quarter of a million tons a year and it was already in the toils of labor troubles. The main work force at the refinery comprised some two thousand Persian coolies from Luristan, not the most pacific sector of that country. On Richard's second day in Muhammerah an Indian loco-motive driver ran over one of the Lurs, all of whose compatriots seized their knives and pistols and surged through the plant looking for Indians to massacre. With only twelve Arab policemen for a security force the British engineers at the refinery called for help when the Lurs began smashing machinery in their fury. It arrived in the person of the consul with a party of Indian cavalrymen and order was restored.

Richard was beginning to wonder whether the curse put on his and Maitland's sacrilegious heads in the unlucky tomb of Jonah might be more than a form of words. The storm that had eventually wrecked their raft, the vicissitudes of a friend from Mosul stranded for two days without water and robbed when his car broke down in the desert, the murder of an Englishman aboard his boat the day they arrived in Basra, the death during an operation of one of Lynch's officials the day they left it, and now the riot at Abadan all seemed to indicate a sinister purpose. When they sailed for India ill fortune continued. As they lay off Bushire, the political agent there shot himself; one of the crew was washed overboard in the storms that followed them down the Gulf, and finally as they arrived at Muscat the Arab who fired the signal gun was transfixed by the ramrod and blown out to sea. "It has indeed been a chapter of bad luck," Richard reflected, not unaware that if the mantle of Jonah really had fallen on him it was at least working its revenge in the same vicarious way that it had originally. Maitland and he got back to Quetta by way of Karachi and there Richard submitted his report to General Headquarters in Simla, shortly evoking the response from the director of intelligence, "first class and most valuable."

The men in Simla and Delhi were not the only ones with a stake in the Middle East. As Richard Meinertzhagen was wallowing in the fleshpots of Muhammerah a young archaeologist called Thomas Edward Lawrence was sitting on the other side of Arabia in an oasis in what he called the Wilderness of Sin (more properly Zin or Sinai), eating turkish delight and the beans his camels fed on. Lawrence and Leonard Woolley* had been digging for the British Museum and casually observing the Germans on their railroad at Carchemish on the Euphrates. At the end of the archaeological season, before snow fell on Carchemish, they were invited south by the Palestine Exploration Fund to accompany one Captain S. F. Newcombe of the Royal Engineers on a survey into Sinai. The request for the survey had come from Lord Kitchener, himself a former employee of the Fund, whose observations in the same area had been interrupted thirty years before by the distant appearance of the Mahdi in the Sudan. Woolley and Lawrence were cover for Newcombe's work, which was the mapping of the area between Aqaba and the southern tip of the Dead Sea. The archaeologists dug up a few well-preserved Amorites who had been buried naked and headless, but Lawrence went further. He discovered routes and passes that he would later use when he led the Arab Revolt toward Damascus. In so doing he was fulfilling the greater purpose of the Fund which, while it had originally been formed in 1865 for the collection of such scientific evidence in the Holy Land as might rebut the attacks on orthodox religion made by Darwinism and free-thinkers, had almost at once been adopted by the War Office as camouflage for intelligence operations of a mild but vital kind. The importance of Sinai in any Egyptian scheme of defense or attack was clear to all, but its significance in the diplomatic climate between Great Britain and Turkey was understood by few. A firman from the sultan in 1892 had acknowledged the peninsula as falling under the administration of the government of Egypt but neither the British nor the Turks frequented it.

In 1906 Lord Cromer had asked a young English officer given

---

* Woolley was Lawrence's senior at Carchemish and an old friend from the Ashmolean Museum in Oxford. During the First World War he was an intelligence officer and spent the latter half of it a prisoner of the Turks. He was later celebrated as the elucidator of the civilization of Sumer and the excavator of Ur of the Chaldees.

to wandering there to discover whether the Hejaz Railway* proposed a branch to Aqaba and thus a strategic threat to Egypt. The young man had fallen foul of Turks outside the town; the ensuing argument caused Lord Cromer to write peremptorily to London and Sir Edward Grey, Secretary of State for Foreign Affairs, to match his mood in a note to the Sublime Porte claiming all of Sinai. A British fleet concentrated in the Piraeus. To most this was the mere movement of a couple of pawns but the disillusioned Wilfrid Scawen Blunt saw it differently. He recognized in it the cause of that friction between London and Constantinople which led to Turkey's alliance with Germany, "a combination which gave Germany its victory over Russia," he wrote. "Not a soul in England understood its importance or cared to understand."

Few realized at the beginning of 1914 where the currents of pressure and counter-pressure were building. There was an awareness in France and Britain that Germany meant war but it was not keen and it was only reluctantly faced. It was still possible and logical for Richard Meinertzhagen, despite a knowledge of the agreements between the Powers dividing them plainly into sheep and goats, to conclude from his Mesopotamian reconnaissance that the threat there was Russian and not German, a sentiment Lawrence was to echo. Richard foresaw Russian ports not only on the Persian Gulf but also on the Mediterranean and the China Sea. "One might as well attempt to dam the Amazon River with a handful of mud as try to stop the expansion of Russia," he wrote.

This suspicion of Russia awoke in Richard almost as soon as he had returned to Quetta a scheme to penetrate to the Helmund River

---

* The railroad had been begun in Damascus in 1904 by Sultan Abdul Hamid with funds subscribed by Muslims all over the world and with a German engineer to build it. Its purpose was to facilitate the pilgrimage to Mecca and, incidentally, the movement of Turkish troops along the shores of the Red Sea, where the sultan's grip was at best palsied. When it reached Medina in 1908 its further progress was opposed by Hussein, the new sherif of Mecca, on political rather than religious grounds. During the Arab Revolt Lawrence harassed it; at least one of the trains he dynamited off it was still lying in the desert as late as 1966.

in Afghanistan. It was a disaster. He had set off with another officer from the Staff College with the commandant's warning that if they were caught they would naturally be drummed out of the army at the very least. They were inexpertly disguised as Pathans. They traveled with camels carrying theodolites and all Richard's bird-skinning equipment and a couple of real Pathans as guides and accomplices. They crossed the frontier at Chaman at night, skirting any habitations and resting by day in the cover of dry watercourses that ran everywhere like the wrinkles on a walnut shell. During the second night one of their camels strayed and though the Pathans searched all day for it, it did not reappear. Since it had been loaded with incriminating European gear Richard decided to retire. They reached Chaman again after a half-hour running fight in the dark with a party of hostile Afghans. "It is no easy matter to shoot accurately from a trotting camel," Richard grumbled.

He was able to work off some of his frustration on one of the instructors at the Staff College whose laziness he deplored. The class was given a scheme to work out and told that the enemy could be of any size. When Richard asked for more helpful detail he was told to be less argumentative and more imaginative. He imagined an enemy of ten modern divisions. The instructor called him impertinent. He reduced it to a cavalry patrol and the instructor turned purple. "Take a bloody division for your enemy and don't play the fool!" he barked. Richard meekly worked out the scheme and arrived at the conclusion: "A bloody division of unknown strength has succeeded in penetrating our line." There was no shortage of amusements at the College. One of the most popular was the Quetta Hunt run by a regiment of Indian cavalry and forced in the absence of foxes from the scenery of Baluchistan to pursue jackals. Richard went out one spring morning and found that not only had the quarry been brought up in a sack but its lips had been stitched up so that it could not bite the hounds. Richard rode back to his quarters in a fury and began a wrathful correspondence that succeeded in ending the practice and brought him sidelong glances at the Quetta Club. Undisturbed, Richard began to make plans for his summer vacation.

In July 1914 Richard was in the mountains breathing the thin but exhilarating air spiced with the scent of junipers of a valley eight thousand feet above sea level. In winter snow closed off the valley from the rest of the world, but now in summer it was cool, clean and peaceful, secluded only by time. For the telegraph penetrated even to Ziarat. On July 24 the Reuters cable had reported nothing untoward in Europe. But on the next day it announced an Austrian ultimatum to Serbia and on the day after that came ominous threats from Russia and counter-threats from Germany. Already the portents were clear but what they led to was, even so, inconceivable. Richard contemplated the splash of lake trout taking the evening drift of flies on the indigo calm of the Kahan Tangi, felt the hush fall on the mountains, and knew the last ebbings of a true peace that would never return.

CHAPTER 11

Meinertzhagen, You're Mad!

It had begun like a dream. High up in Ziarat Richard read the cables that ticked away the rhythm of the march to the abyss with a sense of stupefaction as deep as that of the statesmen whose actions, or lack of them, had set it rolling. The cables merely announced the facts—ultimatum, mobilization, ultimatum, mobilization, ultimatum—with an inevitability too plain to be accepted by a reasoning man. There was a certain familiarity about the game; threat and counter-threat had kept Europe at peace through crises more serious than the casual murder of an Austrian prince somewhere in the Balkans. The statesmen-players knew all the moves: what no player realized until it was too late was that this time the game was different. The pieces were moving themselves. Richard saw the pattern emerging from the cables, concluded that Germany could prevent the holocaust but would not, and rode back to Quetta to be ready.

On Tuesday, August 4, 1914, the British ultimatum concerning the neutrality of Belgium was delivered in Berlin. At eleven-twenty that night, no reply having been received, a telegram was sent to all headquarters ordering "War Germany Act." Thereupon, waving the word honor for a talisman, the British set off with a pathetic decency on the path that led toward their destruction. King George V shortly dispatched a message to his Expeditionary Force bound for France, beginning, "You are leaving home to fight for the safety and honor of my Empire," and promising his deepest interest in their daily progress and welfare. Lord Kitchener, too, gave every man instructions to be gummed into his paybook. "Remember that the honor of the British Army depends on your individual conduct," it exhorted, piling a yet heavier burden on backs already bent under seventy pounds of kit, then continued on a more practical note: "Your duty cannot be done unless your health is sound. So keep constantly on your guard against any excesses. In this new experience you may find temptations, both in wine and women. You must entirely resist both temptations, and, while treating all women with perfect courtesy, you should avoid any intimacy. Do your duty bravely. Fear God. Honor the King." Great Britain, as *The Annual Register* put it, had been "called to be once more the savior of Europe."

Through the last stages of the crisis the nation, arousing, had been restless: on Sunday, August 2, there had been a peace meeting in Trafalgar Square to hear such veterans of the left as Henry Hyndman and Keir Hardie, but it had been swamped by a jingoistic mob. Crowds wandered about London that Bank Holiday weekend clasping miniature Union Jacks and Tricolors, clotting the gates of Buckingham Palace to await some sign of national purpose and to sing the national anthem and the *Marseillaise*. When the word of war came in the warm night there was a massive, formless roar from the throngs spreading from the Palace down the Mall, the bellow of a beast burning with menace and relieved to see at last a tormentor to charge. The cause seemed clear, seemed honorable, and with ease could be accepted. It was as though everyone, grown tired of petty violence and the reiteration in the popular press of ills long since diagnosed, thought he could submerge his malaise in one last dangerous but great adventure. That savage, exultant cry and the solemn masquerade of anthems that followed it were repeated throughout the Empire.

Richard Meinertzhagen heard the paeans to war in the Staff College Mess and in the Quetta Club and was depressed. He had no doubts about the nature of what was coming; the slick predictions that it would all be over by Christmas and that India would not be involved sickened him. He saw the waste of millions in men and gold, but equally clearly he saw his duty, and late one night he sat down to work out his rationale. "I love the naked raw life, bereft of all the trappings and tomfoolery of modern civilisation," he wrote. "Wide horizons in thought and vision, freedom and always more freedom, fresh air and exercise and a contempt for Death—that is what I love. Those are the conditions I understand. Must I leave all that behind and without mercy work night and day to kill my fellow men? Must I take part in unrestrained murder?" The answer he already knew, of course. He could not shrink from duty, however strong his disapproval. So he prayed for victory. "We shall eventually win because our cause is just," he added later. "But Germany will fight well and fight hard. And when Germany is beaten she will look back with pride on the part she played."* For his own part, in spite of his moral reservations, Richard concluded, "I want my chance and I know I shall do a certain amount of damage to the Germans."

On August 17, a Monday, Richard was ordered to report at once to a General Aitken in Bombay. He took the first train out of Quetta next morning, not knowing whither the general might be bound. He suspected it might be East Africa. Portly but agile, his blue eyes alert in a tanned face, Aitken possessed the monumental self-confidence bred by years of command in the old Indian army. His bushy gray moustache and his tightly buttoned uniform marked him the long-service officer who placed more confidence in appearance and convention than in originality. Aitken confirmed Richard's guess about their destination, told him he was to be in charge of intelligence for the force, and left for Simla to get instructions. Richard settled into an office of the force headquarters grandly requisitioned in the Taj Mahal Hotel overlooking the seashore and the Apollo Bunder where he had first trodden Indian soil. The government of India's war plans required the launching of four expeditionary forces. The most important was the contingent for the

---

* Twenty-four years after the German debacle of 1918 a German magazine could still write: "To have created the new warrior, who dared to advance against the products of war techniques was the proud achievement of the German infantry. The German army, crowned with glory, could lay down its weapons unashamed, because it passed on to the coming generation a legacy of the spiritual kind, the science and teaching of the new man."

Western Front in France. Another was for Mesopotamia, a third for the hinterlands of British East Africa, and the fourth was to invade German East Africa from the sea. This last task was assigned to General Aitken, who bustled back to Bombay to put all in readiness, having been told, "The object of the expedition under your command is to bring the whole of German East Africa under British authority." From his subordinate position Richard viewed this design with apprehension; he believed that the strategic purpose should not extend beyond the defense of British East Africa, the most economic course when the war would obviously be decided in Europe. His own plan for this, based on his reconnaissance of the area eight years before, was to build a railroad across the Serengeti, occupy the Kilimanjaro area, and await events in comparative comfort. His interviews with Goanese and Indians just returned from the German colony had provided nothing to counter this theory, and his assessment of the quality of the troops assigned to Aitken's Force B, which he categorized as "the worst in India," made him conclude moreover that an invasion had modest hopes. With the advantage of this intelligence and a pamphlet written by the former British consul in Dar-es-Salaam, General Aitken called a conference at the Bombay Yacht Club and brushed all doubts aside with a hearty "The Indian Army will make short work of a lot of niggers." He then outlined his plans and concluded with the most important business of all. His blue eyes hard and his tone inflexible, he announced, coming to matters of dress, "I will not tolerate the appalling sloppiness allowed during the Boer War."

On October 16 Force B sailed from Bombay in conditions of less than absolute secrecy, for its matériel had been lying about the docks in crates marked, to avoid confusion, "Force B. Mombasa. East Africa." Some of its components had already been aboard for more than two weeks waiting for the convoy to assemble. The German raider *Emden** was terrorizing the Indian Ocean, so Force B's troop-

---

* This exasperating light cruiser had slipped out of Kiauchau before she could be blockaded and was roaming the Orient like a demented sheep dog. Late in September she had the effrontery to bombard Madras, setting some oil tanks afire. At Penang she came across a Russian cruiser and a French

ers were shepherded across in a mass of nearly fifty ships, most bound
for Muhammerah or Suez and beyond. Fourteen of them carried
Aitken's questionable command of eight thousand men organized in
two infantry brigades. The 27th (Bangalore) Brigade included some
British regulars, the 2nd Battalion of the Loyal North Lancashire
Regiment, upon whom the main hope rested, and three battalions of
Indian infantry not one of which had seen action for more than a generation. It had been commanded since 1912 by Brigadier General
Richard Wapshare, formerly of the 30th Lancers (Gordon's Horse)
and the Secunderabad Cavalry Brigade and now in the thirty-fourth
year of a fairly peaceful and entirely gratifying military career. It
was accompanied by the Imperial Service Brigade under Brigadier
General M. J. Tighe, consisting of the 13th Rajputs (a unit attached
two years before to the Royal Fusliers outside Delhi and reported
by them then as unfit for service), the 61st Pioneers, and contingents
of uncertain worth from the princely states of Kashmir and Gwalior;
this brigade was much under strength. For support there was one
battery of mountain guns. Aitken's headquarters and the British
regulars were aboard the P and O ship *Karmala* for a wearisome two
weeks, which Richard spent sizing up his superiors, urging discretion on the general, and lecturing in the saloon on German East
Africa. To Richard's warnings that the German askaris were better
trained, better led, and used to warfare in the bush, Aitken merely
barked the cheerful answer that he would thrash them all before
Christmas. Neither he nor anyone else knew then that the hand that
held the whip belonged to one of the greatest masters of mobile warfare the world had yet seen, soon to be blessed by destiny but in 1914
no more than an obscure name—Colonel Paul von Lettow-Vorbeck,
a Prussian.

---

destroyer and gobbled them up. She snapped up merchant ships where she
found them, capturing thirteen and destroying two million pounds' worth
of Allied property. On November 8, 1914, the heavier and faster Australian
cruiser *Sydney,* convoying Australian troops to Egypt, caught the *Emden*
in the Cocos Islands, set her ablaze with a more powerful broadside, and
sank her. By that time Karl von Müller, her commander, had achieved by
his humanity, as well as by his gallantry and initiative, a reputation only
slightly tarnished by his belonging to the wrong side.

Of all the members of the German officer corps, von Lettow was the only one to emerge from the war undefeated. The reason for this was simple: he was unique. He had a brilliant and original brain that his Junker upbringing had been unable to compress into a stereotype, and it had benefited from his unusually varied experiences as a soldier. These corresponded to Richard Meinertzhagen's but for a German officer they were out of the ordinary. Grounded most thoroughly in the theories of war at the military school at Kassel, experienced in regimental duties in Prussia, von Lettow had gained practice as one of the kaiser's Hunnish contingent in the Boxer Rising, as commander of the troops in the German colony of the Cameroons, and, most important of all, during the Hottentot Rebellion ten years before in German South-West Africa. This insurrection, beginning before and continuing longer than Richard's Nandi Expedition, had raged over terrain as forbidding as anything in East Africa. It had taught the thoughtful von Lettow a great deal about mobility, about how to survive in the most inhospitable surroundings, and about ambushes. He bore scars in the chest and beside the eye to remind him of this last lesson. Though broad-shouldered and stiff in the back von Lettow had none of the brittle arrogance of his class; his face in thought squeezed itself into the quizzical frown of the scholar; his forehead was academic, bulging under a round, bald crown. His mouth was firm but gentle and the wrinkles above it and at the corner of his eyes betrayed humor. He looked, in fact, like a contented and bookish man of affairs on the point of perpetrating a joke comprehensible only to himself. He affected a safari hat swept up on one side quite out of keeping with his nature, but in all else he practiced moderation. Throughout the war he was to display the soundest of judgment, inexhaustible determination, and personal gallantry of an exemplary kind. The campaign had hardly started before he came within inches of being shot by Richard Meinertzhagen.

Richard had depressed his brother officers aboard the *Karmala* by maintaining that the Germans in East Africa might not fight at all, not knowing that von Lettow had already changed the neutral attitude in Dar-es-Salaam into a more pugnacious one. His audiences listened glumly but cheered up when it occurred to them that a quick victory would allow them to reach France before everything was over. They acknowledged that Richard was a clever fellow, more brainy than themselves certainly, but they listened with only half an ear and they mistook his reserve for hauteur and the mist that an inner pain sometimes brought to his brown eyes for introversion. He was, they recognized, a loner. The convoy lazed on through the Indian Ocean at nine knots and on October 28, still out of sight of land, fell in with the light cruiser *Fox* (Captain F. W. Caulfield, R.N.) fresh from Mombasa but bringing little intelligence of use to an invasion force save a vague indication that most of the Germans seemed to be at Moshi. "Whoever is in charge seems to have done the right thing, namely, concentrate," Richard wrote with approval. *Karmala* lumbered away from the convoy leaving thousands of sepoys still sweltering in their torrid hulks with no horizon but the sea, and with H.M.S. *Fox* put in at Mombasa.

The Governor of the British East Africa Protectorate, though he by no means favored the hostilities now in progress, was kind enough to allow the use of part of his residence for a council of war. General Aitken presided, with Colonel Sheppard (known as "Collie"), his chief of staff, and Captain Meinertzhagen, his intelligence officer, in support. Others at the table were Brigadier General Stewart, commanding Expeditionary Force C of the 29th Punjabis and contingents from some native states hurried out from Karachi in August, Colonel Graham from Richard's old battalion of the King's African Rifles, Captain Caulfield of H.M.S. *Fox,* Colonel Ward of the 4th KAR, and of course His Excellency. It was a meeting of talents, though few were really appropriate to the task in hand. Sheppard knew the Northwest Frontier of India like the back of his hand, having first fought in Waziristan twenty years before, won the Distinguished Service Order battling the Mahsuds, and struggled to Lhassa with a company of Sappers and Miners; by training an engineer, he had been an instructor at the Staff College during Richard's studentship and tended to approach a problem very much aware of its inherent stresses and strains. Stewart was preoccupied with his own difficulties to the north, Caulfield was plagued by an irrational fear of mines and the very real threat from the German cruiser *Konigsberg,* still at large, as well as by a political problem he had not yet disclosed. The governor, an expert in the laws of land tenure, felt disinclined to contribute much to plans for enlarging his estate; this was only his second year in the Protectorate, whence he had come from long, serendipitous years in Malaya. Colonel Ward, formerly of the Oxford and Buckinghamshire Light Infantry, confronted by the weight of the Indian army, said little. Colonel Graham, fresh from bush warfare in Jubaland, was equally retiring, though he and Richard Meinertzhagen were the only ones with any relevant experience. General Aitken was full of confidence and would not be stayed; he would go by the book* and the book said quite clearly in Chapter 10 ("Infantry in Attack") Section 121, paragraph 5, "The main essential to success in battle is to close with the enemy, cost what it may." That was what the general would most certainly do, especially when the paragraph continued in slightly heavier type, "The object of infantry in attack is therefore to get to close quarters as quickly as possible." When Colonel Graham offered his seasoned askaris, General Aitken refused them.

He had decided, he announced, not to attack Dar-es-Salaam, which was the first time Richard had heard of that possibility. He would take Tanga. At this point Captain Caulfield unburdened. The Royal Navy had made a truce with the Germans in both these ports guaranteeing no warlike acts so long as those harbors were put only to peaceful uses. There was a thoughtful silence. Richard then asked how the truce had been authorized. Caulfield said the Admiralty had not been told of it, but authorized or not it was a truce and he could not in all honor as an officer and a gentleman break it without warning. All but Richard expressed sympathy with his predicament

---

* The book, unfortunately, had little to offer General Aitken. In 1914 there were available for study such military works as *Manual of Military Ballooning, Part I* (1905), *The Art of Command* by Colonel von Spohn (Translated. Price 1d.), Hans von Kiesling's *The Battle of Encounter (Part I. Practical), The Operation of Large Formations (Translated from the German)* and *Camel Corps Training (Provisional),* but of instructions for amphibious assault there was not a shadow.

and it was decided to proceed to Tanga preceded by *Fox* to give proper warning.

Richard foresaw calamity. Very quietly people began to leave the conference room but Richard was stopped at the door by the governor, who, explaining that he had known the Meinertzhagens at Mottisfont, added casually, "By the way, I have a telegram for you." Richard's mind was far away. He ripped open the flimsy paper with his thumb and unfolded it. It was from the War Office and it read "To Belfield. Tell Captain Meinertzhagen that his mother died two days ago." Richard had not even known that Georgina was ill; she had never been ill in her life. He wished he could weep. Despite the four good years of sympathy and understanding since his father's death, the long tally of sins of ommission and commission lying like jagged shards between him and his mother rose in the memory, irrevocable now. He rehearsed them, impotently, and they made the old wounds bleed again. Later he was to receive a letter written a few months before. In it Georgina told him how when he was born she had been obsessed by grievances against his father that made delusion out of mere suspicion, but even in this last weary attempt at explanation she gave Richard cause to wonder whether she had written it partly to draw his sympathy away from his father. The question perturbed him, along with all the other ambivalences, even though he could still recall every nuance of their reconciliation over his father's death bed. He wrote of her as "one whom I had so deeply respected and loved, and who had influenced me more than anyone I had ever known." Years later he was comforted when his sister Beatrice told him Georgina on the day she died had seen herself in a dream standing on the bank of a golden river with Dan on the other side smiling a welcome and stretching out his arms in love. She had died very peacefully. She was buried with her husband at Mottisfont.

Before his mother was in her grave, Richard in the press of war was forcing his sorrow and his loneliness to the back of his brain. He was plunged at once into the preparations for Tanga, toward which the convoy was now herded with H.M.S. *Fox* for a bell-wether. It was joined en route by lighters crammed with Zanzibari porters, without whose help the Indian infantry would consider itself unable to move. At dawn on November 2 the transports hove to just out of sight of land so that the cruiser could break the glad news to the Germans that the truce was over. They lay in a warm mist as *Fox* slid away through water like a plate of glass and vanished into an opal blankness. Not a man aboard, other than the staff, had set foot on land for more than two weeks, and some not for over a month.

At six o'clock in the morning Captain Caulfield called on the Germans to surrender the town. There was no answer. He began to look for mines and General Aitken called his commanders to *Karmala,* where they were handed a copy of the operation orders and read, "Opposition is not expected." They were reminded, just to be sure, that dress was important and some officers felt a little uneasy at wearing their second-best boots for wading through the salt water. Aitken had decided to launch a night attack, so in the late afternoon some of the troopships drew slowly in toward shore. There rose from the skyline clumps of tattered palms and stunted trees fringing some rock bluffs at whose feet spread mangrove swamps, waterlogged but not too dense. In the center of the swamps gleamed a strip of sand. The ships anchored in a cluster opposite the beach. They were on the seaward side of a curving promontory that protected the great harbor of Tanga. At the tip of the promontory, overlooking the narrows leading into the harbor, they could see a stone tower, crenellated like some medieval keep. It was flying the German flag. Closer to them a white house was perched on the bluff with views out over the ocean, and directly opposite their anchorage, in line with the little beach, was a red house. On the other side of the promontory, about half a mile away, lay the little town itself with a suburb of pleasant white homes scattered up the hillsides that marched away into the hinterland. Alert as ever, *Fox* detected suspicious movement in the town and fired a round of 4.7 inch. There was no response. All these demonstrations and dilatory preliminaries filled Richard with horror; it seemed to him that every German in the colony must know what was intended.

Colonel von Lettow-Vorbeck had known the British plans, in fact, for days. The meanest intelligence would have expected an assult on Tanga, the colony's second port, and his guess had been confirmed in detail by captured mail, by reports from his African agents in British East Africa and the German citizens still living comfortably in Mombasa and Nairobi, and by the articles running in the newspapers there. He had already made his dispositions by the end of October and was now back in Moshi with a sizable reserve ready for anything. Spry as a squirrel and efficient as an accountant, he waited for the British to make their move.

The sun set fast and lurid over Tanga and still practice was separated from theory by a stretch of water. Aitken had chosen as his spearhead the untempered 13th Rajputs of Tighe's Imperial Service Brigade. On legs enfeebled by their long sea voyage, in total ignorance of their whereabouts or the purpose of all this activity, wondering why they were missing their dinners and being flung into an amphibious procedure they had never rehearsed, the Indians stumbled slowly and erratically into the lighters that were to carry them ashore. When the moon rose big and bright they set off for their rendezvous and then, still three hundred yards from the shore, the lighters went aground, beautifully silhouetted on the shining water. The sea came up to a man's chest. A British officer waded all the way to the shore and back as a demonstration and the Rajputs began their assault, lurching as best they could through the water and the noisome mud of the mangrove swamp and, at last dropping exhausted on the first bit of dry land they could find, resolved to do no more for the British Raj until morning. They were joined in an hour or so by the 61st Pioneers, who reached the same conclusion, and by Brigadier Tighe and his staff, who could offer nothing better. It was now midnight; the Germans had been given eighteen hours' notice of the invasion and the first of their reinforcements were clattering confidently down the narrow-gauge railroad from Moshi. Before climbing into his bunk aboard *Karmala* Richard wrote, "We appear to have made a proper mess of today's operations." He slept soundly.

The Imperial Service Brigade welcomed the first gray streaks of light of a new day, though it showed them a wilderness. In front of them lay a tangle of thorn bush and thick grass as high as a man, thickened by clumps of palm trees, and a thoroughly inauspicious place for a battle. The brigadier was not inhibited by it. He had seen many a dawn blood red on equally forbidding fields from the jungle hills of Burma to the rock escarpments of Persia and he had never yet shirked a fight. He sent out a strong patrol. They found a path rough-hewn through the bush and in the silence of the dawn wandered along it in the direction of Tanga. They came out of the bush into a full view of the town, clean and peaceful and apparently as empty as a ruin. When they were well exposed in the open the Germans opened up with machine guns. As undaunted as he was uninformed, Tighe urged his main force forward. They struggled through the bush, disconsolate and savagely scratched, in as close order as the terrain would allow and arrived at the beaches skirting the town by an unhappy chance as the first of von Lettow's askaris from Moshi, put in the best of spirits by the novelty of a train ride, marched briskly in from the other side. An accurate and rapid fusillade began to play upon the 61st Pioneers and the 13th Rajputs. Their British officers, trying at once to rally them and to locate the enemy positions, were toppled over one by one. The line of Pioneers began to shiver and then to crack. The Rajputs hesitated and began to fall back. The fire did not slacken. And then, when bugles and cheering announced the onset of a charge by these fearsome black askaris, the sepoys turned. The Rajputs' porters dropped their loads, including the battalion's machine guns, and made for the beach. They arrived there only just ahead of the sepoys.

From the transports the rest of the advance force saw the tiny figures thronging the area of the red house and were puzzled. An officer watching General Aitken deliberately pacing *Karmala's* bridge was struck by his likeness to Napoleon, but it was Napoleon aboard *Bellerophon*. Signal flags began to flicker from the beach . . . checked by stiff resistance . . . driven back . . . heavy losses . . . half the British officers casualties. Colonel Sheppard suggested landing the rest of the force and General Aitken agreed. But that was easier said than done, for the Bangalore Brigade was hull down on the horizon, waiting where it had been told to wait. With it were all the medical stores, now much needed in the little red house, which had been turned into a shambles of a hospital. Richard was nearby, rushing about trying to restore some order in Tighe's shattered infantry, having been ashore since dawn and still not quite willing to believe what he had seen. Von Lettow was on the railroad with his headquarters and another company of delighted askaris.

Late that afternoon General Aitken established his headquarters in the white house on one point of the promontary. By nightfall the Loyals and two more battalions had landed; the rest would come in at daylight. That night Richard summarized the situation, entirely for his own satisfaction, since no one so far had read any of his intelligence reports. He estimated the German strength at about two hundred and fifty men with four machine guns (in fact he had guessed thirty men too many), though Brigadier Tighe thought he had faced two thousand five hundred. The Imperial Service Brigade had lost about three hundred men, including a high percentage of its officers. Richard was dubious about its prospects. He took a stroll round the outposts, finding them very nervous, and was about to return to headquarters when he heard a single shot and the whole area was suddenly filled with running bodies. A sepoy had fired his rifle by accident, at which the Rajputs and Pioneers had taken off once more at full speed for the beach. "These are jolly fellows to go fighting Germans with," Richard noted gloomily and prepared his bed on the white house lawn. He was using lingerie looted from his hostess' closets as a mattress and he had three German flags and a Union Jack to serve as blankets. "My pillow," he recorded, "is palm leaves stuffed into the corsets of a stout lady whose name I do not know." Von Lettow, still traveling, was some thirty miles from Tanga.

On this second night of British folly the moon still rode full and clear. It shone on a white town where nothing moved at all. Von Lettow stopped his train four miles to the west and took counsel with his local commanders. It was three o'clock in the morning. Von Lettow felt fine. His men, as it transpired, had pulled back from the town itself at the day's end in view of the enormous numbers of enemy now ashore, leaving only pickets there. Exactly where the British were no one could be sure. So von Lettow at once dispatched two patrols under German officers to find out. He himself mounted a bicycle, invited a doctor and a Captain von Hammerstein, an amiable and able member of his staff, to do likewise and pedaled determinedly into the port. Freewheeling through its deserted streets with no sound but the hiss and plop of his tires, von Lettow had time to enjoy the brilliance of the moonlight on the houses and emerged on the far side with nothing to disturb the smoothness of his passage. Then he saw the transports, still unloading men and stores with all their lights blazing and a hubbub of strange tongues echoing across the water. The landings had been shifted to a new beach between the narrows and the stone signal tower. Von Lettow and his companions rode on in that direction but dismounted out of discretion at the German Hospital, propped up their bicycles, and proceeded on foot. They were unaware that they were now beyond the British outposts. Coming to a suitable vantage point von Lettow watched the activity off-shore with a pang of frustration. His two field pieces had not yet arrived; though they dated almost from the Franco-Prussian War, even they could have bitten deep into this succulent target. On the way back to their bicycles the party was challenged by what they supposed must be an Indian sentry but since the language was one they did not understand they ignored it. Nothing happened. They pedaled back the way they had come as the sky began to lighten over the promontory behind them. Von Lettow ordered three field companies of askaris back into the town at once and kept by him a reserve of two companies of Europeans and one of askaris, with seven machine guns. He figured the odds against him would be about twenty to one. He considered for a moment whether he was wise to give battle, but he concluded, "to gain all we must risk all," and sat down to breakfast. He was by no means a gourmand but his appetite always seemed sharp.

Breakfast in the British lines was so prolonged that orders were not issued till ten-thirty. They were very clear, because all they required was for both brigades to advance for rather more than a mile in extended line with Tighe's brigade on the right and Wapshare's on the left. They did not explain how this was to be accomplished across terrain that but for three narrow tracks running along the axis of the advance was almost impenetrable bush. Shortly after noon all was ready. Tighe's Kashmiris were on the right with their flank brushing the harbor and with a company of Gwalior infantry in line on their left. Behind them the 13th Rajputs formed a second line and farther back still the 61st Pioneers provided a support not a few hoped would not have to be called on. The Loyals formed the right of Wapshare's brigade and thus the center of the British line, with the 63rd Infantry on their left and the 101st Grenadiers echeloned still farther left. Wapshare held the 98th Infantry in reserve but too far forward. General Aitken had once more gone by the book. His dispositions completed, he now took heed of Section 115 ("Position and Duties of Commanders in Action") which read in part, "Personal example has undoubtedly an extraordinary influence, especially under heavy fire, and there are times when every other consideration must be sacrificed to leading or steadying the troops." The general's bravery was never for a second in question but it was unfortunate that when he pressed forward to the van he vanished into an undergrowth of such obliterative density that none but his personal staff could see him and draw inspiration from his courageous bearing. Everyone else stumbled forward through thorn and thicket unmindful of anything but the necessity of maintaining some sort of order. About six hundred yards from the periphery of Tanga the undergrowth thinned a little and units began to shake themselves into parade-ground line. It was two o'clock. At that point the Germans opened a concentrated fire.

For the 61st Pioneers and the two companies of Rajputs next to them it was yesterday's nightmare all over again. Joined by the Madrasis of the 63rd Infantry, they began to dash madly back to the beach firing their rifles in all directions. A few were even shooting in their panic at the Loyals advancing to their left front. Richard, with general headquarters, had been marching slightly behind them. "It was too piteous to see the state of the men," he wrote later. "Many were jibbering idiots, muttering prayers to their heathen gods, hiding behind bushes and palm trees and lying down face to earth in folds of the ground with their rifles useless beside them." He spent the next two hours trying to get them back in line, kicking some and pistol-whipping others. One native officer of the Rajputs who attempted to draw his sword on him he shot dead.

The whip of bullets through the trees had brought a new hazard into the battle. The local tribesmen kept long barrel-like hives among the branches for bees to nest in. Now greatly disturbed, they swarmed over the field, not pausing to discriminate between assailant and assailed, construed by the Indians as a divine affliction and by the Loyals as another piece of German frightfulness. Richard was stung twice on his way to the right flank, where he joined a group of Dogras of the Kashmir Rifles who with two equally determined companies of Rajputs were battering their way forward with great success. With a party of twenty-five Dogras, Richard worked his way along the sea front of Tanga until he reached the main street near the Customs House. At their first attempt to cross it a burst of machine-gun fire swept nine of the Dogras writhing into the dust. Away down the street Richard could see a party of the Loyals, but a counter-attack was already coming in between them. Richard could enfilade the German assault and he and his Dogras made smart execution until it became clear that they would soon be enveloped. They pulled back to the Customs House, losing men on the way so fast that only two were left with Richard when he dashed into the building. The firing slackened.

Von Lettow had been walking from one flank to the other encouraging his men and trying to read the battle; he had just begun to realize that Aitken's left flank was open. He had stopped a momentary panic among his askaris by standing in the open laughing at them while Captain von Hammerstein, to drive the point home, threw an empty bottle at an askari running the wrong way. Von Lettow was in full military trim, bandoliers crossing his chest, two pistols at his belt, and a rifle cradled in his arm. As Richard was finding a convenient window in the Customs House, von Lettow was walking toward the main street.

It was comparatively cool in the Customs House. Richard was well back from the window in a pleasant protective gloom. He had a good view of the street, brilliant in the sun but deserted. He waited for a shot. Cautiously von Lettow and his staff approached the main street, so silent now that they could hear the soft crunch of their boots. They peered around a corner. A hundred and fifty yards away lay the Customs House, deserted. They straightened. Richard watched them and waited. Confident now, von Lettow stood in the open peering up and down the street. Richard picked his target, brought the rifle up to his shoulder, held his breath and fired. He saw the splash of the bullet into the wall, high and right. Von Lettow whipped round, seeking the enemy. Richard aimed again and fired. He was still high. The Germans scuttled round the side of a house. "It annoyed me intensely, for two reasons," Richard wrote; "it was my first fair chance at a German and secondly I had shot abominably." Years later von Lettow wrote, "This was my first social contact with my friend Meinertzhagen." For the present, he smelled victory. He sent his reserves swinging round the town and into the British left. Under its charge the British front dissolved into remnants quickly swept up by von Lettow's machine guns. Richard had made his way back from the Customs House, having come across a section of sepoys hiding behind a bank of earth. One of them, ordered to move out, had threatened Richard with his rifle. "I shot the brute as he lay half crazy with fear," Richard reported. He took over one of the Indian machine guns now being served by British officers, but the counter-attack was still being pressed. General Aitken signaled to *Fox,* lying in the narrows, to bombard the town, an activity he had forbidden till this moment in the expectation that he would need the buildings intact to billet his troops. *Fox* opened with her 6 and 4.7 inch and hit the German Hospital. Richard heard the roar above the clatter of his machine gun and was delighted. He got up to fetch more ammunition. There was a sudden flash of fire in front of him and he felt himself lifted and flung through the air. A six-inch shell from the cruiser had blasted him into the fronds of a palm tree.

The explosion dazed Richard for a few minutes but he was unwounded. At about five-thirty he rejoined Aitken's headquarters, a gloomy rendezvous. The Loyals had held together, but without support they had been pushed far back and the firing had become desultory. Then a bugle sounded from the German lines. Richard was standing beside the general. "My God!" a voice cried behind them. "That's the charge!" Richard spoke quietly to the general. "Sir," he said, "that's the retreat. I learned their calls in one of their garrison towns. It's the retreat!" General Aitken ignored him. Still believing that all was not yet lost, Richard went forward to investigate. Von Lettow, equally puzzled, was doing the same thing. An askari had mistaken an order and sounded the wrong call, so von Lettow found his men moving back. It was twilight already and it would soon be dark. Von Lettow walked back into Tanga. Richard moved very cautiously through the bush and was about to emerge when he heard a few sentences of German. There were two or three figures just discernible. He fired and they fired back. Richard withdrew to report to General Aitken that the town was virtually empty. Von Lettow headed in the opposite direction to reorganize.

General Aitken had had enough. Richard looked at him and saw that he was beaten. Orders were to go back to the starting point and entrench; Aitken's concern now was not whether he could win but how to avoid annihilation. Of his India troops, only the Kashmiris had any spirit left, but they had lost every one of their British officers. The Loyals, badly mauled, were still eager to fight. "We don't mind the German fire," one of them explained to Richard, "but with most of our officers and NCOs down and a bloody crowd of niggers firing into our backs and bees stinging our arses, things are a bit hard." But virtue had left Aitken. He gave Richard a long dispatch for the War Office that took him all night to encipher. Richard's next assignment was to carry medical supplies for the wounded in enemy hands, so after a long drink of warm water and rum out of a bucket he set off early in the morning through the bush carrying a white sheet on a pole. On the way he saw the mutilated corpse of a friend from the Loyals and not far away a row of sepoys spread-eagled face down in a ditch, each spitted with his own bayonet through his back. At the German Hospital Richard presented his bandages and chloroform and a letter from General Aitken apologizing for *Fox*'s shelling of the hospital. The Germans were very affable, discussing the previous day's fighting with great zest over an excellent breakfast. Richard began to wonder if he was living a dream. Captain von Hammerstein conducted Richard to the German perimeter and politely bade him goodbye. Before Richard had gone far a bullet cracked through his helmet, grazing his hair. A German askari on picket duty, not knowing what a white flag might signify, had sought to ambush him. Richard rammed his makeshift flagpole into the pit of the askari's stomach, wrenched away his rifle, and stuck him with his own bayonet.

During Richard's absence the headquarters staff had displayed an unwonted alacrity by issuing complete orders for reembarkation. The Loyals and the Kashmir Rifles were to furnish the covering party, and all arms, stores and equipment were to be abandoned. By five o'clock most of the troops had been ferried back to their transports; General Aitken felt able to join them there but detached Richard to carry a second flag of truce to see if the Germans would allow the recovery of the wounded, left, incredibly, at the red house and still within the British lines. Richard was rowed to the Tanga jetty and once more reported to the German Hospital. This time he was given old brandy while he waited for an answer. Von Hammerstein brought von Lettow's agreement to the truce, having by now recovered from the shock given him by Richard's information that the British were back aboard their ships. The truce was to last until six the next evening and Richard was to be back at the hospital at a quarter after nine next morning.

Richard was there early. He and von Hammerstein rode slowly to the end of the promontory on borrowed mules, each arguing without rancor the merits of his country's case. When Richard finally put forward the belief that Britain must win because her cause was right, von Hammerstein countered with "God favors the big battalions. Might is right." Realizing the vanity of further discussion they got down to business, putting the wounded on parole not to fight again against the Germans and starting their evacuation. At the beach they found the quartermaster general miserably taking inventory of his forfeited stores. Richard had just persuaded von Hammerstein not to take him prisoner when some scores of men from the Loyals jumped out of an incoming lighter and began to bathe. Von Hammerstein's military conscience was outraged at such an irresponsible breach of protocol and Richard had to confess, "It was all very embarrassing." At von Hammerstein's insistence Richard went back to the hospital for a breakfast of eggs, cream, asparagus and iced beer, and after a long talk about bird migration with a young German officer from Zanzibar Richard exchanged home addresses with von Hammerstein and promised a reunion after the war. As Richard was finally leaving, von Hammerstein held him confidentially by the arm and whispered that von Lettow wished Richard to know that his old field guns were about to arrive and that when they did he would be compelled to use them on the transports the moment the truce expired. Richard relayed the message to General Aitken. Anchors rattled up and *Fox* led the way north past the signal tower where a Union Jack still innocently flew and under the gaze of von Lettow, who had cycled to the end of the promontory to watch the ships go by—barely in time. When they arrived at Mombasa four white customs officers prevented disembarkation until dues at the rate of five per cent ad valorum had been paid on what equipment was left. Richard overcame this contretemps by threatening to arrest them.

Expeditionary Force B had left behind three hundred and fifty-nine British and Indian dead and a number of Zanzibari porters also extinguished in the battle but not counted. They had left sixteen machine guns, four hundred and fifty-five rifles and six hundred thousand rounds of ammunition, and a quantity of telephone gear. Some of this von Lettow eventually returned, but not until after the Armistice in 1918. A wit in the Secretariat (to Richard's chagrin, an old Aysgarth boy) hymned the shambles with a poem ending:

> *Back to old Mombasa*
> *Steams B Force again.*
> *Are these generals ruffled?*
> *Not the smallest grain.*
> *Martial regulations*
> *Inform us day by day,*
> *They may have foozled Tanga*
> *But they've taken B.E.A.*

The administration of the British East Africa Protectorate did not feel itself deeply committed to such undertakings, as the governor shortly pointed out: "I wish to take this opportunity to make it abundantly clear that this colony has no interest in the present war except in so far as its unfortunate geographical position places it in such close proximity to German East Africa." Hundreds of settlers had ridden into Nairobi the moment war was declared to form themselves into a rough-riding regiment of East African Mounted Rifles and a number of buccaneering smaller units, but none of the officials had been allowed to desert his desk and even the Secretariat roster for home leave was still in force. The governor spent most of his time at Mombasa, where the fishing was excellent. When Richard suggested to him that the German civilians still dotted all over the territory should be arrested, he asked for a reason and huffed grumpily, "I consider nothing less than extreme urgency would warrant the course proposed."

Without the Establishment's blessing Richard went about his business. After a meeting to settle future strategy he had concluded: "Von Lettow is not going to fight it out. He will flit from pillar to post and occupy as many of us as he can. It is downright murder to pit a man of Aitken's ability against such as von Lettow." General Aitken's summation at the meeting had been that, since he was faced by five thousand Europeans and nine thousand askaris with a hundred machine guns, he would need two new divisions to take the offensive or two good new battalions to stay safely on the defensive. Richard's own figures were five hundred Europeans and three thousand askaris; in fact in 1914 von Lettow's forces numbered two hundred and sixty Germans and fewer than two thousand five hundred askaris, distributed in fourteen field companies. No one seemed very interested in Richard's information, so he concentrated on ridding Mombasa of von Lettow's spies and hiring some of his own. At the end of two weeks he had shot two of the former and had begun to spin a spy network using a system he invented, which depended in part on the salvaging of jettisoned documents from the enemy's latrines. Richard called it his "dirty paper" method. By such subterranean means he had a good idea before long of just what forces were at von Lettow's disposal and how that good colonel's mind worked. He believed, correctly, that von Lettow's sole aim was to attract as many British troops as he could to prevent their deployment elsewhere. In this the German was succeeding brilliantly.

The War Office assumed control of operations, recalled Aitken and put him to pasture on half pay, appointed Wapshare to command and warned him not to take the offensive, and began scraping together reinforcements. Richard knew "Wappy," as he was universally called, as "a fatherly old gentleman always ready to listen to reason," but observed how the mention of von Lettow's name made him shiver. He could not resist bringing it up every night just before Wapshare went to bed. General Wapshare had established his headquarters in Nairobi to control Stewart's force opposite Kilimanjaro and Tighe's along the coast south of Mombasa. His apprehensions were confirmed in the middle of January 1915, when von Lettow attacked Tighe's men in the Umba Valley at an outpost they had established in a German plantation near Jasin. It was a hard fight in an area swarming with mosquitoes and tsetse flies, covered with agave that slashed clothing and skin, and blanketed by the wet heat of the coast. Von Hammerstein died there, hit in the belly while walking beside von Lettow. The two were caught in a creek filled with a river of dry sand, which von Lettow described: "The sand was so deep and the heat so great that one could only run, or walk quickly, for a few paces at a time. Most of the time we had to walk slowly across the open and bear the unpleasant fire as best we could. Fortunately it did no serious harm, although one bullet through my hat and another through my arm showed that it was well meant."

Richard had predicted and reported the German troop movements but nobody had paid any attention and Jasin fell. He was sinking deeper and deeper into depression at the chaos and indecision above and around him. "I wish to heaven I could get out of it all and fight in the trenches," he wrote, revealing one of the reasons that drove men of his generation into that maelstrom—the wish to escape from the confusion and decay of everything they had understood and lived for, into the clear-cut, simple confrontation of the front-line trench, the barbed wire and the bayonet. It was this mood that inspired Rupert Brooke's poem significantly entitled "Peace" and superficially a paean to the joy of accepting the challenge thrown down by a callous enemy. "Now, God be thanked Who has matched us with His hour," it began, affording to the insensitive poetic justification for the war: in fact Brooke's vision of the true state of things, as the rest of the poem* bore out, was far ahead of any but that of his fellows in the line of battle. Brooke was turning away from a world "that honor could not move" onto the chastening and the tempering fire, quite conscious of the agony of that flame but preferring it to the dull, lifeless ache of despair. Brooke and his contemporaries lusted for purification.

Despite this deep and morbid disturbance Richard was faintly encouraged by the replacement of General Wapshare by the thruster General Tighe. Wapshare was given command of a brigade in Mesopotamia and departed with a show of force by halting his train to Mombasa in order to open fire on a flock of ostriches peacefully pecking beside the track, bagging a cock and a hen. Oblivious of a double trespass in that hen ostriches were protected and that he had been shooting in a game reserve, Wappy spent the rest of the journey plucking them in the caboose. Richard wrote as his requiem, "I am sorry he has gone for he was a great gentleman and good friend,

---

* Now, God be thanked Who has matched us with His Hour
　And caught our youth, and wakened us from sleeping,
With hands made sure, clear eye, and sharpened power,
　To turn, as swimmers into cleanness leaping
Glad from a world grown old and cold and weary,
　Leave the sick heart that honor could not move,
And half-men, and their dirty songs and dreary,
　And all the little emptiness of love!

Oh! we, who have known shame, we have found release there,
　Where there's no ill, no grief, but sleep has mending,
　　Naught broken save this body, lost but breath;
Nothing to shake the laughing heart's last peace there
　But only agony, and that has ending;
　　And the worst friend and enemy is but Death.

but his removal is for the public good, for he was a public danger."
Richard was trying to work out his frustration by widening and
improving his intelligence and counter-intelligence networks: his
agents, many of them Swahilis reporting through white hunters
Richard had recruited, wandered in and out of German territory
at will, bringing him a flood of information including scraps of
filthy but informative paper from the latrines used by von Lettow's
officers. There were private letters, notes on coding and decoding,
sections of orders and pages from message pads and they told Richard a great deal about von Lettow's progress and plans. By June
1915 more than three thousand men were at work in Richard's
organization and he had destroyed the most effective of von Lettow's
agents. This was an Arab who had been helping to direct the
sabotage of the Uganda Railway. Richard wrote a letter thanking
him for some information (which had really come from intercepted
radio messages) and asking for more on certain points, and enclos-
ing for veracity's sake fifteen hundred rupees. He gave the letter
to one of his own men who he knew was incompetent enough to
be captured by the Germans. Word quickly came that the Arab
had been tried, convicted and shot. Richard felt a pang about the
end justifying his means, but consoled himself with the reflection
that it would all be the same in a hundred years' time and, to
sublimate, went out on some extended patrols.

On one of these, accompanied by four of his agents, he spent
an afternoon stalking a German raiding party. Walking back to
his base he noticed that all the game in the area was very restless,
and he and his party began to crawl in the direction in which the
giraffe and impala were staring. They found a patrol of eight
grouped in the shade of a big baobab. They killed four and wounded
the others. Richard also surprised one of the British defensive posts
on the railroad, walking in through a monumental boma of thorn
and wire past a sleeping sentry. The Indian officer in charge was
washing in a pool on whose surface floated five decomposing hippo-
potamuses he had used for rifle practice. Richard saw to it that
the marksman was cashiered. These wanderings were briefly interrupted by the arrival of a new battalion of Richard's own regiment,

the most baroque collection of soldiery ever to leave the shores of England.

At the outbreak of war the Royal Fusiliers had comprised four battalions of Territorials in addition to its regular battalions; by the time the war ended there would be sixty-five battalions through which nearly a quarter of a million men would have passed. Most of these were humdrum, mute units of the mass of the citizen army, but some, especially those formed in the first rush of enthusiasm for the Great Crusade, were unmatched for their elegance and eccentricity. A casual idea over dinner at the Travellers' Club led to the recruitment in the City of the 10th (Stockbrokers') Battalion, joined almost immediately by a satellite battalion (10b) composed almost entirely of linguists, and relegated to the furthest limbo of Intelligence. Four battalions of graduates of public schools and universities joined en bloc. Then a Mars in petticoats, Mrs. E. Cunliffe-Owen, enrolled in the Hotel Cecil the 23rd and 24th (Sportsman's) battalions, personally measuring the recruits' chests, ordering their food, and superintending their exercises in a street off the Strand, and wiring to Lord Kitchener, "Will you accept complete battalion of upper- and middle-class men, physically fit, able to shoot and ride, up to the age of forty-five?" It was a little late for his lordship to refuse and he accepted with the enthusiasm common at the time. Later came five battalions of Jewish volunteers that were to have an effect far beyond military operations. None of these extraordinary offshoots of the Royal Fusiliers, however, was brewed to as rich a broth as the 25th (Legion of Frontiersmen) Battalion, which arrived in East Africa in May 1915 and was dubbed "The Old and Bold." In its ranks were a millionaire from Park Lane, a servant from Buckingham Palace, a sometime colonel of the Army of Honduras enlisted for political reasons, cavalrymen from a regiment of death-or-glory lancers, a few elderly clowns from a circus, some Texas cowboys, the famous bird- and big-game photographer Cherry Kearton, deserters from the French Foreign Legion, former members of the orchestra at the Empire Theatre, convicts released from the gold mines of Siberia, a lighthouse keeper, a scattering of stockbrokers and—monumental at three hundred and thirty-six pounds, with a sword belt sixty-four inches round—the American sportsman and friend of President Roosevelt, William N. Macmillan of St. Louis, Missouri, and Juja Farm on the Athi Plain. But for Richard the most interesting and welcome of this fascinating collection was his dear friend Selous, come at the age of sixty-four to fight for the territory he loved and soon to die from a bullet through his mouth. He and Richard fell into a lengthy discussion ranging from the peculiarities of the Nakuru hartebeest to the nesting habits of the harlequin duck in Iceland, a matter of some complexity from which Richard was rudely torn by General Tighe's complaint that he had come here to inspect the battalion, not to listen to a debate of the Natural History Society.

The arrival of the Frontiersmen did not herald a change of policy. War Office instructions were quite clear: the posture must be one of vigorous defense until further reinforcements arrived. Since German patrols were still harassing the Uganda Railway, Richard decided to secure at least part of it for good. He had his scouts kill some game and distributed the corpses around a pool at Kasigau, the only water for eighty miles. He then put up a notice warning that the pool was poisoned and arranged to have the supposed victims renewed occasionally. The first German patrol to come there lost one man from thirst on its way home and no others followed. Von Lettow wrote a formal protest which received no answer, though Richard noted after examining his conscience, "surely there is nothing wrong in labelling water as poisoned when it is not so treated?" Such modest victories encouraged Richard to nag at Tighe to *do* something. Tighe was not unwilling and eventually prevailed on the War Office to be incautious enough to allow him a small *jeu d'esprit*. The venue was a small and peaceful village on the shore of Lake Victoria Nyanza, far off on von Lettow's left flank.

The Bukoba Expedition embarked at Kisumu on the night of June 20, 1915, a kind of armada in miniature headed by the armed steamer *Winifred,* whose twelve-pounder in the bows gave British sea power supremacy on the lake. Its arrival off Bukoba the following night was greeted by such a salvo of rockets and flares that

General Stewart turned back again into the watery anonymity of the lake. The fleet reappeared early the next morning in front of a small idyll: a church, a landing stage, a customs house and an unpretentious radio station were Bukoba's chief landmarks, spread in a saucer of land sloping gently down to the water and rimmed with hills covered with the restful dark green of banana plantations. On each side of the town was a swamp of reeds man-high. A detachment of Frontiersmen was first ashore and disappeared toward the hills; some of the Loyals and a mountain battery followed and at last the general and his staff with part of the 3rd Battalion of the King's African Rifles. By noon the force was drawn up within a mile of the town and Stewart had committed two of the errors that had helped cause Aitken's downfall at Tanga; he had not retained a reserve and he was himself in the firing line. The Loyals' advance was so reluctant that Richard waded across to them to discover what was wrong. He found their colonel "shaking like a blancmange" and so deaf to pleas for a more forceful approach that Richard flashed a heliograph message to Stewart, who replied with a peremptory order to advance. The colonel advanced. The day was passing, however, so when dusk came the attack halted where it was and went to sleep as best it might. No one had thought to land any food.

Richard was in unkindly mood next morning, cold, hungry, still wet from the swamp and impatient of delay. He was watching the battle's resumption from the mountain battery's position atop a little rocky hill, when the whole site was suddenly swept by fire from a wood on their flank. Half a company of the King's African Rifles, guarding the guns, charged straight for the wood with Richard alongside for a brisk and bloody five minutes. Four British askaris were killed and five on the German side. "I got one man at only five paces and pricked another, though he got away with a dangling arm," Richard wrote. He went back to his hilltop to watch the Fusiliers' advance and noticed a German officer up to his waist in mud and water some fifteen hundred yards off in the swamp. The German was steadily picking off the Fusiliers from his excellent cover. Richard slid quietly into the swamp to stalk him, heading for the sound of his shots. He came to within a few paces before he nuzzled his rifle through the reeds and fired, feeling less guilty about it when he discovered that the German had been using soft-nosed expanding bullets. Bukoba fell shortly after one o'clock and at the Fusilier colonel's extraordinary request was given over to looting. Richard supervised the demolition of the radio station and was amazed to discover the town full of drunken soldiery threatening their officers and violating women while the African porters watched, dressed in women's underclothes sacked from European homes and drinking champagne by the bottle. Leaving this carnage with "It makes me ashamed to think of what von Lettow and his officers will say," Richard went to the fort to blow it up. There were two tame and rather svelte pelicans waddling about its little parade ground. They delayed the demolition party for some time but when neither force nor blandishment could evacuate them Richard decided they must go to glory with their quarters, and blew up the magazine. He spent the night on the jetty persuading his bold warriors to reembark, which eventually, festooned with the fumes and spoils of war, they did and hiccuped away north toward Kisumu. Richard cooked himself an enormous lentil curry and slept all the way home. It had been a microcosm of war and a futile little demonstration.

Nothing was being decided in East Africa. The petty skirmishing went sputtering on; once a week the Uganda Railway was blown up; the strength of the troops was steadily drained by bouts of malaria, blackwater and dysentery; patrols and outposts were menaced by marauding rhino and lion. There was nothing like a grand design for victory, while in France there was at least the illusion of one. There the brutal pattern had already been set, first faintly penciled in ten days after the war started when the Schlieffen Plan wavered and the first German troops dug holes in the ground where they were, set up their machine guns and waited. Before ever Richard had set eyes on Tanga the old British army he had known had fallen back from Mons, advanced again to the Marne, and clashing head-on with a full-scale German attack in the first battle of Ypres at the end of October 1914, had been blown to the winds. Its survivors were little more than yeast for the new divisions being formed out of the volunteers that flooded the recruiting offices at the rate of a thousand a month after the initial tidal wave of half a million men in the first rapturous month of the war. In the London music halls young ladies with rosebud lips were still singing:

> *On Sunday I walk out with a soldier,*
> *On Monday I'm taken out by a Tar.*
> *On Tuesday I'm out with a baby boy scout,*
> *On Wednesday a hussar.*
> *On Thursday I gang out wi' a Scottie,*
> *On Friday the captain of the crew—*
> *But on Saturday I'm willing,*
> *If you'll only take the shilling,*
> *To make a man of every one of you.*

and back from the trenches came the echo:

> *Far, far from Ypres I long to be,*
> *Where German snipers can't snipe at me.*
> *Damp is my dugout,*
> *Cold are my feet,*
> *Waiting for whizz-bangs*
> *To send me to sleep.*

which was not, as it superficially appeared, a mutedly mutinous complaint, but merely the kind of melancholy rune with which the common soldiery by incantation kept up their own spirits. Morale was still high, for it had not yet occurred to anyone (save Lord Kitchener, and that briefly) that by now the Germans in the west were in effect inside an impregnable keep against which might pound waves of the most gallant of men without achieving its reduction. The grim grinding of the machinery of attrition had not yet crunched into its steady gear; nevertheless, during the three days of the battle of Neuve Chapelle the British lost fifty thousand men to the Germans' twenty thousand, and it was beginning to dawn on some that total victory could only be won by total effort and beyond that perhaps only by some crystallization of the nation's war aims. The mood reached Richard Meinertzhagen in his backwater and in one of his moments of self-examination he wrote: "To lose this war is quite unthinkable. We have jolly well got to win it, even though this generation perishes in the attempt." He considered the real reasons for fighting the war, concluding that it was not for Belgium, for the maintenance of British sea power supreme, nor in defense of property but, with the voice of Herbert Spencer in his ear, because "we have to struggle for existence. We have to show the world that we who are fittest shall survive. We are fighting so that our race may continue, we are fighting for our homes and our womenfolk and our future generations."

Richard was then deep in inconclusive warfare with the Royal Navy in the person of an admiral with a face like a plowed field whose patrols had been allowing supply ships to reach von Lettow. After one of his engagements with the admiral Richard wandered into the Mombasa Club, "a pot-house dedicated to Bacchus and Dame Rumor," where a general meeting was discussing the expulsion of the German members. The chairman was a judge whose servant, as it chanced, had been one of the spies upon whom Richard had visited a lethal justice: the judge requested Richard to leave the meeting as it was confined to members. Pointing out that he was the most senior member present, Richard suggested to the Club's owner that the Germans, if removed, might well sue him after the war. This prompted the owner to propose to the meeting that each member should guarantee his support in such an event to the extent of a check for ten pounds. The meeting closed without a vote. "It is surprisng," Richard remarked mildly, "what effect money has on principles." A few days later the xenophobia became a little more personal. *The Leader* of Nairobi ran an editorial asking, "Even the head of our intelligence section boasts a typical German name. Is this to be tolerated when we have so many spies among us?" Richard sent for the editor, berated him for not being in uniform, suppressed his newspaper, and the following day hauled him before a court-martial. But more than brute force would be needed to arouse in the British East Africa Protectorate a fervor that would match von Lettow's. The Colonial Office finally urged the governor to his most energetic efforts to induce every settler available to join the colors. He invited the Nairobi Defense Force to parade at Government House, Nairobi, a singularly affable gesture they answered by marching with music and banners up the drive as asked, where in a cloud of dust they met the governor head on, traveling at full speed in his car to catch the train for Mombasa and a few days' fishing. In His Excellency's absence the valiant E. S. Grogan, himself an early settler and now in Richard's employ, called a mass meeting in Nairobi with Richard's clandestine assistance. The meeting resolved to demand compulsory service and the colony as a result became the first part of the British Empire to enjoy that doubtful privilege. It was, whatever the outcome, an extraordinary psychological advance and Richard recorded with some satisfaction, "The colony has found itself."

On the heels of this success came better news yet. The War Office announced that the force in East Africa was to be brought up to a strength of two divisions under the command of General Sir Horace Lockwood Smith-Dorrien, late of France. One of the five officers who had escaped the Zulu assagais of Isandhlwana, Sir Horace had made the best of that lease of life against Arabi Pasha outside Alexandria, on the Northwest Frontier, at Omdurman and with Kitchener as Fashoda. He had ended the Boer War a major general and had then been given command of the Quetta Division (a sure sign of advancement), where it was said that he probably knew by sight every subaltern in the division and certainly every subaltern's pony. He had commanded in France with distinction from the start, his turning at bay at Le Cateau having probably saved the retreat from Mons from becoming a rout by crippling the Germans so severely that they could not follow. Richard looked forward to his arrival for he was a man of vigor and sense, yet even this Lochinvar out of the west could hardly achieve alone what in Richard's view was needed. "If he thinks he is going to conquer German East and bring von Lettow to terms, he is mistaken," Richard predicted. "He would be even less likely to do it with ten divisions. In fact, I cannot imagine how it can be done except by long attrition at the expenditure of thousands of malaria cases and many millions of money. Civilised warfare in tropical Africa is quite off the picture."

While waiting for the new dispensation Richard went off to practice a little uncivilized warfare inside von Lettow's domain southwest of Lake Victoria Nyanza. He took with him into the wastes a junior officer called, not inappropriately, Major J. J. Drought, and fifteen men of his private army of intelligence scouts. They crossed the border on Christmas Day 1915 and almost at once got wind of a German patrol. Not long before dusk they came upon the enemy camp in holiday atmosphere: they counted fourteen askaris squatting unarmed by their campfires and not bothering to post sentries. There were four tents, indicating the presence of at least one German. Richard's party crawled near enough to attack without firing and rushed silently in upon the camp with bayonets glinting. Richard killed one man and Drought managed three while Richard dashed into the nearest tent. A fat German officer was lying on a camp bed on the point of rousing himself to eat a Christmas dinner spread out on the table beside him. Richard covered him with his rifle and harshly ordered him to put up his hands. Foolishly and far too slowly the German groped under his pillow. Richard shot him dead. By then the encounter was over; Within minutes Richard's men had killed fifteen of the enemy, wounded two, captured seven, at no loss to themselves and with only a single shot having been fired. They had used bayonets. Drought tended the wounded, Richard covered over the dead and set out sentries, and then Drought announced that he was very hungry indeed. So was Richard. Not minding the body in the bed, they worked their way through its Christmas dinner, ending with a delicious Christmas pudding. Before leaving the camp Richard searched the officer's kit for documents, finding in a pocket a letter addressed with the honorific "Graf." Impressed, Richard wrote: "So I must have shot a Duke. The first Duke I have killed." His elation was cooled years later when he met the man's brother in Amsterdam and was innocently asked whether by chance, since he had served in East Africa, he had any knowledge of the circumstances of the nobleman's death. "I felt an utter brute and was unable to tell him the truth," Richard confessed then. "It revealed the revolting and cruel nature of war."

On New Year's Day 1916 a mounted brigade of South Africans arrived in Nairobi as harbingers of the new troops that were to bring victory. General Jacob Louis van Deventer, their commander, was not a talkative man; a throat wound from a British bullet made speech difficult for him, but he had captured one of Smith-Dorrien's convoys during the Boer War, so a wordy introduction would not be necessary. Before long it became clear that even this formality would not take place, for Smith-Dorrien fell ill during his voyage and was replaced by Richard's old acquaintance General Jan Smuts. The new commander greeted Richard pleasantly, recalling their hours together in the Union Club at Pretoria and asking for news of Richard's Potter aunts. Richard spread out his maps for the general and was delighted to find a good listener; he wrote enthusiastically, "He is a fascinating little man and one leaves him after an interview with the impression that he has a first class brain." Richard also carried away an uneasy suspicion that Smuts and his South Africans were underestimating the problem facing them. They referred to von Lettow's askaris as "kaffirs," boasting that they would drive them with a whip, and they proposed to outmaneuver von Lettow in the true, hard-riding Boer fashion of wide out-flanking movements. Richard tried to explain that thick bush inhibited that kind of tactic, that the climate and the diseases caused ten casualties to every one from a bullet, and that they would soon come to respect the fighting qualities of von Lettow's blacks. Not sure that his advice had been heeded, he busied himself while the buildup continued with his scheme to discredit von Lettow's currency. Some months before he had captured a few twenty-rupee notes and sent them to the Standard Printing Press in England with an order for several million duplicates. These he was now spreading out in the sun, crumpling and rubbing them with dirt to give them a credible appearance.

By the first week of March 1916 Smuts and his army were ready. Their numbers—approaching nineteen thousand men—indicated that strategically at least von Lettow was succeeding. They were disposed in three divisions: one was under Stewart and one under Tighe, both polyglot formations of Indians, East African settlers, Rhodesians, British, Africans and some Boers; the third division, van Deventer's, was South African. Against them von Lettow could bring eleven thousand askaris, three thousand Germans, and vastly greater experience. Smuts took his headquarters out of Nairobi and into the fighting zone opposite Kilimanjaro, where Richard was able to survey the enemy positions from an airplane. At his request the pilot climbed up the shoulder of the mountain until at seventeen thousand feet, four hundred feet below their ceiling, they skimmed the snowy crater of Kilimanjaro's summit. After a leisurely glide over von Lettow's positions Richard ended his first flight stone deaf, with his brain "wobbly" and too excited to settle right down to work. He found that he loved flying.

Slowly and at cost Smuts pushed southwest into von Lettow's line without achieving an envelopment. Von Lettow gave ground, having decided during the months of inaction to fall back into the fertile center of his colony where he could sustain a guerrilla action. It was his purpose by mobility and aggressive feints to keep as many of the enemy as possible pursuing him through the bush until they were exhausted. He would still be succeeding in this policy when the Armistice was signed, by which time Smuts and Richard Meinertzhagen would be far away. At present, however, von Lettow's grand design was not yet clear to the British, for when attacked he resisted and when presented with an open flank he bit it. Moreover, patrolling by Smuts's forward troops was not providing enough illumination. Richard decided once more to make his own reconnaissance. Starting by moonlight from Moshi, von Lettow's former base, he struck straight through the bush to the big German posts at Kahe and Pangani Bridge, and lay within touch of their sentries until he had estimated their strength. He cut back home by swimming a river full of crocodiles and was hurrying down a path when a sentry challenged him from very close by. Richard had thought he was beyond the German picket line, but he realized that the askari could not recognize his uniform in the darkness so he began to speak in Swahili as he walked softly forward. Before the man could raise the alarm Richard lowered his rifle and put his bayonet through him. When Richard reported his findings to Smuts, the general listened with his usual noncommital expression. Then he said, "Meinertzhagen, you're mad, stark, staring mad! It isn't your business to undertake this sort of risk. Don't do it again." Richard explained that he was not only more qualified for this kind of work than his subordinates but that he also enjoyed it. Smuts's red beard twitched. "You're mad!" he said again. Richard saluted and left.

When the rains came in April Smuts made a bold move. He sent van Deventer to a hilly place called Kondoa Irangi, so placed that von Lettow was bound to attack it to maintain the logic of his own plans for constant and uniform maneuver. Van Deventer's horsemen were a knife pointing at his stomach. Richard joined the Boers at Kondoa and found them a less formidable weapon than he had hoped. Horses were dying fast of swarms of tsetse fly, many of the troopers were sick with fever, and the ammunition reserves were low. Richard's spies told him that von Lettow was massing his companies within two days' march. Van Deventer rasped, "Let them attack!" but he had dug only a few yards of trench, he sent out no patrols, and his barbed wire was still lying in bundles where it had been dumped. "Von Lettow," Richard observed uneasily, "is never late for an appointment." At four in the afternoon of May 9, 1916, von Lettow called. A shell bursting close by von Deventer's headquarters awoke everyone, and Richard, collecting the fragments, identified them as coming from one of the *Konigsberg*'s guns, which von Lettow had long since dismounted and had used in all his serious battles. Nothing more happened until suppertime. The entire east face of the camp began to flash and spit with volleys. Richard, who liked nothing better than a fight at night, for he could see perfectly in the dark, ran across the ridge toward the firing. He paused for a moment, caught by the sparkling beauty of the rippling line of musketry and machine guns and the star shell and flares arcing and spluttering over the bush. Gathering the nearest platoon, Richard, "just bursting for a bayonet charge," led it at full speed against the nearest machine-gun post, which was silenced in minutes. Richard broke his bayonet, so used the rifle as a club and shattered the stock. The main enemy body came up the hill in a rush, the few that survived it dropping into a short stretch of trench near Richard, now unarmed. There was a confused, choking welter of bodies which he approached with fists and boots at the ready. Suddenly he realized there was a man beside him. He asked in Swahili, "Who are you?" but heard only the whistle of air as the man struck at him with a club. It smashed into Richard's shoulder but that was not enough. Richard kneed the man hard in the stomach and snatched at the weapon in a fury, then hit him savagely on the head until he dropped. When quiet came he found he was holding a long, beautiful knobkerrie. He carried it with him from that day on until at the end of his life he presented it to his old regiment, who placed it in their museum in the Tower of London.

That same month he acquired a second souvenir he had long coveted. The *Konigsberg* had eventually been sunk in her hideaway in a creek of the Rufiji River, her guns supplying von Lettow with some unwieldy but powerful artillery and her crew a company of troops, who carried with them everywhere her ensign. Richard lusted after this flag but it was too well guarded to be stolen by his agents, and for a long time all he could do was stare hungrily at a photograph of it had had captured. At last he heard that the sailors were about to embark on a raid, swiftly set an ambush with a hundred and sixty of his agents led by a Boer officer in his confidence. They told nobody about the scheme. The Boer machine-gunned the sailors at a river crossing, brought the flag to Richard, and split a bottle of champagne. Richard kept the flag in his safe but in later years hung it on a wall in his London home, where it was admired by von Lettow among others.

A new flag, that of England's oldest ally, now appeared on von Lettow's southern frontier. Portugal had entered the war on the Allied side and had promptly launched an expedition from her colony to the south of German East Africa, despite Richard's warnings of its obvious dangers, and had suffered a defeat even more ludicrous than that of the British at Tanga. "What a change from the days of Vasco da Gama," Richard sourly commented, having anticipated no other result. "Their colonies are a scandal, the natives being much worse off than they ever were before. Except for introducing every European vice and withholding every European virtue, they had done nothing." The only effect of this act of folly was to give von Lettow more room to maneuver, since he could now feel free to cross the Portuguese frontier.

The sagacious colonel was now proving very difficult to pin down. Every time Smuts launched what he believed was an enveloping attack on one of von Lettow's main positions, the Germans managed to slip away before they could be crushed. This was due to the fact that the maneuvers were not flank attacks at all, but merely exaggerated extensions of Smuts's own flank, which had no more effect on von Lettow than an arm thrown round a shoulder. No one had yet thought to get astride the Germans' lines of communication, and no one ever did. With operations constantly mobile Richard's work became very strenuous. He now employed twenty-five hundred scouts for patrolling as well as hundreds of agents on espionage work, so the assessment of reports alone was an immense task. The reports made it clear to Richard that von Lettow was being out-maneuvered but certainly not defeated, and in a wild fit of fancy he imagined the only conclusion would be that Smuts would "outflank" von Lettow all the way through Portuguese East Africa, winding up somewhere around Pretoria. At the end of August 1916 he predicted, "I think we are in for an expensive hide-and-seek, and von Lettow will still be cuckooing somewhere in tropical Africa when the cease-fire goes."

By the end of August both Tanga and Dar-es-Salaam had been relinquished by the Germans, and general headquarters moved to the larger port in September. Just north of the passage into the harbor of peace, the Germans had maintained an old coastal defense gun and quite frequently used it. One afternoon Richard heard that the admiral commanding this sector of the Indian Ocean was expected in his flagship, so with a friend he made for the old emplacement, charged the gun with a quantity of black powder, and when the flagship was well into the narrows lit it. There was an expensive bang and a great volume of smoke. When it cleared Richard and his friend were staring straight down the barrels of ten six-inch guns at point-blank range. It was lucky that the admiral was not trigger-happy; Richard expressed due gratitude for that at dinner that night. Perhaps what had caused Richard's high spirits had been the arrival in the mail of a big package of decorations from His Imperial Majesty the Tsar of All the Russias, in which Richard took a modest but becoming share.

At the beginning of October Richard could neither eat nor sleep and found himself concocting crazy plans. For months he had been working from six in the morning until the early hours, often without a break for food. Smuts ordered him to Nairobi for a rest. Richard enjoyed meeting friends there, including the wise and gentle Selous, but the doctors studied him and concluded that he was in such bad shape that if he stayed in East Africa he would die. Smuts ordered him home with a handsomely laudatory report that brought him a degree of fame in the higher reaches of the War Office. Richard had begun to be recognized as one of the more spectacular intelligence experts; the cornerstone of his reputation had been laid.

When Richard embarked at Mombasa on December 10, 1916, he left behind a situation not significantly better from the Allies' point of view as far as tactics were concerned, and worse strategically, than at the beginning of the year. As von Lettow saw it at the time, "I regarded the military situation in the Colony as remarkably favorable, for I knew that the South African troops were for the most part worn out with battle-casualties and sickness, while a large portion of the remainder were returning to South Africa at the end of their engagements." He stopped fighting on November 13, 1918, two days after the end of hostilities. By that time he had cost the British seventy-two million pounds and over sixty-two thousand lives (four out of every five from disease), a figure which did not include the tens of thousands of patient natives of the country who expired, carrying loads along the line of march, from bullets, from disease, or from sheer exhaustion.* In military terms von Lettow was quite clearly the victor.

---

* These dead, though never counted, were not entirely forgotten; there still stands in what used to be Delamere Avenue (now renamed for President Jomo Kenyatta) in the center of Nairobi a bronze group of three heroic Africans. On its base is inscribed in English and Swahili, "This is to the

Richard Meinertzhagen's long return home by way of Cape Town and Sierra Leone was both slow and relaxing, so that when at last he reached London on January 19, 1917, he was well. He was put to work at once in the War Office, where he immediately realized that the butcher's bill in France made his own experiences seem like kiss-in-the-ring. What had started as a brief campaign of maneuver was now bogged solidly from one end of Europe to the other. For a year the British commander-in-chief had been Douglas Haig, whom Richard had last seen one carefree morning during his golden days with the yeomanry. Haig was an extremely handsome man whose expression was invariably so sincere as to appear almost wooden. His breeches were of a cut that struck Court tailors dumb with awe, the peak of his cap hid his direct blue eyes under a halo of proud red, his boots had the liquid gleam of pure crystal, and he managed always to stand, feet at an angle and clean chin up, in the pose of the hero. He had never seen the front line and he never would. But what happened there, save for minor details, was all his doing, and he was convinced that the Germans could be defeated by sheer brute force, head on across the mud. One more battle would do it.

On July 1, 1916, thirteen divisions of British infantry, knowing nothing but how to stay shoulder to shoulder and not to flinch, almost every man a volunteer, went over the top. The first wave was mowed down; the second wave lapped a little further and seethed to a stop; the third passed through that writhing debris and was itself lashed from the German trenches; the fourth trod on bodies all the way across no man's land. By nightfall sixty thousand men lay in that small compass, one in every three of them stone dead. It was the greatest day's blood-letting any army anywhere had

---

memory of the native African troops who fought: to the carriers who were the feet and hands of the army: and to all other men who served and died for their king and country in Eastern Africa in the Great War of 1914–18. If you fight for your country even if you die, your sons will remember your name." Below this is the footnote, under the earlier dates, 1939–45. Across the street is a plain stone obelisk commemorating the white dead with a simple "To our glorious dead."

ever suffered, or ever would. General Haig, however, was not convinced that one more push would not do it.

On July 14, by a kind of accident, a night attack succeeded where the battering had failed, and a gap was torn in the German lines. This was the very thing the British army had been created for—this was the moment to realize the dream. This was the moment to loose the cavalry! After some difficulty in picking their way over the riven ground three divisions of cavalry launched themselves with bugles chanting and lances glancing in the sunlight into the cornfields behind the German trenches. It was the summation of all the best thinking, the culmination, the martial orgasm. They were cut down by machine guns slashing through the corn—the horseflesh and the men—before they had gone from the gallop to the charge. On September 15 General Haig reluctantly tried tanks. They failed and proved his point. The last attack on the Somme came on November 13. In four months General Haig had advanced, at the maximum point, five miles. For this he had spent four hundred and twenty thousand men; the French, fighting rather incidentally on his right at the same time, had lost two hundred thousand men. At this point General Haig paused to ponder how to achieve his object. It was beginning to look a bit tricky.

Though the commander in chief was happily able to hold fast to his vision, the views of those in his care were changed by their labors in the valley of the Somme. They did not question the wisdom of those set over them. But the fire had melted from them all the sweet fat of idealism and left them stark, enduring professionals. There grew from then on in France a society apart, a kinship of men in battle, altruistic and strangely noble, that could outface unimaginable horror but which, though holding bitterness toward none, extended no farther back than the reserve trenches and was mute in the presence of those not a part of the mystery. Thus the flower of Richard Meinertzhagen's generation held its tongue, bent its back, did its duty and died. And with its passing finally whispered into history the Century of Hope.

CHAPTER 12

No Advance Without Security

few weeks in the War Office among time-servers, sycophants and dullards were enough to make Richard Meinertzhagen long for action elsewhere. The main occupation within its martial halls seemed to him to be an unremitting pursuit of honors and awards and in mute protest he stopped wearing his own modest but honest decorations. His transfer to an intelligence job in the Egyptian Expeditionary Force then nibbling at the frontier of Palestine came therefore as a release and a promise of a milieu that at worst would be congenial. On May 3, 1917, Richard embarked with three thousand four hundred troops at Marseilles on the transport *Transylvania*.

Richard came aboard with a minimum of baggage, in a dark mood at having been parted from his camera, books and luncheon basket through the officiousness of an embarkation officer. The transport was so solid with men that life-boat drill was judged impracticable, the decks being further obstructed by some fifty horses tethered there. The morning of the second day was heavenly. Sea and sky were brilliant and the ship was close enough to shore for the breeze to carry out to it a dry scent of pines and heather from the hills of Italy. Comfortable in the sun, *Transylvania*'s passengers crowded her rail gazing cheerfully at the land and with casual interest at a fishing boat moored inshore with its crew energetically hauling in their catch. A few of the watchers noticed a sleek dark shape sliding toward them and called out to friends to watch the dolphin, but a voice from the bridge yelled, "Torpedo!" and in seconds there was a thunder in the bow. Before the first orders to lower the boats took effect three more torpedoes rammed into the transport. *Transylvania's* escort was two Japanese destroyers; these now raced back to where she wallowed to pick up her troops and incidentally to sink the fishing boat which, it was later discovered, had been captured by a German submarine which then hid beneath it, having replaced the Italian fishermen with some of its own crew who reported *Transylvania's* arrival by portable telephone line. The transport began to list after the first strike; the succeeding impacts drove her so far over that it was possible to walk down her sloping deck into the Mediterranean.

Richard viewed the chaos with some detachment. He had refused to board one of the few boats launched and now watched most of them founder. An animal-lover had cut loose the horses, which were plunging in terror among the mass of swimming and drowning men. Richard noticed no panic anywhere—everyone seemed to be in the best of spirits, as the British were wont to be in supreme adversity, and song filled the air—but the lack of any central control of affairs disquieted him. He was wearing a life-jacket so he waited for the crowd to thin out a bit, helped himself to a couple of bottles of brandy from the ship's bar, tucked them under his arm, and then, knobkerrie in hand, strolled composedly into the water.

Then the trouble with the horses began. Unable to see land they were milling about trampling anything solid in attempts to climb onto it. Most of the solid objects were men. Richard managed to stun a number of horses with a stroke between the eyes but one came at him awkwardly and kicked him hard in the stomach before he could strike. He was left on the edge of oblivion but the brandy saved him. *Transylvania* sank in half an hour but it was four hours before Richard was pulled out of the sea in a net. He was rolling drunk, for apart from a couple of slugs he had given to soldiers in passing he had emptied both bottles. He was in hospital for two days before the shock wore off, by which time four hundred of his companions had died of exhaustion. Richard returned to Marseilles by train, recovered the possessions he thought he had lost, and, thus prompted to think it an ill wind that blew nobody good, set out once more on the seventh crusade.

The struggle against Turkey with its overtones of holy war had not as yet been conspicuously blessed. The landings at Gallipoli, Churchill's concept and the only one of any genius in the entire war, had failed through the inept decisions of a fearful admiral and a handful of dodo generals. An Anglo-Indian army sweltered in the badlands of Mesopotamia and died of disease more rapidly than from Ottoman bullets; suffering greatly and almost forgotten, it had captured Baghdad but it was very far from disabling the Turks. On the most important front—that of the Palestine border with Egypt in Sinai—there appeared to be a stalemate.

At the beginning of the war the Turks had crossed the impassable desert using ingenuity and sheer peasant muscle to make roads through the sand for their howitzers by digging parallel ditches and filling them with brushwood. They had held part of the east bank of the Suez Canal for a while and occupied El Arish, confounding the British commander who had prophesied, "The desert is our great ally and it will beat the Turk in the end."* But the Turks were not long to enjoy the fruits of their audacity: by the beginning of 1917 they had been pressed back to a frontage extending from Beersheba to Gaza, famous as the temporary residence of Samson.

When Richard Meinertzhagen finally arrived in Cairo on May 24, 1917, the situation was by no means clear. The outbreak of the Russian Revolution had aborted a Russian design to drive from the Caucasus toward Mosul and had permitted the withdrawal of the Turkish divisions contesting their passage. These were now to

---

* In the end what made the desert more amenable to the British than to the Turks was a water supply carried through an American pipeline. Standard Oil of New York had been prospecting in Palestine before the war. At its outbreak the company dumped its pipeline in Alexandria to await better days.

be concentrated at Aleppo in northern Syria with other forces, supported by a German contingent known variously as Pasha II or the Asia Corps, a brigade of selected and highly trained infantry with auxiliary arms. This Turko-German body, comprising two army corps, was to be employed in the recapture of Baghdad in an operation christened *Yilderim* (Thunderbolt), directed by that same General Erich von Falkenhayn who had conceived the nightmare of Verdun and whose inflexible mental habits were to have as much cohesive effect on the Turks as a bar of iron laid upon quicksilver. He would never understand why the immaculate arrangements of his German staff never blossomed into action, for the dilatory and devious workings of the minds of his oriental allies defied the comprehension of a mind as bony and narrow as his.

Coincident with these shiftings and realignments David Lloyd George, now Prime Minister, made queasy by the massive cost of Haig's Western policy in Flanders and desperate for an alternative in the east, had demanded Jerusalem for Christmas. Though not disposing of sufficient strength for such an accomplishment, Sir Archibald Murray, the commander in Egypt, dutifully attacked Gaza for the first time on March 26 and was repulsed. Thereupon the Turks not only reinforced Gaza but also greatly strengthened their defenses as far as Beersheba. When Sir Archibald renewed his assault on April 17 he was again held off.

In these sullen and doubtful circumstances Richard reported to general headquarters of the Egyptian Expeditionary Force in the Savoy Hotel, Cairo, a caravanserai only slightly less sumptuous than the immortal Shepherd's, and was assigned to the intelligence section at advanced headquarters in northern Sinai, about two hundred miles from the Egyptian capital geographically and half a world away in temperament. Though beyond the desert proper, Deir-el-Belah remained an arid place during the summer months; in spring it shimmered green with fields of young barley and corn and the buds of almond, apricot and orange trees, and the rain brought anemones like glowing scraps of satin, little purple irises, narcissi and sweet clover. Richard much preferred it to Cairo; a cool clean breeze freshened the camp and only some dunes separated him from the beach and a perfect swim. Though physically at ease and with plenty of work to occupy him, he was worried about the general state of things. Most of his family actively supported the Russian Revolution, but Richard saw it as a disaster not only to the Allied cause but to Russia herself, not because he was politically conservative but because, holding a dark view of human nature, he feared anarchy. "Revolution results in the shedding of buckets of innocent blood, senseless destruction of property, chaos, anarchy and cruelty more typical of wild beasts than of human beings," he wrote in June 1917, "and in a reactionary despotism or dictatorship infinitely less tolerant than the very tyranny which caused the revolution."

Since the Revolution neutralized the Russian threat to Turkey from the Caucasus, its effect on British policy toward the Turks was immediate. It was clear that the Turkish forces released from that area would be launched in the Yilderim operation against the Anglo-Indian army in Mesopotamia. An enemy success there would menace British oil supplies from Abadan and at length the security of the Persian Gulf and even of India. These strategic dangers, and Lloyd George's thirst for a palpable victory somewhere, prompted the British to plan an attack toward Jerusalem to draw the Yilderim divisions away from the road to Baghdad and the glittering prizes of the Orient. This vital objective was entrusted to a new commander who was to write of Richard Meinertzhagen, "This officer has been largely responsible for my successes in Palestine." Generous as it was, this opinion was something of an overstatement of the facts, for though Richard played a great part in breaking the Turks, it was Sir Edmund Allenby who ground them under his heel.

The blood of Cromwell ran cold and commanding in Allenby. He was a dragoon, a pale, fleshy Englishman with nothing exotic in his nature or his experience. He had commanded the Cavalry Division in the first days in France, then a corps and finally the Third Army, carrying out Haig's rescripts without question, though he respected neither Haig nor his methods and though his own slow opinions were cut short by that dapper demagogue. Allenby possessed that brutal nerve to commit many men to their deaths that was essential to good generalship, but it was balanced by a practical judgment that measured the prize shrewdly against the cost and it was only exercised when he was certain that everything had been done to mitigate loss. He was thought of as a spiller of blood, a battering ram, and this reputation was crystallized by the readiness of his choking rage to burst flashing and thundering on the slightest deviation from orders. He was nicknamed "The Bull," not out of affection. Thus Allenby the archetype: beneath was something more complex and brilliant. Allenby had been schooled in the straight English tradition; at Haileybury, in the house named for Sir Bartle Frere, he had been shown his duty (which lay in service through leadership) and taught indifference to mere popularity; above all, he had been trained to be thorough. Richard's mentor Bishop Welldon once wrote of Allenby, with the dispassionate insight of the born schoolmaster looking at the master of men and seeing still the growing child: "Edmund Allenby would not, I think, have been regarded as a boy of outstanding distinction, either in work or in play. But in his lessons, as in his games, he was always painstaking and thoroughgoing. He was a quiet, strong, manly, conscientious boy, of singular modesty, who never put himself forward. Among his qualities I think I should place first his high ideal of duty: he was one upon whom it was possible to rely in boyhood as in manhood for entirely faithful service." Allenby was loyal not only upward, but downward as well and expected his subordinates, whom he chose with great astuteness, to take responsibility and stood firmly by them as long as they did so. Those close to him loved him. Those who only saw him at a distance were impressed by his size, his energy and his obvious solidity. Few saw behind the master strategist the scholar who could cull from Greek sources the history of his battlefield, behind the ruthless attacker the collector of wild flowers and birds, behind the annihilator the shy lover of young children.* What everyone recognized

---

* Allenby's only child, Michael, had served as an artillery officer in his Third Army in France. Not yet twenty-one, Michael Allenby was killed in July 1917 when a shell fragment smashed through his steel helmet. The Bull showed no signs of grief but Edmund Allenby wrote to his own mother: "He was all that one could desire as a son; and I am proud to have been his father. . . . There is not a day of his life I could wish to be otherwise

was a professional who looked, striding through inspection after inspection and apparently tireless in his preparations, like a winner. They began to realize that his temper struck only when some detail intended to contribute to victory or to improve the welfare of his men had been overlooked and when people tried to fob him off with butterfly answers. Part in fear, part in affection, a warning "BL" would be flashed to the units he intended to visit, meaning "Bull Loose."

Richard Meinertzhagen welcomed his truculent new chief, discerning in him the unusual directness he practiced himself. "His manner is brusque almost to rudeness," he wrote with approval after their first meeting, "but I prefer it to the oil and butter of the society soldier." Soon after Richard had arrived he had suggested the reorganization of the intelligence section, and it was being carried out. In the meantime he had begun collecting agents for his own system to supplement the network already operating out of Cairo, and had established a counter-espionage organization. One of his first coups was a repetition of the trick he had used in East Africa to dispose of the opposing champion; he wrung the name of their chief from some captured small fry, wrote the chief a letter of thanks, enclosed a reward and made sure it would be intercepted. Taking advantages of the wonders of Egypt, Richard also popped a bijou radio station atop the Great Pyramid to monitor Turkish messages, and its operator never failed to decode what he received.

In addition Richard was on the trail of a shadowy figure who had attained the stature of a myth. He was a supposed German agent called Fritz Franks who crossed back and forth through the lines at will in the guise of an English or Australian officer. There were many stories about his bravery and effrontery, none of which Richard believed, for no one had actually set eyes on Franks. More to suppress the rumors than to capture the ghost, Richard sowed a crop of fictitious reports about Franks's habits and issued a false description, warning all troops to be on the alert. The result was a flurry

than as he lived it. In simplicity, gentleness, cheerfulness and honor he walked from his birth until his death. I rejoice in every remembrance of him." The strong, careful script was blotched with tears.

of false arrests, including that of Richard himself while out with a friend crawling after the bird life of the Wadi Ghuzze. Visiting the prisoner of war camp at Alexandria, Richard was astonished to find a Greek deserter from the Turks who claimed that he had worked for Franks. Richard made a deal. The Greek was to bring Franks to a dry wadi three miles east of Deir-el-Belah.

At four in the morning of the day appointed, Richard rode out to the rendezvous. The Greek was already there, alone. He explained that Franks and an orderly would soon join them. A while later a single horseman trotted into the gulley, slim in an Australian trooper's uniform, and after handing some papers to the Greek explained that Franks had had to go back to the Turkish lines. The Greek suggested that they should meet in a week's time. Richard agreed but announced that he must arrest the orderly. The Greek asked Richard if he would be kind enough before he did so to ride out of the gulley and check whether his own escape route to the Turks across the plain was clear.

Richard had kept his hand in his pocket all this time, resting on a heavy automatic. He walked to his horse and was mounting when the Greek and the orderly fired simultaneously. Richard's horse reared and made him miss the Greek but he slammed the orderly to the ground with a bullet in the neck. The Greek was beyond pursuit almost at once with the orderly's horse galloping behind him. The orderly was writhing in the dust of the gulley floor and screaming shrilly. When Richard came closer he discovered in horror that he had shot a woman. She died before he could do anything and in utter confusion and shame he buried her among some boulders. He told no-one what had happened but months later in Jaffa when he searched Franks's house he found the rest of the story in some photographs. They appalled him. The Greek had been Franks himself and the woman his wife, whom he loved greatly.

Richard's more orthodox intelligence activities were fortunately more successful than the Franks fiasco. He soon collected thirty agents, half of them Arabs or Egyptians, half of them Jews. These last brought him much more than information; they brought him a cause. Until the middle of 1917 Richard's only conscious association with Jews had been with the Rothschilds. Then in Cairo he encountered the fiery spirit Aaron Aaronson, a true believer. Born in Rumania but raised on a kibbutz at Zichron Jacob low on the foothills of Mount Carmel, Aaronson had begun the war as an officer in the Turkish army. His desertion to England by way of Germany had been eased when he was captured at sea by the Royal Navy; once in London he had argued his worth so vehemently that he had been sent to Egypt and there won the support, though qualified, of the galaxy of brains that sparkled in the courses of the Arab Bureau,* which was prepared for the moment to use any means—even Zionists—to further the British and the Arab cause against the Turks. Impressed by Aaronson's vigor, Richard agreed to employ him and his group of kinsmen and friends and was astonished to find them all when they reported fair-haired and blue-eyed. Their daring soon captivated him and they did not find it difficult to make of him a passionate Zionist. For Zionists it was the moment of rebirth; Aaronson's clandestine enterprises had been preceded by the first practical manifestation of progress toward a National Home for the Jews in Palestine, the formation of a quaint but significant body known as the Zion Mule Corps. It had been organized by Vladimir Jabotinsky, a journalist turned politician and a kind of Caliban to Chaim Weizmann's Prospero, who had assembled his Russian compatriots in Cairo, joined them with refugees from the settlements of Palestine, and with British approval shipped them off to Gallipoli under the command of Colonel J. H. Patterson, that martinet from the Indian army who had slain the man-eating lions of Tsavo. They did not achieve sufficient glory on those bloody beaches to receive more than

---

* Not officially so called, the Arab Bureau had begun as the office of the perspicacious Captain Gilbert Falkingham Clayton, chief of military and civil intelligence in Egypt. It became the center for Arab sympathizers and the inspiration of the Arab Revolt. Within its orbit, officially or otherwise, came and went such luminaries as T. E. Lawrence and his mentor, D. G. Hogarth; Leonard Woolley, the excavator of Ur; Philip Graves, an expert on the Turkish army and brother of the warrior-poet Robert Graves, who wrote a biography of Lawrence; Aubrey Herbert, whose brother was to find what was left of King Tutankhamen; and, inevitably, Ronald Storrs, the Oriental Secretary.

a nod from history but their successors, the Jewish Legion, won more.

Prompted by Jabotinsky and others, the British government decided on the eve of the Balfour Declaration, itself the somewhat incoherent statement of an ill-defined policy, to raise a force among the large communities of Jews (mostly recent refugees and many not yet British citizens) in British cities. The purpose, though not at the time explicit, was threefold. A Jewish Legion would instill in its members a sense of service, it would symbolize support of Britain's cause against the Turks and, of course, it would provide more fodder for the cannon. Accordingly the 38th, 39th and 40th Battalions of the Royal Fusiliers were created out of some two thousand men from England and, later, enthusiasts from the United States, Canada and the Argentine. Their motto, it was said, probably for the first time by themselves, was "No advance without security." Their alumni included David Ben-Gurion, Jacob Epstein and Major James de Rothschild; Jabotinsky was a sergeant in the 38th Battalion, shortly to be commanded by Colonel Patterson. Patterson was a man of violent enthusiasms and fulminating decisions, one of which was to bring him into contact with Richard Meinertzhagen after the fighting had ended. The battalions had arrived in Egypt too late for the capture of Jerusalem but they fought in Allenby's campaign to Megiddo, sometimes called Armageddon, in a manner that drew both praise and condemnation, somewhat depending on the commentator's attitude toward Jew or Arab. When all was over, Patterson's battalion was inspected by a brigadier known to detest Jews. Finding something amiss with the appearance of one of the men, the brigadier called him "a dirty little Jew." Patterson, close behind, wheeled round in a moment of blistering rage and yelled out the command to fix bayonets. There was a hiss and click of steel. Patterson then ordered his companies to form square round the stupefied brigadier and held him in that menacing hedge until he apologized. Naturally there were recriminations. Allenby ordered Richard, by now very much a partisan, to investigate, and as a result of his report booted the brigadier back to India and disbanded the battalion.

In the middle of August 1917 however, Richard was less con-

cerned with matters of high policy or with causes than with preparations for battle. Allenby moved his headquarters out of Cairo and
close up to the line; from that desert camp he could see the Mediterranean below Gaza and the faint mass of the hills of Judaea
dark beyond Beersheba. The nearest geographical feature to the camp
was Umm-el-Kelab (The Mother of Dogs), a cluster of wells, and
it lay on the edge of the wilderness of Edom, once the frontier
of the Shepherd Kings, those Hyksos who had roamed from Central
Asia to rule the delta of the Nile. Allenby camped beside the great
nomadic highway of the Middle East: the dry watercourse of the
Wadi Ghuzze where he and Richard Meinertzhagen sought migrant
birds or desert flowers was the road trodden by Canaanites, Philis-
tines, Egyptians, Assyrians, Persians, Greeks and Romans. Allenby
did not know that his outpost in the high dunes of Tel-el-Fara
stood atop a fortress built by Ramses, nor had Ramses seen beneath
the sand the buried walls the Hyksos left. Yet Allenby was conscious that he followed an ancient route on this, the last crusade.

His plan was not his own. It had been conceived at a Corps
headquarters and Allenby adopted and adapted it and brought Guy
Dawnay, its begetter, into his own headquarters. He faced, looking
into Palestine, the strongly held positions around Gaza on his left
and the less formidable but entrenched settlement of Beersheba
on his right. Between the two were strongly defended localities in
difficult country. Gaza itself was a patchwork of gardens, cactus
hedges and white, undistinguished buildings, by no means an obstacle to an army; but southward ran low spurs on which the Turks
had dug redoubts, threatening an assault with the effect of break-
waters dividing and sapping the onset of the sea. Beersheba was
less imposing as a dwelling place or fortress and was held in part
by Arab troops thought to be less than zealous in support of their
Turkish overlords, but to outflank Beersheba meant a desert march
and, if the Turks were given time to destroy Beersheba's wells, the
end of mobility through the death of thousands of Allenby's horses
and camels. Dawnay's plan therefore afforded Allenby a great deal
of flexibility; basically it was a double punch, right at Beersheba and
left at Gaza, but it gave him successive choices as the battle de-

veloped as to which fist he would swing harder. It was of course vital to hide from the Turks which was to be the knockout blow. This task of obfuscation aptly fell to Richard Meinertzhagen and in carrying it out he achieved what the official history described as "an extraordinary effect, hardly to be matched in the annals of modern war."

There were both long-range and short-range deceptions. The former included the construction of camp sites and the sowing of rumors on Cyprus to give the impression that a seaborne invasion was intended. There were enough warships along the coast to lend credence to the possibility. Radio messages began to hint at a reconnaissance in force toward Beersheba and at Allenby's absence from Sinai at the end of October, which was in fact the time set for the attack. As a result of his delirious flight up and down Kilimanjaro Richard had begun a habit of aerial patrolling every morning just after dawn. He learned much from these excursions, one day more than he really cared to know. He was piloted by a cheerful youth called Sandy Machintosh, who usually managed to avoid unpleasantness but whose luck and judgment failed him one morning. An enemy fighter caught them and Machintosh was wounded in the stomach. The plane tumbled into a series of gyrations so spectacular that the enemy plane stopped firing, convinced of a kill, and flew away. His rudimentary knowledge of flying suddenly and sharply stimulated by terror, Richard clambered into the pilot's cockpit, sat on top of his unconscious friend and made for home. Reaching the airfield he dropped a message, "Sandy hit. How do I land?" and circled hopefully. Below him strips of cloth began to spell out, "Touch down here at eighty." Richard had never landed a plane before but any action was better than surrendering tamely to certain death. He thought he could recall the essentials and put her nose down. The plane careened right off the field and fetched up by pure luck against a convenient palm tree.

Richard was so shaken by the episode that he could not work for the rest of the day, but it did not destroy his faith in the uses of air power. He had elicited from prisoners that there was a great dearth of tobacco in the Turkish army, so he provided them with

some comfort by detailing a daily sunset flight that scattered pack-
ages of cigarettes over the enemy lines accompanied by a few words
of propaganda. The Turks became so used to this infidel insanity
that they would run out of their trenches in readiness when they
heard the evening plane. There was, however, a darker purpose.
Richard intended at the appropriate moment to substitute for the
usual mixture his own brand, made principally of opium. When
Richard, as he must, brought forth this concept, Dawnay's con-
spiratorial mind seized on it but Allenby, though admiring, deprecated its practice as coming too close to the use of poison. Richard
concluded that he must deceive his commander-in-chief as well as
the Turks and dropped the cigarettes anyway. He was never sure
whether Allenby knew what he had done, but it was at least suspicious that Allenby remarked to him after Gaza had fallen, "Those
Turks at Gaza put up a jolly poor fight," and years later offered him
a cigarette at lunch with a rather pointed, "They aren't doped!"
Richard tried one himself after the battle and noted: "They were
indeed strong. The effect was sublime, complete abandonment,
all energy gone, lovely dreams and complete inability to act or
think." Such abandon being quite foreign to his nature, Richard did
not smoke the few he had left, but after the war if he found himself traveling by train with an inescapably loquacious companion
he would offer one. One of the recreations listed under Richard's
name in *Who's Who* was silence.

At the end of September Richard began to compose his magnum
opus. Its components, all false, were a notebook supposedly the
property of a staff officer, an agenda for a meeting at Allenby's
headquarters, some rough notes about a cipher, twenty pound notes
(a sum Richard, never one to throw money around, deemed large
enough to convince the Turks that its owner would be most reluctant
to lose it), a letter announcing the birth of a son to the staff officer,
orders for an attack on Gaza, and a telegram announcing a reconnaissance around Beersheba. All these were very cunningly devised
and amply detailed; the letter in particular was a model of its kind.
It had been written expressly by Richard's sister Mary and it ended
with cosy brilliance: "Good-bye, my darling! Nurse says I must not

tire myself by writing too much—so no more now but I will write again soon and then it will be a longer letter than this. Take care of your precious self! All my love and many kisses. Your loving wife, Mary. Baby sends a kiss to Daddy!" On October 10 Richard stuffed the documents into a haversack spattered with fresh blood and rode into the wastes toward Beersheba. At length he was spotted by a patrol of Turkish cavalrymen who pursued him for a little over a mile but then reined in six hundred yards behind him. So Richard reawakened their interest by dismounting and opening fire. The Turks bit, galloping forward with a wild fusillade. As the chase resumed Richard suddenly lurched sideways as if hit and dropped his field glasses, rifle, water bottle and haversack.*

The Turks behind Gaza and Beersheba accepted the gift of Richard's haversack with more reserve than their German colleagues on the staff. The Germans, perhaps considering the Turks so intricately subtle that they could not really bring themselves to believe anything at all, made dispositions to meet an attack on Gaza and a reconnaissance at Beersheba. Allenby's plan, with Richard Meinertzhagen's help, was beginning to work. On October 31, 1917, Allenby started to develop it with six infantry and three cavalry divisions. His massed artillery opened on Gaza, boosted by a heavy naval bombardment, and seemed to the enemy to fit the Allenby

---

* The official historian of the campaign later wrote, "The officer who planned and carried out this ruse has requested that his name should not be made public, and though it is well known not only in the British Army but to the Turks, it has seemed reasonable to comply with his desire." Sixteen years later Richard happened to be passing through Constantinople. One night two officers of the Turkish General Staff called upon him, having recognized his name in the list of visitors published by tradition in the newspapers. They insisted on entertaining so famous a guest and dragged him off to a night club featuring a European cabaret, the first Richard had ever beheld. "There were eight semi-nude girls," he wrote, "varying in age from nineteen to thirty, flinging themselves about the room, embracing all and sundry and generally brightening things up. There were Russians, French and Austrians among them, no English, thank God." Richard discovered that the Turkish official history had spent an entire chapter discussing his triumph and his hosts were so effusive and admiring that he did not get to bed until dawn.

style, for they knew that on the Western Front he had favored a ponderous but short barrage as his prelude. While the guns spoke in this acceptable rhythm, however, Beersheba was put under sudden assault by a corps that had marched all night across Allenby's front. Australian horsemen charged and the vital wells were captured intact. Thereupon while the Turks were looking apprehensively (and perhaps, because of Richard's free cigarettes, bemusedly) to their left, Allenby plunged through Gaza and pressed on up the coast road. It was then that he exerted the maximum pressure on his own troops, forcing exhausted men and horses into the pursuit, whipping them far forward to prevent the Turks from digging in and obliging him to assault again in a set-piece battle. Tactically the battle was moving like a machine and it was beginning to have a strategic effect. The first of the Yilderim divisions moved south from Aleppo, followed by von Falkenhayn and his entourage. One night Richard's radio station intercepted his order for a counter-attack. The German commander to whom it was addressed asked for it to be repeated as his version was garbled; by the time the German got a clean copy Richard had deciphered the original message and given it to Allenby. The counter-attack was brushed off by a flank brigade. On November 16 Jaffa fell. A port and a historic stronghold roughly halfway between Gaza and Haifa, Jaffa could now serve as a base for further operations northward along the coast. Allenby's advance had cleared the whole Plain of Philistia between the Judaean hills and the sea; the fall of Jaffa meant that he had virtually split the Turks in two, pushing some northward and some east into the hills. Ten thousand of them with a hundred guns were his prisoners.

After a day's rest Allenby, relentless, swept up into the hills of Judaea in the rain. It was his intention to force the enemy out of Jerusalem by cutting their supply road from Nablus and so avoiding having to fight among the most precious sites in Christendom. Many before Allenby had failed in those harsh hills; Saladin had broken Christian hearts among them and Richard Coeur de Lion had stood on a commanding peak and turned his back on Jerusalem out of anguish at his impotence. But in mist and rain, cold and

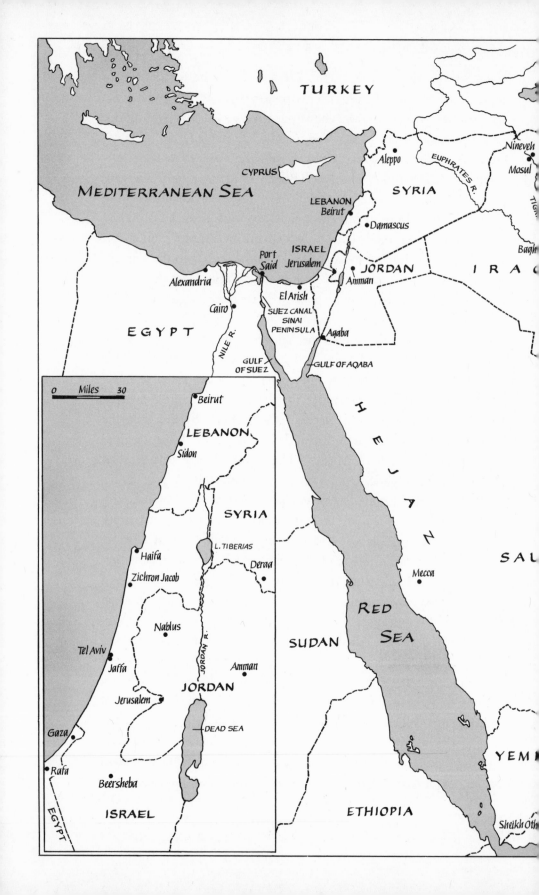

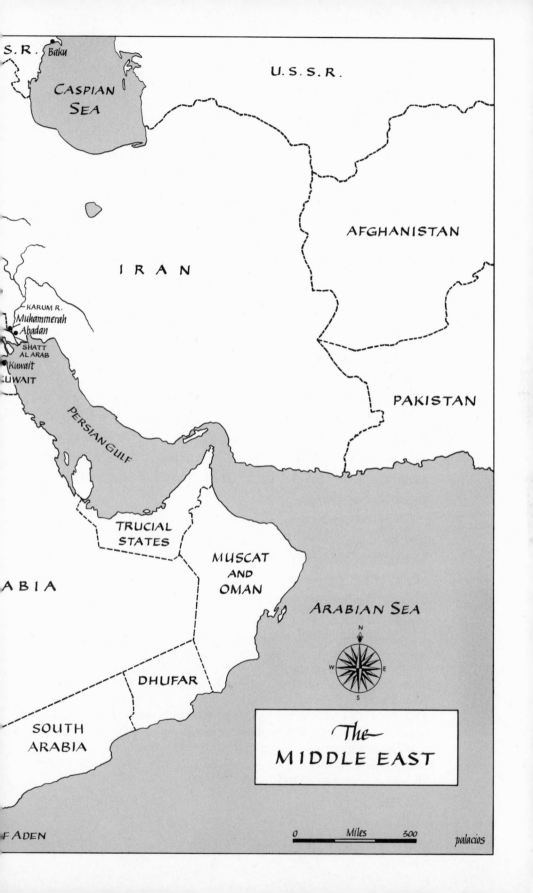

poorly rationed, Allenby's infantry struggled on their bitter way crest by crest, storming where they could not infiltrate, until they came dour and implacable over the skyline and saw the city. At dawn on December 8 the Nablus road was cut and there was an uncomfortable pause while the British waited in the rain. Early next morning there sallied from the gate the moustached mayor of Jerusalem, most solemn in his long black coat, striped trousers and fez. He carried with him the keys of the city and he was accompanied by a flunkey with a large white flag. His Worship met two stray sergeants of infantry and smoked a cigarette and had his picture taken with them but could not by any means persuade them to accept the Holy City. He was passed from pillar to post in growing disconsolation until eventually a divisional commander made so bold as to accept the mayor's gift. On December 11 Allenby fulfilled a prophesy,* strode majestically into Jerusalem as its first Christian overlord since the Dark Ages and set the bells of Rome, Paris and London ajangle for holy joy. Just behind him stepped a small and awkward major in a disreputable uniform whose name, through the agency of an American journalist, would be wondered at when Allenby's was forgotten. Richard Meinertzhagen thought the major an impostor, an opinion that years of friendship and affection did not altogether change.

Lawrence of Arabia had come to Richard's tent out of the darkness the night before. Working by the light of a kerosene lamp, Richard had been interrupted by "an Arab boy dressed in spotless white, white headdress with golden circlet; for the moment I thought the boy was somebody's pleasure-boy." Then Richard remembered that Lawrence was in the camp and turned his hard face and fierce eyes on the apparition. It shifted under his stare and

---

* It had been said that the Turkish yoke would be lifted from Jerusalem when the waters of the Nile came to Palestine, which indeed the pipeline from the Sweet Water Canal could be said to have effected. Concurrently a prophet, one El Nebi, would walk into Jerusalem by the Golden Gate. It happened that Allenby's name in Arabic script closely resembled El Nebi and certainly came from Arab lips with much the same sound. The Golden Gate being bricked up, Allenby entered by the Jaffa Gate, very wisely on foot. He was an exceedingly careful man.

announced softly, "I am Lawrence, Dalmeny sent me over to see you." Richard asked levelly, "Boy . . . or girl?" Lawrence smiled, blushed and murmured, "Boy." He was a figure out of a mirage, seeming in dress a prince of Mecca, yet diffident, not easy to define, evasive even. He carried about him like a ghostly advertisement rumors of the Arab rising in the vast wilderness of the Hejaz; it was said that no Bedouin would pit himself against Lawrence in a ride of any distance and yet he had come to Palestine to confess to Allenby his failure to demolish a bridge protected by a mere handful of Turks. His reputation in the Middle East was shadowy and as yet had not spread into the world outside. To Richard Meinertzhagen, as to all Allenby's junior staff, Lawrence was an amateur and something of a nuisance. But he had the ear of Allenby and he could be useful, so Richard stopped work, stretched in his chair and invited Lawrence to make himself comfortable. Lawrence sat primly down on Richard's camp bed and they began the first of many talks that would leave Richard after eighteen years as confused about the reality behind the dancing image as he had been before this first encounter. Richard's judgment in any case plumped heavily for black or white; the coruscant, shifting vision now in front of him was unique. Lawrence was the first psychedelic public figure and Richard was left, like everyone else, with the enigma.

Lawrence had not instigated the Arab Revolt, though he was to ride into Damascus the Golden with Feisal, the revolt's princely general. In fact it was six months old before he joined it and puffed its feeble embers into flame. It had begun more from a combination of circumstances than from a single stroke of British policy; the British could have no firm policy in a place where a wandering white man was likely to be shot. Quite elegant Englishmen were to be spat on as kaffirs or dismissed as mere Franks by their proud allies from Mecca. At the beginning of the twentieth century, Arabia proper was still a blank space on European maps and terra incognita except for a few miserable gulf ports. The Romans with their penchant for tri-partition had divided it into Arab Petraea (Sinai and the highlands to the east), Arabia Felix (the coast of Yemen and the smaller principalities) and Arabia Deserta. It was this last that caught the romantic mind, a dream of immensity and emptiness not yet lived but hinted at by Byron singing the rich passions slumbering beyond Athens and Alexandria. Richard Francis Burton, wandering far, had mined the untapped lode of Arab stories and sent a delicious tremor through Victorian parlors bold enough to open his shocking books. The desert sands took on a golden glow and their lean inhabitants a dangerous mystery that attracted the bold, the original and the bored away from the blue-serge proprieties of the West. The handful of travelers who reported the reality confirmed the half-seen legend; when they spoke of the black tents, of a natural aristocracy, of a society hard and unsentimental, stripped of the superficialities of London or Paris, yet bountiful of hospitality in a wasteland, they created an image of pride, freedom and fierce individuality strikingly in contrast to the dreary commonplaces of a culture becoming less and less aristocratic and more and more vulgar. For a few in fact, for most in the mind only, the desert became an escape route, the last challenge. Burton wrote, looking for gold in Midian, "At last once more it is my fate to escape the prison life of civilized Europe, and to refresh body and mind by studying nature in her noblest and most admirable form—the nude. Again I am to enjoy a glimpse of the glorious desert, to inhale the sweet, pure breath of translucent skies that show the red stars burning upon the very edge and verge of the horizon and to strengthen myself by a short visit to the wild man and his home." To ride into the desert was to journey back to innocence. It was this wondrous, aching fantasy of Arabia that Lowell Thomas began to feed when in March 1919 he began his lectures in the Century Theatre in New York and introduced an unknown amateur soldier as romantic as Valentino but more real.

To Lawrence Arabia was a challenge, so he both loved and hated it. To Richard Meinertzhagen it was something of a bore. He tended to the view of Gibbon that "The life of a wandering Arab is a life of danger and distress; and though sometimes, by rapine or exchange, he may appropriate the fruits of industry, a private citizen in Europe is in the possession of more solid and pleasing luxury than the proudest emir who marches in the field at the head of ten thousand horse."

Richard considered the Arab Revolt a sideshow and he was not alone. It had had its beginning nearly a century before with the arrival in Beirut of the American Presbyterian Mission that by printing books in Arabic (a language suppressed for three centuries in favor of Turkish) lit the first flicker of a cultural enlightenment that was to turn into political consciousness and nationalist societies. The idea of an Arab nation built out of the factions and tribes under Ottoman domination waxed and waned, hindered from fruition not least by the brotherhood of both Turk and Arab in Islam. While the sultan of Turkey strove to draw about him the robes of religious leadership, it was undeniable that the real keeper of the faith was he who guarded the Black Stone of Mohammed in the closed city of Mecca. This was in 1914 the Sherif Hussein ibn Ali, a Hashemite.

In April 1914 the sherif sent an embassy to Lord Kitchener, then the ruler of Egypt, in the person of his plump and sleepy second son, the Emir Abdullah, a quick politician. Kitchener deputed his Oriental Secretary, Ronald Storrs, to seek out the sherif's desires. Storrs presented himself at the Abdin Palace and for a couple of hours listened politely as Abdullah, sipping coffee, delighted him with soft and exquisite passages from *The Glories and the Lament of Antar ibn Shaddad*. Delicately Abdullah came to the point. His father wanted some machine guns. With relations between Turkey and Britain still nominally of a friendly kind, Storrs was bound to regret his inability to satisfy the request, though he was careful to display no signs of disquiet. Just before Turkey entered the war Kitchener, a warlord in London, wrote to inquire the sherif's intentions. The answer was ambivalent. There practical matters rested: the sherif refused to declare a jehad as the sultan of Turkey wished and waited for the wind to settle, while the British wondered what comfort they might get from the Arab secret societies in Syria, a matter of some complexity not lightened by their ignorance of what was really happening. In July 1915 the sherif began to negotiate by letter with Sir Henry McMahon, high commissioner in Egypt.

The sherif promised a revolt in the Hejaz and in Syria in return for British recognition of an Arab state taking in all the Arabian peninsula save Aden and all the lands between Persia and the Mediterranean as far north as Mersina and Adana. The correspondence grew as Hussein reduced his demands and Sir Henry became more specific about what he could offer. Neither mentioned Palestine and Sir Henry maintained that the reason for the omission was that both parties understood that Palestine would be the subject of special British arrangements. Sir Henry was careful, moreover, to warn the sherif that French interests must certainly be protected. Sir Henry was not aware that a Sir Mark Sykes and a Monsieur Charles François Georges-Picot* were already arranging these post-war matters to the satisfaction of the Foreign Office and the Quai d'Orsay. Messieurs Sykes and Picot were methodical and meticulous and reached agreement by February 1916 without announcing it, naturally, to the world. By that time Sir Henry and the sherif had come to an understanding too. There ensued a pause.

It was broken by circumstance. News came from the north that the Turks were forming a column with artillery and machine guns to demonstrate in Mecca. On June 5, 1916, the Arabs of the Hejaz thronged to the sherif's crimson banner in open rebellion, whereupon, reacting slowly, the Turkish garrison of Mecca in a gross lapse of gunnery and diplomacy shelled the holy Ka'aba, outraged Islam, and gave the sherif the mantle of a savior. Until Lawrence arrived and met the Emir Feisal, the sherif's eldest son, the Arabs gained little but prestige. It was Lawrence and the fabulous Abu Tayi, chief of the Howeitat, every inch the Bedouin warrior and slayer of seventy men not counting Turks, who brought them into Aqaba. To the Arabs, to Lawrence and to posterity the fall of Aqaba was

---

* M. Picot had been French consul-general in Beirut when war came. He left with the American consul there a sealed package which the Turkish police could not be prevented from opening despite the favored status of its guardian. It contained long lists of Syrians and Palestinians actively hostile to the Turks. Hundreds of these were deported, thirty-four of their leaders were hanged in public, and the Turks felt authorized to indulge in a little massacring here and there. What the Arabs thought was not recorded.

a momentous victory. To the British in Sinai it was an interesting little exercise.

This Richard Meinertzhagen explained to Lawrence that first night of their meeting on the road to Jerusalem. "I told Lawrence that the Arabs were just looters and murderers," he wrote, "they would not stand casualties and were well understood by the Turks who refused to enlist them in combatant units." Smiling and blushing Lawrence met Richard's harsh judgments with a rush of words. He claimed Allenby's right flank as his province, and though Richard scoffed at his vaunt that he could sweep clean the desert with seven thousand camelmen there was that about him that charmed and beguiled. It was an attraction of opposites. Lawrence was blue-eyed, sensuous about the lips, frailly made, with a skin whipped red by the desert sun; Richard's dark eyes and raw-boned power overshadowed him. Yet there was a strength in Lawrence that Richard detected through the troubled veil of bombast and false humility, and clutched at, for he sensed in Lawrence a visionary daring of a sort he could never have. Before long Lawrence had outlined his dream of an Arab empire stretching from the Taurus south to Aden and from the eastern boundary of Iraq across to Aqaba. When Richard, his new sympathies aroused, asked what might be the fate of Palestine and the Zionists who were to settle there, Lawrence said it would be a self-governing province of the Hashemite kings. "Really," Richard noted not unprophetically, "I cannot see the Jews being overlorded by Arabs." Richard and Lawrence parted friends, Lawrence to prepare for Damascus and Richard to help plan Allenby's next move.

Before Richard could accomplish much more for his master, however, he was recalled to England. Though it meant promotion to colonel on the general staff, he was not altogether pleased about it. His time with Allenby had been one of the happiest since his boyhood days at Mottisfont: he loved the curious interplay of harshness and luxuriance in Palestine, he felt no ties in England, and he detested the War Office. No one told him that he was being groomed for greater things. Richard's leave-taking of Allenby passed with felicitations on both sides. Allenby's chief of staff had said of Richard: "He has great determination and is not easily turned from his convictions, he has an excellent influence over and is popular with his subordinates. He has on more than one occasion shown great personal courage in the face of the enemy, whilst his total disregard for ambition or personal reward make his work all the more worthy of merit. I should without hesitation give this officer charge of the intelligence section of any Force, small or large." Allenby had concurred fully in these golden opinions, while Richard for his part had written: "If any one man has by his personality and influence won a campaign it is Allenby. The spirit of the whole force is his and I regard him as the greatest soldier we have in these troublous times."

Troubled the times certainly were. Richard's orders arrived on January 3, 1918, and it did not seem to anyone then that the war could be over very soon, unless it were to end in Germany's favor, for 1917 had not been the Allies' year. In the spring General Nivelle had evolved a master-stroke, though how it differed from the ineffectual battering-ram tactics of previous years no one could quite explain. In two weeks of senseless assault on the Aisne he succeeded in losing a hundred and twenty thousand men and giving the quietus to the last spasm of France's warrior spirit. Not without relief, Haig assumed that it was now up to him and planned for the late summer the ultimate attack that would get him to Ostend, a mere thirty miles behind the German lines. He chose a golgotha in the area of Vimy near a village called, poignantly, Passchendaele. There he crucified three hundred thousand of his men by sending them against an only slightly smaller mass of Germans immovably entrenched on the other side of some impassible terrain. Haig's annihilating bombardment made of the assault area an ocean of mud deep enough to drown a man. Men, wounded or whole, ammunition, tanks, horses, stretcher bearers, guns—everything sank into it and was engulfed without a bubble. When it was all over Ostend was still thirty miles away and Haig's chief of staff, General Sir Launcelot Kiggell, was able to drive over to view the morass for the first time. Though still on the road he could appreciate what he saw, burst into tears, and cried, "Good God! Did we really send men to fight in that?" General Kiggell was not known as an excitable fellow and when it was shortly found that he must be ill he was gently sent home.

While the British and French were thus letting out their own life-blood, the Germans saw their own position improving. Russia had dissolved into a jelly of Bolshevism and civil war, so the Germans were able to switch a few divisions from the east to the south to annihilate the Italians at Caporetto. Their prospects for Paris in 1918 began to look rosy, even though America had been in the war since February 1917. Black Jack Pershing had been photographed clumping purposefully up and down a number of gangplanks but his boots and bellicosity were no substitute for guns, and the heroics of doughboys in the Argonne and at Belleau Wood were still to be enacted. No one doubted, friend or foe, that America's entrance with her masses of men and her multitudinous factories would prove decisive, but as 1918 began no man saw how or when.*

In this gloomy fog Richard Meinertzhagen returned reluctantly to the Olympus whence were handed down to the British army its noblest thoughts and most ingenious ideas, and there he was berated for wearing the wrong color of socks. A brigadier passing him in a War Office corridor barked, "Why aren't you wearing regulation socks?" Richard, not pausing, answered gaily, "Damned if I know." Next morning he was summoned to the brigadier's office for admonishment but lost his temper at the brigadier's vulgarity and walked out as the brigadier screamed after him, "Come back, you bloody young swine!" Instead of complying Richard burst into his chief's office to complain about these indignities. General Sir Frederick Maurice, the director of military operations, was a man of freezing reserve. Remarking only, "What can you expect from a

---

* The arguments that 1917 marked the emergence of the United States as a world power are strong. Militarily, however, it was hardly an avalanche. She was woefully equipped; the government bought back naval cannon from an arms dealer who had stored them on an island in the Hudson River since the Civil War, and though much was promised from her mighty industry her infantry had to fight with the backing of French-made field guns and British heavies. In the middle of February 1918 the French were maintaining ninety-nine divisions in the line and the British fifty-nine. The Americans had one, but expected a total of twelve by the beginning of 1919.

pig but a grunt?" he took Richard's part and savaged the brigadier.

Richard stayed in Maurice's directorate as head of one of its planning sections long enough to witness Maurice's fall through an honest but inappropriate letter to *The Times* following Lloyd George's statement to the House of Commons that the strength of the British army in France was greater in January 1918 than it had been in January 1917. Maurice's letter threw doubt on the Prime Minister's veracity and caused a parliamentary debate which Lloyd George won by revealing with Celtic sagacity that his statement had been based on figures supplied by Maurice's own directorate. What Lloyd George did not reveal was that as he spoke he had other figures from the same source that told the true story: though the total of troops in France was indeed larger it contained a far higher number of noneffectives such as Chinese coolies, African pioneers, Italian labor companies, and even working German prisoners of war. Though Lloyd George's terminological inexactitude must have set his spiritual forefather Gladstone groaning in his grave, it saved his government, incidentally ended Maurice's career, and provided Richard Meinertzhagen with a lesson in administrative finesse.

Political jobbery nauseated Richard but fortunately did not involve persons of his humbler sort. He was thought to have expertise in the Middle East and East Africa, so his early days at the War Office were occupied in dealing with suggestions from and plans for those parts and in briefing the King on such matters. From time to time Richard presented himself at Buckingham Palace meticulously dressed—for the Monarch, like all his House, was a stickler more expert far than the oldest sergeant major—to deliver progress reports. He found His Majesty more interested in personalities than in the dry dust of maneuvers and inclined to talk for rather longer than he listened. Richard gained a strong feeling that King George V anticipated the accession of German East Africa, Mesopotamia and Palestine to his Crown at the war's end as a matter of course. His Majesty divertified extensively on this prospect and expressed particular pleasure on biblical grounds in the acquisition of Palestine. When Richard mildly and with great respect murmured that the territory had been promised to the Jews for a National Home the royal monologue scarcely halted: of course the Jews would be members of the Empire and a good thing too for all concerned. "I thought that a splendid idea," Richard wrote loyally. From these geographical considerations the King moved quite naturally to his stamp collection and, knowing Richard's brother Louis' collection, invited Richard to see his own world-famous one. They were joined among the albums by Queen Mary, who questioned Richard quite closely about his old antagonist von Lettow, whom she distantly admired. "I came away impressed by the homeliness of Buckingham Palace and the very fatherly attitude of the King towards us all," Richard wrote. In both observations he was correct: King George's domestic life was felicitous and unpretentious, yet stately, and as a sovereign he was the last to command, though at no pains ever to appear anything but the ordinary man he really was, the respect and awe-struck love a people accords its patriarch. George V was The King; his successors, after the promise of his eldest son had been quenched, were only Royalty and the property of the nation.

There was little of a practical nature Richard could do about his briefs at the beginning of 1918, for General Smuts had grown to such intimacy with Lloyd George that he was dispatched as an extra-mural military expert to discover what Allenby's further policy might best be. Richard prepared schemes to suit whatever Smuts suggested, though his own preference was for a reduction of strength in Palestine and Mesopotamia and a concentration of as much power as could be scraped together on the Western Front, where it was clear that a German stroke of the greatest weight was about to fall. With authority, however, Richard allowed himself a digression in the direction of the oilfields of Baku on the Caspian Sea. He had not initiated the adventure but he pressed for its execution. The scheme was known in Baghdad as the "Hush-Hush Push" when its participants were observed in their secret camp making obvious preparations for a sally deep into Persia. Their objective—the establishment of a foothold on the Caspian and the domination of the oilfields*—was laudible but the means provided to achieve it were lamentable. The force was propelled through a roadless, famine-stricken wasteland in which Bolsheviks, Armenians, Turks and roving Kurds organized local governments that tumbled as swiftly as they had been formed, and miraculously established itself for a while on the Caspian shore until a greater tide swamped its destiny.

On March 21, 1918, the German offensive that had thrown its shadow over the War Office for months burst upon Sir Hubert Gough's Fifth Army, the one least prepared to meet it. General Gough had been so famous as a "thruster" that divisions had been known to request to be excused from serving under him. He was now to discover what thrusting really meant. The German prelude belched from the mouths of nearly six thousand guns. The stinging smoke from their cascade of shell mingled with and made more acrid the dense fog that had settled on the battlefield and through which came pouring the finest troops in Germany, the best men picked from every unit, the new stormtroopers. In the first day of battle the British identified fifty German divisions already committed. There were twelve more to come. It was the climactic moment of the war and, it seemed for a few days, of victory for Germany too.

Richard watched with fascination the effect of the huge German offensive on his colleagues, most of whom began openly to discuss the evacuation of the Channel ports and even of France entirely. On the ignorant mass of the people, however, Richard saw a wholly different effect. What had seemed to him a dissolution of the national spirit suddenly hardened into a massive im-

---

* At the end of 1917 there had traveled from Baghdad into Persia an American errand of mercy calling itself "The Persian Famine Relief Commission," which alleviated much suffering and simultaneously relieved the Persians of some oil rights in favor of Standard Oil of New Jersey. These rights were naturally contested later and became part of exceedingly complicated dealings extending over all the Middle East. The affair indicated, however, that the subject of oil in those parts was growing in importance and that American philanthropists were not such fools as they might seem.

placable purpose: Richard was uplifted by it. Even his family abandoned their incessant arguments to join in the universal prayer for a British victory. In the end the Germans lost through their own mistakes, having learned nothing from the Allies' abortive methods, which had been the same, though they hammered first the British then the French and in one pathetic episode the Portuguese, they nowhere broke the line into fragments. Where they made a breach they exploited it only locally and without a grand strategic plan; everywhere their advance was contested tenaciously and they bled freely both in body and in mind, for they found their enemy well supplied with goods they had long been deprived of by the naval blockade, so the further they stormed the more aware they became that the stories their generals had told them of a weak and starving foe were cynical lies. In the moment of crisis General Foch had been placed in a sort of supreme command. His use of reserves for counter-attack instead of for plugging the line succeeded in driving back the Germans until their slow yielding became a morose retreat and the British and French armies began themselves to counter-attack.

Richard happened to be lecturing at the Cavalry Corps School in Dieppe on August 8 as a sideline to his War Office duties. A British attack was in progress east of Amiens, so he motored casually in that direction till he found some Canadian armored cars bound for the battle and persuaded them to give him a ride. "I seldom enjoyed myself so much," he wrote that night, "chasing the Hun in standing corn." The armored cars in their ardor had passed the trudging infantry and shortly overtook some tanks and marauding cavalry. British planes were buzzing in front of them spotting such positions as the Germans had been able to dig. It was open country, quite unlike the old battlefields so pulverized into moon landscapes. Knowing themselves uncovered by the planes and seeing the tanks' approach, the Germans bolted. Richard had been given a Hotchkiss gun in the turret of one of the cars and killed twenty-three Germans with it during the day, "besides taking part in the utter destruction of the headquarters of a German battalion as they sat at breakfast under a small shelter." Richard's party next swooped upon a German staff car containing two officers who gallantly but foolishly gave battle with their pistols. The car and one of the officers were given their quietus with the machine guns but the other officer leaped out and ran. Richard went after him with his knobkerrie but was balked as he was about to strike by a Hotchkiss chopping down his prey. That night Richard was back in London claiming a record for things achieved in a single day by a General Staff Officer, Grade 1.

On the last day of September 1918 Richard took up an appointment at Haig's general headquarters in France, another step toward the goal for which others intended him. He was not told what it was until ten years after the war, when he learned that he was to have been brigadier in charge of intelligence. For the moment he was advised vaguely to "get the hang of things" because there were to be many changes. Most of the junior staff resented his presence and Richard was not greatly impressed by the state of the intelligence work he saw. "It was in a groove," he wrote, "and stagnant." But he kept busy. He spent November 10, 1918, on special assignment waiting in a railroad car in the leafless winter forest of Compiègne for the German emissaries of peace to accept the Allied terms. The German armistice commission had crossed the fighting zone three nights before, scared into action by a mutiny of the Grand Fleet at Kiel and by Ludendorff's announcement that the war was lost. In fact the German army was not yet beaten and remained still on foreign soil, nor was the naval mutiny virulent, but with the example of Russia the threat of anarchy was enough. At five o'clock in the morning of November 11, while Richard sat with Foch's chief staff officer waiting for a copy, the Germans signed the terms of the armistice. When Foch had done so, sitting in his greatcoat by an open window to oblige the photographers, the Germans handed him in exchange for their copy a foolish Declaration. It concluded, "A nation of seventy millions of peoples suffers, but it does not die." Foch glanced at it. "Very good," he snapped. "Well, gentlemen, that's it. Beat it!" and walked away without further civilities.

Richard set off by car with Haig's copy of the armistice. Haig was in his advanced headquarters north of Cambrai and of course already knew the major provisions, the most important of which was the cease-fire at eleven o'clock. The word came to the troops at ten and the result was a last tremendous cannonade of hate in which every weapon in the British line blasted forth a valediction of rapid fire. Suddenly the front of Richard's car seemed to explode, his chauffeur burst in a red pulp and he was hurled into the road. When he woke he found he was not bleeding though there was an agony in his stomach at the place where the horse had kicked him. A shell fragment had hit him there, but without penetrating. A truck picked him up and delivered him in some pain late in the afternoon at the headquarters. He spruced himself up, bolstered his insides with a good slug of brandy, and reported to the commander in chief. Hearing Richard's name Haig kindly asked if he were related to a wild young officer in the Hampshire Yeomanry he had met twenty years before. Richard explained that indeed he was and politely thanked Haig for his good advice on that occasion. On that day Haig's command numbered nearly two million men: his recognition of Richard was powerful evidence of the strength and closeness of that professional brotherhood of regular officers to which they both belonged.

That night the sky flashed and roared as battery after battery loosed its star shell in celebration. Rockets and Verey lights snaked across fields where troops had built great bonfires they fed with the contents of eight-inch shells and roads were made dangerous with necklaces of guncotton that cracked to split the ears. In this harsh illumination Richard wrote page after page of his diary not only in summary of his final duties in the war but also in contemplation of the shadow that remained still across many minds. The Russians had succumbed to it, the Germans had surrendered for fear of it, and Richard's own sisters, as he believed, were preaching it. "I feel that the whole world is now standing exhausted on the brink of some deep abyss, into which some insignificant cause might plunge us," he wrote. "That abyss is the Bolshevik idea, the Rule by Terror, the Rule of the Beast and the Uneducated Mass, a rule which thrives on hunger and misery, which preys on civilization, but which is a highly infectious disease for which the remedy is as yet imperfectly understood." Physically weakened more than he knew by his invisible wound and with his intellect fogged by his effort to disregard the constant pain, Richard's perception became confused. He wrote, oddly, "I regard Zionism as only another form of Bolshevism, though an ordered form," and in support recalled lunching with Chaim Weizmann at the Ritz in London some months before. It had been a political affair attended by overdressed men and women busy with quantities of food and more concerned with social pleasantries than with causes. Richard had stared round the room, then asked Weizmann what he thought of the scene. Weizmann's face was angry. "This is what I want to sweep off the face of the earth," he said.

Less than two weeks after the Armistice Richard was told that his name had been submitted as British commissioner in Cologne with the rank of major general. He was pleased at the possibility of promotion but not at the nature of the appointment, so he was delighted when orders came through giving him charge of all intelligence work in the occupied zone of Germany. That was much more to his liking and in high spirits he went off to see a doctor about his stomach. He was ordered into hospital at once, examined, and told that an operation might already be too late. The surgeon feared a punctured intestine and peritonitis. Half an hour before he was to be wheeled into the theater Richard made what he thought might well be the last entry in his diary: "it will all be over one way or the other in a few hours and it is not such a bad period of one's life just to retire quietly into peace. I certainly should not very much regret it for I have naught to live for and I certainly do not fear death." He could not end without a defensive show of detachment, however, so he described what could have been his last joke, and a poor one at that. The hospital was run by a kindly but humorless noblewoman who had asked Richard what she could do for him. In sardonic mood he had affected to object to being washed by any nurse of lower social standing than the daughter of a duchess. The Lady Margaret Scott, daughter of the duchess of Buccleugh, was dispatched to his side at once, ruining his joke. Richard concluded with the hope that in the next world there would be sense more humorous and a limp, "If not, I shall apply for permanent leave in Hell. Adieu."

His recovery took time but it was fortunate that he survived because he was about to enter, at the age of forty-one, upon the most productive period of his life, for others as well as for himself. He was told during convalescence that he had been selected in the rank of full colonel as a member of the British Delegation at the Peace Conference at Versailles. On January 25, 1919, he reported for duty, on crutches, and found himself in a madhouse.

CHAPTER 13

The Uniform of the Heart

On Memorial Day 1919 President Wilson carried a wreath from the Boy Scouts of America to one of God's acres hard by Mount Valerian in France. There he stood in the sun among acacias looking at the new white crosses of an American cemetery and asked in his careful way what these fallen comrades might say if they were alive again. Soldiers wept as he furnished his own answer: "We command you in the names of those who, like ourselves, have died to bring the counsels of men together, and we remind you what America said she was born for. She was born, she said, to show mankind the way to liberty. She was born to make this great gift a common gift. She was born to show men the way of experience by which they might realize this gift and maintain it. Make yourselves soldiers once for all in this common cause, where we need wear no uniform except the uniform of the heart, clothing ourselves with the principles of right, and saying to men everywhere: 'You are our brothers and we invite you into the comradeship of liberty and peace.'" These were noble words springing from a noble heart and a nobler tradition, robed in the purest morality. But between the word and the deed yawned a terrible gulf. Their author would find his prophet's mantle turned by the black arts of his colleagues into a shirt of Nessus. Tragically, his own weaknesses permitted this perversion.

President Wilson had left New York drunk with the loftiest ideal ever borne across the Atlantic and supported by the most expert

group of advisers of any nation attending the Congress. But in believing himself the emissary of the people he discounted both the
power of the people's representatives on Capitol Hill and also the
effect upon his European colleagues at Versailles of the mandate of
their own peoples. Every European statesman at the Congress was
conscious of the great incoherent mass of his voters staring over his
shoulder, so in secret he sought to wrest by guile, by threat, and out
of fear the biggest piece of spoil he could carry home to satisfy, as he
thought, the democratic charge laid upon him by the popular will.
So President Wilson paraded across France through cheering crowds,
unconsciously marked for martyrdom in a century when martyrs had
lost not only their significance but their popularity. The Peace Congress began without ideals, degenerated at once into a welter of expedients, and tore apart Wilson's dream and the peoples' best hopes.

It was just the kind of climate Richard Meinertzhagen detested.
He arrived in Paris after a boring convalescence on January 25, 1919,
a week after the first session of the Congress. By then the French
press had already begun to complain that President Wilson's "open
covenants of peace, openly arrived at" had died aborning. Very soon
Richard was writing: "Never before have such vital decisions, affecting millions of persons, hung in the balance. Seldom have such in-
trigues and immoral principles had such fair ground on which to
work. My eyes are sore with the falling scales of disillusion." He felt
the depression that fell on everyone, attributing it to the absence of
sufficient men of brilliance, to the lack of principle of the politicians,
and to the cumbrous machinery that toiled so slowly to produce so
little. Richard was one of twenty-eight soldiers in the British Delegation, which numbered in all two hundred and seven people. The
Delegation had sequestered the Hotel Majestic* on the avenue

---

* Harold Nicolson, a junior member of the Foreign Office contingent
of the Delegation, reviewed the scene in his *Peacemaking, 1919* and recalled
that the Majestic was staffed with British recruits from solid provincial hotels
with obvious effects upon the menu and the coffee. A very eminent obstetrician
had been engaged as medical officer and a chaperone was provided for the
female staff. "The atmosphere of the Majestic," Nicolson reported, "was in
this way one of cheerful and comradely anglicanism."

Kléber, an edifice whose ramifying public chambers were reminiscent of nothing so much as the interior of some deep grotto of the sea, being made almost exclusively of onyx for the delight of the South American matrons and heiresses who had been its chief patrons as well as Monsieur Worth's.

It chanced that Richard's room was directly below Lawrence of Arabia's; the two had resumed the friendship begun outside Jerusalem and Lawrence began to take Richard more and more into his confidence. They lunched together often, walked in the Bois de Boulogne and at night sometimes conducted a strange correspondence. If Richard had something to say to Lawrence he whacked his ceiling with his knobkerrie; Lawrence on his part would bang on the floor and let down a string from his window with a message tied to it. One night the string delivered part of a manuscript of a book.

Lawrence had first mentioned the book while strolling one afternoon along a quiet walk. He was troubled by it and gradually, encouraged by Richard's noncommittal expression, he revealed the crux of his problem. "He told me," Richard wrote, "that ever since childhood he had wanted to be a hero, that he was always fighting between rushing into the limelight and hiding in utter darkness but the limelight had always won." What frightened him, Lawrence said, was that he had embroidered quite commonplace events in the Arab Revolt until they looked like minor epics and now he could not decide whether to brazen out his deceit or run away and hide. Unconscious that this ambivalence in itself was difficult to construe, Richard offered him the straightforward advice that he should "write a truthful book and not a fairy tale." Grateful for this plainness, Lawrence joined Richard for dinner and cheered up enough to accept a little champagne.

Piece by piece in the evenings that followed, the chapters of the first draft of *Seven Pillars of Wisdom* came sliding through the dark. Then one night the string bore a desperate note: it read, "My mind is afire with all kinds of forebodings; may I come in?" Anticipating a crisis, Richard met Lawrence at the door, saw a terrifying intensity in his face and tried to divert him by raising the subject of Lawrence's description of him in his book. Lawrence had called him "a student of migrating birds drifted into soldiering, whose hot immoral hatred of the enemy expressed itself as readily in trickery as in violence," and had continued "Meinertzhagen knew no half measures. He was logical, an idealist of the deepest, and so possessed by his convictions that he was willing to harness evil to the chariot of good. He was a strategist, a geographer, and a silent laughing masterful man; who took as blithe a pleasure in deceiving his enemy (or his friend) by some unscrupulous jest, as in spattering the brains of a cornered mob of Germans one by one with his African knobkerrie. His instincts were abetted by an immensely powerful body and a savage brain, which chose the best way to its purpose, unhampered by doubt or habit." Richard protested that the portrait was inaccurate, exaggerated and misleading, and begged Lawrence to expunge it. His tactic failed. Far from being diverted Lawrence seized on Richard's point as further evidence of the book's lack of integrity and his own duplicity. The dam burst.

In an agony of mind that haunted Richard ever afterward Lawrence told Richard how his illegitimacy filled him with shame, whereupon Richard offered the somewhat inconsequential comfort that Jesus after all was born out of wedlock and added that in these enlightened times bastardy was no more than a peccadillo. Lawrence was not to be soothed. He raced on, pouring out admission after admission, and came shivering to the core of his travail, the incident at Deraa that was to remain so enigmatic and which all who sought to understand him must probe. Richard sat silent and sick while Lawrence told the story, or at least a version of it. Disguised as a Circassian peasant he had been captured on a reconnaissance of the Turkish garrison of Deraa, stripped, bound, sodomized by the governor of the town and then by the governor's servants, and finally flogged. At the end of the account he told Richard he would never publish the true narrative of this incident because it was too degrading. However, his account as finally published was significantly different: in this Lawrence told how he was captured, how the governor attempted to seduce him but failed and had him whipped until he vomited and passed out. There was neither specific mention of sodomy nor implication of it, but after a detailed description of his own reaction

to the flogging Lawrence admitted that "a delicious warmth, probably sexual, was swelling through me." It was quickly chilled when
the corporal of the guard lashed him with brutal accuracy full in
the groin. Lawrence concluded the chapter, "that night the citadel
of my integrity had been irrevocably lost," leaving his critics to
construe from that many things: that secret homosexual longings
had been exposed, that he had been crushed under an unacceptable
vice, or that he had enjoyed the sadistic torture. Richard did not
speculate on the point, for Lawrence's tale that night in the Hotel
Majestic, pitched in a state of the highest tension, rang true.* By
midnight Lawrence's spirit had ceased its excited flutterings. Seeming drained, he suddenly asked Richard if he might bathe, since his
own quarters had no bathroom. When he took off his shirt there
were red weals crisscrossed on his ribs like cicatrices. Richard cried
out, "Good God! Whatever are those?" But the mask was back on
and Lawrence answered indifferently. "A camel accident at Azraq.
I was dragged across barbed wire." Richard saw no bullet wounds.
After his bath Lawrence was still so depressed that Richard offered
his spare bed. He tucked up the hero of Arabia, gave him two sleeping pills and sat silently by him until he fell asleep.

By day and officially, Richard's relationship with Lawrence was
different. Prince Feisal had been admitted rather reluctantly as Dele-
gate of the Hejaz to attend the Congress and Lawrence sat in white
Arab robe and headdress at his elbow striving against the odds to
realize his dream of an Arab empire. Lawrence's responsibility was
vague but in practice he was the chief lobbyist for the Arab case.
Richard's duties, on the other hand, were very clearly defined; they
included matters in the German colonies in Africa and the settlement
of the Middle East, but they were very strongly affected by Richard's

---

* It is interesting to speculate, however, whether Richard might not have
been totally misled. The description of himself he had recently read occurs
in Book VI of the first edition of *Seven Pillars of Wisdom* not far before
the description of the Deraa episode. It is at least conceivable that Lawrence
had just readied that part of his manuscript and, out of the anguish of recall
or (to put it more cynically) out of some need to rehearse the tale, had stopped
writing and rushed to talk to his friend. It was in any case Lawrence's habit
to change his stories incessantly for reasons never satisfactorily explained.

adherence to Zionism. What had begun as a faint sentimental bias suddenly changed into a hard conviction that he must work positively for the Jews. The process had been a long one, but when it culminated he acted, as was to be expected, with all his energy and faith. A week before the fall of Jerusalem in 1917 Richard had stayed over briefly in a Jewish hotel in the settlement of Richon, which was not unnaturally in a state of high emotional excitement. He found the little colony most congenial and though he wrote ingenuously, "The true Zionist has no politics or political activity," he also noted, "The Jew, however small his voice, however mild his manner, will in the end be heard and he will succeed. The Arab will trumpet and bluster, others in Europe and America will sing his praises if the local orchestra breaks down, but he will remain where he is and has for ever been, an inhabitant of the east, nurturing stagnant ideas and seeing no further than the narrow doctrines of Mohammed." Two months later, hoeing his reluctant plot at the War Office, Richard was invited to a lunch at which the other guests were Herbert Asquith, the former Prime Minister, Walter Rothschild, the huntsman with whom Richard shared a passion for birds, and Arthur Balfour, the Foreign Secretary. Lord Rothschild's mind could not concentrate on his favorite topic that day. He took from his pocket a folded copy of a letter he had received from Mr. Balfour on November 2, 1917, and of which Richard had heard by now. It read:

I have much pleasure in conveying to
you on behalf of His Majesty's Government,
the following declaration of sympathy with
Jewish Zionist aspirations which has been
submitted to, and approved by, the Cabinet.
His Majesty's Government view with
favor the establishment in Palestine of
a national home for the Jewish people, and
will use their best endeavors to facilitate
the achievement of this object, it being
clearly understood that nothing shall be
done which may prejudice the civil and
religious rights of the existing non-Jewish

> *communities in Palestine, or the rights*
> *and political status enjoyed by Jews in*
> *any other country.*
> *I should be grateful if you would bring*
> *this declaration to the knowledge of the*
> *Zionist Federation.*

This last request had not been difficult to fulfill, since Dr. Chaim Weizmann had been sitting outside the Cabinet Room while the letter was being completed* and Sir Mark Sykes had rushed out to him with the merry news, "It's a boy!"

Richard read the Balfour Declaration slowly and with care and concluded immediately and correctly that it was an ambiguous document susceptible to many interpretations. He could not see how any Jewish society could be established that did not prejudice the civil and religious rights of the Palestinian Arabs. The others were enjoying their hostess's excellent food and chatting about the letter's effect. At a suitable pause Richard asked Balfour whether his letter was a reward to the Jews for past services or a bribe to win their full support for the war. Lord Rothschild and the hostess gasped but Balfour replied with the slightest indication of heat that both the Prime Minister and he wished only to give the Jews their rightful place in the world. In this there was some truth, for Lloyd George's Celtic sentimentality tended to gush forth in sympathy with a people he identified to some extent with his own downtrodden Welsh forebears, while Balfour eleven years before had been first pricked by Chaim Weizmann, who had recognized the romantic fire held deep below that urbane exterior.

Pleased by Balfour's answer, though far from satisfied, Richard pressed closer. He asked whether there was an implication that the

---

* The original draft had referred to "the reconstitution of Palestine as the national home of the Jewish people." At the insistence of Edwin Montagu (anti-Zionist on the grounds that Jews assimilated into British society might find themselves regurgitated), supported by Lord Curzon (fearful of the effect of a pro-Zionist policy on the Muslims of India), this was changed to "the establishment in Palestine of a national home for the Jewish people," and the proviso about the civil and religious rights of non-Jews was added. This change was the root of all the difficulties that followed.

Declaration would be the charter for Jewish sovereignty in Palestine, or whether the intention was merely to graft a Jewish population onto an Arab Palestine. Balfour thought about that while everyone looked at his plate, then he said carefully, "My personal hope is that the Jews will make good in Palestine and eventually found a Jewish State. It is up to them now: we have given them their great opportunity." Asquith had added nothing to this exchange and Lord Rothschild was by now quite discommoded. Richard said quietly to Balfour, "That scarcely answers my question." Balfour was too old a fox to be put out. With great charm, as if complimenting a vastly superior theoretician, he ventured that Richard was a most persistent young man but he really thought his answer was perfectly clear. Grumpily Richard insisted that if the Declaration did lead to a Jewish State it would be the only good thing to come out of the war, then the conversation glided on to pleasanter topics. That night, having recorded the encounter in his diary, Richard ended, "I want to meet Weizmann."

Weizmann's stock with the British was currently very high. With C. P. Scott of *The Manchester Guardian* for an advocate and friend he had long been the principal Zionist in England. His single-ness of purpose had been made evident early when he had been fore-most among those who opposed Herzl's suggestion to accept the Uasin Gishu as a temporary home. Weizmann's arguments had slowly gained support but it was a crisis in the war that indirectly gave him his strongest lever. As a chemist at the University of Manchester he had discovered a means of extracting acetone from corn, a success that Winston Churchill hailed with relief, for Mr. Churchill needed great quantities of acetone to make explosives for his shells and Germany held the monopoly. Churchill asked Weiz-mann to engineer large-scale production: Weizmann did so and gained an ally.

Richard met Dr. Weizmann for the first time, as he had long wished to do, on August 10, 1918, but not until after one false alarm. Some months earlier Richard's chief at the War Office warned him that the head of a Zionist organization would be coming to see him. So when a dark foreigner was brought into his office at the appropriate time Richard assumed that he was now going to be told all about Zionism, and settled down to listen with pleasure. Somehow or other, his visitor kept on returning to the subject of Armenians and the appalling massacres they had suffered at the hands of the Turks. Armenians, as it happened, were among Richard's antipathies. "They are troublesome, unattractive, stupid and will not cooperate with anyone," he wrote severely. As often as Richard tried to discuss Zionism his visitor returned to the Armenians. Suddenly Richard said, "I'm not much interested in the Armenians," grinned savagely, drew a finger across his throat, and added confidingly, "The Turk knows how to treat them." The visitor rose, looked at Richard with a face of doom, and announced, "I am an Armenian." Richard's apologies were not really adequate.

With Weizmann, too, at their first meeting there was a misunderstanding. Weizmann had called with a request for an increase in the number of Jewish battalions being formed to serve under Allenby, but Richard prolonged the visit by asking Weizmann a number of questions about his real intentions. Weizmann's answers did not drive out Richard's notions about the nature of Zionism, for that night his diary read: "He is an enemy of society and his real aims go further than Zionism, for they encompass the destruction of all society which hinders revolutionary ideas." Years later Richard scribbled after this entry, "First impressions are often wrong." He first began to realize just how wrong he had been when he invited Weizmann to dinner in Paris early in the Peace Congress and Weizmann set out the practical details of his aspirations, dispersing some of Richard's wilder imaginings, and at least partially allaying Richard's suspicion that he was a Bolshevik pretending to be a second Moses. But it was not Weizmann's logic that changed Richard's attitude. Less than two weeks later Richard defined two reasons for supporting Zionism: the first was his old sympathy with the right of the Jewish nation to claim a home; the second was that a Jewish state in the heart of the Middle East would lend great strength to the British Empire. Neither of those reasons, Richard was aware, had much to do with the Balfour Declaration. Richard was now committed. On February 12, 1919, he sought out Weizmann and advised him to press with all his power for nothing less than Jewish Sovereignty in Palestine while there was still time. Weizmann shook his head dubiously. But now Richard had the bit between his teeth and resolved, with or without the Zionist leader, to hew out of the tangled thickets of the Peace Congress a Jewish sovereign state. He began to seek allies.

After a preliminary hesitation Smuts agreed with Richard. Venizelos, prime minister of Greece, was next. Lloyd George was of course amenable and President Wilson seemed inclined to follow. Sir Henry Wilson, chief of the general staff, sensing strategic profit, became a zealot. The Arabs would accept anything now while their own fate hung in the balance and on March 1, the day following the submission of the Zionists' proposals to the Peace Congress, the Emir Feisal and Lawrence sat down with Dr. Weizmann and Richard to draft a letter from Feisal to Felix Frankfurter as leader of the American Zionists. Frankfurter, too, was present at the drafting, for the letter was no more than an exercise in public relations for use in the United States. Nevertheless it was interesting as some indication of the state of Feisal's mind; it raised no objection to Zionism as a national movement and declared that there was room in Palestine for both Arab and Jew. As an instrument of policy, however, it was without effect, chiefly because President Wilson's "open covenants" were being replaced—if they had ever existed—by expedient and unpublicized decisions reached in private and in haste in a small room by three powerful men hovering above a map with which they were none too familiar. The Council of Ten that had begun the Congress had now shrunk to a trinity of Wilson, Clemenceau and Lloyd George. Accordingly Richard sought the ear of his Prime Minister: toward the end of March he suggested over lunch with Lloyd George that his government should annex Sinai. The Prime Minister was greatly taken with Richard and was to write of him: "He struck me as being one of the ablest and most successful brains I had met in any army. That was quite sufficient to make him suspect and to hinder his promotion to the higher ranks of his profession." So he listened to Richard's plan and asked him to put it on paper, but he would not by any means declare his intentions in the question of Jewish sovereignty.

Richard's private memorandum to Lloyd George achieved some local fame, for it predicted the spread, as a result of President Wilson's passion for self-determination, not only of Jewish nationalism but of Arab nationalism from Mesopotamia to Morocco. "Palestine," Richard claimed, "is the corner-stone of the Middle East; the Jews have moreover proved their fighting qualities since the Roman occupation of Jerusalem. The Arab is a poor fighter though an adept at looting, sabotage and murder. The Egyptians, even in superior numbers, are no match for an inferior Jewish army. But as modern weapons—tanks and aircraft—develop, offensive power rests more and more on weapon proficiency than on human bravery and endurance. That is why I regard Egypt as Palestine's potential enemy." This extraordinary piece of prevision was read by Lord Curzon and by Arthur Balfour and was persuasive enough to propel Lloyd George in the direction of President Wilson with the proposal that the British should take over Sinai. The President would not hear of it: it ran counter to the principles of his Fourteen Points. Richard could not help suspecting that it also caused resentment in the hearts of some members of President Wilson's professional staff, because, though the United States had not been at war with Turkey, they felt that any extension of western influence in the former Ottoman Empire should be American, not British. Richard's memorandum disappeared into the void. There it joined other proposals and other schemes still circulating, like cherubim awaiting incarnation, in the ether of high policy and sheer horse-trading which remained, an atmosphere apart, long after the tight-lipped German delegates had signed the Treaty in the Hall of Mirrors.

That ceremony was arranged for three o'clock on June 28, 1919, a Saturday. The Huns were to be humbled, a peace was to be signed that would last forever and the brave new world would immediately begin. The broad avenue that climbed up to the Arc de Triomphe had been lined with captured cannon, mute but still deadly, behind which gendarmes were standing with red flags to block every street that debouched into the avenue. Richard Meinertzhagen's car swept between the guns with sufficient speed, its Union Jack flickering, toward Versailles among other cars bearing the flags of twenty-seven nations all hastening west. There were no crowds to see them pass, for all the world was at Versailles. It had been leaden gray that morning, but slipping out of the quiet city Richard could see a light blue sky with clouds racing. Shortly, thirteen miles to the west, the avenue du Château began, a double row of trees blessedly green leading to the Place d'Armes and to the most majestic palace in the world rising beyond. For Richard and for those who knew, today it was more a place of humiliation than of hope. Louis XIV, mounted and inescapable, towered among his captains, a bronze reminder of all the glories of France. Twenty thousand men, eleven regiments, horse and foot, lined the approach with a haze of horizon blue. A blue mass of infantry packed the Court of Honor, long bayonets glinting in continuous salute as delegation after delegation arrived. The people were far off, thronging the great park in expectation of a miracle that would be signaled by gunfire and by the eruption of the fountains of the Sun King into white triumphant fleurs-de-lys.

Richard stepped out of his car, saluted the guard of honor, and saw in front of him the route to the Hall of Mirrors picketed by men of the Garde Républicaine. Their plumes were bright as blood and their swords at the present flashed with liquid purity. The Hall was already crowded; at one end surged four hundred guests come to watch the execution, and on the other an equal number of journalists there for the same reason. Richard scanned the guests, dismissed them as over-dressed and over-scented, and looked toward the center of the great mirrored room. On a small ornate table lay a volume bound in tooled leather, watered silk ribbons and seals dangling from its luxurious pages of Japanese paper, and beside it a box of goose quills sharpened by the expert pen-pointer of the French Foreign Office. Behind the Treaty and under the marble gaze of Minerva, goddess of learning and handicrafts, the great men of the world were beginning to take their places at the long Delegates' table. They were somber in black formal clothes, but here and there color flashed—Pershing's scarlet sash of the Legion of Honor, the bright jumble of Foch's medals—and the tension was palpable. Three groups of private soldiers, fifteen each to represent the fighting men of America, Great Britain and France, looked on quietly from beside the window embrasures. Every one of them had borne at least one wound. Sentries of the Garde Républicaine stood by the doors, and closer to the Treaty itself, very conspicuous, was a group of grizzled veterans of the War of 1870. In them the sense of history most violently expressed itself, for where they stood Prussian grenadiers had once witnessed the degradation of France and the proclamation of a German emperor and before that, in 1783, British ambassadors had signed there the armistice that had relinquished for ever their American colonies. Yellow-faced, his hands covered with lavender gloves to hide his eczema, Clemenceau declared the session open in a few cold sentences, then ordered in his harsh peasant's voice, *"Faites entrer les Allemands!"* The Garde Républicaine troopers sheathed their swords in disdain, a door opened, and in an icy silence the German delegates clicked across the parquet and signed the Treaty. No one rose. Richard noticed that the French poilus spat on the floor as the Germans signed; "I thought the insult unworthy of a great nation, and wholly undeserved for a beaten enemy who comes to sign a disgraceful peace," he wrote.

Only those who had worked for months to fashion that historic instrument could know how lamentably it had fallen short of the ideal and how faultily it had been executed. The rest of the world felt only relief and expressed it. Paris dined early and then took fire. There were impromptu orchestras on every corner and people dancing and kissing quite promiscuously in every street. The occasional bodies of troops marching by were bombarded with flowers and confetti and strings of citizens bearing blazing torches followed and engulfed them. Maroons and fireworks boomed and sparkled from every arrondissement. Caught up in spite of himself in the rejoicing, Richard ventured into the Champs Élysées, a walpurgis night, where, as he put it, "I was run into and over by a drunken American motorist, which sent me to bed with a twisted and painful foot." So Richard concluded his sojourn at the greatest Peace Congress of all time as he had begun it—partially disabled. It was ironic, but in a way it was apt.

A month after that ceremonial day Richard was still in Paris. He had watched the Victory Parade drumming and trumpeting through the Arc de Triomphe and down the Champs Élysées. There was one color from every regiment in the British army, but in Richard's view, "The American detachments were, from a purely military standard of excellence, the best, and excited everyone's admiration." There were too many generals and staffs and too few troops for Richard's taste, which was later supported in the Majestic Hotel, a bloodbath of scarlet gorgets, by Field Marshal Sir William Robertson. Asked for his opinion of the Peace Conference, Wully rumbled, "These 'umbuging staff officers gives me the 'ump." Apart from this one interlude of historic ceremonial, Richard's task was a monotonous procession of adding detail to what had been decided in rather vague principle. Then, on the last day of July 1919, he was informed that he had been appointed chief political officer for Palestine and Syria on the staff of his old master and friend Allenby.

Richard stared at his orders. He had no idea what his new duties might be, nor did he know what policy he would be expected to execute. Deciding that Arthur Balfour might be informative if not actually specific, he invited himself to lunch. Balfour unbent enough to say that though personally he was not in favor of a British Mandate for Palestine under the League of Nations he would not oppose it. He defined the government's policy for all purposes of development other than political as the support of the Jews as the "most-favored nation." He thought that the boundaries of Palestine must be decided by economic, rather than by military or strategic necessities, particularly by the need for water for irrigation. Richard was encouraged if not greatly enlightened by this exchange, and flattered by Balfour's parting good wishes and expressions of personal esteem, but he left the table without very much in the way of a clear brief.*

---

* It was never easy for ordinary intellect to distinguish whether Balfour was being vague or extraordinarily precise. An exposition was once sent to him outlining two possible courses of action, each described in great detail

He had enjoyed the sensation of being close to the center of power and in the confidence of the men who exercised it, but the frustration of watching his predictions come true and yet of seeing his best advice ignored made him glad of the chance to go abroad again.

The soft malodorous wind of Egypt greeted Richard once more on September 1, 1919, as he arrived not without a touch of pride to report as chief political officer to Field Marshal the Viscount Allenby of Felixstowe and Meggido, now high commissioner for Egypt and occupant of the unpretentious but mighty throne once occupied by Cromer and Kitchener and latterly by Sir Reginald Wingate, father of the Sudan. Though pleased by the reunion and respectful as ever of Allenby's capacity, Richard had already foreseen trouble. He had been given a double responsibility: he was to advise Allenby, the soldier, on political matters affecting Syria, Transjordan and what was officially called "Occupied Enemy Territory-South" and more popularly, Palestine; on the other hand he was to maintain a direct correspondence with the Foreign Office and ensure that its policy was carried out. "This dual loyalty," he wrote grimly, "is not going to be easy and must end in friction." There were perquisites in his new situation that helped alleviate a sense of doom and he was soon riding about the babbling streets of Cairo in a Rolls Royce limousine. His other Rolls, fitted with a bed, he used for journeys out of town where there were few, if any, hotels.

The Emir Feisal, as putative ruler of Syria, was in Damascus already coldly raging against the French, who expected—as a result of the Sykes-Picot Agreement—to control Syria, and particularly at the awkward M. Laforcade, head of the French Mission. Before he had been a week in Cairo Richard, an unlikely emollient, motored up to Syria to try to soothe both parties. Though the eye of a politi-

---

and one exactly the opposite of the other. The memorandum ended, "Which of these two alternative courses do you wish us to adopt?" It emerged from his office with the endorsement, "Yes. A.J.B." Dismayed, his private secretary took the paper back to his master and complained that his answer was not very useful. Balfour was a little surprised, but patiently explained, "I merely meant that I agreed that there were only two courses open. I still agree with that proposition."

cal whirlwind, Damascus was still a haven offering soft and rich protection after the puritan austerities of the open desert, the silken
sound of its name still an invitation. Its enveloping narrow streets,
hardly too wide to be spanned by a man's stretched arms, still bore
their timeless traffic of veiled women and voyaging Bedouin. Doors
of dark wood studded with hand-hewn bolts of iron gave onto shady
gardens where fountains rippled and fragrance wafted from black-
stemmed Persian lilacs.

Walking east through the city Richard could enjoy the freshness
of early morning and find blackbirds, jays and woodpeckers busy
among the apricots. It gave him easement from the tiresome and
difficult squabbles between M. Laforcade and Feisal. At the end of
five days he was able to report to the Foreign Office that he had
averted the threat of Arab aggression but that Laforcade held to the
terms of the Sykes-Picot Agreement, while Feisal totally rejected it
and retained the desperate hope that the British would take the
Mandate for Syria in place of the French. Affairs in the Middle East
were so far from any real settlement that even this insignificant
achievement could be thought a success.

A few days later Weizmann was denied entry into Palestine, in
Allenby's absence, by the military in Cairo on political grounds.
Suspecting anti-Zionism or, as he called it, "hebraphobia," Richard
remonstrated with the acting commander. Balked, he cabled directly
to the Foreign Office. The military were admonished, Weizmann
traveled on, and Richard had created the first bit of friction between
his separate loyalties.

"Intelligence is a Jewish virtue," Richard once wrote, "intrigue
is an Arab vice." To take advantage of both vice and virtue he
organized a private spy service, both Arab and Jewish, to keep himself informed; its existence was unknown to anyone but its control,
a bright young lady in Richard's office. Much of the underground
knowledge garnered was inaccurate, but enough of it could be
checked to make it useful. Richard was shocked to discover numbers
of British officers not only in sympathy with the Arabs but actively
plotting on their behalf against the British government. The chief of
these was a colonel on the staff of the British Administration of

Palestine whose wife Richard had almost shot, purely by accident, while she was bathing in the Mediterranean. The lady exhibited a few eccentricities, particularly of dress. "Her early morning attire is her husband's jodhpur breeches and his pajama tops," Richard noted. "She then rides down to Haifa beach where she bathes in her husband's shirt and shorts."

Driving south along the magnificent coast road from Beirut Richard came one day to a headland near Sidon and saw, bobbing in the sea about four hundred yards out, what he took to be a very rare Mediterranean seal. He stopped the car, took out his rifle and clambered as inconspicuously as he could down through the rocks. He drew a bead on the glistening head of his seal but chanced to glance at the beach before squeezing the trigger. A pile of clothing and the colonel placidly smoking a cigar behind it bore the awful truth to Richard. He realized that his rare mammal was the colonel's lady, bathing without clothes. "She must have seen me stalking her," he wrote that evening, "and heaven knows what she thought my purpose was." His purpose with her husband was to discredit him, for he had information that the colonel was in contact with Feisal and the Arab Notables of Jerusalem, chief among whom was the Haj Amin el Husseini, a genuine villain. Richard's spies told him that the colonel's wife was frequently to be seen in her Arab outfit passing through the Mufti's portals. When Richard reported these doings to Allenby, accompanied by some observations about an Arab bias in the attitude of Ronald Storrs, now military governor of Jerusalem, Allenby was upset but believed a purge, even if justified, would do more harm than good to his administration.

Once again Richard had been abrasive. But his personal relationship with Allenby continued warm and mutually respectful. They had much in common. Neither was a learned man yet each in his way thought deeply and doggedly about the ideas he cherished. In the first week of January 1920 they spent an evening together talking about the future of the Empire, a concept and an entity in which they both believed with a true devotion already slightly anachronistic. Allenby pondered the inevitable dissolution of the Empire as those ruled became educated, but wondered whether they were really being taught the integrity that alone would ensure proper self-government. Richard proposed the picture of a British Empire in sixty years' time compromising only Canada, Australia, New Zealand and a few fortress islands. In Africa, he thought, "especially in Somaliland and among the more intelligent tribes of East Africa such as the Kikuyu and Nandi, we shall find the urge to govern themselves too strong for us; and this will be inflamed by the way we have stolen and occupied native land." Allenby and Richard were both too practical to busy themselves long with such projections and they soon turned to more immediate matters. Richard had discovered that in 1906 Turkey had granted administrative rights to Egypt over that part of Sinai west of a line from Rafa to Aqaba. Allenby himself had overrun all of Turkish Sinai, so Richard held that Sinai east of the line Rafa-Suez was British, mainly by right of conquest. Occupation of this area would give England a stranglehold on the Suez Canal, create a buffer between Egypt and Palestine and offer the possibility of another canal between the Mediterranean and the Gulf of Akaba. Allenby's interest was caught and he promised to suggest annexation. Richard was not unduly encouraged, however, for he had proposed the identical plan to Lloyd George in Paris without any conviction that the Prime Minister had understood a word of what he was saying.

More and more he was feeling himself isolated in his championship of Zionism. He knew that many in the Middle East believed him a Jew, a circumstance he found ironic in the extreme, for he knew himself in some ways and partially emotionally to be anti-Semitic. "The idea of fighting for Jews against Christians and my own people is most distasteful to me," he wrote on one of those nights of self-analysis that marked crises of action, "but it is what I have had to do out here for the last few months. And I feel that the best in Zionism is an ideal well worth fighting for, an ideal which must eventually materialize and win. It was indeed an accursed day that allowed Jews and not Christians to introduce to the world the principles of Zionism, and that allowed Jewish brains and Jewish money to carry it out, almost unhelped by Christians save a handful of enthusiasts in England." He added, "it annoys me that Weizmann should be a Jew, it annoys me that he should be so far ahead of Christians in intelligence and general purity of mind." The entry followed some discussions with Dr. Weizmann during his visit to Palestine at the end of 1919 which it seemed at the time might not only have united the Zionist faction there but, by virtue of Weizmann's clarity in argument and obvious sincerity of purpose, might have cooled the multitudinous angers rising against them.

The spring of 1920 came to Jerusalem tense as an electric storm so that the slightest explosion of energy might boil up into a tempest. The Feast of the Passover, Easter Day and the Muslim festival of Nabi Musa fell into rough coincidence that promised trouble if fervor were allowed to burgeon into hatred. Richard knew from his clandestine sources that Haj Amin el Husseini had been inciting his following against the Jews. Storrs had summoned some leading Muslims for a warning about the dangers of turning religion into politics, but declined to address the Muslim population of the city because he thought it commonly held that he was a friend of the Jews, though the opposite was the fact. Four days before Easter Sunday, the critical day, Feisal's British colonel visited Haj Amin and advised him to show the world that the Jews could not and must not dominate Palestine. On the morning itself disreputable notices were scrawled all over the city. "The Government is with us, Allenby is with us, kill the Jews!" they exhorted; "there is no punishment for killing Jews." The sinister colonel had left Jerusalem for the day, having warned the Mufti and Haj Amin by way of farewell that the Jews planned to assassinate them both. Easter Matins had ended and the English congregation were strolling away from St. George's Cathedral pleasantly occupied with anticipations of refreshment when word came of an outbreak at the Jaffa Gate and a man mortally hurt. Tumult spread through the climbing, twisting alleyways of the Old City with drawn knives and slaughter at the heart. Commanded by a lieutenant and woefully weak in numbers, the police ended the rioting before there could be too great a loss on either side. But blood was spilt, property was destroyed, and the repercussions reached Whitehall where, at a distance, the outbreak seemed more venomous than it really was.

On April 14 Richard sent a dispatch to Lord Curzon as it was his duty to do, detailing the sequence of events and furnishing evidence of the complicity of some pro-Arabists in the British Administration. The letter though precise was extremely long. It was also heavily biased in everything but matters of fact, as Lord Curzon would expect when he saw its origin, for Richard had always been anxious to reveal his affiliation. The document was one of the most explosive ever composed by a government official and was never again allowed into the light of day by the Foreign Office but it had its effect. Richard received personal letters of congratulation from Lloyd George and Lord Curzon. A month later he received a summons to Allenby's office and a broad intimation that, like many before him, he was for home. Allenby was as friendly as ever, but he showed Richard the cable he was about to send to London, complaining that since Richard as one of his staff had criticized his administration he could not remain in office if a precedent had thus been created. Richard was not blind to the outcome of a Cabinet choice between Allenby and himself. He accepted Allenby's invitation to lunch gladly, passed a delightful hour or so in friendly talk, and left for the cable office and a little private business. Hoping that Whitehall would now be approaching some kind of realignment, he fired off a telegram each to Lloyd George and Curzon suggesting the replacement of the military administration of Palestine with a civilian one under the control of the Foreign Office and recommending Sir Herbert Samuel as high commissioner. That done, he reflected that Allenby was really a most charming man and an excellent ornithologist, for an amateur.

At one o'clock on the afternoon of June 30, 1920, to a salute of seventeen guns firing from a knoll where the Hebrew University was to rise, His Excellency Sir Herbert Samuel, the new high commissioner for Palestine, a Jew, stepped out of his car outside Government House in Jerusalem and assumed the obligations of a ruler. The ceremonial finished, the outgoing chief administrator (General Bols, formerly Allenby's chief of staff, and a cheery fellow) handed Samuel a slip of official paper on which he had written, "Received, one Palestine in good order." Samuel read it, did not smile, signed it and added "E. & O.E.," meaning "Errors and omissions excepted."

Richard felt that he had struck a small blow for freedom. He visited Samuel in Jerusalem and found him modest to the point of shyness but admired the quickness of his mind and the warmth of his nature. Undeniably the change was for the better. He summed up: "The Arab has been surrounded by that same halo of romance with which our East African officials used to clothe the Masai. I have dared to tear down this halo and expose the Arab and his so-called government as rotten and never likely to be anything else. So I have won, lost my appointment and got six months leave." He went to say goodbye to Allenby, who complimented him on his singleness of purpose and the integrity he had shown in a difficult situation and then revealed his admiration for the way in which he had struggled to wreck his career on the rocks of his own convictions. Richard parried. He complained that Allenby had given him less notice than he would give a housemaid. Allenby's vast frame rocked with laughter. They lunched expansively, still friends, and absorbed themselves as usual in the inexhaustible subject of birds. At the time Richard thought he could now retire from the contest and what had been "most unpleasant work, entailing fighting my own colleagues and my own religion on behalf of the Jew." He felt free. "The world is large," he wrote, "and I can live with or without the leave of Jew or Government Office."

Richard sailed home by way of Crete, which he reached on a small Greek steamer. Most of his fellow-passengers were Greek women, "whole continents of unsteady flesh and to watch some of them being ill was like the convulsions of a mountain range when heaved by volcanic eruption." Landing at Candia after a restless night sleeping on deck with a calf and a protesting turkey tied to his bed, Richard hired mules to carry him to the top of Mount Ida, where he knew he would find peace, silence, solitude and space, his favorite pastimes. He was warned by the townsfolk that there were brigands above the tree line, especially the notorious George Nikolokakis, a prototype of Zorba. The encounter was a happy and violent one. Laughter bubbled from the gnarled and muscle-knotted bulk of Nikolokakis unbidden. Richard anticipated his handshake with such violence that he winced; recovering, he roared with laughter and in comradeship gave Richard a pat on the back that sent him reeling. They became firm friends, conducting long conversations, the one in a Cretan dialect and the other in English, that generated much merriment even though they provided not a scrap of information.

After two weeks the idyll was cut short. A policeman came toiling up the mountain with a telegram calling Richard to London with all speed for interview at the Foreign Office. There he was offered the charge of the Palestine Section of the Middle East Department. His friends advised him to accept this chance of an important new career but Richard's horror of government offices prevailed over his currently diminished interest in oriental affairs and instead he demanded six months' leave. At the end of January 1920 he dined with his old friend Freddie Guest and Winston Churchill, who asked kindly whether he would care to go to Japan as military attaché. Richard jumped at the offer, whereupon Churchill continued that he himself was about to move from the War Office to the Colonial Office, where he would create a new Middle East Department that would certainly require Richard's services. The offer of Japan was therefore withdrawn. As soon as Churchill had changed hats Richard began to lobby for Tokyo but without much confidence for he knew Churchill's bulldog tenacity. Besides, he was engaged to a girl who did not greatly relish beginning her marriage in so alien a city. She was Anne Constance Jackson, daughter of a soldier-landowner living quietly in remotest Swordale in Western Scotland. Annie, as Richard called her, was a quiet girl, compliant but self-reliant, and she offered Richard the deep springs of affection he had always craved. She had a fresh beauty of face and mind and a calm spirit that promised to bring him ease. Like Richard, she loved the open air and the creatures of the wild; she was more at home on a moor side than in a ballroom, which was much to Richard's taste.

On the eve of their marriage Richard received a letter from the Director of Military Intelligence, his superior at the War Office. It asked him in terms of the warmest respect and esteem to bend to

Churchill's will in behalf of the chief of the Imperial General Staff and all his host, who would feel much happier if a man they knew were in Churchill's bosom. Richard could only accept graciously but declined an invitation to enjoy his honeymoon with Annie as part of Churchill's entourage on an official tour of Egypt and parts north. He began work in the Colonial Office on May 9, 1921, with a whisper from Sir Henry Wilson, Chief of the Imperial General Staff, still buzzing in his ears. "You've got to keep Winston on the rails," Sir Henry had warned in his outrageous fashion. "He might do anything stupid and his military judgment is always at fault. He thinks he's the Duke of Marlborough."

Richard arrived in his office to find an old friend sharing it; he took the desk assigned to the military adviser and smiled a welcome to the Arab adviser at the other desk, the small and now legendary Lawrence of Arabia. Lawrence, Richard soon recognized, exercised an extraordinary influence over Churchill, which forced Richard once more into his familiar role as antagonist of the pro-Arabists. Wearily he remounted his Zionist charger and cantered into his first skirmish over that latter-day Saladin, the Haj Amin el Husseini. Amin had fled across the Jordan after the Easter riots of 1920 in Jerusalem and had been sentenced in his absence to ten years' imprisonment. Allowed an amnesty, he had returned to Jerusalem and had now been appointed mufti in his brother's place. The mufti's delicate figure and elfin expression of innocence enhanced the air of stillness he was careful to preserve about him and seduced many who had dealings with him into believing him a frail saint sustained only by a particularly pure spirituality. Richard was especially annoyed by the mufti's accession because he had taken the trouble to warn Sir Herbert Samuel about him: Richard knew the mufti's flinty purpose and had seen the slow unslakable fires of hatred burning behind the luminous brown eyes. When Richard in wrath tackled Churchill about rescinding the appointment, he could arouse no interest. "I warned him without mincing words," Richard wrote, "of the harm we must expect from such a scoundrel." Eight years later he was proved correct beyond doubt: at the end of August 1929 rioting and massacres probably engineered and certainly encouraged by the mufti seared across Palestine. Six Jewish settlements were destroyed and one hundred and thirty-three Jews were killed.*

During Richard's tenure at the Colonial Office the fires of hatred smoldered subterraneously; they had last flared at Jaffa on May Day in 1920 when Jewish workers parading behind a red flag had incited an Arab attack with consequences as bloody as that pogrom at Kishineff in 1903 that had appalled the world. But to a world still numbed by a Great War the Jaffa riot was no more than a minor horror: if Wilson's uniform of the heart had ever been worn it had now been shrugged off in favor of the armor of insensitivity. The brave new visions that had glowed so vividly two years before had faded and now the jaded, flickering torch of expediency was all that led the statesmen stumbling toward a goal they could not discern. The antipathies of Arab for Jew were echoed not only in Palestine among the administration there but in the Colonial Office itself and among the masses upon whom the politicians thought themselves dependent for their strength. The French, with a stake in Syria and a tradition of popular anti-Semitism, opposed the progress of Zionism, and the pope, for subtler reasons, supported them. The British government, torn between its obligations to the Arabs and its vague promise to the Jews, and burdened by the apathy of a public no longer interested in what might seem to be a minor imperial adventure, had grown hesitant and unsure, and between principle and practice there spread a void. Uneasy, Richard wrote to engage the sympathy of Smuts and to direct pressure on the Prime Minister, Lloyd George, whom Dr. Weizmann was to meet for a lunch Richard felt might have considerable post-prandial effects. Weizmann had just returned from a successful fund-raising raid in America with the gloomy intelligence that the American public not only rejected any European entanglements

---

* One of the causes of the outbreak was the erection on the eve of the Day of Atonement by a Jewish beadle (by name William Ewart Gladstone Noah) of a screen of cloth to separate male from female worshipers at the Wailing Wall. Since the site was equally sacred to Muslims Mr. Noah had, knowingly or not, perpetrated a desecration. The mufti, of course, made the most of it.

but was beginning to ponder the possibility of a war with England.

He unburdened himself of these tidings at Arthur Balfour's house on July 22, 1921, and Lloyd George professed himself very interested. When the discussion turned to the Middle East Weizmann complained that the intent of the Balfour Declaration—the achievement of a Jewish majority in Palestine—was not being accomplished by Samuel's announcements and administrative measures in Jerusalem. Both Balfour and Lloyd George reiterated that they had always proposed a Jewish State there. Not unduly heartened, Weizmann became more specific, regretted the limitation of immigration, the slow rate of development of essential projects, and the lack of protection for Jewish communities against Arab desperadoes, and lamented the gun-running which the settlers had started and of which he could not approve. Churchill broke in. "We won't mind it, but don't speak of it," he said.

There were others who did mind. Richard's own intelligence sources had revealed these operations, now grown ambitious enough to import machine guns. In his pragmatic fashion he pointed out that the traffic could be ignored, stopped or legalized, and recommended the last course; then passing from the symptom to the disease, suggested a course of treatment in five parts. Those British officials in Palestine who could be identified as anti-Zionist should be removed; the military command of Palestine should be severed from GHQ in Egypt; immigration should be resumed; the Jews should be treated as Most-Favored Nation and given concessions; and there should be closer liaison between Zionists, the Colonial Office and the high commissioner. Richard's memorandum was forceful enough to persuade his superiors to present it to Churchill, who readily agreed to place it before the Cabinet. Richard dashed away to have the document printed as a Cabinet Paper and this lent it an illusion of permanence its subsequent fate did nothing to confirm, for the Cabinet was preoccupied with troubles in Ireland, with belligerent Turks and bellicose Greeks, with a swift increase of unemployment, with relations with the United States, and with other complexities more pressing than the plight of Zion. Before the winter of 1921 set in Richard had begun to feel the familiar ache that came from pounding his head against an invisible but adamant brick wall.

On July 22, 1922, the League of Nations, sitting in the dark brick recesses of St. James's Palace, passed the Palestine Mandate to the British. In celebration Dr. Weizmann bought Richard and his wife dinner at the Carlton and it seemed briefly that the tension was ended and that the Mandate would, as Richard put it, "once and for all convince the Arabs and their English friends that the Zionist policy has come to stay and that all their obstruction has been of no avail." In fact the Mandate did nothing of the kind; neither altering nor clarifying the issues, it merely imposed on a government already harassed a fairly specific responsibility. What profit the British might draw from it was never elucidated, though it was obvious there might be strategic dividends. As to the moral obligations implied in the Mandate, they were accepted without much comment, for it seemed in a dim way that the task in Palestine was not too different from bringing enlightenment into the dark corners of the world, a mission the British had been cheerfully executing for years. Unfortunately no one envisaged two factors in the situation relatively unknown to the nineteenth century: the British did not command all the time in the world to accomplish their pacific task, and what in the past might have been dismissed as traditional antipathy now began to emerge as race-hatred. The British and others had yet to discover that in the twentieth century things not only happened faster, they happened with greater violence. For the time being, however, there was comparative peace and Richard, believing his point of principle accepted, turned from the general to the particular and set out on a tour of inspection of Palestine and Mesopotamia.

He left London early in October 1922, but with his usual pleasure at escaping office routines and the power game clouded by a novel sensation. He was leaving behind not only his wife but also an infant daughter, Anne, and she was a needle in his heart. At the age of forty-four he had won distinction; he was a busy man pursuing important business, affairs of consequence, a man to whom a baby in a household full of servants would pose no practical problems. It was still possible for a man of means to be made no more aware of a child than as a glittering and more valuable piece to add to the mosaic of a full life. But to Richard Meinertzhagen in early middle age his daughter Anne already held enormous potential. So his leaving her and her mother meant pain, and his launching on a new journey was less boisterous than had been customary with him. He reached Jerusalem, honey-colored in the Mediterranean light, on October 11, 1922, and held hopeful conversation with Samuel, his host at Government House on the Mount of Olives. His main purpose being military, he visited Trans-Jordan and then crossed the desert to Baghdad in a convoy of four armored cars loaned him by the Royal Air Force. En route a message came crackling from Amman that the government had fallen, and with it Churchill. Richard asked who had been appointed colonial secretary in his place, to which came the answer, singing over the dark rock ridges of that joyless place, "The Duke of Devonshire, thank God a gentleman." Reserving comment, Richard pressed on to Baghdad and sad-faced Feisal, now king of Iraq.

It was April before he got back to London to assess the quality of the new colonial secretary for himself. His tour had taken him to such strange outpost garrisons as Bentinck's Battalion of Assyrians in southern Kurdestan and the Yemen Infantry based at Sheikh Othman north of Aden, whose members, being subjects of the imam, were regularly imprisoned for a spell when they went home on furlough as a token of that eminence's displeasure. Richard had seen the glowing orange of Petra and the deadly flat horizons of reeds of Mesopotamia where he had lived for two weeks with the Marsh Arabs. He found, back in London, that such exotica lay far outside the experience of His Grace. "The Duke," Richard wrote after his first interview, "appeared sleepy but pleasant." These characteristics had been noted in at least one of His Grace's forebears, the former more markedly than the latter, and they were usually accompanied in that noble line by an ever-present shrewdness and a placidity of the most comforting kind. Richard was not far wrong when he added in summary, "I should say that his main assets are integrity and solid common sense with little originality or drive." The significance of the duke, however, lay less in these admirable attributes of his kind than in the fact that he represented, four-square and true-blue, the maintenance of the status quo. It was unlikely that, with the duke at the helm, the ship of colonial state would steer toward anything resembling a squall. Under his dispensation Richard completed his tour of duty in relative calm though the recurrent assaults by partisans of the Arabs necessitated regular fulminations on his part in behalf of the Zionists. Though nothing basic had changed, the surge of sympathies with one side or the other provoked a Cabinet Committee with the Duke of Devonshire in the chair charged with advising the government about the correct policy to adopt in Palestine, and coinciding with a meeting of the Committee of Imperial Defense assembled to discuss Palestine's strategic importance. The most noteworthy item to emerge from these deliberations was that the First Sea Lord, a jaunty commander of battle squadrons in the late conflict, had not been aware until confronted with the fact that Haifa was a port in Palestine.

Richard left the Colonial Office without fanfares and without regrets early in the spring of 1924. While working there he had retained his rank, but in the process of reorganizing the army two battalions of his own regiment, the Royal Fusiliers, had been disbanded and Richard had therefore been transferred to the Duke of Cornwall's Light Infantry, in military terms a transformation comparable to the appointment of an Episcopalian priest to a ministry in a Methodist chapel. The Duke of Cornwall's Light Infantry not only marched with the jerky celerity of their kind and used a less deliberate form of drill but cherished customs and traditions with which Richard was quite unfamiliar. Richard was not unbalanced by these differences in ritual because he remained at heart a Royal Fusilier and knew he could instantly revert to type, but approaching his new regiment's barracks in Cologne, where it formed part of the British army of occupation, he was troubled by the thought that he had done no regimental soldiering for twelve years.

Almost at once he found the army at the regimental level greatly changed. The immaculate machine he had known in 1913 and 1914 had long since been blown into fragments. Most damaging, the noncommissioned officers, who had been the marrow and bone of the old army, were all dead or retired and the troops themselves were young and green. The duties of the forces occupying Germany were not onerous and Richard found himself, with some reluctance, relaxing into a life of peacetime soldiering that carried none of the bite or glamour he had enjoyed in his youth. Though he did not recognize it at once, he was grown too experienced to find much satisfaction in the duties of second-in-command of a battalion of infantry. In the fall of 1924 there came one brief flash of glory when he was given command of the "enemy" for brigade maneuvers, the culmination of summer training. His force comprised four aircraft, six tanks, a squadron of cavalry, and a sprinkling of soldiers representing two battalions of infantry. With a rising sense of pleasure and a resurgence of his old craftiness Richard made his dispositions along a low ridge and awaited attack by an infantry brigade supported by a battery of guns and a squadron of cavalry. The brigade advanced in good order and Richard watched their deliberate preparations to assault him with interest. He allowed them to deploy in the approved fashion and then, exposing his devious counter, made their orthodoxy ridiculous. At the moment when the extended brigade expected the signal to launch the assault Richard's cavalry thundered out of a wood on the flank, the tanks at the foot of the ridge clanked forward through the haystacks piled around them, and Richard's aircraft, summoned by radio, roared in from the rear at low level and disgorged hundreds of tennis balls Richard had had the foresight to buy in Cologne. The effect was novel. The gun horses took fright and snapped their traces, the gunners took refuge under their guns and the infantry milled about in pandemonium, then ran back whence they had come. At the conference later Richard found himself less than popular with his colleagues, though the commanding general commended his originality. He was unmoved by either praise or blame, for he was beginning to realize that the enchantment of what he had once thought would be his career and his whole life had begun to fade.

At the beginning of the next year Richard started to reach a decision about the future. He had been posted to regimental duty in India, and crossing the Arabian Sea, alone in his cabin, he debated his life in the army and weighed it against his new responsibilities toward a family. Annie had never sought to influence him one way or another, but by now he knew her preferences. These, moreover, were now growing more important, for she was on the point of bearing a second child. So Richard Meinertzhagen, approaching forty-seven, reviewed his life and his prospects and came, being a courageous man, to some truths. Since his marriage he had rejected or spurned appointments—among them the post of military attaché in Tokyo, the directorship of intelligence in Ireland, and the governorship of the Falkland Islands—that would have advanced his career and kept him forever from returning to regimental duty. He felt the strain of transfer from his old regiment into one where he knew no one and which, professionally excellent as it might be, warmed none of the old strains planted in his blood by the Fusiliers. The leisure of former days had been stolen away from the peacetime officer; all was now business and responsibility unrelieved by the old joys of shikari and days filled with nothing more serious than polo practice. Then there was his age; he could bear the heat of Indian cantonments with less fortitude; if he retired now he would still be young enough to do the things he wanted to do. He had discovered at last that his old love of natural history and travel had become more real than his drive for success in the army. And finally, weightiest of all, was the attraction of his family. All this Richard set down methodically but without conclusion in his diary on January 6, 1925. On the following day his first son was born, a boy called Daniel, the eighth of his line. He was to grow into the image of that brother of the same name Richard had so loved, so that his father would see in him again with pride the courage, the intelligence and the pure heart he thought he had lost forever in that snowstorm so many winters before.

Within two weeks of arriving in the bosom of his new battalion in Lucknow Richard had tendered his formal resignation of his commission and was faintly surprised to find that his major sensation was one of relief. He decided at once to carry principle into practice and made plans for a journey by way of Kashmir and

Ladakh to western Tibet, with birds and flowers for business and whatever intelligence he might gather en route for savor. Weeks later he discovered he was not yet totally free of the army, for a letter reached him high in the Himalayas. In it the command paymaster at Meerut asked Richard for a receipt for some back-pay. Richard was glad to oblige, though he was forced to provide the receipt on the only paper he could find in that remote place. There shortly returned a remonstrance from the paymaster deploring the use of toilet paper for official business and announcing his intention of reporting such a breach of good taste to the government of India. Undismayed Richard plodded further into the mountains. But no peak in Asia was high enough to fend off the long arm of Simla; one day there arrived a missive from the adjutant general himself requiring answers and explanations and outlining some rules for the more gentlemanly conduct of some officers. Richard took up his pen to write with military formality for the last time. It was a relatively penitent, a meticulous and a punctilious composition. It fitted one of his last sheets of toilet paper beautifully. "And so," he wrote in his diary that night, "ends my Army career."

EPILOGUE

When he left the army Richard Meinertzhagen was already middle-aged, at a point in life when an affluent man might well drift through the doldrums of retirement considering his service ended and his duty done. Richard's generation, blown apart in Flanders, was represented now by men whose bodies were more or less intact but whose minds were anesthetized by the aftermath of terror and by disillusionment. They lived apart from the hectic, aimless posturings of the twenties. There was no going back and ahead lay only banks of fog. Richard had been lucky; he was still fit and hard and his brain was as sharp as ever. Though out of sympathy with the tone of the times, abhorring lacquered fingernails and wailing saxophones, he set himself to spend his considerable energy on four interests—his family, ornithology, travel (and the gathering of what incidental intelligence he might for his country) and Zionism.

He was blessed with seven years of happy marriage. It was never a passionate affair of youth but there was absolute trust, and Annie provided the haven he had always needed for she was self-sufficient enough to sustain Richard's sometimes prolonged absences. It was not a marriage of proximity on either part yet it was buttressed by devotion of great strength which seldom expressed itself openly. Much between Annie and Richard was so well understood that it needed no words. Neither made demands on the other that could not be met. The result for Richard was years of content and fulfillment during which Annie bore him a daughter, Anne, and two sons, Daniel and Randle. Shortly after giving birth to Randle in the summer of 1928, she died in a shooting accident at Swordale. Richard was silent, but later he brought himself to write, "It is fortunate that children do not suffer such grief as older people do." Masking his sudden loneliness as best he could, he tried, knowing himself remote and uncommunicative, to give the children the comfort of a parent's love. As they grew they adopted his enthusiasms and his independence of spirit and Daniel in particular became very close to him.

Many of their visitors were adults, Richard's friends and, in one case, a former enemy. General von Lettow-Vorbeck* came to stay with the Meinertzhagen household in 1929, and while he and Richard fought over their old battles in East Africa and particularly their duel in deserted Tanga, little Daniel listened with enough comprehension to conclude, "Oh Daddy, I wish you'd killed him!" Daniel's first public appearance was at von Lettow's side when the general laid a wreath at the foot of the Cenotaph in Whitehall. From time to time Lawrence of Arabia would appear without warning, sometimes when no one was at home. Then the children would return to find their toy train all laid out in the drawing room and Lawrence waiting with bags of flour to demonstrate the best way of blowing up the Turks and looting their train. When the children had retired sated to bed, Richard and Lawrence would discuss the vast scheme they had begun at their desks in the Colonial Office between 1921 and 1924. It was the unification of all British political and military intelligence services in a single directorate, spinning into one strand the organizations in the Foreign Office, the War Office, the Air Ministry and Scotland Yard. The plan envisaged a training college in London and another less public in the

---

* Von Lettow had been saluted by his nation when he rode through Berlin at the end of the First World War; he was the only German general with any claim to victory. In the anarchy that followed he put down a Communist rising in Hamburg and, supported by Hindenburg, took part in a short-lived military putsch. Though right-wing in politics and for some years active in the Reichstag, he abhorred the National Socialists and retired to private life in Hamburg-Altona. His sons were killed in the Second World War and, his resources exhausted, he was forced to accept charity from old friends, among them Smuts and Meinertzhagen.

country. But Lawrence's erratic way of life during the first decade of Richard's retirement slowed development of the plan; by the time it was all worked out and just as they were applying to the Treasury for funds Lawrence reached the end of his troubled life. One spring day in 1935 his motorcycle hurled him through a hedge on a quiet road and crushed his head. Sadly, with Lawrence's memory wandering through his dreams, Richard let the scheme die.

He did so reluctantly, for he was already aware of the very likely danger of another war. From the first Richard had been concerned with the effects of the Treaty of Versailles on Germany and though he had never been overly fond of the German nation he felt that the Treaty's provisions had been both vindictive and impractical. In the early fall of 1934 Richard was in Berlin for ornithological work at the Museum, now his main pursuit and one for which he was famous. Unaware as yet of the perversions lurking behind the efficiency and vitality of Adolf Hitler's new regime, Richard conceived that Germany should be wooed by the West and encouraged to help defend Europe against Russia, the real enemy. Accordingly he called on Joachim von Ribbentrop, the former cavalry officer and wine salesman who had risen through the S.S. to become the Nazis' expert on foreign affairs and president of the German half of the Anglo-German Association. A lunch followed at von Ribbentrop's home in circumstances of such domestic felicity that Richard—who in his antique way set great store by such appearances—withheld judgment of a man he instinctively distrusted. Ribbentrop arranged a meeting with Hitler that very afternoon.

Richard was so startled by the size and silence of Hitler's office that he checked for a moment in the doorway. At the far end of the room a man was getting to his feet. He wore a chocolate-brown tunic open at the neck, a brown tie and black pants. An Iron Cross hung over the left pocket of his tunic and a broad, brilliant red band stamped with a black swastika on a white ground blazed from his left arm. Richard caught a sensation of physical strength and immense mental force as the man began to walk toward him, then moved forward himself. They met, staring at each other with the fixed intensity of two predators, in the center of the room. The

Fuehrer stopped, threw up his right arm in a limp backward wave, and grated "*Heil* Hitler!" Thinking it a little odd that the man should *heil* himself, Richard raised a hand and replied with a hearty "*Heil* Meinertzhagen!" No one smiled.

With Ribbentrop interpreting, Richard began by exchanging memories of the Great War with this phenomenal new leader of Germany. Then the platitudes came trotting out. Hitler loathed war, Germany must expand but only by peaceful means; France was inimical though Germany intended no aggression; Hitler desired friendship with Britain beyond all else in spite of the vilification poured on him, the Jews were not being persecuted but admittedly they were being treated as aliens. It was all quite persuasive and the tone was so sweetly reasonable that Richard left in a decided mood of optimism.

A year later the mood began to change. Chaim Weizmann arrived in London and as usual came to Richard's house. He was so agitated that Richard was disposed to question his objectivity. What was happening to the Jews in Germany, Weizmann said, was monstrous; they were not allowed to remain except under durance and they could not seek refuge in Palestine unless they stripped themselves of their possessions. Richard could not be convinced that Hitler was opposed to Zionism, so Weizmann challenged him. He asked Richard to approach the German government on the Jews' behalf with a scheme to permit emigration at once. Stirred by Weizmann's passion Richard agreed. He met Hitler for the second time in Berlin on July 15, 1935. As on the first occasion the conversation was extraordinarily calm. Hitler deprecated the bellicose intentions of Mussolini toward Ethiopia, when everyone else was working so hard for peace. For himself and his policies, though he found suspicion and calumny in every quarter, he was full of hope. He grew confidential: he was about to change his ambassador in London and was looking for someone who would be popular with the British, perhaps an admiral. Inspiration flashed in Richard's head and he blurted out, "Von Lettow-Vorbeck!" Hitler thought for a moment, then slapped his thigh in approval.

Encouraged, Richard broached the subject of Jewry. This time the fist came slamming down, instantly, in insane rage. Hitler's face suffused, the voice that had been so gentle rose to a strangled scream, and the eyes flamed into an unseeing crazed stare. The transformation effected what all Weizmann's anguish had not done. When Rudolph Hess walked in, seemingly phlegmatic, to deliver a message and stem the harangue, Richard gladly made his adieus.

When Richard got back to his hotel he found two Jews waiting for him. Still numbed, he took them up to his room and concentrated only partially on the story they began to unfold. They spoke of concentration camps, of rape, torture, mutilation and death. Richard could not believe what they said; it was unreality piled on unreality. But they talked for two hours rehearsing detail after detail, authenticating, pouring forth facts and specifics in such profusion that what had appeared fantasy hardened into hideous reality. The men left, but they were the first of many. The telephone in Richard's bedroom rang incessantly all the time he was in the city, and every voice that spoke was Jewish, every story atrocious, every plea one of despair. He saw Ribbentrop and some correct officials at the Reichsbank who assured him that any proposals for assisting Jews to emigrate to Palestine would be most welcome; there could even be special agricultural schools and classes in Hebrew for intending emigrants. But Richard read the signs on the official notice boards. *"Wer den Juden kennt, kennt den Teufel,"* they said and he knew, though he could not admit it, that he was out of his depth.

Four years later, on the eve of war, there occurred to him a much simpler solution, one more suited to his own disposition. It was June 28, 1939, and he had just finished a Berlin breakfast of good bread and preserves and coffee when a telephone call summoned him to a meeting with Hitler at the Chancellery at eleven o'clock. Though he had considered refusing he was there punctually and again he was led into the enormous room and again Ribbentrop interpreted. But Ribbentrop's former smile had changed into a snarl and this time Richard was aware that the man with the swastika on his arm was a fanatic. This time, too, something else was different: in the right pocket of his capacious coat Richard carried a loaded automatic pistol. The voice that by now was infamous dispensed with greetings and swept over him a tirade. It went on for forty minutes, until at last Richard stood up, held out his hand in silence and left. He was puzzled, for he could not explain to himself why he had carried the automatic, unless it was merely out of bravado or to prove that he had had the opportunity to dispatch both Hitler and Ribbentrop. He had considered doing so several times during the harangue in a dispassionate way but he had not acted. "I am seriously troubled about it," he wrote that night in his diary. "If this war breaks out, as I feel sure it will, then I shall feel very much to blame for not killing these two."

When the second world war of his lifetime began, Richard was sixty-one years of age, old enough to see history repeat itself and courageous enough to accept the likelihood of his elder son's becoming embroiled in it. Daniel was in school at Winchester; as his father expected, the war lasted long enough for him to become a soldier and to Richard's delight he became a fine one. Daniel was killed on October 2, 1944, at the age of nineteen. A subaltern in an armored battalion of the Coldstream Guards, he was reconnoitering near the Maas River in Holland when he and his companions were caught in a sudden flurry of mortar bombs. His body was found in a foxhole next to that of an American soldier. "He had done his duty," Richard wrote, omitting volumes.

Richard himself was recalled to the War Office at the declaration and occupied himself with intelligence planning. Once more the Jews offered their services to the British and the idea was brought to Richard by Vladimir Jabotinsky, the ruthless and vigorous leader of the radical left wing of the Zionists. The two had first met early in 1920, when Richard had jailed Jabotinsky.* At this second meeting in 1939 Jabotinsky proposed to Richard over lunch at the Carlton Club, one of the more opulent nurseries of Conservative

---

* Shortly after the Armistice of 1918, suspecting that the British administration of Palestine might not be competent to prevent a massacre of the Jews by the Arabs, Jabotinsky had begun to gather adherents whom he trained and armed, and so fathered Haganah. He was arrested after the Easter Riots of 1920 and thrown into Acre prison. Partly because of Richard's intercession his savage sentence was later reduced and eventually quashed.

thought, the raising of a Jewish army of two hundred thousand men and the instigation of a propaganda campaign in the United States. For these services the Jews would expect a seat at the peace table. Richard was not of course in a position to offer a guarantee of any kind and the concept was not pursued. But Jabotinsky was a man of exquisite fancy and continued to present Richard with less ambitious devices. At the end of the year he reappeared with a design for blowing up German oil barges on the Danube and asked Richard to provide the explosives. They visited the arsenal at Woolwich, where a sticky bomb (a contrivance notoriously eccentric filled with what Richard described as "nasty green jelly") so convincingly punctured a piece of armor plate that Jabotinsky threw his arms around his benefactor and kissed him, a recompense not usually accorded a British colonel in full uniform. The bombs were shipped and Jabotinsky's agents put them to use.

Richard's personal participation in the war was less active than he would have wished. His one taste of real battle was unofficial. In the clear, beautiful early summer of 1940 he managed to get aboard a unit of the cockleshell fleet sent to recover the British Expeditionary Force from Dunkirk. With the rest of that amateur navy Richard crossed the Channel, navigating by the black smoke columns on the beaches. He suffered a flesh wound from a shell fragment and hardly mentioned it. Then, to occupy his spare time, he joined the Home Guard so as to be of some use during the blitz.

The end of the war brought Richard a dilemma, for it left in Palestine antagonisms of the most violent kind which the Powers seemed reluctant to solve by the political means at their disposal. Unshaken in his belief in Zionism and the propriety of the National Home, Richard was nevertheless torn between that loyalty and his love of his own country. Extremists were attacking not only the Arabs but the reluctant garrisons left behind under the British Mandate. He persisted in his conviction that all the British government need do was honor the Balfour Declaration and he could not understand the reference of the whole question early in 1947 to the United Nations. "It is the complete abdication of Britain's moral influence in the world," he wrote, with some truth. Richard still believed in the simple principle that a promise is a promise. He felt ashamed that there were still British troops in Palestine to keep order, he resented the supply of arms to the Arabs, and he suspected that the government was preparing to abandon the Jews to their fate. It was a relief when at the close of 1947 the United Nations voted and it seemed that at last Jewish sovereignty would become a reality, though over a territory smaller than that envisaged so long before by Balfour and Lloyd George. Richard was touched when a telegram came from Chaim Weizmann in New York. It said, "To you dear friend we owe so much that I can only express it in simple words—May God Bless You," and it caught up with Richard as he was within four miles of Mecca.

He had been crossing Arabia from east to west studying birds in the preparation of a book, *The Birds of Arabia,* that became the standard work on the subject. This was the first of two similar trips and both were means of observing matters other than ornithological. His old antipathies were still strong: "I suppose a slightly unbalanced mind and a craving for romance or solitude is attracted by the dirt, squalor, dishonesty, inefficiency, laziness, intolerance and unreliability of the Arab," he wrote, "and no doubt the romance of the desert and the nomad has its attractions; it certainly attracts me. I suppose the truth is that a man slightly abnormal is in search of something abnormal and in the Arab and the desert he finds just what he wants, people and places out of the ordinary and an atmosphere where his eccentricities find full scope and expansion and where he can with ease become a whale among the smaller fry." Richard took every chance he could to sound out Arab opinion about Palestine, without revealing his own views. At dinner in Kuwait he asked an Arab guest, "Why don't you Arabs, with all your resources from oil, do something for these wretched refugees from Palestine?" The man took the bait. "Good God," he said. "Do you really think we're going to destroy the finest propaganda we possess? It's a gold mine." Richard found similar sentiments everywhere, and everywhere he felt the vast changes that had taken place in the old Arabia Deserta. When he had first seen its fringes it had been nothing, an emptiness. But after the First World War the desert prince Ibn Saud had begun to make a kingdom of the waste, had broken the power of the sherif of Mecca and proclaimed himself King of Saudi Arabia, and had slowly entered into a profitable relationship with an American oil company. Though as late as 1939 the Arabian peninsula had not been accounted one of the world's great oil-producing areas, by 1944 American initiative had established in Ibn Saud's possessions an industry capable of meeting almost any demand. This development, with all its political implications, Richard viewed with disfavor.

At the end of his first crossing of Arabia he left for England by way of Egypt, embarking at Alexandria on April 22, 1948. The ship happened to be carrying as fellow passengers a company of Coldstream Guards, his son Dan's former regiment. The officers spoke of Daniel with affection, greatly to Richard's joy, and he arrived in Haifa in high spirits. There a vigorous battle between Jews and Arabs was in progress, necessitating the departure of Richard's new friends to protect official stores. The ping of bullets and the sporadic crack of rifle fire struck a chord in Richard's bosom, languishing aboard, and he quickly persuaded himself where his duty lay. One of the guardsmen had been left behind, sick, so Richard borrowed his rifle and uniform and marched ashore in the briskest Guards style as if following the detachment ahead. For all his seventy years he looked smart enough.

Once inside the town Richard abandoned the Coldstream and walked toward the firing. He soon found the Haganah lying in a shallow trench beyond the outskirts, flopped down alongside a group of twenty of them, and began in soldierly fashion to prepare for action. First he sighted his borrowed rifle with a few rounds at a barrel a couple of hundred yards away, thoughtfully scanned the opposition with his field glasses, and noted the location of some Arabs who had unwisely sniped at him during his approach. Then he began to crawl forward like a stalker. Three of the Haganah accompanied him at a distance, looking a little puzzled and yelling at him briefly in Hebrew, which he ignored. His first shot rolled over one of the Arabs. Advancing a little further he discovered he could enfilade the rest of the Arabs and killed two more, at which point his friends caught up, assisted in the demise of five more and accepted the surrender of the solitary Arab who put up his hands. There were still twenty or more Arabs left, much further off, and it took an hour to account for them. By that time a Coldstream officer had arrived to investigate; he recognized Richard and ordered him back to the ship at once in tones more of anger than of sorrow. Richard obeyed, feeling a little sheepish but not objecting, because he had fired off all his two hundred rounds. He returned the uniform, cleaned the rifle, and split a bottle of champagne with his benefactor. Later he made an entry in his diary that belonged in spirit to his youth half a century before. "Altogether I had a glorious day," he wrote. "May Israel flourish!"

It was his last significant act in the cause of Zionism. Henceforth he was an observer, though with bias. "No matter what equipment one gives the Arab," he wrote, "they run no chance against the Jews. It is the man behind the gun who counts, not the gun." He was to live to see events bear him out. From time to time he grumbled at the idiocies of a world grown suddenly too complicated, huffing when a resolution in the United Nations carried the names of Uruguay, Paraguay, Bolivia, China and Ethiopia, "Good God! What utter tomfoolery it is." When he had been in his prime not one of those countries could have made any decision at all that the presence of a timely gunboat could not have altered.

As Richard observed the flow of events, much swifter in the twentieth century than in the nineteenth, it was almost as though he was living his life a second time. When the Kikuyu rebellion began in 1952 he could only reflect on what he had predicted forty years before when he had—following, as he thought, his duty—helped sow the seeds of it. When Gamal Abdal Nasser in pique seized the Suez Canal in 1956, Richard recalled that summer in 1882 when Arabi Pasha, the first great Egyptian nationalist, had threatened to destroy the canal and thus had brought down on his head Gladstone's thunder and the broadsides of the Mediterranean Fleet. After Eden's feebleness of will had turned the invasion of Egypt into a farce, Richard wrote, "Never did Britain stand so low since the death of Gordon in Khartoum"; he could remember the newsboys crying that strange martyr's death in the streets, though he had lived so long that martyrdom had lost its significance, along with other things Richard had been taught were the very pillars of the world. The old puritanical standards that had forged an empire in his lifetime had dissolved and might never return.

In 1964 Richard Meinertzhagen reviewed his life. He was eighty-six but his mind was as sharp and as painfully honest as it had ever been. He felt a proper nostalgia for all that he had lost, that simpler world of the late Victorians and the Edwardians, and he revived with tenderness all he had loved from his boyhood on. In some ways he had not been very lucky. Yet he had lived fully, even passionately, in his curious fashion. He had been honest and he was not ashamed. But at the close he felt alone. "We are now entering a world of indecision, dishonesty and irresponsibility," he wrote in 1964, "a world I shall not be sorry to leave." And so, gentle at the last, on June 17, 1967, he died.

BIBLIOGRAPHY

his brief bibliography is meant more as a guide to those wishing to pursue an interest in Richard Meinertzhagen's times than as a piece of scholarly apparatus. The narrative framework of the book came from Colonel Meinertzhagen's papers and diaries held in Rhodes House, Oxford, parts of which have already been published:

> *The Life of a Boy* (Oliver and Boyd, 1947)
> *Birds of Arabia* (Oliver and Boyd, 1954)
> *Kenya Diary 1902–6* (Oliver and Boyd, 1957)
> *Middle East Diary 1917–56* (Thomas Yoselof, 1960)
> *Army Diary 1899–1926* (Oliver and Boyd, 1960)
> *Diary of a Black Sheep* (Oliver and Boyd, 1964)

As a general guide I have relied greatly on two volumes of The New Cambridge Modern History: Volume XI, *Material Progress and World-Wide Problems 1870–1898,* edited by E. H. Hinsley (Cambridge University Press, 1962); and Volume XII, *The Era of Violence 1898–1945,* edited by David Thomson (Cambridge University Press, 1960). Among the periodicals consulted were *The Listener, The Times, The New York Times* and *The Illustrated London News.*

Books are listed under the chapters in which they were first used.

PROLOGUE

DUNDONALD, THE EARL OF. *My Army Life.* London: Edward Arnold, 1926.
MAUROIS, ANDRÉ. *The Edwardian Age.* London: D. Appleton-Century, 1933.
MAXWELL, SIR H. *Sixty Years a Queen.* London: Harmsworth Brothers, 1897.

PRINCESS MARIE LOUISE. *My Memories of Six Reigns.* London: Evans Brothers, 1956.

ST. AUBYN, GILES. *The Royal George.* New York: Alfred A. Knopf, 1964.

WILLIS, FREDERICK. *Peace and Dripping Toast.* London: Phoenix House, 1950.

CHAPTER I

BERESFORD, LORD CHARLES. *Memoirs* (2 vols.). London: Methuen, 1914.

BRIGGS, ASA. *Victorian People.* Chicago: University of Chicago Press, 1955.

BRIGGS, ASA. *Victorian Cities.* New York: Harper and Row, 1965.

BRITISH BROADCASTING CORPORATION. *Ideas and Beliefs of the Victorians.* 1949.

COLLIER, RICHARD. *The Sound of Fury.* London: Collins, 1963.

LONGFORD, ELIZABETH. *Queen Victoria.* New York: Harper and Row, 1965.

MAGNUS, PHILIP. *Gladstone.* New York: E. P. Dutton and Co., 1964.

MEINERTZHAGEN, GEORGINA. *From Ploughshare to Parliament.* London: John Murray, 1908.

PETRIE, SIR CHARLES. *The Victorians.* New York: David McKay, 1962.

PLOMER, WILLIAM (ed.). *Selections from the Diary of the Reverend Francis Kilvert.* 3 vols. London: Jonathan Cape, 1938–1940.

RAVERAT, GWEN. *Period Piece.* New York: W. W. Norton, 1962.

ROBBINS, MICHAEL. *The Railway Age in Britain.* London: Routledge and Kegan Paul, 1962.

WINGFIELD-STRATFORD, ESME. *Those Earnest Victorians.* New York: William Morrow and Co., 1930.

YOUNG, G. M. *Victorian England.* Oxford, England: Oxford University Press, 1936.

CHAPTER II

ABBOTT, EVELYN, AND LOUIS CAMPBELL. *The Life and Letters of Benjamin Jowett.* 2 vols. London: John Murray, 1897.

ASQUITH, MARGOT. *An Autobiography.* 2 vols. New York: George H. Doran, 1920.

BALSDON, DACRE. *Oxford Life.* Fairlawn, N.J.: Essential Books, 1958.

BOND, BRIAN. *Victorian Military Campaigns.* London: Hutchinson, 1967.

DUTTON, RALPH. *The Victorian Home.* London: B.T. Batsford, 1954.

GRETTON, R. H. *A Modern History of the English People. Vol. I, 1880–1898.* New York: Small, Maynard and Co., 1913.

LACOUTURE, JEAN AND SIMONNE. *Egypt in Transition.* London: Criterion Books, 1960.

LINDER, LESLIE (ed.). *The Journal of Beatrix Potter.* London: Frederick Warne, 1966.

NUTTING, ANTHONY. *Gordon of Khartoum.* New York: Clarkson N. Potter, 1966.

SYMONS, JULIAN. *England's Pride.* London: Hamish Hamilton, 1965.

CHAPTER III

BLUNT, WILFRID. *Cockerell.* New York: Alfred A. Knopf, 1965.

CHURCHILL, WINSTON S. *My Early Life.* New York: Charles Scribner, 1930.

MUGGERIDGE, KITTY, AND RUTH ADAM. *Beatrice Webb, A Life*. London: Secker and Warburg, 1967.

STANLEY, A. P. *The Life and Correspondence of Thomas Arnold*. Ridgewood, N.J.: Gregg International, 1968.

THORP, ELLEN. *Ladder of Bones*. London: Jonathan Cape, 1956.

WEBB, BEATRICE. *My Apprenticeship*. London: Longman's, Green, 1926.

CHAPTER IV

CECIL, LADY GWENDOLYN. *Life of Robert, Marquis of Salisbury*. 4 vols. London: Hodder and Stoughton, 1921–1932.

CHAPLIN, E. D. W. *The Book of Harrow*. London: Staples Press, 1948.

CHURCHILL, RANDOLPH S. *Winston S. Churchill: Youth, 1874–1900*. Boston: Houghton Mifflin, 1966.

EVANS, GEORGE EWART. *Ask the Fellows Who Cut the Hay*. London: Faber and Faber, 1960.

EVANS, GEORGE EWART. *The Horse in the Furrow*. London: Faber and Faber, 1960.

FERRIS, PAUL. *The City*. New York: Random House, 1961.

FRYER, PETER. *Mrs. Grundy: Studies in English Prudery*. London: Dobson Books Ltd., n.d.

KENNEDY, A. L. *Salisbury 1830–1903: Portrait of a Statesman*. John Murray, 1953.

KIPLING, RUDYARD. *A Farmer's Year*. London: Longman's, Green, 1899.

LAVER, JAMES. *Manners and Morals in the Age of Optimism 1848–1914*. New York: Harper and Row, 1966.

MARCUS, STEVEN. *The Other Victorians*. New York: Basic Books, 1966.

SAMPSON, ANTHONY. *Anatomy of Britain Today*. New York: Harper and Row, 1965.

STANLEY, H. M. *Through the Dark Continent*. Sampson Low, 1878.

———. *In Darkest Africa*. Sampson Low, 1890.

CHAPTER V

BADEN-POWELL, COLONEL R. S. S. *The Matabele Campaign, 1896*. Methuen, 1897.

BALFOUR, MICHAEL. *The Kaiser and His Times*. Boston: Houghton Mifflin, 1964.

COWLES, VIRGINIA. *The Kaiser*. New York: Harper and Row, 1963.

DEWAR, GEORGE A. B. *Wild Life in the Hampshire Highlands*. London: J. M. Dent, 1899.

HILL, JOHN WALLER. *A Summer on the Test*. London: Geoffrey Bles, 1946.

MAXWELL, SIR HERBERT (ed.). *Chronicles of the Houghton Fishing Club, 1822–1908*. London: Edward Arnold, n.d.

MILLIN, SARAH GERTRUDE. *Cecil Rhodes*. New York: Harper and Brothers, 1933.

PAKENHAM, LADY ELIZABETH. *Jameson's Raid*. London: Weidenfeld and Nicholson, 1960.

ROBINSON, RONALD, AND JOHN GALLAGHER. *Africa and the Victorians*. New York: St. Martin's Press, 1961.

TURNER, E. S. *All Heaven in a Rage*. New York: St. Martin's Press, 1964.

WARNER, REX. *English Public Schools.* London: Collins, 1945.
WILLIAMS, BASIL. *Cecil Rhodes.* London: Constable, 1938.

CHAPTER VI

CHURCHILL, WINSTON S. *The River War.* London: Eyre and Spottiswoode, 1899.
MAGNUS, PHILIP. *Kitchener: Portrait of an Imperialist.* New York: E. P. Dutton, 1959.

CHAPTER VII

BADEN-POWELL, LT. GEN. SIR ROBERT. *Memories of India.* New York: David McKay, n.d.
GEE, E.P. *The Wildlife of India.* New York: E. P. Dutton, 1964.
JARVIS, MAJOR C. S. *Arab Command.* London: Hutchinson, 1942.
KIPLING, RUDYARD. *From Sea to Sea.* 2 vols. Doubleday and McClure, 1899.
KRUGER, RAYNE. *Good-Bye Dolly Gray.* London: Cassell, 1959.
McGUFFIE, T. H. (ed.). *Rank and File.* New York: St. Martin's Press, 1966.
MALLET, VICTOR (ed.). *Life with Queen Victoria.* London: John Murray, 1968.
PANTER-DOWNES, MOLLIE. *Ooty Preserved.* London: Hamish Hamilton, 1967.
RICHARDS, FRANK. *Old Soldier Sahib.* London: Faber and Faber, 1936.
SIMSON, FRANK B. *Letters on Sport in Eastern Bengal.* London: R. H. Porter, 1886.
SPEAR, PERCIVAL. *A History of India.* Vol. 2. Baltimore, Md.: Penguin, 1965.
WARDROP, MAJOR A. E. *Modern Pig-Sticking.* London: Macmillan, 1914.
WILLIAMS, L.F. RUSHBROOK (ed.). *A Handbook to India, Pakistan, Burma, Ceylon.* London: John Murray, 1965.
WOODRUFF, PHILIP. *The Men Who Ruled India. Vol. 2: The Guardians.* London: Jonathan Cape, 1964.

CHAPTER VIII

BEARD, PETER H. *The End of the Game.* New York: Viking, 1965.
HARDY, RONALD. *The Iron Snake.* London: Collins, 1965.
HOBLEY, C. W. *Kenya from Chartered Company to Crown Colony.* London: H. F. and G. Witherby, 1929.
HUXLEY, ELSPETH. *White Man's Country.* 2 vols. London: Chatto and Windus, 1935.
JACKSON, SIR FREDERICK. *Early Days in East Africa.* London: Edward Arnold, 1930.
MORGAN, W. T. W. (ed.). *Nairobi, City and Region.* Nairobi: Oxford University Press, 1967.
MOYSE-BARTLETT, LT. COL. H. *The King's African Rifles.* Aldershot, Eng.: Gale and Polden, 1956.
MUNGEAM, G. H. *British Rule in Kenya 1895-1912.* Oxford, Eng.: Clarendon Press, 1966.

CHAPTER IX

CRANWORTH, CAPTAIN, THE LORD. *Profit and Sport in East Africa.* Macmillan, 1919.
FLEMING, PETER. *Bayonets to Lhasa.* New York: Harper and Brothers, 1961.

Huntingford, G. W. B. *The Nandi of Kenya*. London: Routledge and Kegan Paul, 1953.

Nowell-Smith, Simon (ed.). *Edwardian England 1901–1914*. Oxford, Eng.: Oxford University Press, 1964.

Petrie, Sir Charles. *The Edwardians*. New York: W. W. Norton, 1965.

CHAPTER X

Boulanger, Robert. *The Middle East*. Paris: Hachette World Guide, 1966.

Kirk, George E. *A Short History of the Middle East*. New York: Frederick A. Praeger, 1960.

Lewis, Michael. *The History of the British Navy*. Baltimore, Md.: Penguin, 1957.

CHAPTER XI

Bonham Carter, Victor. *The Strategy of Victory*. New York: Holt, Rinehart and Winston, 1964.

Carew, Tim. *The Vanished Army*. London: William Kimber, 1964.

Clark, Alan. *The Donkeys*. New York: William Morrow, 1962.

Gardner, Brian. *On to Kilimanjaro*. Philadelphia, Pa.: Macrae Smith, 1963.

Green, Lt. Col. Howard. *The British Army in the First World War*. Privately Printed, 1968.

Hordern, Lt. Col. Charles. *Official History of the Great War, Military Operations, East Africa*. Vol. 1. London: Her Majesty's Stationery Office, 1941.

Lettow-Vorbeck, General von. *My Reminiscences of East Africa*. London: Hurst and Blackett, n.d.

Marcus, Geoffrey. *Before the Lamps Went Out*. London: George Allen and Unwin, 1965.

O'Neill, H. C. *The Royal Fusiliers in the Great War*. London: William Heinemann, 1922.

Pound, Reginald. *The Lost Generation*. London: Constable, 1964.

Taylor, Edmond. *The Fossil Monarchies*. London: Weidenfeld and Nicholson, 1963.

Terraine, John. *Ordeal of Victory*. Philadelphia, Pa.: J. B. Lippincott, 1963.

Wynn, Wynn E. *Ambush*. London: Hutchinson, 1937.

CHAPTER XII

Aldington, Richard. *Lawrence of Arabia*. Chicago: Henry Regnery, 1955.

Barker, A. J. *The Neglected War*. London: Faber and Faber, 1967.

Gardner, Brian. *The Big Push*. New York: William Morrow, 1963.

Gardner, Brian. *Allenby*. London: Cassell, 1965.

Falls, Cyril. *Armageddon, 1918*. Philadelphia, Pa.: J. B. Lippincott, 1964.

Garnett, David (ed.). *The Letters of T. E. Lawrence*. New York: Doubleday, Doran, 1939.

Graves, Robert. *Lawrence and the Arabs*. London: Jonathan Cape, 1927.

Lawrence, A. W. (ed.). *T. E. Lawrence by His Friends*. New York: Doubleday, 1937.

LAWRENCE, T. E. *Seven Pillars of Wisdom.* London: Jonathan Cape, 1935.

LIDDELL HART, B. H. *T. E. Lawrence: In Arabia and After.* London: Jonathan Cape, 1934.

LONGRIGG, STEPHEN HEMSLEY. *Oil in the Middle East.* Oxford, Eng.: Oxford University Press, 1961.

MacMUNN, SIR GEORGE, AND CYRIL FALLS. *Official History of the Great War, Military Operations, Egypt and Palestine.* 5 vols. London: Her Majesty's Stationery Office, 1928.

MASSEY, W. T. *The Desert Campaigns.* London: Constable, 1918.

NUTTING, ANTHONY. *Lawrence of Arabia.* New York: Clarkson N. Potter, 1961.

OCAMPO, VICTORIA. *338171 T. E.* Paris: Librairie Gallimard, 1947.

PATTERSON, LT. COL. J. H. *With the Judaeans in the Palestine Campaign.* London: Hutchinson, 1922.

PITT, BARRIE. *1918. The Last Act.* New York: W. W. Norton, 1962.

RICHARDS, VYVYAN. *Portrait of T. E. Lawrence.* London: Jonathan Cape, 1936.

ROBINSON, EDWARD. *Lawrence.* Oxford, Eng.: Oxford University Press, 1935.

STIRLING, LT. COL. W. F. *Safety Last.* London: Hollis and Carter, 1953.

STORRS, SIR RONALD. *Orientations.* London: Ivor Nicholson and Watson, 1937.

THOMAS, LOWELL. *With Lawrence in Arabia.* London: Hutchinson, 1925.

WAVELL, A.P. *The Palestine Campaigns.* London: Constable, 1928.

——. *Allenby.* London: George G. Harrap, 1940.

CHAPTER XIII

BENTWICH, NORMAN AND HELEN. *Mandate Memories, 1918–1948.* New York: Schocken Books, 1965.

ESCO FOUNDATION FOR PALESTINE, INC. *Palestine, A Study of Jewish, Arab and British Policies.* 2 vols. New Haven, Conn.: Yale University Press, 1947.

LEIGHTON, ISABEL (ed.). *The Aspirin Age 1919–1941.* London: The Bodley Head, 1950.

MARWICK, ARTHUR. *The Deluge.* London: The Bodley Head, 1965.

SAMUEL, MAURICE. *Harvest in the Desert.* New York: Alfred A. Knopf, 1945.

SAMUEL, VISCOUNT. *Memoirs.* London: Cresset Press, 1945.

SYKES, CHRISTOPHER. *Crossroads to Israel 1917–1948.* New York: The World Publishing Co., 1965.

WEISGAL, MEYER M., AND JOEL CARMICHAEL (eds.). *Chaim Weizmann, A Biography by Several Hands.* New York: Atheneum, 1963.

WEIZMANN, CHAIM. *Trial and Error.* New York: Schocken Books, 1966.

EPILOGUE

CROSSMAN, RICHARD. *Palestine Mission.* London: Hamish Hamilton, 1947.

LORCH, NETANEL. *The Edge of the Sword.* New York: G. P. Putnam, 1961.

INDEX

About the Author

JOHN LORD was born in Lancashire in 1924. He was an infantry platoon commander from the Normandy invasion to the Rhine and later served in the Sudan and East Africa. He came to the United States in 1960 and now works as a producer for NBC in New York.